Communications
in Computer and Information Science   161

David Obdržálek   Achim Gottscheber (Eds.)

Research and Education in Robotics – EUROBOT 2011

International Conference
Prague, Czech Republic, June 15-17, 2011
Proceedings

 Springer

Volume Editors

David Obdržálek
Charles University Prague
Faculty of Mathematics and Physics
Prague, Czech Republic
E-mail: david.obdrzalek@mff.cuni.cz

Achim Gottscheber
SRH University Heidelberg
Electrical Engineering
Heidelberg, Germany
E-mail: achim.gottscheber@fh-heidelberg.de

ISSN 1865-0929   e-ISSN 1865-0937
ISBN 978-3-642-21974-0   e-ISBN 978-3-642-21975-7
DOI 10.1007/978-3-642-21975-7
Springer Heidelberg Dordrecht London New York

Library of Congress Control Number: 2011929867

CR Subject Classification (1998): I.2.9, I.2, I.4, I.6, H.4-5

Typesetting: Camera-ready by author, data conversion by Scientific Publishing Services, Chennai, India

Printed on acid-free paper

Springer is part of Springer Science+Business Media (www.springer.com)

Preface

This volume contains the selected papers presented at the International Conference on Research and Education in Robotics, EUROBOT 2011, held at Charles University in Prague (Faculty of Mathematics and Physics), Czech Republic, June 15–17, 2011.

Besides the conference presentations, invited talks were given by:

- Alexander Hildebrandt, Mechatronic Systems Research, Festo AG & Co. KG, Germany
- Ivan M. Havel, Center for Theoretical Study of Charles University in Prague and the Academy of Sciences of the Czech Republic, Prague, Czech Republic
- Jana Horáková, Masaryk University, Brno, Czech Republic
- Josef Průša, RepRap core developer

We would like to thank all the people involved in the conference organization. We also thank all authors who submitted their work and the reviewers who helped to select the papers to be presented at the conference. Last, but not least, we want to thank the developers of the EasyChair system, which was used as the main management tool for the conference papers.

June 2011

David Obdržálek
Achim Gottscheber

Organization

EUROBOT 2011 was organized by:

- EUROBOT Association
- SRH University Heidelberg, Germany
- Charles University in Prague, Czech Republic

Executive Committee

Conference Chair	Achim Gottscheber (SRH University Heidelberg, Germany)
Program Chair	David Obdržálek (Charles University in Prague, Czech Republic)

Program Committee

Richard Balogh	Slovak University of Technology in Bratislava, Slovakia
Kay Erik Böhnke	SRH University Heidelberg, Germany
Branislav Borovac	University of Novi Sad, Serbia
Jean-Daniel Dessimoz	Western Switzerland University of Applied Sciences, HESSO HEIG-VD, Yverdon-les-Bains, Switzerland
Heinz Domeisen	Hochschule für Technik Rapperswil, HSR/IMA, Rapperswil, Switzerland
Achim Gottscheber	SRH University Heidelberg, Germany
Boualem Kazed	University of Blida, Algeria
Agathe Koller	Hochschule für Technik Rapperswil, HSR/IMA, Rapperswil, Switzerland
Markus Kottmann	Hochschule für Technik Rapperswil, HSR/IMA, Rapperswil, Switzerland
Tomáš Krajník	Czech Technical University in Prague, Czech Republic
Giovanni Muscato	Università degli Studi di Catania, Italy
David Obdržálek	Charles University in Prague, Czech Republic
Pavel Petrovič	Comenius University in Bratislava, Slovakia

Table of Contents

Looking Backward at the Robot 1
  Jana Horáková

VEX Robotics: STEM Program and Robotics Competition Expansion
into Europe 10
  Irene Alvarez Caro

Educational Environment for Robotic Applications in Engineering 17
  Silas F.R. Alves, Humberto Ferasoli Filho, Renê Pegoraro,
  Marco A.C. Caldeira, João M. Rosário, and Wilson M. Yonezawa

EmbedIT – An Open Robotic Kit for Education 29
  Dorit Assaf and Rolf Pfeifer

Semantic Simulation Engine in Mobile Robot Operator Training Tool... 40
  Janusz Bedkowski and Andrzej Masłowski

Mobile Robot Localization Using Beacons and the Kalman Filter
Technique for the Eurobot Competition 55
  Oliver Bittel and Michael Blaich

A New Programming Interface for Educational Robotics 68
  Javier Caccavelli, Sol Pedre, Pablo de Cristóforis, Andrea Katz, and
  Diego Bendersky

An Attempt to Teaching Programming with Robots 78
  Petr Čermák and Jozef Kelemen

Domestic Service Robots in the Real World: More on the Case of
Intelligent Robots Following Humans 88
  Jean-Daniel Dessimoz and Pierre-François Gauthey

Designing an Omni-Directional Infrared Sensor and Beacon System for
the Eurobot Competition 102
  Valentin Durst, Daniel Hagel, Jan Vander, Michael Blaich, and
  Oliver Bittel

How to Teach Robotics to Children (12 - 16 Years Old) 114
  Achim Gottscheber, Andreas Hochlehnert, and Lukas Mairon

Model-Based Nonlinear Control of 2-WMR 123
  Gernot Grabmair

Obstacle and Game Element Detection with the 3D-Sensor Kinect 130
Matthias Greuter, Michael Rosenfelder, Michael Blaich, and
Oliver Bittel

Identification Based Model of Ultrasonic Sensor 144
Jaroslav Hanzel, Marian Kl'účik, Ladislav Jurišica, and Anton Vitko

RoboCoP: A Protocol for Service-Oriented Robot Control Systems 158
Dmitry Kononchuk, Victor Kandoba, Sergey Zhigalov,
Pavel Abduramanov, and Yuri Okulovsky

AR-Drone as a Platform for Robotic Research and Education.......... 172
Tomáš Krajník, Vojtěch Vonásek, Daniel Fišer, and Jan Faigl

Team Development of an Autonomous Mobile Robot: Approaches and
Results 187
Andrey Kuturov, Anton Yudin, Igor Pashinskiy, and
Mikhail Chistyakov

An Autonomous Robot Localization System Based on Coded Infrared
Beacons 202
Milan Lukic, Miodrag Brkic, and Jovan Bajic

An Omnidirectional Mobile Robot for Large Object Handling.......... 210
Lenka Mudrová, Václav Jahoda, Oliver Porges, and Tomáš Krajník

A Practical Mobile Robotics Engineering Course Using LEGO
Mindstorms 221
Ana C. Murillo, Alejandro R. Mosteo, Jose A. Castellanos, and
Luis Montano

An 8 Year Old Educational Robotics Program – Structure, Methodology
and Goals... 236
Othon da Rocha Neves Jr., João Bosco da Mota Alves, and
Josué J.G. Ramos

A New Three Object Triangulation Algorithm Based on the Power
Center of Three Circles 248
Vincent Pierlot, Maxime Urbin-Choffray, and
Marc Van Droogenbroeck

Humanoid Robot Reaching Task Using Support Vector Machine 263
Mirko Raković, Milutin Nikolić, and Branislav Borovac

Development of a High Speed 3D Laser Measurement System for
Outdoor Robotics.. 277
Jens Schlemper, Lars Kuhnert, Markus Ax, and
Klaus-Dieter Kuhnert

A Robot Competition to Encourage First-Year Students in Mechatronic
Sciences 288
    Johannes Stier, Gero Zechel, and Michael Beitelschmidt

Engineering Education Program at Kanazawa Institute of Technology:
A Case Study in Department of Robotics 300
    Ryoichi Suzuki and Nobuaki Kobayashi

Autonomous Robot Navigation Based on Clustering across Images 310
    Tomas Vintr, Lukas Pastorek, and Hana Rezankova

Distributed Control System for a Mobile Robot: Tasks and Software
Architecture... 321
    Anton Yudin and Mikhail Semyonov

University Education in Robotics and Advanced Automation:
A Certified Lectures Perspective and Strategy for Development of
Didactical and Technical Course Model 335
    Duško Lukač and Werner Schollenberger

Author Index 349

Looking Backward at the Robot

Jana Horáková

Masaryk University, Faculty of Arts, A. Novaka 1, 602 00 Brno, Czech Republic
horakova@phil.muni.cz

Abstract. The paper is dedicated to the 90th anniversary of Karel Čapek's drama *R.U.R., Rossum's Universal Robots* (1920) first stage production at the National Theatre in Prague (1921), in which robot, in a form of drama character, was introduced to the world for the very first time. Robot had transgressed the realm of fiction to become part of realm of facts and in a form of mechanical curiosities soon became the central figure of myth of technological progress and work automation.

Keywords: robot; robotics; Karel Čapek; R.U.R.; myth; mechanization; automation.

1 Introduction

In the year 2011 we celebrate the ninety years anniversary of Karel Čapeks drama R.U.R., Rossum's Universal Robots (1920) officially first stage production.[1] In the staged drama, the neologism robot[2] was coined to name artificial workers of utopian R.U.R. factory, and robots, in form of drama characters, were introduced

---

[1] The official first night of the play in National Theatre in Prague was in fact not the historically first stage production of the play. The world first stage production of the R.U.R. was, despite protests of National Theatre representatives, held in Hradec Králové, January 2, 1921. The R.U.R. was staged by Theatre amateurs society – Klicpera: director Bedřich Stein: by profession inspector of State railways.

The official first stage production of R.U.R. was held at National Theatre in Prague, January 25. Director: Vojta Novák; stage designer: Bedřich Feuerstein; Costume designer: Josef Čapek, for whom it was the first opportunity to make theatre costumes.

[2] The word robot, suggested to Karel Čapek by his brother Josef, is neologism made from the old Czech word of Slavonic origin "robota" that means drudgery, corvee, or hard work. The meaning of the word robot is broader than by Karel Čapek originally planned word Labors (Labořì) [1]. Labor is man reduced to the work, but Robot etymologically refers to an orphan (child without mother) too. The word Robot better resonates with notion of artificial man, the man that was not naturally born (see Homunculus, Golem or artificial humanoid creatures in movies like Blade Runner (1982) or Artificial Intelligence: IA (2001)).

D. Obdržálek and A. Gottscheber (Eds.): EUROBOT 2011, CCIS 161, pp. 1–9, 2011.

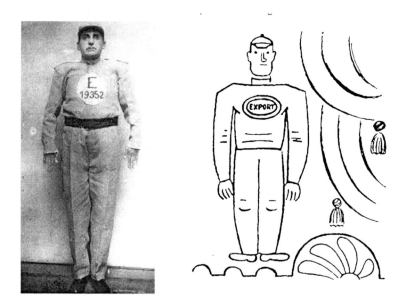

Fig. 1. *Left*: Robot from the R.U.R. stage production in National Theatre in Prague, 1921.
Right: Robot on stage. Illustration of paragraphs dedicated to Karel Čapeks R.U.R. in the artistic essay Homo Artefactus (1924) by Josef Čapek

to the world.[3] The play gained immediate popularity and was staged all around the world.[4]

The R.U.R. popularity among broad public brought about rather disdain of Czech theatre professionals of the period than their recognition. Yet in the year 1929, Miroslav Rutte, remarkable writer and journalist of the time, recalled critical reactions to the R.U.R. first stage production in National Theatre in Prague that took place eight years before:

"Čapek was often rebuked that success of R.U.R. was based on calculated use of the period atmosphere, and thus, that his collective drama was just kind of skilful handle of mental demands." [4]

According to many Czech reviewers, it was the atmosphere of the time that was the main coefficient of R.U.R dramatic effect and popularity. These voices blamed Karel Čapek usually for taking advantage of the common and conventional theme of the period – the "robotisation" of man.

However, the play gained the biggest popularity not at home, but in an Anglo-Saxon cultural context, where not so much theme of "robotisation of man",

---

[3] About the origin of Robot in context of brothers Čapeks work I wrote in [2].

[4] For more information about the stage production and reception of the R.U.R. play in Prague (1921), Berlin and Vienna (1923), New York (1922), London (1923), and Paris (1924) see [3].

Fig. 2. *Left*: Newspaper illustration referring to London stage production of R.U.R. in 1923.
Right: Newspaper review referring to New York stage production of R.U.R in 1922

but other qualities of the drama – it's melodramatic, adventurous plot and fascinating artificial men – were stressed in its stage productions. R.U.R. stage productions in New York (1922) and London (1923) affected transformation of the drama reception from dystopian drama into Frankensteinian melodrama on man made monsters that got out of control of their creators and annihilated humankind, as well as they initiated the world attention and fame of the R.U.R.

Czech writer and translator Jan Čep wrote about his impression from the London R.U.R. stage production, which he visited in St. Martin's Theatre only three month after its first night at April 24, 1923:

"(...) We were embarrassed both by the way it was staged, and by the way it was receipted. (...) For them, the theatre is above all entertainment (...), relaxation, fun. (...) The audience was the most impressed by curiosity and sensation of the story, unusual idea of artificial men, they burst into laugh for accidental jokes in absolutely inappropriate moments, that man was hiding his face with shame and bitterness."[5]

It was the melodramatic, sci-fi interpretation that gained to the R.U.R. and to its author the world fame. This way understood the Čapek's play Isaac Asimov too. We can deduce it from his writing in which he was commenting on sci-fi production of 20s and 30s, he wrote that authors of these stories repeated again and again the R.U.R. plot based on a conflict between human heroes and robots: "During 20s and 30s, R.U.R. helped to strength Frankensteinian complex (...) hordes of noisy and killing robots appeared in one story after another (...)."[6]

2 Robot – Figure of Technological Progress

Looking back to the beginning of the 20th century we can see, that the robot became soon a figure working in service of the modern myth of technological progress, which goes bravely beyond boundaries and limits of natural, biological humanity. Robots had not only colonized pages of science-fiction novels and short stories very soon, they were quickly transposed into the physical world too.

Fig. 3. Mr. Televox (USA): Robot in service of televox device advertising with his inventor R. J. Wensley, 1928

By their crossing from realm of science fiction into the realm of science-facts, robots have got shapes of man made from metal and steel and they were presented to the public as curiosities serving to popularization of the concept of technological progress and automation of work (see Fig. 4).[5]

In the year 1929 already, Stuart Chase, economist and engineer, wanted to describe advantages of work automation in the contrary to mechanical work symbolized by assembly lines, used two meanings of Karel Čapek's neologism robot as rhetoric figures.

He wrote: "In one of the great establishments manufacturing automobiles, there is a room filled with punching machines. In front of each machine stands

---

[5] Erkki Huhtamo in his article From Cybernation to Interaction: A Contribution to an Archeology of Interactivity wrote that there is still missing research on relationship between development of human – machine interface and interaction (from mechanization, through automation to cybernation of the working process, which has transformed itself into discourse about interactivity of new, digital media).[7]

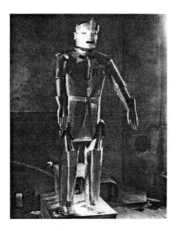

Fig. 4. *Left*: Robot Eric (UK) with R.U.R. on his chest. His construction was supported by Captain Richardson.
Right: The Robot Eric was the main attraction of the Exhibition of the Society of Model Engineers opening ceremonial, London 1928

a worker, feeding it pieces of steel by hand. A lever is geared to the mechanism, and to this lever the man is chained by a handcuff locked to his wrist. As the punch comes down, the lever moves back, taking the hand with it. (...) To look down the long room is to see machines, levers and men in unison – feed, punch, jerk back; feed, punch, jerk back ... I have heard of no other single task today which so closely approximates the gloomy prophets' picture of the robot – the mechanism of flesh and blood first heard of in a Czechoslovak play, towards which, it is alleged, all men are moving."[8]

However, Chase's argument didn't lead towards refusal of industrial revolution and machine based civilization. The solution, he is offering as a remedy of the situation of the enslaved worker by his/her work at assembly lines, has shape of robot again. It is not the "the mechanism of flash and blood" anymore, but an automatically working machine, that is able to replace man in all instances where it is possible.[6] According to Chase man becomes robot in a process of mechanical production, but automation of work puts man into position in which he/her enslaves the engine.[8]

3   From Robot as Automaton to Robot as a Means of Work Automation

The concept of work automation by means of replacing man with machine (robot) in working process, appeared in 1915 already, when Spanish inventor

---

[6] More precise and appropriate definition of robot we can find in a book The Robotic Primer by Mataric: "a man created system which exists in its own physical environment, is able to sense this environment and act in it in order to achieve its goals or to accomplish its own missiles."[9]

Leonardo Torres y Quevedo thought about possibility to transform useless automatons (e.g. androids) into apparatuses, which will not resemble outer human appearance and gestures, but which will be able to resemble man in work.[10]

We can find marks of the process of artificial man transformation into the autonomous machine even earlier, in Golem legend of Prague from the end of the sixteen century, according to which the Golem was made by historical person, rabbi Judah Loew ben Bezalel. The Golem legend is originally connected with mystical initiation. However, in the Prague variety of the Golem legend we can find certain marks of the artificial man reduction into the practically useful artificial servant of its creator. In other words, the figure of Golem, artificial man, is transformed into a figure of an autonomously working tool. We can say that already in this moment Golem became robot – the perfect (universal) servant or worker, able to do hard work and to serve to man.

Zdeněk Neuabuer noticed that in this moment appeared new qualities of artificial man too: Its unpredictability and potentially its potential to get out of its creator control:

"Unpredictability of Golem's behaviour is really un-predictable/in-calculable, (...) it is not possible to prevent it by better specification of commands – by 'program development'. The Golem is something im-perfect, un-formed in its very substance: his repetitional aberrations – deviations from order of presumptions and common sense – were in fact warning marks of threaten danger."[11]

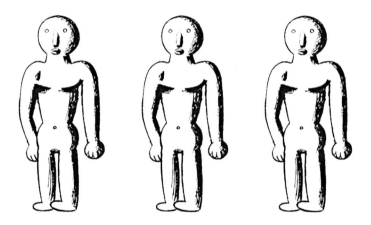

Fig. 5. Golem. Drawing by Josef Čapek: An illustration from artistic essay Homo Artefactus, 1924 [12]

Karel Čapek sow correspondences between his Robot characters and Golem too. He wrote in Prager *Tagblatt*, September, 23 1935, that: "R.U.R. is in fact a transformation of the Golem legend into a modern form. However, I realized this only when the piece was done. 'To hell, it is in fact Golem, I said to myself. 'Robots are Golem made in factory mass production.'"[13]

Čapek's robots, as modern, serially reproduced Golems, with their double meaning of mechanized man and autonomous machine; refer as far as to the Aristotle's utopian vision of an ideal social system supported by intelligent machines described in *Politics*:

"For if every instrument could accomplish its own work, obeying or anticipating the will of others, like the statue of Daedalus, or tripods of Hephaestus, which, says the poet, 'of their own accord entered the assembly of Gods'; if, in like manner, the shuttle would weave and the plectrum touch the lyre without a hand to guide them, chief workmen would not want servants, nor master slaves." [14]

4   Myth of Robot

Going back to the beginning of the 20th century we can see, that robot has become soon a symbol working in service of the modern myth of technological progress, which goes bravely beyond boundaries and limits of natural, biological humanity.

Robots have colonized pages of science-fiction novels and short stories very soon, and they were quickly transposed into the physical world too. They have got shapes of man made from metal and steel and they were presented to the public as curiosities serving to popularization of the concept of technological progress (see Fig. 3 and 4).

Robot became popular means of articulation of myth of modern times. To understand the way the modern myths, in which service robot is working, is structured, we can use methodology and observations of Roland Barthes [15]. According to him: a) Myth often uses neologisms derived from generally known words; and b) The sign system of myth works as a second order sign system using first order sign system (words, sentences, images) as its source material which he transforms into the myth narrative. The meaning of the source material of the myth narrative is inevitably deformed as it is on a one side reduced and on the other side it is replaced with or integrated into new meanings of the myth.

The neologism robot gained big popularity and spread especially over English language countries very soon. The play R.U.R. was translated info English by Paul Selver in 1923 and in 1933 already we can find many variations of word robot, that became part of English language, listed in Oxford English Dictionary supplements: "robotize, robotizing, robotization, robotry, robotism, robotian, robotesque and so on". Frantiek Chudoba reported about it in Czech newspaper with sigh that the word robot has richer life abroad than at home.[16]

However, the most influential neologism derived from the word robot – robotics – was coined later on by Russian-born American writer Isaac Asimov. He used the word robotics, as well as three law of robotics, for the first time in his short story *Runaround*, published in pulp magazine *Astounding Science Fiction* in 1942. The author, who calls himself "father of the modern robot story" inspired many scientists and engineers working in robotics laboratories in their effort to construct humanoid robot.

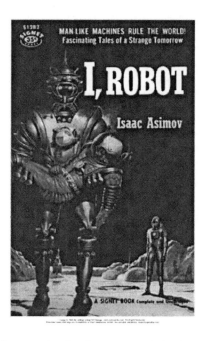

Fig. 6. I. Asimov: I, Robot. 1950 The first print of the book collection in which the short story *Runaround* was published.

5 Conclusion

Robot – the subject of the interest of scientists and engineers working in the field of robotics – as well as the main figure and even symbol of technological progress – hides its broad and ambivalent cultural meaning. In the myth of technological progress, the robot works rather as a super-machine, symbol of rapid technological development. However, under the simple and evident message of the myth, whole cluster of other meanings of robot still lives and animates our approaches to robots: Robot as character from R.U.R., which is an ambivalent metaphor of state of humanity in Machine age; Robot as a man reduced to an engine of factory production (see Charlie Chaplin's movie The Modern Times, 1936); Robot as an intelligent (living) tool (Aristotle's *Politics*); Robot as a mannequin, about which Freud wrote in his article *Das Unheimliche* (1919)[17]. – All these meanings are not going against the modernist myth of progress. In opposite, the myth integrates them into itself. The dizziness, fascination and fear we feel when we are facing robots, the creatures with deep and rich cultural consciousness, are transformed into our experience of and attitudes towards the products and effects of technological progress.

References

1. Čapek, K.: O slově robot. Lidové Noviny 24(12), 12 (1933)
2. Horáková, J., Kelemen, J.: The Robot Story: Why Robots Were Bor nand How They Grew Up. In: Husbands, P., Holland, O., Wheller, M. (eds.) The Mechanical Mind in History, pp. 283–306. The MIT Press, Cambridge (2008)
3. Horáková, J.: Robot jako robot (Robot as a robot; in Czech). Koniasch Latin Press, Prague (2010)
4. Rutte, M.: Královské divadlo na Vinohradech. Národní Listy 16. 11., č. 314, 9 (1929)
5. Čep, J.: Dojmy z Anglie. Sternberg, Šternberk (2007)
6. Asimov, I.: The Robot Chronicles. In: Gold – The Final Science Fiction Collection. HarperPrism (1995)
7. Huhtamo, E.: From Cybernation to Interaction: A Contribution to an Archeology of Interactivity. In: Lunenfled, P. (ed.) The Digital Dialectic: New Essays on New Media, pp. s.96–s.110. MIT Press, Cambridge (1999)
8. Chase, S.: Man and Machina. The Macmillan Copany, New York (1929)
9. Mataric, M.J.: The Robotic Primer. The MIT Press, Cambridge (2007)
10. Fleck, G. (ed.): A Computer Perspective. Harvard University Press, Cambridge (1973)
11. Neubauer, Z.: Golem a další příběhy o kabale, symbolech a podivuhodných setkáních. Malvern, Prague (2002)
12. Čapek, J.L.: Umělý člověk. Dauphin, Prague (1997)
13. Čapek, K.: R.U.R. Prager Tagblatt, Prague 23. 9 (1933)
14. Aristotle. The basic Works of Aristotle, McKeon, R. (ed.), vol. 1. Random House, New York (1941)
15. Barthes, R.L.: Mythologies. Vintage Books, London (1972)
16. Chudoba, F.: Národní dílo. In: Lidové Noviny, s. 9, 15 and 16. 12 (1933)
17. Freud, S.: The Uncanny. Penguin Books, London (2003)

VEX Robotics: STEM Program and Robotics Competition Expansion into Europe

Irene Alvarez Caro

Spanish Robotics Competition Organization (A.R.C.E.),
Calle Magnolia 12, 28260 Galapagar, Spain
http://www.arcerobotica.org

Abstract. VEX Robotics is a competition and an educational system for STEM (Science, technology, engineering and mathematics) programs. It was started in 2005 in the USA and was introduced in Europe in 2007 in England. Currently three European countries are using VEX Robotics system: United Kingdom, Sweden and Spain and it is expanding to France and Germany. In this paper we analyze VEX Educational robotics and we cover the main aspects of the European Expansion.

Keywords: Educational, Competition, VEX Robotics, STEM programs, Teaching with robotics.

1 Introduction

VEX Robotics has become one of the biggest competitions and educative robotics system in North America and is steadily expanding around the world. In this paper we focus on what makes this system so popular and interesting for STEM programs and why its expansion into Europe is still in its incipient phase. Details of the VEX Educational Robotics (EDR) and the VEX Robotics Competition are included along with an analysis of the European situation and how VEX might be integrated to help the growth of STEM programs there.

2 VEX Educational Robotics (EDR)

VEX educational robotics (EDR) was started in 2005 to provide an affordable, accessible and sustainable option for students, educators, and professionals to get excited about STEM education and involved via hands-on robotics programs.

At the time VEX was started there were already other robotics competitions that had left some needs unmet which VEX tried to solve. For example in the FIRST (For Inspiration and Recognition of Science and Technology) Robotics Competition, because of the material used, the teams had to invert around $6,000 to $10,000 each year to get a basic robot. There was a more reasonably priced competition in the FIRST Lego League (FLL) with a yearly cost of about $500. The problem here is that while Lego Mindstorms is a really useful system for elementary and young middle school students when it comes to high school

D. Obdržálek and A. Gottscheber (Eds.): EUROBOT 2011, CCIS 161, pp. 10–16, 2011.

students there is a lack of mechanical complexity in the system and a lack of design intricacy in the FLL challenge.

Those were the reasons that prompted the creation of VEX Robotics design system as an adaptable robotics kit. As Marty Mechsner, adjunct professor at Cal State Universtity and president of the Small Manufactures' Institute (SMI), said in an interview for Robot Magazine: "With the VEX System, you can sponsor a team for a minimum $750 to $1000, and you'd need to provide that team with $300 to $500 a year thereafter for continuing competitions. A small business can more easily do this and it's reasonable. Middle schools and high schools, teachers and students love the VEX Robotics kits. Their affordability, educational materials and curriculum and that the robots can be built in a classroom without any need for a machine shop make VEX perfect for getting robotics into schools. The huge network of competitions and events for VEX teams to participate in is also a huge incentive."[1]

2.1   STEM Programs

STEM (Science, Technology, Engineering, and Mathematics) programs are a new way to get students as interested in scientific and technical fields as they are in sports and movies. The term is mostly used in English speaking countries and it has become popular because of the decrease in STEM university graduates.

These programs try to show that STEM can be fun and interesting by focusing on a hands-on approach more than a theoretical one. "The constant breakthroughs in chemistry, medicine, materials and physics reveal a new set of challenges and create an even greater opportunity for problem solving through technology. These problems are not academic; the solutions could help save the world and those technology problem solvers will be the ones to make it possible."[2] In the end it becomes a pedagogical issue as until now STEM has always been taught similar to other fields (languages, literature, philosophy, etc). In these fields receptive learning may be enough; however when it comes to STEM has been shown to be insufficient. On the surface, students appear to know the theory because they perform well on classroom exams, but struggle when asked to apply the concepts to the real world. The conceptual difficulties can often drive them away from continuing studies in STEM fields.

Most STEM programs have the philosophy of "Learning from Discovering", which simply means learning from what you actually do. These programs face students with different problems and give them the material (theoretical and physical) to solve them; and they have to do it helping each other, trying different methods and looking for information related to the problems in their resources. With this method students understand the nature of the problem and better assimilate the theoretical concepts used in solving the problem.

2.2   VEX Educational Robotics as Part of STEM Programs

Robotics is widely used by STEM programs because it provides a chance to integrate applied physics, mathematics, computer programming, digital prototyping and design. Practicing robotics as a team also provides the students with experiences related with problem solving, teamwork and leadership that help them to develop their soft skills.

VEX Educational Robotics includes all of these characteristics it provides pre-manufactured and easily formed structural metal and user-programmable microprocessors combined with a wide range of sensors and mechanical parts. While the students work also learn interdisciplinary teamwork by having to integrate mechanical systems with sensors for electronics and programming, as they normally work as separated subgroups. According to Indiana Robotics Educators, a group that provides workshops on VEX Robotics for middle and high school teachers: the program is success because "robots are entertaining and fun to build, operate and compete with, and students progress more quickly in their studies and become more aware of technical career opportunities along the way."[3]

In addition VEX has made partnerships with numerous companies and organizations, such as Autodesk, Intelitek, Carnegie Mellon Robotics Academy and VisualEdge to provide one of the most complete robotics and STEM curriculums. As we mentioned before there are other STEM robotics programs, for example Lego, however when we compare the range of ages to which Lego and VEX EDR are applicable we found that the Lego system is only effective until the students are about14 years old, whereas VEX EDR is challenging enough for students from 12 to 18 years old and can be extended to Universities and Colleges with VEX Robotics Competition and VEX PRO (a line of large-scale powerful competitive robotics components), This sets VEX Robotics apart from other STEM programs that are limited by age or by the possibility of adding components not from the same brand of products.

3   VEX Robotics Competition

The VEX robotics competition is the largest competition of its kind for middle and high school students with more than 3,600 teams from 20 countries playing in over 270 tournaments worldwide. It started as the FIRST Technology Challenge with the demonstration in 2005 and pilot season the following year. After the 2007 season VEX separated from FIRST and Bridge Battle was the game played in the first VEX Robotics World Championship celebrated in Northridge, California (USA), in March 2008. The goal of the competition is to engage students with robotics and STEM by means of competitiveness, teamwork, and collaboration with teams. This is achieved by offering different awards that promote life values and quality work. From this they obtain a complete cooperation between the students, mentors, organizations and companies that collaborate with VEX.

The competition is composed of one main challenge and two optional ones. The main challenge consists of a 20 second autonomous period and a 2 minute driver controlled period in which students have to play a game that changes yearly. The two optional challenges consist of a one minute of autonomous or driver controlled period both playing the same game as in the main challenge except with one team on the field at a time.

Matches of the main challenge are composed of two alliances, blue and red, that compete to get the higher score. Each alliance consists of two teams during the preliminary wounds and three during the direct elimination rounds. The winner of regional competitions earns the right to compete at the World Championships.

Apart from yearly game each, each season various online challenges proposed, such as promotion videos, designing a game, digital prototyping, designing a robot, team website, educational video, etc. These online challenges promote the diversification of students and as they are awarded with VEX gift certificates teams with few resources can work on these challenges to try to get new vex parts.

One of the main pillars of the VEX Robotics Competitions is the team combination of mentors and students. VEX team's normal structure is between 5 to 10 students and at least one mentor or teacher and in teams with more resources one teacher for each of the two main areas, mechanics and programming. The mentors, who are mostly volunteer and do not receive any salary, take care of the administrative team issues and in collaboration with the students' parents they raise the money needed to keep the team working. Meanwhile students work on their robots sometimes splitting into smaller groups to concentrate on their favorite subsystem always with the goal of building and programming a good robot while having fun and learning. For beginning teams, the internet is a great resource to connect with experienced teams who share information, ideas, tips, photos/videos and help solve problems. VEX Robotics promotes this networking by providing online forums and tutorial information on their website to support the community.

The other main pillar in the VEX Robotics Competitions is the events and the volunteers that run them. Usually events are sponsored by a company and an organization. The company provides the event with judges for the award, media visibility, funds, etc. and the organization is in charge of getting volunteers, the previous planning, the announce of the event, etc. This competitions have a duration of 1 to 3 days, depending if they are local, national/state or continental/worldwide. Their schedule is divided in registration; robot inspection; practice and qualifying matches, in which alliances are raffled for each match preciously to the beginning of the competition; alliance selection, in which the top highest seek teams choose their alliance partners; final matches and award ceremony. After the competition some events celebrate a team party in which teams can interact without the competition's pressure.

4   Expansion in Europe

VEX Robotics started to expand in Europe in 2006-2007 when Alan Fuller, a communications manager at MBDA, desired to start some robotics activity in his community. They found VEX as an affordable system to sponsor and easy to implement for schools. They sponsored schools and in collaboration with Barclay School, Stevenage (UK), they founded Robot Rumble, the qualifying event for British teams.

Lately VEX expanded to Sweden where two teams were founded at Stockholm International School. They started working with VEX components in 2007 but they did not compete until the season of 2008-2009, becoming Europe and VEX champion in Galapabot in the 2009-2010 season. The last country in which VEX has expanded is Spain in 2008, when Irene lvarez (author of this paper) came back from US where she had spent one year studying at Granada Hills Charter High School where she joined their robotics team, the Robodox. Upon returning to Spain she was sponsored by the team and one of the mentors, Chris Siegert. The first team started in Spain, Yehabots, competed in Robot Rumble II becoming European VEX Champion of the 2008-2009 season (its rookie year).

All of the above activity has been self-generated by individuals who have been aware of the VEX platform in the United States and imported product to compete because of a true passion for Robotics. It is only from the start of 2011 that Innovation First has begun to actively market the VEX Robotic Design System in Europe. Based out of an office and distribution centre in the UK, the company is signing up local partners across several countries to help establish the platform both in competition and education.

4.1   Competitions in Europe

The expansion of VEX Robotics Competition into Europe has been slow due in part to the travel expenses to compete in events hosted mainly in America and Asia. Because of this British and Spanish VEX teams have started organizing their own competitions as a possible solution.

The first VEX Robotics Competition was held in Stevenage under the name of Robot Rumble I in the 2007-2008 season. After having a team competing in the USA the previous season, Robot Rumble was sponsored by MBDA, and 12 teams also sponsored by MBDA competed. In the next season, 2008-2009, Robot Rumble II was presented and it became the European Qualifying Tournament ought to the participation of the Spanish Team Yehabots. After that season, Robot Rumble Committee decided to convert the event to a middle school event only and has celebrated another two editions, Robot Rumble III and IV.

After the Yehabots competed at Robot Rumble II, as they were a middle and high school mixed team, they decided to try to start a new competition open to students of any age. A.R.C.E. (Spanish Robotics Competitions organization) was founded as the organization committee of the event that by a partnership with Galapagar, Madrid, City Council and adopted the name of Galapabot. The first tournament, held under the name of Galapabot'10 for 2009-2010 season, became the European Qualifying Tournament as Robot Rumble had limited the age and ought to the participation of the two Swedish teams. It was a one and a half day tournament with 6 teams competing, 2 Swedish and 4 Spanish, held on the 28th and 29th of January 2010. For the current season, 2010-2011, Galapabot'11 had

to reduce its budget and held only the Spanish Qualifying Tournament as they could not afford the expenses of hosting foreign teams.

The current situation is a competition in the United Kingdom, Robot Rumble, and a competition in Spain, Galapabot. Right now there are projects for new competitions and teams in France, Germany, United Kingdom and Spain; with extra-curricular classroom competitions based around the 'Swept Away' game and World Championship qualifying games on the 2011-2012 game 'VEX Gateway'. The medium-term goal for VEX expansion in Europe is to generate enough interest and teams that a true 'European Championship' will be held annually.

4.2   Difficulties for the Integration of STEM Programs

North American educational systems are open systems in the way that leave students to pick different classes depending in their progress and likes. This structure of different classes leaves space for the student to choose classes outside the regular curriculum such as auto shop, wood working and robotics. These characteristics promote the introduction of STEM programs also have the possibility of university/college credits.

European educational systems are completely different from the North American ones. In Europe students have to take specific classes to be able to graduate and only in their last years of pre-university studies can choose one or two optional classes in the best of cases. This, in conjunction with many bureaucratic problems, makes the approval of new optative classes, like robotics, almost impossible. Because of this most robotics teams end up working as an extracurricular activity.

Statistically Europe has a higher percentage of students in STEM fields (26.6%) than the international average for the ratio of STEM to non-STEM degrees. That ratio was 26.4% in 2002 while in North America it was only 18.7%. This is the reason North America has seen the necessity of enhancing STEM programs while in Europe it is less urgent.[4]

5   Conclusion

The VEX Educational Robotics (EDR) program perfectly integrates all the concepts of STEM programs, along with the VEX Robotics Competition. VEX shows potential to be a way to start integrating STEM in Europe as it can be developed as an extracurricular activity. Its affordability and new projects from VEX are helping the expansion in Europe and it is getting more companies, schools and individuals in general involved in working for a new generation of STEM workers.

Acknowledgments. I would like to thank my mentor, Chris Siegert, for his support since I started thinking about starting the first VEX Robotics team in Spain, for being more than a mentor for me and his help while developing this paper; Jamie Moran for his support as a mentor when I was in Robodox, as a friend all this years and for his review of the paper; all my teammates and friends from Robodox that inspire me to do keep doing robotics; and also VEX Robotics for understanding the difficulties of starting teams and a competition in a new area.

References

1. Atwood, T.: VEX Robotics Taking Off in California Classrooms. Robot Magazine (September/October 2008)
2. VEX Robotics Competition - Round Up manual, VEX Robotics (June 12, 2010)
3. Atwood, T.: 560 Indiana teachers receive VEX robots & training Thousands of additional students learning robotics & competing. Robot Magazine (July/August 2008)
4. Kuenzi, J.: Science, Technology, Engineering, and Mathematics (STEM) Education: Background, Federal Policy, and Legislative Action. CRS Report for Congress (March 21, 2008)

Educational Environment for Robotic Applications in Engineering

Silas F.R. Alves[1], Humberto Ferasoli Filho[2], Renê Pegoraro[2],
Marco A.C. Caldeira[2], João M. Rosário[1], and Wilson M. Yonezawa[2]

[1] Laboratory of Integrated Automation and Robotics, Mechanical Engineering Dep.,
State University of Campinas, P.O. Box 6122, 13083970, Campinas, São Paulo, Brazil
{silas,rosario}@fem.unicamp.br
[2] Laboratory of Integration of Intelligent Systems and Devices, Computer Dep.
Sciences Faculty, University of São Paulo State, P.O. Box 473, 17033360,
Bauru, São Paulo, Brazil
{ferasoli,pegoraro,caldeira,yonezawa}@fc.unesp.br

Abstract. This paper describes an initiative which uses low-cost mobile robots to create both robotics courses and learning environment to support the teaching of computing and many other related disciplines. The pursued principle is that lower cost alternatives that can meet the educational needs, since it is accompanied by an environment with friendly software interface. In this sense, the hardware interface was developed to allow the computer to process data from the sensors and actuators of the mobile robot. This architecture is adequate because of the acceptance of students in their use, since the environment is developed within a familiar platform to them.

Keywords: Mobile Robot, Engineering Teaching, Educational Environment.

1 Introduction

Today, the engineering education in universities faces new challenges. Traditional approaches do not capture attention of students and college dropout not only undermines the pedagogical practices, but also wastes resources [1].

One approach that has shown success in different levels of education is the Robotics. As a pedagogical tool for teaching engineering, robotics has several interesting aspects. It is inherently multidisciplinary, encourages teamwork and promotes a real visual feedback in an exciting and motivating manner [2]. However, the high cost of robots sometimes forbids the use of robotics in the classroom. In this sense, the Systems Integration Group and Smart Devices (GISDI), Department of Computer Science (DCO), UNESP, Bauru develops initiatives that uses an open control architecture and are low-cost, flexible and aligned to the teaching of Engineering and Robotics itself.

This paper describes three LISDI robots: Michelangelo; AEDROMO; and the C2-25. The paper also discusses the implementation details of the software and

D. Obdržálek and A. Gottscheber (Eds.): EUROBOT 2011, CCIS 161, pp. 17–28, 2011.

hardware that composes these projects, as well as it presents some activities that can be developed with these platforms.

2   Open Control Architecture

The control architecture is based on a Personal Computer (PC), a Communication System and a Robot, as shown in Fig. 1. The PC is responsible for controlling the robot, therefore it does the planning of the tasks that the robot must perform. In turn, the robot performs these tasks which define the way it will acts over the world, while it senses the world state and sends the sensory data to the computer, ensuring that the planning is carried with updated data on the environment. The communication between the computer and the robot is performed through the Communication System, which is established in a wired or wireless manner.

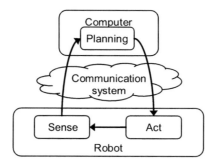

Fig. 1. Open Control Architecture of LISDI Educational Mobile Robots

The Open Control Architecture is implemented as shown in Fig. 2. The computer runs the user software which is responsible for controlling the robot. To ease the software development, an Application Programming Interface (API) is developed for each robot. These APIs provides the function calls and procedures needed to access the robot embedded hardware. In other words, the API serves as an interface for the robot, and therefore it abstracts the communication system and its protocol. On the robot side, a supervisor system responds to the API calls through the communication system, and is responsible for accessing the robot's sensors and actuators.

This choice of architecture approximates the student to robotics at the same time it reduces the cost of the system. The computer plays a key role within the architecture. Being familiar to most students, who have access to PCs in schools or at home, the computer bring them closer to robotics through the use of tools they already known. Moreover, it is the computer that gives the flexibility of the architecture through modular and open software. In addition, the computer is already inserted into existing computing infrastructure in universities, which have computers in their laboratories.

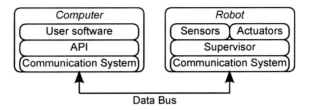

Fig. 2. Implementation of the Open Architecture

As the computer is responsible for the robot task planning, it is on the computer where data processing occurs more intensively. As consequence, the Robot does not need huge processing power, requiring only digital and analog input and output devices.

Finally, since there is data exchange between computer and robot, a Communication System is necessary. This system can be either wired (as the RS232 or USB standards) or wireless (eg Bluetooth, WiFi, Zigbee, etc).

Another important aspect observed in the robots developed by the GISDI is their small dimensions. Little robots do not require large space to set in the workspace, facilitating its implementation in different laboratories and eases the handling and transport of these robots. Other common feature of these robots is the differential drive system, adopted by its efficiency, ease of implementation and relative low-cost.

3 Robot Platforms

3.1 Michelangelo

The Michelangelo robot, shown in Fig. 3, is a small mobile robot with differential drive system and four infrared sensors. Its main goal is being a simple platform that involves the basic concepts of electronics and computing, providing different experiments that demonstrate these concepts. To this end, this robot uses few sensors and actuators, so its hardware and software architectures are simple. The control circuit uses only discrete components studied in the disciplines of Digital Circuits and Digital Circuits Laboratory. Therefore, the robot also serves as a practical demonstration of the concepts studied in classroom.

This robot is used in different educational activities within the Computer Science course from UNESP. In the disciplines of Digital Circuits Laboratory and Introduction to Mobile Robots, it is used as a platform for demonstrating the concepts studied in the classroom. It is also used in interdisciplinary activities of the course's pedagogical plan. Moreover, it is also available for the students to use in their major papers.

The Michelangelo robot embeds four infrared (IR) reflective sensors, used to find black lines on the floor, and two motor, which are controlled by a supervisor system implemented on a microcontroller. This supervisor system is commanded by the student software running on the computer, where is also the robot's API

Fig. 3. Michelangelo Robot

and the communication layer. To establish the communication between the robot and the computer, a Bluetooth communication system is used. Originally, this robot was based on the Parallel Port, but this communication port fell into disuse and sometimes it is no longer found in newer computers, such as notebooks. Furthermore, the Parallel Port uses a cable for transferring data, which affect the robot's mobility and limits their field of actuation. In this sense, though it raises the robot cost, Bluetooth provides greater mobility to the robot, besides being a standard present in current personal computers mainly notebook models. Computers that do not have integrated Bluetooth can utilize a low cost adapter, which provides the same operation capability.

The group made of the computer, the robot and the communication system composes the Michelangelo's Architecture, shown in Fig. 4.

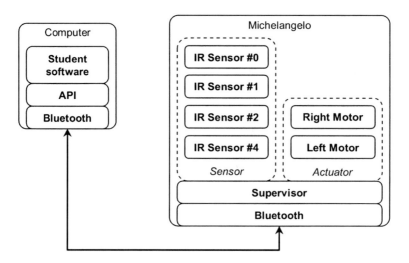

Fig. 4. Michelangelo's Control Architecture

3.2 AEDROMO

The AEDROMO is an Didactic Experimental Environment with Mobile Robots, consisting of two robots (or more), one computer, one global camera (a webcam) and one transmitter, as shown in Fig. 5. The main goal of the design and development of this environment was provide an environment with more than one robot that had flexibility of adaptation and use. The experiment on this environment can be motivated for research, learning or merely entertainment [3].

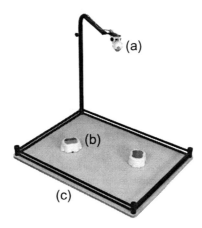

Fig. 5. AEDROMO environment: webcam (a); robots (b); and the workspace (c)

The AEDROMO also has two versions. The first version of AEDROMO, shown in Fig. 5, used small robots. The second release of AEDROMO uses the robots shown in Fig. 6. This version was size reduced to be easily manipulated by children.

Fig. 6. The second version of AEDROMO robot held by an adult

AEDROMO's Architecture uses a computer to control the robots and a global camera which allow the computer to trace the robot's positions. The images captured by the camera are sent through USB (Universal Serial Bus) to the computer. In the computer, these images are acquired and processed to determine information about the Cartesian positions (x, y, θ) of individual objects (robots, balls, blocks, etc.) inserted on the workspace. These information are used by the strategy module according to the rules of the running application - the student software. Thereafter, commands are sent to the robots so they can act on the environment according to these rules. These commands are interpreted by the supervisor system that controls the robot motors. The occurred changes are seen by the camera, and then the process repeats at a rate equivalent to the camera capture rate, which usually varies from 15 to 30 Hz. Fig. 7 illustrates this architecture.

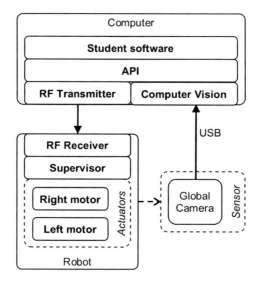

Fig. 7. AEDROMO's Control Architecture

This kind of architecture, which uses global vision, gives great versatility to the system since it allows small robots to react to the environment in complex ways without the need to include sophisticated sensors. At the same time, it enables a wide variety of pedagogical applications for both teaching and research.

3.3   C2-25 Robot

The C2-25 robot [4], shown in Fig. 8, is a mobile robot aimed to bring students closer to the robot through an already known environment: the computer. Environments composed by personal computers and graphical operating systems, as the one used by this robot, are not only known by most students, but are also used by them in curricular activities, such as programming. Thus, the development environment is within the scope of programming already known by the student. This reduces the time required to develop control algorithms for the robot, thanks to the familiarity with the environment. In this sense, this robot embeds a netbook, where the students can implement their control architectures or which may serve as server which allows its remote control. Moreover, the programming of C2-25 is facilitated by an API written specifically for the robot. This API contains the classes and methods needed to acquire sensory data and trigger its actuators. This tool allows the quickly development of practical activities involving, for example, system software, control theory, robotics, instrumentation or sensor networks. It provides a simple interface for students to acquire data and drive actuators without knowing the hardware interface or communication protocols. This reduces the time spent to resolve the activities making them more dynamic.

Another possibility already covered by the development architecture is provided through a network of computers. A server installed inside the robot allows access to its sensors and actuators via a remote computer, whose development API is similar to the robot API.

The architecture of the C2-25, shown in Fig. 9, consists on the onboard electronics, an embedded computer and a remote computer.

The onboard electronics of the robot is responsible for driving the motors and reading the sensors. There are two DC motors, responsible for the traction, the odometry sensors coupled on the motors, and a servo motor whose function is to change the heading of the infrared range sensor. These sensors and actuators are controlled by an supervisor system implemented on a microcontroller, which

Fig. 8. C2-25 Robot

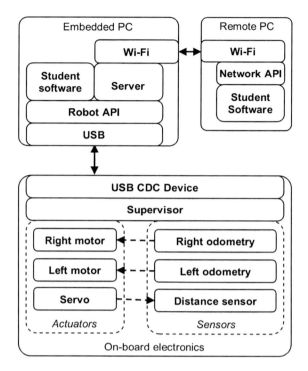

Fig. 9. C2-25 Control Architecture

also provides the USB CDC (Communications Device Class) device that allows the data exchange between the supervisor system and the computer.

The control of electronics is made through the embedded computer (netbook) with the API is available for the onboard electronics. In this sense, the student can develop the control software on the embedded computer itself, since it uses a common operating system. Using a familiar computer platform, students can develop their work in programming environments they learned in other disciplines, thus speeding up the programming process.

The embedded computer also provides a server that allows remote access to the robot via an IEEE 802.11 (WiFi) link. To use this resource, an API that abstracts to the user both the network layer and the robot services has been built. This way, students can also develop the control software on other computers. This option eases the access control to the robot when several students are working at the same time with it.

4   Proposed Activities

4.1   Michelangelo

Despite the limited amount of sensors and actuators, it is possible to develop different didactic activities with Michelangelo. The main objective of these activities is to demonstrate in a practical fashion the application of digital circuits and provide a platform for the development of software programming skills.

The goal of one activity performed with the robot is to demonstrate the robot programming and get the students used to the robot control architecture. The activity consists on driving the motors through the keyboard while the state of the sensors is printed on the screen.

Another activity is to keep the robot inside an area surrounded by a black line. To this end, students should be able to read the sensors and trigger actuators automatically.

It is also proposed programming of Michelangelo to operate similarly to an AGV (Automated Guided Vehicle), so it should follow the black line that forms the enclosure. The difficulty of the software lies on the amount of intersections of the line, which may form a maze.

It is important to note that these activities are always proposed in the end of the Digital Circuits and Digital Circuit Laboratory courses, for this stage of the course students already knows all the components used by the robot and have more knowledge of programming.

4.2   AEDROMO

The AEDROMO environment presents several options of applications for teaching, as well as for research and entertainment .The ability to recognize two robots and various colored objects through the camera provide the means for activities that involve collaborative and multiagent systems.

The objective of the proposed activities with AEDROMO is to experiment more complex aspects of robotics and computing.

The activity, entitled *Collecting Stuff*, deals with the basic aspects of the environment. Several balls of different colors are placed on the desktop. The task is to collect balls of the same color (*stuff*) to a reserved area. The time to collect the balls is the goal of this activity. There are two situations for this application. The first is characterized by a robot at a time working on the Environment, and the second with two robots. The latter situation is richer due to the dynamism imposed by the environment and the possibilities of variants of the experiment.

On the activity *Hunt and Hunter*, the two robots are placed in the environment and with different goals. The first robot runs away from the second one, while the second one tries to catch the first one. The environment can be improved with objects to ease the escape or hunting.

One activity that can involve the disciplines of graph theory or artificial intelligence is *Solving the Maze*. Obstacles are placed on the workspace providing alternative paths to a given area. The goal is to find this area and return to the home in the shortest time or shortest path. In this case, only one robot is used. A hunter and hunt situation and can be implemented with the two robots.

Another activity consists on a *Tennis Game*, where students are divided in groups to develop the strategy of the robot. The workspace is divided in half and each robot occupies one area. Then, a ball is released and the objective of the game is to push the ball across the line without going over it, allowing the ball to reach the bottom of the opponent's court. It is up for the opponent to prevent this from happening and to return the ball to other court. A little competition is held at the end of the activity so the performance of each solution presented is discussed.

4.3   C2-25

As the C2-25 robot has more onboard sensors and do not rely on external computer for the task planning, it enables varied activities. For the same reason it is recommended for students with more experience on programming.

The *Navigation* activity demonstrates the difficulties of moving a mobile robot throughout the world and what techniques were developed to address these difficulties. It is possible to experiment, for example, navigation with odometry and landmarks (through the use of markers recognized by the camera).

The activity *Follow the Master* proposes controlling of robot using computer vision and the distance sensor. Through the camera, the robot should identify a colored object, align itself with it and move on until it reach a predetermined distance. After that, the object is exchanged for colored clothing so that the robot should follow the person wearing these clothes.

The activity *Interaction with People* uses open source libraries for recognition and speech synthesis to create scenarios of interaction between the robot and a person. In this interaction, one can ask the robot to take objects from one side to another side of the room, or for it to show the path to a known area.

5   Concluding Remarks

Just like computers, robotics is an assistant technology resource usable in the educational process that may contribute to the cognitive development of students and of specialized intellectual skills. It is offered as an educational tool interesting on several aspects and it should be understood and exploited as such [5]. The presence of the robot in our society in the near future is undoubtedly. It is also undeniable the need to get acquainted and to demystify this technology that supports many other fields of knowledge.

Therefore, the use of robotics in education is mainly motivated by the active learning that it provides, and this happens in two ways. The first, in the use of robotics for education, in other words, for teaching particular or general concepts of the involved disciplines with robotics itself, and as a testbed for the teaching of this area, as outlined before. The second, in the use of robotics in education as an motivating element and experiments testbed to teach and verify concepts of disciplines from related areas [6]. In this sense, robotics is an educational tool, a teaching object.

Robotics in education should be seen as a pedagogical tool, as a learning environment to study new technologies, as an aid to programming, as a laboratory for Artificial Intelligence and many other disciplines, promoting active learning and enabling students with different levels of knowledge to achieve, even in a different time, an effective and motivating learning.

Mobile robots built by schools and universities can produce good results, mainly because they have been designed and tuned to pursue the initiative educational goals. However, the obtained results, although reportable, cannot usually be shared and used by other similar initiatives in other institutions, unless the entire experiment or environment is carefully replicated and the goals or purposes are equal or, in worst case, similar [7].

In parallel, the efficiency of using robotics to teach programming is relative to the care given to the adopted teaching strategy. In other words, robotics, as well as computers, are powerful educational tools, and should be understood as such, but its effectiveness is dependent on the model, on the objective and on the imposed educational strategy.

Robotics in education cannot be seen as a panacea, but as a support tool that should be properly explored. Schools cannot stay apart from this tool, as well as they cannot use it without well-established criteria.

Anyway, robotics is increasingly present in schools, whether as part of the curriculum, as in parallel courses, or even as entertainment. In this sense, GISDI has been working in educational environments with mobile robots. From the technological point of view, the presented environments support a wide variety of educational practices, as for teaching problems related to robotics itself, as well as for supporting other disciplines, such as teaching of programming, modeling, control, signal processing, or even behavior.

This paper presented and discussed the application of three didactic environments adopted by GISDI. Currently, they are applied within the curriculum of the course of Computer Science of the Faculty of Sciences in the form of activities in specific disciplines or as a biannual pedagogical project. The implementation details of each of the environments described here are available in the group's website.

References

1. Nogueira, F.: País perde R$ 9 bilhões com evasão no ensino superior, diz pesquisador (2011),
   http://g1.globo.com/vestibular-e-educacao/noticia/2011/02/
   pais-perde-r-9-bilhoes-com-evasao-no-ensino-superior-
   diz-pesquisador.html
2. Avanzato, R.: Mobile robotics for freshman design, research, and high schooloutreach. In: 2000 IEEE International Conference on Systems, Man, and Cybernetics (2000)
3. Ferasoli Filho, H., Pegoraro, R., Caldeira, M.A.C., Rosário, J.: AEDROMO- An Experimental and Didactic Environment with Mobile Robots. In: Proceedings of The 3rd International Conference on Autonomous Robots and Agents (2006)
4. Alves, S., Rosário, J.M., Ferasoli Filho, H., Pegoraro, R.: Environment for Teaching and Development of Mobile Robot Systems. In: Electronics, Robotics and Automotive Mechanics Conference (CERMA), pp. 302–307 (2010)

5. Papert, S.: Mindstorms: children, computers, and powerful ideas. Basic Books, Inc., New York (1980)
6. Barker, B.S., Ansorge, J.: Robotics as means to increase achievement scores in an informal learning environment. Journal of Research on Technology in Education 39, 229–243 (2007)
7. Borenstein, J., Everett, H.R., Feng, L.: Where am I? Sensors and Techniques for Mobile Robot Positioning, 1st edn., ch. 2, pp. 28–35, 71–72. AK Peters, Ltd., Wellesley (1995)

EmbedIT – An Open Robotic Kit for Education

Dorit Assaf and Rolf Pfeifer

Artificial Intelligence Laboratory
Department of Informatics
University of Zurich
Switzerland
{assaf,pfeifer}@ifi.uzh.ch

Abstract. Robots have often been used as an educational tool in class
to introduce kids to science and technology, disciplines that are affected
by decreasing enrollments in universities. Consequently, many robotic
kits are available off-the-shelf. Even though many of these platforms are
easy to use, they focus on a classical top-down engineering approach.
Additionally, they often require advanced programming skills. In this
paper we introduce an open robotic kit for education (EmbedIT) which
currently is under development. Unlike common robot kits EmbedIT
enables students to access the technical world in a non-engineering focused way. Through a graphical user interface students can easily build
and control robots. We believe that once fascination and a basic understanding of technology has been established, the barrier to learn more
advanced topics such as programming and electronics is lowered. Further
we describe the hardware and software of EmbedIT, the current state of
implementation, and possible applications.

Keywords: Robotic Kits, Educational Robotics, Edutainment, Embedded Systems, Rapid Prototyping in Robotics.

1 Introduction

The number of students showing interest in pursuing a career in Science, Technology, Engineering or Math is decreasing in the USA [1] as well as in Europe
[2]. In order to maintain economical competitiveness, education in these disciplines is crucial. This phenomena has gained a lot of attention from teachers,
researchers, politicians, authorities and other stakeholders. Consequently, a vast
number of initiatives have been developed to improve the situation. A popular
educational approach to motivate young people in learning is based on the con-
structivist/constructionist paradigm, where learning through play can contribute
to the construction of knowledge [3][4]. Active learning environments through the
use of interactive lessons, friendly competitions, and trial and error are therefore
preferred. Robots have been used in the last decade to introduce kids and especially girls [5] to science and technology [6]. Class activities with robots range

D. Obdržálek and A. Gottscheber (Eds.): EUROBOT 2011, CCIS 161, pp. 29–39, 2011.
© Springer-Verlag Berlin Heidelberg 2011

from kindergarten to high secondary school. A large number of robot competitions emerged such as the FIRST Lego League or RoboCupJunior, all with the aim to engage young people in these disciplines [7]. Consequently, many robot kits have been developed in research projects as well as in commercial companies. A popular robot kit used in educational robotics courses is the LEGO NXT [8]. Even though this platform is very easy to use, it focuses on a classical top-down engineering approach, where the actual robot has to be planned, built out of predefined parts and programmed using classical programming routines. Many other educational robotic platforms require advanced programming skills in C/C++.

In this paper we describe an open robotic kit (EmbedIT) that we are currently developing. The aim is to provide an open-source platform that enables teachers and students to easily build and control robots. In addition, our robot kit can be used as a rapid prototyping tool for researchers. With EmbedIT we try to overcome the constraints of classical engineering focused toolkits. We believe since young people are used to user-friendly applications in their everyday life, we should incorporate such interfaces in our kit. The user should be able to play with sensors and actuators without having to deal with the technical details. Furthermore, he should be able to build and implement a robot within a short time, and consequently, while testing and revising it, getting a deeper understanding about these sensors and actuators. We believe that once fascination and a basic understanding of technology has been established, motivation is increased to get familiar with more advanced topics such as programming and electronics. However, we don't solely target one group of users. EmbedIT is completely open-source and therefore technically more skilled users can reprogram and adapt the platform as they wish.

In the rest of this paper, besides the related work, the EmbedIT's hardware and software is described. This is followed by application examples, discussion, conclusion and future work.

2   Related Work

The field of educational robotics is growing due to the fact that robots are a proven effective learning tool [7]. A widely used robotic platform for educational robotics is the LEGO NXT [9][10]. It provides actuators, a variety of sensors, building blocks as well as an easy-to-use graphical programming language. Additionally, the LEGO NXT platform can be programmed using higher programming languages, such as JAVA.

A low cost educational robotic platform is the Asuro robot [11]. By soldering all electronic components to the PCB the user has to assemble the robot from scratch. Asuro is designed to be a wheeled robot, thus the user has no much flexibility to modify the default shape. It is programmed with C/C++ programming language. Other educational robotic platforms [12] use the popular Arduino boards [13]. We also used a small custom made wheeled robot based on the Arduino board to teach robotics to secondary school teachers [14]. Arduino is an open-source electronics prototyping platform based on flexible, easy-to-use hardware and software. Furthermore, the Arduino project provides custom C/C++ libraries to program the on board microcontroller. Hardware design and software is open-source and a large community grew around the platform contributing libraries, tutorials, hardware designs etc. Meanwhile, several Arduino control board designs have been developed, each suited for different applications. However, even though there are plenty of well documented online tutorials, skills in electronics are needed in order to attach sensors and actuators to these boards (which have to be purchased separately). The Arduino boards can be damaged easily by connecting additional components in the wrong way.

A fairly new project, but very related to the EmbedIT platform is .NET Gadgeteer of Microsoft research [15]. It is a rapid prototyping platform for small electronic gadgets and embedded hardware devices. It combines object-oriented programming and solderless assembly of electronics using a kit of hardware modules. Unlike the Arduino platform .NET Gadgeteer provides all kinds of sensors and actuators that can be plugged into the main board. This prevents problems caused by wrong connections.

Phidgets offers similar to .NET Gadgeteer a variety of sensors and motor controller modules which are all connected through an USB interface to the computer [16]. Additionally, the Phidgets libraries support the most common programming languages.

Nevertheless, Asuro, Arduino, .NET Gadgeteer as well as Phidgets require advanced programming skills.

3   EmbedIT – An Open Robotic Kit

Currently we are implementing the robot kit's hardware (electronics) and software. Building blocks such as structural material, wheels etc. will not be provided by EmbedIT. However, it is planned to provide design solutions to interface EmbedIT's electronics together with recommended motors and sensors with off-the-shelf mechanical construction kits such as LEGO blocks [17], Stokys [18], Meccano [19] etc.

The components of the EmbedIT platform are hardware modules consisting of small embedded systems (individual printed circuit boards equipped with an Atmel AVR microcontroller). Each module is an independent entity that serves either a control, sensory, actuation or communication purpose. According to a module's purpose a specific control program is running on its microcontroller. Additionally, each module carries its own unique identification number. A CAN data bus (two conductor cable) is the connecting piece between the modules. Each module can easily be attached and detached from the bus. The master module, which is a control module, controls the communication traffic on the bus. In addition, the master module serves as an interface to the user. A Java application, the EmbedITApp, running on the user's PC connects to the master module through a communication module, that can either be a Bluetooth, USB or serial (RS232) interface. In Fig. 1 the master module is attached to the CAN bus and a Bluetooth module is attached to the master module (communication modules are not attached to the bus directly, they have to be attached to a module). The EmbedITApp connects to the master module through the Bluetooth communication module. Additionally in Fig 1, one actuation module (servo) and two sensor modules (accelerometer, ultrasonic sensor) are connected to the bus.

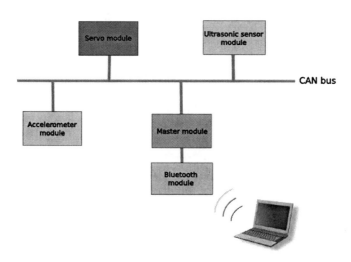

Fig. 1. A master module is attached to the CAN bus and a Bluetooth module is attached to the master module. The EmbedITApp running on the PC connects to the master module through the Bluetooth communication module. Additionally, a servo module, an accelerometer module and an ultrasonic sensor module are connected to the bus.

Fig. 2 shows the real modules, a Bluetooth module, a master module, two sensor modules (accelerometer, ultrasonic), the CAN bus, a power supply and a servo module with one servo attached. Once a connection between the EmbedI-TApp and the master module has been established, the master module returns the ID and module type (sensor type, actuator type) of all hardware modules that are physically connected to the bus.

Fig. 3 shows an example of the EmbedITApp where a servo module and three sensor modules (gyroscope, ultrasonic, accelerometer) are listed. Each available module is represented with its ID, icon and a button within the application. While clicking on a module's button, its control panel opens.

Fig. 4 shows the control panel of the servo module. The servo module is able to control four servos at the same time. From this control panel commands such as connect/disconnect servos or move to discrete servo positions can be sent. Another possibility is to let the servo motors change positions in a continuous, sinusoidal way (alternating from 0 to 180). Different sine parameters such as amplitude (servo angle range), offset (shift of the servo middle axis), phase lag (synchronization of all servos) and frequency can be applied. The EmbedITApp

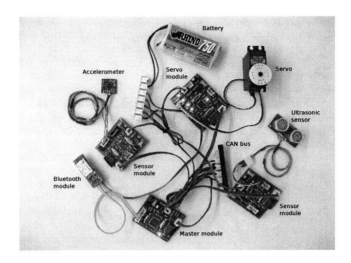

Fig. 2. Some EmbedIT modules: A Bluetooth module, a master module, two sensor modules (accelerometer, ultrasonic), the CAN bus, a power supply and a servo module with one servo attached.

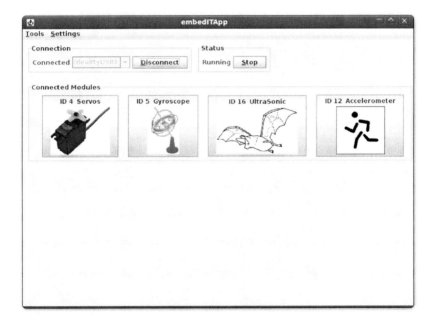

Fig. 3. An example of the EmbedITApp where a servo module and three sensor modules (gyroscope, ultrasonic, accelerometer) are listed. Each available module in the application is represented with its ID, icon and a button.

sends the commands to the master module which forwards them to the target module on the bus. Servo positions can be changed while dragging the servo position sliders. After pushing the apply buttons on the control panel, the servo positions are changed physically.

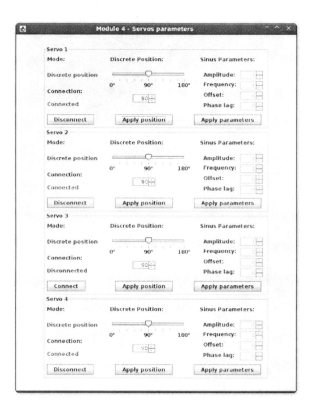

Fig. 4. The control panel of the servo module. The servo module is able to control four servos at the same time. From this control panel commands such as connect/disconnect servos, move to specific servo position as well as continuous position change in a sinusoidal way can be applied.

For each module on the bus a control panel can be opened where module specific commands and settings can be applied. The master module manages the requests coming from the EmbedITApp and forwards them to the specific hardware modules. These targeted hardware modules execute the requests (motor position, get sensor data) and reply to the master module which acknowledges the EmbedITApp's commands. To achieve robustness the EmbedITApp resends the request three times in case of unacknowledged commands. To minimize traffic on the CAN bus only high level commands are being sent to the individual modules (e.g. start, stop motors etc.). Since each module has module specific algorithms implemented computation is reduced for the master module.

Through the plug and play nature of the hardware modules on the bus as well as the possibility to acquire sensor data and to control modules through a GUI, usability increases significantly. With other platforms a user has to program a lot of code in order to be able to do similar tasks. At this state the user is able to remote control and monitor the hardware. By means of a graphical programming environment which is currently under development the user will be able to define the control of sensors and actuators such that the hardware will be able to run autonomously. It has to be mentioned that the preprogrammed source code of each EmbedIT module is not hidden. A more experienced user can easily change code (C/C++) and upload it to the modules.

EmbedIT's hardware designs and source codes are completely open and will be free available on the project website [20] with the release of the stable version. Inspired by the Arduino project, we would like to enable a community to extend and adapt the hardware and software once it is released. The main goal is to encourage users from all kinds of backgrounds to use this kit. By means of the EmbedITApp users with no background in electronics or programming are able to access and control the modules. In addition, more advanced users have the possibility to extend the source code by themselves. Since the hardware and software interfaces are open and common standards are used, it is possible to interface the modules with other kits or projects, for example with an Arduino board. By adding the required CAN components to the Arduino board and including our CAN library on the software side, the board is easily connected with EmbedIT.

4   Application Examples

As we are currently developing the hardware and software of EmbedIT, more modules are being added to the kit. Currently in addition to the servo module common sensor modules exist such as light sensors, ultrasonic sensors, accelerometers, potentiometers, gyroscopes. The goal is to have a repertoire of many different kinds of sensors and actuators, also unusual ones such as shape memory alloy, whisker sensors [21] etc. There are many possible applications for this kit and they are not limited to education only. Other uses could be e.g. a rapid prototyping tool for researchers as well as a playground for hobbyists.

In this section we describe application examples where two different robots (a quadrupedal running robot and a skating robot) are controlled by the same EmbedIT modules. Both robots use in addition to the master and Bluetooth modules a servo module that controls four servos in a sinusoidal positioning mode. Each robot requires its specific sine parameters that had to be tuned manually by trial and error using the EmbedITApp interface. These two examples show how easy and with no programming knowledge one can already control a robot. Furthermore, the EmbedIT control interface eases the exploration of control parameters in cases where this kind of approach is required.

4.1   A Quadrupedal Running Robot Controlled with EmbedIT

Iida et al. [22] applied a parsimonious control strategy for a running quadrupedal robot. The motors were controlled by a simple oscillatory position control without additional sensory feedback. The robot had four identical legs each of which consisted of one servo motor and a series of two limbs connected through a passive elastic joint.

We rebuilt a similar puppy robot based on the same concept and controlled by EmbedIT modules (Fig. 5). By means of the EmbedITApp's servo control interface different sine parameters could be applied to the robot and therefore different running gaits could be achieved.

Fig. 5. A quadrupedal running robot controlled with EmbedIT modules (a master module, a Bluetooth module, a servo module, a battery). The robot has four identical legs each of which consists of one servo motor and a series of two limbs connected through a passive elastic joint.

4.2   A Skating Robot Controlled with EmbedIT

The same EmbedIT modules used for the quadrupedal running robot (Fig. 5) were reused to control a skating robot (Fig. 6). The two servos on the hips control the bending and stretching movement of the legs and the two other servos above the hips adjust the angle between the feet. The goal was to control the robot such that it achieves a forward skating movement while alternately relocating its center of mass from one leg to the other (that, in a simplified way, is what skaters actually do). Therefore discrete positioning has been applied to the feet angle servos while the hip servos were controlled in a sinusoidal positioning mode.

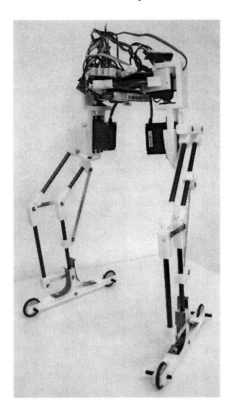

Fig. 6. A skating robot controlled with EmbedIT modules (a master module, a Bluetooth module, a servo module, a battery). The two servos on the hips control the bending and stretching movement of the legs and the two other servos above the hips adjust the angle between the feet.

5 Discussion

EmbedIT differs from other robotic kits with respect to usability and user-friendliness. Our goal is to enable users from different kinds of backgrounds and interests to explore the world of technology while accessing it in a creative, playful and non-engineering focused way. We believe that building own robots result in a basic understanding about how they work. This can lower the barrier to move on to more advanced topics of engineering such as programming and electronics which can be explored with the kit as well.

EmbedIT is contributing to education in such a way that it provides an alternative to common robot kits on the market. The goal is the same - teaching technology - but the approach is different. The user-friendliness of EmbedIT can encourage teachers to incorporate it in class as a learning tool. We intentionally chose EmbedIT to be open source to encourage the growth of a contributing community. This could consequently lead to the availability of cheap hardware from which schools can profit as well.

6   Conclusion and Future Work

In this paper we referred to the problem of decreasing enrollments in science and technology disciplines in Universities. The field of educational robotics is growing due to the fact that robots are a proven effective learning tool for education in these disciplines. Consequently, many robot kits have been developed in research projects as well as in commercial companies. However, most of them focus on a classical top-down engineering approach, where the actual robot has to be planned, built out of predefined parts and programmed using programming languages such as C/C++. We are developing EmbedIT, an open robotic kit that enables users to build robots in an easy and user-friendly way. This can be highly motivating and may lower the barrier to move on to more advanced topics in engineering.

Right now we are developing, testing and revising the hardware and software of EmbedIT. More modules have to be added to the repository. At the moment servos can be controlled through the EmbedITApp interface and sensor data can be read. To combine sensor data and servo commands a graphical user interface has to be implemented. In addition, interface solutions for attaching EmbedIT's modules to mechanical structures (for instance by using mechanical toolkits) have to be developed. Since we are interested in including the end-users feedback in our design process, it is important to communicate and publish the project idea as well as to test the kit with students at an early stage. In order to evaluate the approach workshops using EmbedIT in upper secondary schools are planned. A survey will be conducted to investigate the impact EmbedIT produces upon students, regarding change of attitude and self-confidence towards studying technology. Once the EmbedIT hardware and software achieves a first stable release state, it will be available under an open-source license on the project website [20].

Acknowledgments. We would like to thank Emanuel Benker, Juan Pablo Carbajal and Konstantinos Dermitzakis for providing the body design of the quadrupedal running robot (Fig. 5). Furthermore, we thank Wolfgang Pils and Andreas Bertschi for the idea and the design of the skating robot (Fig. 6).

References

1. Miller, J., Ward, B., Sienkiewicz, F., Antonucci, P.: ITEAMS: an Out-Of-School Time Program to Promote Gain in Fundamental Science Content and Enhance Interest in STEM Careers for Middle School Students. In: Proceedings of The 8th Intl. Conf. on Education and Information Systems, Technologies and Applications, EISTA 2010 (2010)
2. Rocard, M., et al.: Science Education now: a renewed pedagogy for the future of Europe. EUR22845, European Communities, Brussels (2007) ISBN 978-92-79-05659-8
3. Piaget, J.: The origins of intelligence in children. International Universities Press, New York (1952)

4. Piaget, J.: The construction of reality in the child. Basic Books, New York (1954)
5. Bredenfeld, A., Leimbach, T.: The Roberta Initiative. In: Workshop Proceedings of Intl. Conf. on Simulation, Modeling and Programming for Autonomous Robots (SIMPAR 2010), pp. 558–567 (2010) ISBN 978-3-00-032863-3
6. Alimisis, D., Moro, M., Arlegui, J., Frangou, S., Papanikolaou, K.: Robotics & Constructivism in Education: the TERECoP project. In: Proceedings of EuroLogo 2007, Bratislava (2007)
7. Bredenfeld, A., Hofmann, A., Steinbauer, G.: Robotics in Education Initiatives in Europe Status, Shortcomings and Open Questions. In: Workshop Proceedings of Intl. Conf. on Simulation, Modeling and Programming for Autonomous Robots (SIMPAR 2010), pp. 568–574 (2010) ISBN 978-3-00-032863-3
8. LEGO NXT, http://mindstorms.lego.com
9. Kabatova, M., Pekarova, J.: Lessons learnt with LEGO Mindstorms: from beginner to teaching robotics. AT&P Journal Plus 2, Robotics in Education, 51–56 (2010) ISSN 1336-5010
10. Menegatti, E., Moro, M.: Educational Robotics from high-school to Master of Science. In: Workshop Proceedings of Intl. Conf. on Simulation, Modeling and Programming for Autonomous Robots (SIMPAR 2010), pp. 639–648 (2010) ISBN 978-3-00-032863-3
11. ASURO robot, http://www.arexx.com/arexx.php?cmd=goto\&cparam=p_asuro
12. Balogh, R.: Acrob – an Educational Robotic Platform. AT&P Journal Plus 2, Robotics in Education, 6–9 (2010) ISSN 1336-5010
13. The Arduino project, http://www.arduino.cc/
14. Assaf, D., Pfeifer, R.: Robotics as Part of an Informatics Degree Program for Teachers. In: Proceedings of Society for Information Technology & Teacher Education International Conference 2011, pp. 3128–3133. AACE, Chesapeake (2011)
15. The Gadgeteer project, http://research.microsoft.com/en-us/projects/gadgeteer/
16. Phidgets, http://www.phidgets.com/
17. LEGO, http://www.lego.com
18. Stokys, http://www.stokys.ch/
19. Meccano, http://www.meccano.com
20. The EmbedIT project, http://www.embed-it.ch
21. Lungarella, M., Hafner, V., Pfeifer, R., Yokoi, H.: Artificial Whisker Sensors in Robotics. In: Proceedings of the IEEE/RSJ International Conference on Intelligent Robots and Systems, IROS (2002)
22. Iida, F., Gomez, G., Pfeifer, R.: Exploiting body dynamics for controlling a running quadruped robot. In: Proceedings of the 12th International Conference on Advanced Robotics, ICAR 2005 (2005)

Semantic Simulation Engine in Mobile Robot Operator Training Tool

Janusz Bedkowski and Andrzej Masłowski

Institute of Automation and Robotics, Warsaw University of Technology,
Warsaw, Poland,
Institute of Mathematical Machines, Warsaw, Poland
januszbedkowski@gmail.com,
a.maslowski@mchtr.pw.edu.pl

Abstract. In the paper the semantic simulation engine and its role in multi level mobile robot operator training tool is described. Semantic simulation engine provides tools to implement mobile robot simulation based on real data delivered by robot observations in INDOOR environment. It is important to emphasize that real and virtual part of the training system is integrated. The supervision of real objects such as robots is performed by association with its virtual representation in the simulation, therefore events such as object intersection, robot pitch roll are defined. Semantic simulation engine is composed of data registration modules, semantic entities identification modules (data segmentation) and semantic simulation module. The data registration modules delivers 3D point clouds aligned with ICP (Iterative Closest Point) algorithm accelerated by parallel computation to obtain on-line processing. Semantic entities identification modules provide implementation of methods for obtaining semantic entities from robot observations (already registered). Semantic simulation module executes rigid body simulation with predefined simulation events. It is implemented using NVIDIA PhysX engine. The simulation can be easy integrated with real part of the system with an assumption of robust localization of real entities, therefore Augmented Reality capabilities are available.

Keywords: Semantic mapping, operator training, mobile robot.

1 Introduction and Related Work

Semantic simulation engine is an extension of framework for designing tools for mobile robot operator training [1] and it is related to semantic mapping. Semantic information [2] extracted from 3D laser data [3] is recent research topic of modern mobile robotics. In [4] a semantic map for a mobile robot was described as a map that contains, in addition to spatial information about the environment, assignments of mapped features to entities of known classes. In [5] a model of an indoor scene is implemented as a semantic net. This approach is used in [6] where robot extracts semantic information from 3D models built from a laser scanner. In [7] the location of features is extracted by using a probabilistic

D. Obdržálek and A. Gottscheber (Eds.): EUROBOT 2011, CCIS 161, pp. 40–54, 2011.

technique (RANSAC RANdom SAmple Consensus) [8]. Also the region growing approach [9] extended from [10] by efficiently integrating k-nearest neighbor (KNN) search is able to process unorganized point clouds. The improvement of plane extraction from 3D Data by fusing laser data and vision is shown in [11]. The automatic model refinement of 3D scene is introduced in [12] where the idea of feature extraction (planes) is done also with RANSAC algorithm. The semantic map building is related to SLAM (Simultaneous Localization and Mapping) problem [13]. Most of recent SLAM techniques use camera [14], laser measurement system [15] or even registered 3D laser data [16]. Concerning the registration of 3D scans described in [17] [18] we can find several techniques solving this important issue. The authors of [19] briefly describe ICP (Iterative Closest Point) algorithm. In [20] the mapping system that acquires 3D object models of man-made indoor environments such as kitchens is shown. The system segments and geometrically reconstructs cabinets with doors, tables, drawers, and shelves, objects that are important for robots retrieving and manipulating objects in these environments.

In this paper new idea of semantic simulation engine is proposed. Semantic simulation engine combines semantic map with rigid body simulation to perform supervision of its entities such as robots moving in INDOOR environment composed by floor, ceiling, walls, door etc. Automatic detection concerning these entities are based on robot's observations, the relations between them are defined by semantic net. A detailed description of computer based simulators for unmanned vehicles is shown in [21]. Also in [22] the comparison of real-time physics simulation systems is given, where a qualitative evaluation of a number of free publicly available physics engines for simulation systems and game development is presented. Several frameworks are mentioned such as USARSim which is very popular in research society [23] [24], Stage, Gazebo [25], Webots [26], Matlab [27] and MRDS [28]. Some researchers found that there are many available simulators that offer attractive functionality, therefore they proposed a new simulator classification system specific to mobile robots and autonomous vehicles [29]. A classification system for robot simulators will allow researchers to identify existing simulators which may be useful in conducting a wide variety of robotics research from testing low level or autonomous control to human robot interaction. Another simulation engine - the Search and Rescue Game Environment (SARGE), which is a distributed multi-player robot operator training game, is described in [30]. To conclude this section it can be stated that there are many available sophisticated mobile robotic systems, in the same time the ergonomic solutions for HMI (Human Robot Interface) are necessary to perform complex tasks. Based on this observation advanced training systems are needed to improve operators' skills. It this paper multi level training is introduced and the role of components of semantic simulation engine for each training level is described.

The paper is organized as follows: section *Semantic simulation engine* describes the structure of semantic simulation engine and its components, section *Mobile robot operator training tool* describes training tools in RISE (Risky

Intervention and Surveillance Environment) developed during project, named A platform for design of computer trainer-simulators for operators of inspection-intervention mobile robots. Section *Role of semantic simulation engine in training* shows main experiments performed in real and simulated environment, and the role of semantic simulation in multi level training is discussed, section *Conclusion and future work* gives final discussion and shows areas of future work.

2   Semantic Simulation Engine

The concept of semantic simulation engine applied in mobile robot operator training is a new idea, and its strength lies on the semantic map integration with mobile robot simulator. Semantic simulation engine is composed of data registration modules, semantic entities identification (data segmentation) modules and semantic simulation module. It provides tools to implement mobile robot simulation based on real data delivered by robot and processed on-line using parallel computation. Semantic entities identification modules can classify door, walls, floor, ceiling, stairs in indoor environment. Data can be delivered by robot observation based on modern sensors such as laser measurement system 3D and RGB-D cameras. Real objects are associated with virtual entities of simulated environment.

2.1   Data Registration

Data registration performed on-line is very interesting research area, therefore many researchers are focused on such studies. Alignment and merging of two 3D scans, which are obtained from different sensor coordinates, with respect to a reference coordinate system is called 3D registration [31] [32] [33]. Range images are defined as a model set M and data set D, where N_m and N_d denotes the number of the elements in the respective set. The alignment of these two data sets is solved by minimization of the following cost function:

$$E = (\mathbf{R}, \mathbf{t}) = \sum_{i=1}^{N_m} \sum_{j=1}^{N_d} w_{ij} \left\| \mathbf{m}_i - (\mathbf{R}\mathbf{d}_j + \mathbf{t}) \right\|^2 \tag{1}$$

w_{ij} is assigned 1 if the i-th point of M correspond to the j-th point in D as in the same bucket (or neighbor bucket). Otherwise $w_{ij}=0$. $\mathbf{R}$ is a rotation matrix, $\mathbf{t}$ is a translation matrix. $\mathbf{m}_i$ and $\mathbf{d}_i$ corresponds to the i-th point from model set M and D respectively.

Solving equation 1 is related to Nearest Neighborhood search. The distance between two points in Euclidean distance metric for point $p_1 = \{x_1, y_1, z_1\}$ and $p_2 = \{x_2, y_2, z_2\}$ is defined as:

$$distance(p_1, p_2) = \left[(x_1 - x_2)^2 + (y_1 - y_2)^2 + (z_1 - z_2)^2 \right]^{\frac{1}{2}} \tag{2}$$

To find pairs of closest points between model set M and data set D the decomposition of XYZ space, where x,y,z $\in\; < -1, 1 >$, into 2^8x2^8x2^8 buckets is

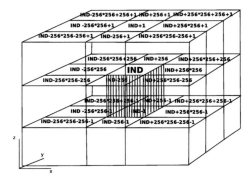

Fig. 1. Cubic subspaces - neighboring buckets, the way of indexing

proposed. It should be noticed that in case of 2^8x2^8x2^8 buckets cubic subspace length,width,height $= 2/2^8, 2/2^8, 2/2^8$. Each bucket that does not belong to border has 26 neighbors. The 27 neighboring cubic subspaces are shown on figure 1 where also the way of indexing in CUDA GPU is given. The approach is new idea that differs from [34] [35] (improved ICP procedure fast searching algorithms such as the k-d tree) by no need of building complex data structure, therefore computation time is decreased. The ICP point to point algorithm using CUDA parallel programming is shown in algorithm 1. It should be noted that all computation is implemented in CUDA architecture, therefore the time needed to transfer data between host and device is decreased.

Algorithm 1. ICP - point to point parallel computing approach

allocate the memory
copy data from the host(M_{host}, D_{host}) to the device(M_{device}, D_{device})
for $iter = 0$ to $max\_iterations$ **do**
    select closest points between M_{device} and D_{device}
    calculate (R, t) that minimizes equation 1
    transform D_{device} by (R, t) and put the results into $D_{deviceRt}$
    copy $D_{deviceRt}$ to D_{device}
    if D_{device} is aligned to M_{device} **then**
        break
    end if
end for
copy D_{device} to D_{host}
free memory

2.2 Data Segmentation

Segmentation based on image processing methods. Figure 2 illustrates the projection of 3D cloud of points obtained by RGB-D camera (kinect) onto OXY and OXZ planes. During the preprocessing, the pitch and roll parameters

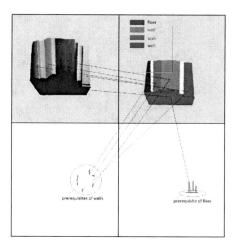

Fig. 2. Range image segmentation based on image processing techniques

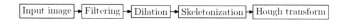

Fig. 3. Image processing methods used for prerequisites computation (input for segmentation)

are compensated using 3DOF accelerometers integrated with mobile platform. Therefore projected wall, doors and stairs determine the line on the considered binary OXY image. The same assumption can be applied to ceiling and floor detection in case of 3D data projection onto OXZ plane.

We consider the region 10m x 10m because of the acceptable distance between closest measured 3D points. Additional, in figure 2, the corresponding image coordinates in (x, y) and (u, v) coordinates are given. The image size is 512 pixels width, 512 pixels height, therefore one pixel occupies the rectangle region approximately $20cm \times 20cm$. Line extraction algorithm depends on computing the table of number of all projected points for each pixel (sum_{uv}).

Computed sum_{uv} (Input image see fig. 3) where values are normalized to the range $< 0, 1 >$ is used for prerequisites generation (segmentation) based on image processing methods. The implementation is based on OpenCV image processing library [36]. Procedure is presented in figure 3. Input image box represents the computed sum_{uv} image transformed into binary image using simple thresholding. Filtering box reduces noise from image. The structuring element used for this operation is

$$strel = \begin{bmatrix} 1 & 1 & 1 \\ 1 & 0 & 1 \\ 1 & 1 & 1 \end{bmatrix}$$

For each pixel $p_{k,l}$ from binary image, where $k = 1 : 510$, $l = 1 : 510$, following equation is solved.

$$p_{res(k,l)} = \sum_{i=-1}^{1} \sum_{j=-1}^{1} strel_{i,j} \cdot p_{k+i,l+j} \cdot (|i| + |j|) \tag{3}$$

if $p_{res(k,l)} > 0$ and $p_{k,l} = 1$ then $p_{out(k,l)} = 1$, else $p_{out(k,l)} = 0$. Dilation operation increases the width of the binary objects in the image. The function cvDilate [36] dilates the source image using the specified structuring element that determines the shape of a pixel neighborhood over which the maximum is taken. Neighboring objects are connected to improve the accuracy of the hough transform. Skeletonization is based on classical Pavlidis [37][38] algorithm. It provides thin lines that are used by Hough transform box to obtain line segments. The used Hough transform variant is $CV\_HOUGH\_PROBABILISTIC$ - probabilistic Hough transform - more efficient in case of picture containing long linear segments. It returns line segments rather than the whole lines. Every segment is represented by starting and ending points. At this stage we can consider each line as prerequisite of wall, floor or ceiling, therefore segmentation of range points can be performed as shown on figure 2. Each line segments that are parallel and in defined distance are prerequisite of stairs.

Segmentation based on normal vectors computation. The procedure of normal vectors computation for registered range images uses CUDA for robust nearest neighbors search. The parameter $maxnumberofplanes$ in algorithm 2 is assigned experimentally as 10. This value guarantee robust procedure execution with satisfying heuristic of random planes generation.

Algorithm 2. Compute normal vectors (r,g,b)

---

  for all range points (x,y,z) in parallel **do**
    $bucket$ = findbucket(x,y,z)
    for $allneighboringbuckets$ **do**
      add points from bucket to $listofpoints$
    end for
    for $i = 0$ to $maxnumberofplanes$ **do**
      compute plane based on 3 random points
      $sum_i = 0$
      for all points in $listofpoints$ **do**
        sum_i += distance(point,plane)
      end for
    end for
    $normalvector$ = plane for min(sum_i)
  end for

2.3   Walls and Stairs Detection

The procedure of prerequisites generation using image processing methods is used. The set of lines is used to obtain segmentation of $3D$ cloud of points, where different walls will have different labels. For each line segment the orthogonal $plane_{orth}$ to $plane_{OXY}$ is computed. It should be noted that the intersection between this two planes is the same line segment. All $3D$ points which satisfy the condition of distance to $plane_{orth}$ have the same label. In the first step all prerequisites of walls were checked separately - it is data segmentation. To perform the scene interpretation semantic net is used (figure 4). The feature detection algorithm is composed by the method of cubes generation (see figure 5 right), where each cube should contain measured 3D point after segmentation (see figure 5). In the second step of the algorithm wall candidates are chosen. From this set of candidates, based on relationships between them, proper labels are assigned and output model is generated (see figure 6 left).

The image processing methods are also used for stairs prerequisites generation. It is important to emphasize that the set of parallel lines (obtained by projected single 3D scan onto OXY plane) in the same short distance between each other is prerequisite of stairs. Possible labels of the nodes are L = {stair}. The relationships between the entities are R = {parallel, above, under}. Figure 6 right shows resulting model of stairs generated from 3D cloud of points. In this spatial model each stair (except first and last one obviously) is in relation

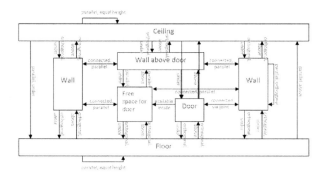

Fig. 4. Semantic net defined for semantic entities identification

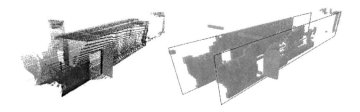

Fig. 5. Left - segmentation of 3D cloud of points, right - boxes that contain measured points

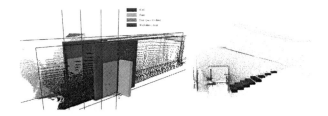

Fig. 6. Scene interpretation left - door, walls, right - stairs

r=above&parallel with the previous one and in relation r=under&parallel with next one.

2.4   Semantic Simulation

Assuming that we have accurate positioning of mobile robots, accurate encoders of inspection robot arm and satisfying tracking system we can update virtual entities position during real robots task execution. The semantic simulation engine from semantic map of INDOOR environment point of view is composed of: semantic map nodes(entities) L_{sm}={Wall, Wall above door, Floor, Ceiling, Door, Free space for door, Stairs...}, it is important to noticed that the L_{sm} set can be extended by another objects, what is dependent on robust and accurate 3D scene analysis, robot simulator nodes(entities) L_{rs}={robot, rigid body object, soft body object...}, semantic map relationships between the entities R_{sm} = {parallel, orthogonal, above, under, equal height, available inside, connected via joint...}, robot simulator relationships between the entities R_{rs} = {connected via joint, position...}, semantic map events E_{sm} = robot simulator events E_{rs} = {movement, collision between two entities started, collision between two entities stopped, collision between two entities continued, broken joint...}. Our robot simulator is implemented in NVIDIA PhysX. The entities from semantic map correspond to actors in PhysX. L_{sm} is transformed into L_{rs} based on spatial model generated based on registered 3D scans i.e. walls, doors and stairs correspond to actors with BOX shapes. R_{sm} are transformed into R_{rs} with remark that doors are connected to walls via revolute joints. All entities/relations R_{sm} has the same initial location in R_{rs}, obviously the location of each actor/entity may change during simulation. The transformation from E_{sm} to E_{rs} effects that events related to entities from semantic map correspond to the events related to actors representing proper entities. It is important to emphasize that following events can be noticed during simulation: robot can touch each entity, open/close the door, climb the stairs, enter empty space of the door, damage itself (broken joint between actors in robot arm), brake joint that connects door to the wall. It is noteworthy to mention that all robot simulator semantic events are useful for operator training, where computer has to monitor simulation events judge them and report for the grading purpose.

3 Mobile Robot Operator Training Tool

Training tools in RISE (Risky Intervention and Surveillance Environment) is given by the project, named A platform for design of computer trainer-simulators for operators of inspection-intervention mobile robots, realized by the authors of the paper in the Institute of Mathematical Machines, Warsaw, Poland. Development of such computer platform, intended to enable designing trainers-simulators for training in operation of different types of mobile robots - finding their application in inspection-intervention missions conducted in municipal or industrial environment, as well as in missions of military or police character - and creation of software for them, is the aim of this project. One can anticipate that diverse types of robots, differing by kind of traction, load capacity, range, manipulation ability, equipment with sensors will be applied in these missions. A need to train significant number of persons in operation of these robots, and obtaining high proficiency in operation, will come into being particularly in police and military forces for the sake of possible contact with explosives and toxic substances creating dangers for operator, population, and environment. Training tasks require many hours of exercises with different types of robots. Conducting of such training with use of real robots would be unprofitable, and probably unfeasible for the technical and organizational reasons for difficulties of creation of all possible situations and coincidences with which an operator of robots has to cope. The use of trainers, simulating robots behavior in different situations and circumstances, will be a necessity. Such trainers, for different types and variants of robots, will have to be designed, manufactured, delivered to users and serviced, so establishing of an innovative enterprise of adequate profile will be justified.

3.1 Multi-level Training

The first research task was drawing up a methodology of multi-level training with use of trainers of different grade of perfection, taking advantages of technologies of virtual reality (VR) and augmented reality (AR). Application of multi-level training, introductory one with use of simplest and not so costly trainers, and at next levels more and more complex, closing to real robot operation, will enable reduction of training costs and facilitate training organization. For multi-level training the following types of trainers are to be used: Trainers of the Level 1 built with use of typical PCs. VR technology is applied. Robot, its environment and control console are simulated. Trainers of the Level 2 built with use of PCs with real robot control consoles connected. VR technology is applied. Robot and its environment are simulated. Trainers of the Level 3 trainers of the Level 1 or 2 with application of AR technology - real robot in the real environment with simulated elements added. A trainee uses special helmet or advanced control base station. Every program of training is a sequence of training tasks. An exemplary training task for mobile robots operators is lifting, with use of the robots gripper, of a certain object, and putting it in a certain container. At the beginning of the training session the trainee is informed on the task to perform, as well as on time limits, grading scale, and penalty points for causing wrong events (e.g.

collisions of robot with objects in its environment). The trainee, using virtual or real control console, performs training tasks of the character of a computer game, and after finishing them is informed about the score obtained. During execution of training tasks, the knowledge about trainees progress is gathered, and on this basis a choice of the next task, or decision on the end of training is made.

4   Role of Semantic Simulation Engine in Training

The most important role of semantic engine is being the core of ranking system. Ranking system is based on events detected in the simulation. There are pre-defined events such as intersection, triggering and yaw pitch supervision. Also time is important during task execution. An extended role is related with level 3 of training where augmented reality techniques are applied for merging real and virtual agents during task execution where on-line processing is needed.

4.1   Level 1 and 2 - Training Based on Computer Simulation

The difference between level 1 and level 2 is the usage real control pane in training of level 2. The role of simulation engine is the same for both levels, where all entities are simulated. As an example the semantic simulation built based on autonomous robot observations (3D laser measurement system) is shown on figure 7. It should be emphasized that semantic simulation engine was used to simulate robot climbing stairs with pitch and roll supervision and robot entering door. Operator will be punished when robot bump the wall or fall down from stairs.

4.2   Level 3 - Training with Augmented Reality

The proposed AR training system is composed by Augmented Reality agents and Real agents that interact each other. The semantic simulation applied in

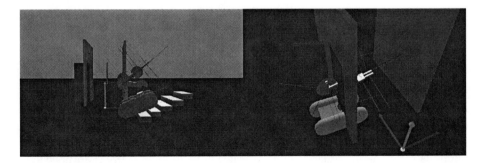

Fig. 7. Left - Climbing the stairs, pitch and roll supervision. Right - Entering opened door.

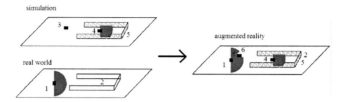

Fig. 8. General idea of AR approach in LEVEL 3 training. 1: real robot equipped with laser range finder, 2: real obstacles, 3: virtual robot, 4: virtual robot equipped with simulated laser range finder 5: virtual 3D model of the real obstacles obtained by real robot, 6: augmented real laser range finder measurement with additional virtual measurement of virtual robot chassis (1+3).

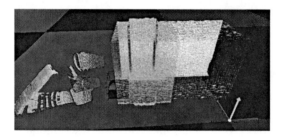

Fig. 9. Visualization of the mobile robot and 3D environment. Red points correspond to time of flight 3D camera measurement, green triangles - registered 3D map based on vertically mounted LMS SICK laser range finder, gray triangles registered 3D map transformed into PhysX model.

NVIDIA PhysX engine is used to perform AR agents simulation. The fundamental assumption is that the position of each agent is known, therefore data fusion from real sensors and simulated is possible. In the global localization of the real robot the SLAM algorithm based on LMS SICK 200 and odometry data is used. The global position of AR agent is given from simulation. To simulate laser range finder the environment 3D model build from 3D data acquisition system is transferred into simulation engine. Figure 8 shows general idea of proposed AR approach.

The augmented reality system dedicated to mobile robotic system operator training is composed of real autonomous mobile robot equipped with 3D map building system, real base station with real remote control robot console, simulation of remotely controlled robot with simulation of laser range finder. The system composites real video feedback from mobile robot with simulation view. Figure 11 shows control base station where operator can control each robot, real and virtual one. It is important to emphasize that virtual robot is visible in autonomous robot main camera view. Another advantage of proposed approach is the possibility of summarizing all system components in the main HMI program that visualizes robots position and sensor data.

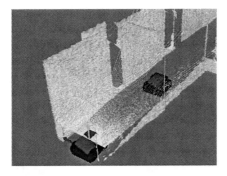

Fig. 10. Simulation of virtual laser range finder LMS SICK 200 in virtual environment

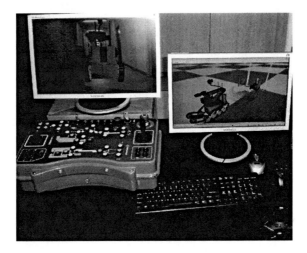

Fig. 11. The augmented reality training system

5   Conclusion and Future Work

In the paper new concept of semantic simulation engine applied for multi level mobile robot operator training, composed of data registration modules, semantic entities identification modules and semantic simulation module is proposed. Compared to the State of The Art new approaches of parallel computing applied for data registration is proposed. Semantic simulation engine provides tools to implement mobile robot simulation based on real data delivered by robot and processed on-line using parallel computation. Semantic entities identification modules can classify door, walls, floor, ceiling, stairs in indoor environment. Data can be delivered by robot observation based on modern sensors such as laser measurement system 3D and RGB-D cameras. Semantic simulation uses NVIDIA PhysX for rigid body simulation. By the association between real objects and simulation entities it is possible to supervise them by prediction of possible collisions and dangerous motion (pitch, roll). Future work will be related to AI techniques applied for semantic entities identification (furnitures, victims, cars, etc...), localization and tracking methods. The Augmented Reality system will be improved by using AR helmet. It should be noticed that the challenge and still opened issue is the implementation of virtual camera of virtual robot working in real environment, therefore it is new research problem.

References

1. Bedkowski, J., Kacprzak, M., Kaczmarczyk, A., Kowalski, P., Musialik, P., Maslowski, A., Pichlak, T.: Rise mobile robot operator training design. In: 15th International Conference on Methods and Models in Automation and Robotics, Miedzyzdroje, Poland, CD-ROM, August 23-26 (2010)
2. Asada, M., Shirai, Y.: Building a world model for a mobile robot using dynamic semantic constraints. In: Proc. 11 th International Joint Conference on Artificial Intelligence, pp. 1629–1634 (1989)
3. Nüchter, A., Wulf, O., Lingemann, K., Hertzberg, J., Wagner, B., Surmann, H.: 3d mapping with semantic knowledge. In: Robocup International Symposium, pp. 335–346 (2005)
4. Nüchter, A., Hertzberg, J.: Towards semantic maps for mobile robots. Robot. Auton. Syst. 56(11), 915–926 (2008)
5. Grau, O.: A scene analysis system for the generation of 3-d models. In: NRC 1997: Proceedings of the International Conference on Recent Advances in 3-D Digital Imaging and Modeling, p. 221. IEEE Computer Society, Washington, DC, USA (1997)
6. Nüchter, A., Surmann, H., Lingemann, K., Hertzberg, J.: Semantic scene analysis of scanned 3d indoor environments. In: Proceedings of the Eighth International Fall Workshop on Vision, Modeling, and Visualization, VMV 2003 (2003)
7. Cantzler, H., Fisher, R.B., Devy, M.: Quality enhancement of reconstructed 3D models using coplanarity and constraints. In: Van Gool, L. (ed.) DAGM 2002. LNCS, vol. 2449, pp. 34–41. Springer, Heidelberg (2002)
8. Fischler, M.A., Bolles, R.: Random sample consensus. a paradigm for model fitting with apphcahons to image analysm and automated cartography. In: Baurnann, L.S. (ed.) Proc. 1980 Image Understanding Workshop, College Park, Md. Scmnce Apphcatlons, McLean, Va, pp. 71–88 (1980)
9. Eich, M., Dabrowska, M., Kirchner, F.: Semantic labeling: Classification of 3d entities based on spatial feature descriptors. In: IEEE International Conference on Robotics and Automation (ICRA 2010), Anchorage, Alaska, May 3 (2010)
10. Vaskevicius, N., Birk, A., Pathak, K., Poppinga, J.: Fast detection of polygons in 3d point clouds from noise-prone range sensors. In: IEEE International Workshop on Safety, Security and Rescue Robotics, SSRR, pp. 1–6. IEEE, Rome (2007)
11. Andreasson, H., Triebel, R., Burgard, W.: Improving plane extraction from 3d data by fusing laser data and vision. In: Proceedings of the IEEE/RSJ International Conference on Intelligent Robots and Systems (IROS), pp. 2656–2661 (2005)
12. Nüchter, A., Surmann, H., Hertzberg, J.: Automatic model refinement for 3D reconstruction with mobile robots. In: Fourth International Conference on 3-D Digital Imaging and Modeling 3DIM 2003, p. 394 (2003)
13. Davison, A., Cid, Y.G., Kita, N.: Real-time 3D SLAM with wide-angle vision. In: Proc. IFAC Symposium on Intelligent Autonomous Vehicles, Lisbon (2004)

14. Castle, R.O., Klein, G., Murray, D.W.: Combining monoslam with object recognition for scene augmentation using a wearable camera 28(11), 1548–1556 (2010), doi:10.1016/j.imavis.2010.03.009
15. Thrun, S., Burgard, W., Fo, D.: A real-time algorithm for mobile robot mapping with applications to multi-robot and 3d mapping. In: ICRA, pp. 321–328 (2000)
16. Magnusson, M., Andreasson, H., Nüchter, A., Lilienthal, A.J.: Automatic appearance-based loop detection from 3D laser data using the normal distributions transform. Journal of Field Robotics 26(11-12), 892–914 (2009)
17. Magnusson, M., Duckett, T., Lilienthal, A.J.: 3d scan registration for autonomous mining vehicles. Journal of Field Robotics 24(10), 803–827 (2007)
18. Andreasson, H., Lilienthal, A.J.: Vision aided 3d laser based registration. In: Proceedings of the European Conference on Mobile Robots (ECMR), pp. 192–197 (2007)
19. Besl, P.J., Mckay, H.D.: A method for registration of 3-d shapes. IEEE Transactions on Pattern Analysis and Machine Intelligence 14(2), 239–256 (1992), doi:10.1109/34.121791
20. Rusu, R.B., Marton, Z.C., Blodow, N., Dolha, M., Beetz, M.: Towards 3d point cloud based object maps for household environments. Robot. Auton. Syst. 56(11), 927–941 (2008), doi: http://dx.doi.org/10.1016/j.robot.2008.08.005
21. Craighead, J., Murphy, R., Burke, J., Goldiez, B.: A survey of commercial and open source unmanned vehicle simulators. In: Proceedings of ICRA (2007)
22. Boeing, A., Bräunl, T.: Evaluation of real-time physics simulation systems. In: GRAPHITE 2007: Proceedings of the 5th International Conference on Computer Graphics and Interactive Techniques in Australia and Southeast Asia, pp. 281–288. ACM, New York (2007), doi: http://doi.acm.org/10.1145/1321261.1321312
23. Wang, J., Lewis, M., Gennari, J.: Usar: A game-based simulation for teleoperation. In: Proceedings of the 47th Annual Meeting of the Human Factors and Ergonomics Society, Denver, CO, October 13-17 (2003)
24. Greggio, N., Silvestri, G., Menegatti, E., Pagello, E.: A realistic simulation of a humanoid robot in usarsim. In: Proceeding of the 4th International Symposium on Mechatronics and its Applications (ISMA 2007), Sharjah, U.A.E (2007)
25. Rusu, R.B., Maldonado, A., Beetz, M., Systems, I.A., Mnchen, T.U.: Extending player/stage/gazebo towards cognitive robots acting in ubiquitous sensor-equipped environments. In: Accepted for the IEEE International Conference on Robotics and Automation (ICRA) Workshop for Network Robot System, April 14 (2007)
26. Hohl, L., Tellez, R., Michel, O., Ijspeert, A.J.: Aibo and Webots: Simulation, Wireless Remote Control and Controller Transfer. Robotics and Autonomous Systems 54(6), 472–485 (2006)
27. Petrinić, T., Ivanjko, E., Petrović, I.: Amorsim a mobile robot simulator for matlab. In: Proceedings of 15th International Workshop on Robotics in Alpe-Adria-Danube Region, Balatonfred, Hungary, June 15-17 (2006)
28. Buckhaults, C.: Increasing computer science participation in the first robotics competition with robot simulation. In: ACM-SE 47: Proceedings of the 47th Annual Southeast Regional Conference, pp. 1–4. ACM, New York (2009), doi: http://doi.acm.org/10.1145/1566445.1566472
29. Craighead, J., Murphy, R., Burke, J., Goldiez, B.: A robot simulator classification system for hri. In: Proceedings of the 2007 International Symposium on Collaborative Technologies and Systems (CTS 2007), pp. 93–98 (2007)
30. Craighead, J.: Distributed, game-based, intelligent tutoring systems the next step in computer based training? In: Proceedings of the International Symposium on Collaborative Technologies and Systems, CTS 2008 (2008)

31. Huber, D., Hebert, M.: Fully automatic registration of multiple 3d data sets. Image and Vision Computing 21(1), 637–650 (2003)
32. Fitzgibbon, A.W.: Robust registration of 2d and 3d point sets. In: British Machine Vision Conference, pp. 411–420 (2001)
33. Magnusson, M., Duckett, T.: A comparison of 3d registration algorithms for autonomous underground mining vehicles. In: Proc. ECMR, pp. 86–91 (2005)
34. Nuchter, A., Lingemann, K., Hertzberg, J.: Cached k-d tree search for icp algorithms. In: Proceedings of the Sixth International Conference on 3-D Digital Imaging and Modeling, pp. 419–426. IEEE Computer Society, Washington, DC, USA (2007)
35. Rusinkiewicz, S., Levoy, M.: Efficient variants of the ICP algorithm. In: Third International Conference on 3D Digital Imaging and Modeling (3DIM) (2001)
36. http://opencv.willowgarage.com/wiki/
37. Lee, S.-W., Kim, Y.J.: Direct extraction of topographic features for gray scale character recognition. IEEE Trans. Pattern Anal. Mach. Intell. 17(7), 724–729 (1995), doi: http://dx.doi.org/10.1109/34.391416
38. Wang, L., Pavlidis, T.: Direct gray-scale extraction of features for character recognition. IEEE Trans. Pattern Anal. Mach. Intell. 15(10), 1053–1067 (1993), doi: http://dx.doi.org/10.1109/34.254062

Mobile Robot Localization Using Beacons and the Kalman Filter Technique for the Eurobot Competition

Oliver Bittel and Michael Blaich

University of Applied Sciences Konstanz, Germany
Laboratory for Mobile Robots
Brauneggerstr. 55 D-78462 Konstanz
{bittel,mblaich}@htwg-konstanz.de
http://www.robotik.in.htwg-konstanz.de/

Abstract. The objective of this work is to propose a landmark based localization system for the Eurobot contest, which enhance the positioning accuracy compared to an odometry based localization. To detect the landmarks a visual sensor which measures the angle between the robot and these landmarks is used. Based on these measurements two approaches to determinate the robot's position are presented: a triangulation method and an extended Kalman filter (EKF) approach. The extended Kalman filter approach combines the landmark measurements and the odometry. A robot from the Eurobot 2010 is used to carry out experimental results for the EKF based localization and present the enhancement of this approach.

1 Introduction

The localization problem is one of the most challenging tasks for all mobile robots, because the knowledge about the own position is a basic requirement for high level tasks. At the Eurobot contest the robot's localization on the playground is necessary for path planning and navigation. Based on this high level tasks like collision avoidance with alternative path planning or the depositing of collected objects at predefined targets are possible. Generally there are two practical approaches to locate the robot's position on the playground: dead reckoning and landmark based localization methods. Our approach combines both methods with an extended Kalman filter to get an improved position estimation.

Dead reckoning systems usually use the measurements of wheel encoders to estimate the rotation of the wheels. Based on these measurements the calculation of the covered distance is straight forward. This position estimation method is also called odometry. The disadvantage of this method is the unbounded accumulation of errors. To reduce these errors an exact estimation of the wheel diameter and the wheel distance is necessary. An approach to precisely collect these parameters and calibrate the robot to reduce these errors is presented in [3]. But errors like wheel slipping can not be handled with this method and

D. Obdržálek and A. Gottscheber (Eds.): EUROBOT 2011, CCIS 161, pp. 55–67, 2011.

thus much research is carried out to improve dead reckoning systems by adding acceleration and gyroscope sensors [4,13,14,16,21].

Another approach to estimate the robot's position is to use landmarks. A standard method is to place landmarks in the robot's workspace at known positions. In this case the robot needs sensors to detect these landmarks and to measure the distance or the angle to these. For many sensors such as cameras or wireless hardware the bearing is easier to measure than the distance. Thus, we focus on these approaches which use the bearings for localization. If the robot is able to measure the angle to at least three landmarks every time, the position estimation in the plane is possible using a triangulation algorithm as shown in [1,10,15,12,2,9]. An approach for an omni-directional camera which only needs two landmarks is presented in [5]. They additionally use a distance measurement to the landmark based on the visual information. All these approaches have three major difficulties to deal with. The first one is the imprecise measurements based on the senors inaccuracy. The second one is the occlusion of one or more beacons which leads to a lack of measurements. The third one is an ineligible arrangement of the landmarks. The arrangement influence is analyzed in detail in [17].

For the Eurobot competition, we present a landmark based localization approach. The competition rules define that every team can put three beacons around the playground at known positions. We use active infrared markers with an unique id as landmarks. As sensor, an omni-directional camera array with an infrared filter is used. The design of this sensor is presented in [8]. The sensor provides an angle measurement between the robot and the landmarks with an accuracy of about ± 0.6 degree. Based on these measurements we analyze two methods for the position estimation. First a triangulation method which only uses the angle information is presented. This method needs the angle to all three beacons to estimate the robot's position.

In a second step we improve this method by applying an Extended Kalman filter to combine the angle measurements with the odometry. An advantage of this approach is that the position can be estimated at all times even if the landmarks are not detected. A second benefit is that the robot's position can be improved by the angle measurement even if only one beacon is detected. The idea of the Kalman filter is presented in [11] and a practical introduction to the discrete and Extended Kalman filter is given in [22].

2   Triangulation Method

The coordinate system fixed with the Eurobot playground is called the global coordinate system. Three beacons are assumed at the positions $B_i = (x_i, y_i)$ for $i = 1, 2, 3$. This beacon configuration is illustrated in Figure 1. The local coordinate system is fixed with the robot, where the x-axis is aligned with the robot's orientation. The robot measures three angles ϕ_i between the beacons B_i and its local x-axis where i is the index of the beacon. The goal is to find the unknown robot position (x_R, y_R) and its orientation θ_R.

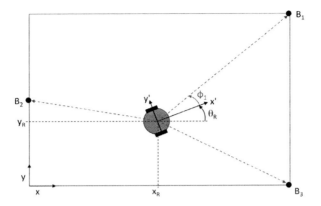

Fig. 1. Robot at position (x_R, y_R, θ_R) and the beacons $B_1 = (3m, 2.1m), B_2 = (0m, 1.05m)$ and $B_3 = (3m, 0m)$. The robot measures the three angles ϕ_1, ϕ_2 and ϕ_3. In the figure, angles ϕ_2 and ϕ_3 are omitted.

From Figure 1 the following equations can be deduced:

$$\phi_i = atan2(y_i - y_R, x_i - x_R) - \theta_R, \; i = 1, 2, 3. \tag{1}$$

This leads to a nonlinear equation system, which can be solved for the unknown x_R, y_R and θ_R numerically (e.g. the trust-region dogleg algorithm [7]). It should be noted that exactly three angle measurements are needed in order to determine the unknowns. This localization system is easy, but unfortunately it is not reliable enough for solving one of the Eurobot tasks. There are two reasons for this.

1. The occlusion of one of the beacons (e.g. by the opposing robot) or some error in the sensors do not allow to compute a position. We estimate that each of the beacons cannot be recognized at about 20% of the times.

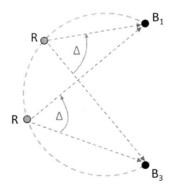

Fig. 2. The angle difference $\Delta = \phi_1 - \phi_3$ determines an unique arc from B_1 to B_3 where the robot must lie on. This results from the inscribed angle theorem.

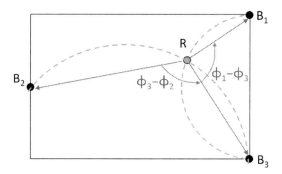

Fig. 3. The position of the robot can be determined by the intersection of two arcs resulting from three angle measurements

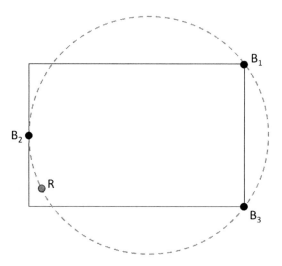

Fig. 4. In this extreme case the robot and all beacons lie on the same circle. No unique intersection point between the arcs is possible. Therefore, localization is ambiguous.

2. Due to the geometric constellations of the beacons there are regions on the playground where localization is very deficient. This can be seen by the following property of the triangulation method. For each pair of angle measurements ϕ_i and ϕ_j the angular difference $\phi_i - \phi_j$ determines an unique arc, where the robot must lie on. This fact is shown in Figure 2. Thus, the position of the robot can be determined by computing the intersection of all arcs, as can be seen in Figure 3. Figure 4 depicts the extreme case where all beacons and the robot lie on the same circle. Therefore the intersection point is not unique and the equations system (1) is not solvable. If an error in the angle measurements is assumed, this leads to a positioning error, which depends on the position on the playground. Based on a measurement error of

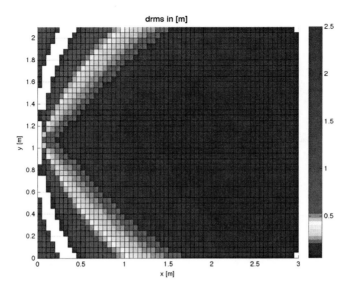

Fig. 5. DRMS (distance root mean square) $= \sqrt{(\sigma_x^2 + \sigma_y^2)}$ in meter at all positions on the playground. σ_x and σ_y are standard deviations of the robot position and are computed by doing some error propagation in equation (1). For the angle measurements we assume a standard deviation of $\sigma_\phi = 0.6°$. Only the right half of the playground guarantees accuracy better than $5cm$.

about 0.6 degree this error is estimated for every position of the playground and the result is presented in Figure 5.

Therefore, we combine the triangulation method with the well known odometry by applying the Kalman filter technique. This leads to an accurate and highly available positioning system.

3   Extended Kalman Filter Localization

Odometry data is usually obtained by integrating some wheel encoder. From odometry data the robot computes $u_t = (d_t, \delta_t)^T$ at each time step, where d_t is the driven distance and δ_t is the change in orientation in the time interval $(t, t+1]$. The odometry data are considered as control signals as presented in [19]. The robot advances from position (x_t, y_t, θ_t) to $(x_{t+1}, y_{t+1}, \theta_{t+1})$ by integrating the control signal $u_t = (d_t, \delta_t)^T$, which leads to the following nonlinear system model:

$$\begin{pmatrix} x_{t+1} \\ y_{t+1} \\ \theta_{t+1} \end{pmatrix} = \begin{pmatrix} x_t + d_t \cos(\theta_t + \delta_t/2) \\ y_t + d_t \sin(\theta_t + \delta_t/2) \\ \theta_t + \delta_t \end{pmatrix} \qquad (2)$$

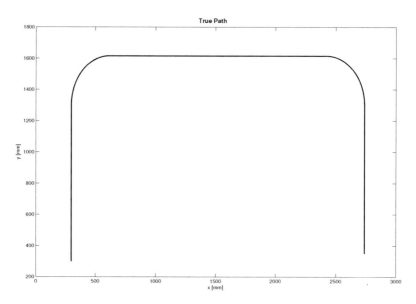

Fig. 6. True path of the robot in the Matlab simulation. The robot starts in the lower left corner and ends in the lower right corner in about 10 seconds.

As described in the previous section the robot measures angles ϕ_i, to the three beacons at each time step t. With the given system equation (2) and the measurement equation (1), the extended Kalman Filter technique [11] can now be applied. The Kalman filter receives a series of control and measurement data and yields an optimal estimation of the robot position. The technical details can be found in [6,22]. This localization method is called EKF localization in the following. It should be noted that the availability of all three measurements in each time step is not necessary. In the extreme case no sensor data is available, odometry only is used. It should also be mentioned that an error model for the control data and the measurement data is assumed as zero-mean Gaussian with some variance. These variances can easily be determined by some measurements with the sensors and the odometry. Some simulations in Matlab are carried out for the true path as shown in Figure 6. The position distance error for the pure odometry comparing to the Kalman filter approach is shown in Figure 7. A scenario with a 50% sensor outage is shown in Figure 8.

4   Experimental Results

In this section the results of several test runs with a real robot on the Eurobot playground are presented to show the performance of the EKF localization system. To get the ground truth position of the robot, a reference system based on a laser ranger installed next to the playground is used. This reference system covers the whole playground and measures the robot's position with an accuracy

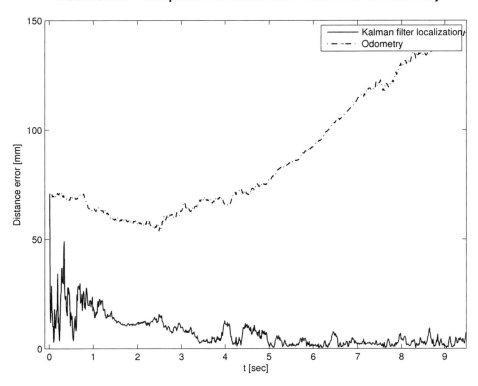

Fig. 7. The position distance error in [mm] comparing pure odometry (i.e. complete outage of beacon signals) with our Kalman Filter approach. In all simulation start with an initial position error of about $7cm$. Unlike the Kalman filter approach, pure odometry cannot compensate for this. For all simulation we assume $\sigma = 1°$ for the angle measurement, $\sigma = 1cm/m$ for the odometry distance error, $\sigma = 1°/m$ for the drift error and $\sigma = 1°/360°$ for the turning rate error.

of about $\pm 5mm$. The beacon configuration is the same as explained above. For all test runs only one robot is used. Thus, the angle to every beacon can be measured from every position on the playground. All test runs shown in this section start at the lower left corner of the playground. To show the improvement and the limitations of the EKF localization approach, the position determinated by the odometry and the EKF localization are compared. To estimate the position estimation accuracy all experiments in this section are analysed in the root mean square error (RMSE) form. The odometry of the robot is precisely calibrated. Thus, the resulting odometry errors are small for short distances. First test runs are carried out with a slow driving-speed to avoided wheel slipping. This leads to a small error for the odometry position estimation. Figure 9 shows the ground truth track, the odometry track and the EKF localization track for this test run. The localization system measures continuously all three angles and corrects the

Distance error with Kalman filter in dependance of beacon outage

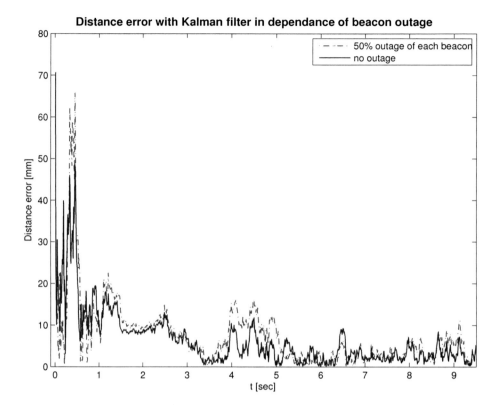

Fig. 8. The Figure shows how robust our approach is about beacon outage. In that case beacon outage of about 50% for each beacon is simulated and compared with no beacon outage.

position estimation. Both systems the EKF localization and the odometry run with an update rate of $50Hz$. The RMSE for the odometry is $0.082m$ with a variance of $0.0017m$. The improved localization has a RMSE of $0.066m$ and a variance of $0.0013m$, which shows that the robot's localization can be improved even if the odometry works well.

In the competition the robot should drive as fast as possible. Thus, all the following test runs are carried out with a faster speed of up to $1m/s$. We tested a stop and go drive to get wheel slipping during the acceleration and the breaking. The resulting tracks are shown in Figure 10. The odometry position drifts far away from the ground truth track but the EKF localization is still close to the ground truth track. This leads to a RMSE of $0.4121m$ with a variance of $0.0815m$ for the odometry and a RMSE of $0.0678m$ with a variance of $0.0009m$ for the EKF localization. This shows an apparent improvement for the localization by the EKF system.

During the competition bad conditions for the angle measurements as described above can be occur. The results of such a test run with no angle measurement on the left half of the playground is shown in Figure 11. The position

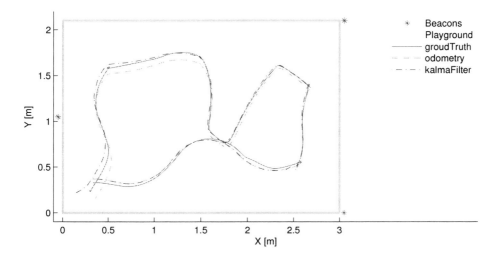

Fig. 9. The figure shows a real robot test run with calibrated odometry. A slow driving speed of about $0.15m/s$ is chosen to avoid wheel slipping. The robot starts at the lower left corner. The red line is the ground truth track, the green line is the odometry measured track and the blue line is the track estimated by the EKF localization.

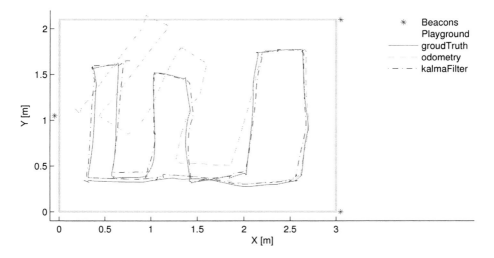

Fig. 10. Test run with fast speed of up to $1m/s$ and wheel slipping. The robot starts at the lower left corner. The red line is the ground truth track, the green line is the odometry measured track and the blue line is the track estimated by the EKF localization.

corrections when angle measurements are available is clearly shown at the position $(1.3m, 0.4m)$. In this case the position is corrected by the EKF to the ground truth path. For the track on the right half of the playground the angle

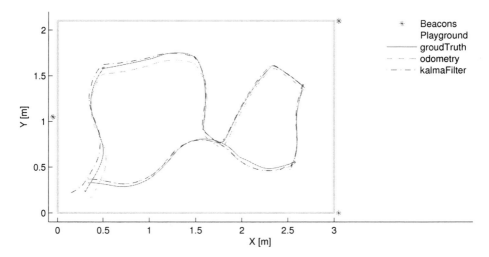

Fig. 11. Test run with occluded beacons on the left side of the playground. The robot starts at the lower left corner. The red line is the ground truth track, the green line is the odometry measured track and the blue line is the track estimated by the EKF localization.

measurements are continuously available. This leads to an EKF position estimation which is close to ground truth track. If the robot reaches the left half of the playground at the position $(1.3m, 1.5m)$ no more angle measurements are available. This experiment shows that a fast improvement of the position is possible even if the odometry has a large error and the angle measurements are not available continuously. The resulting errors for the odometry are a RMSE of $0.624m$ with a variance of $0.172m$ and for the EKF a RMSE of $0.149m$ with an variance of $0.011m$.

To evaluate the system fifteen test runs with different conditions are carried out. The resulting errors over all these experiments show a great improvement of the robot's localization by the EKF. We assume an average RMSE improvement, comparing the odometry and the EKF localization from about $0.3m$ and

Table 1. Overview of the EKF localization RMSE and the odometry RMSE with the corresponding variances for the presented experiments. The last row shows the average RMSE and the corresponding variance for all fifteen experiments.

Description	Odometry only		EKF Localization	
	RMSE [m]	σ [m]	RMSE [m]	σ [m]
Slow robot speed (Figure 9)	0.0820	0.0017	0.0334	0.0009
Slow robot speed long run	0.3481	0.0511	0.0502	0.0008
Fast robot speed (Figure 10)	0.4121	0.0815	0.0483	0.0006
Fast robot speed long run	0.7041	0.1860	0.0715	0.0022
Average over all 15 experiments	0.3719	0.0862	0.0511	0.0016

a variance improvement of about $0.035m$. Analysing all experiments leads to an EKF localization accuracy of $0.0511m$ for the RMSE and a variance of $0.0016m$. For a subset of test runs the resulting errors are shown in detail in Table 1.

5 Conclusion and Future Work

The goal is to apply a simple method which improves the localization of an autonomous mobile robot during the Eurobot contest. We use a visual sensor to measure the angle between the robot and three fixed active beacons. First, a triangulation method for the position estimation based on angle measurements is intended. This has the disadvantage that it falls out for two reasons. The first reason is that this method needs at least three visible landmarks to estimate the robot's position and if the opponent robot covers one of the beacons the localization fails. The other reason is an ineligible geometric beacon configuration which leads to an insolvable system of equations for some regions on the playground. Thus, we decided to combine the angle measurements and the odometry information by an extended Kalman filter which leads to an enhanced localization. In our experiments using the EKF localization we obtained an enhancement of about $0.3m$ for the RMSE and about $0.04m$ for the variance, compared to the odometry localization alone.

If at least one angle to a beacon is measurable we obtain for the EKF localization a position root mean square error of $0.051m$ with a variance of $0.0016m$. The main enhancement of this system is that the unbounded odometry errors can be corrected even if only the angle to one beacon is measurable. This precise localization of the robot allows to receive high level tasks like gripping and depositing game elements, based on their own global position. This provides a benefit for the path planning and navigation. Based on the robot's accurate localization a precise object detection is possible and offers the possibility for a complex game strategy development.

For future work we will extend our robot with a sensor to measure the distance to the beacons and combine this measurements with the beacons angle and the odometry information. With this enhancement the ineligible geometric beacon configuration will be avoided, because the system of equations for the distance measurements differs to them from the angle measurements. This will provide a precise localization at every point on the playground. Additionally, we will compare the results obtained by the EKF localization with other probabilistic localization approaches like unscented Kalman filter (UKF) [20] or Monte Carlo localization [18].

References

1. Bekris, K.E., Argyros, A.A., Kavraki, L.E.: Angle-based methods for mobile robot navigation: reaching the entire plane. In: Proceedings of IEEE International Conference on Robotics and Automation, ICRA 2004, pp. 2373–2378 (2004)

2. Betke, M., Gurvits, L.: Mobile robot localization using landmarks. IEEE Transactions on Robotics and Automation 13(2), 251–263 (1997)
3. Borenstein, J.: Measurement and correction of systematic odometry errors in mobile robots. IEEE Transactions on Robotics and Automation 12(6), 869–880 (1996)
4. Borenstein, J., Feng, L.: Gyrodometry: a new method for combining data from gyros and odometry in mobile robots. In: Proceedings of IEEE International Conference on Robotics and Automation, pp. 423–428 (1996)
5. Calabrese, F., Indiveri, G.: An Omni-Vision Triangulation-Like Approach to Mobile Robot Localization. In: Proceedings of the 2005 IEEE International Symposium on, Mediterrean Conference on Control and Automation Intelligent Control, pp. 604–609 (2005)
6. Choset, H., Lynch, K.M., Hutchinson, S., Kantor, G., Burgard, W., Kavraki, L.E., Thrun, S.: Principles of Robot Motion: Theory, Algorithms, and Implementations (Intelligent Robotics and Autonomous Agents). The MIT Press, Cambridge (2005)
7. Conn, A.R., Gould, N.I.M., Toint, P.L.: Trust Region Methods. Society for Industrial and Applied Mathematics, Philadephia (2000)
8. Durst, V.: Construction of a wii 360 degree infrared sensor. Bachelor's thesis, University of Applied Sciences Konstanz (May 2010)
9. Hanebeck, U.D., Schmidt, G.: Set theoretic localization of fast mobile robots using an angle measurement technique. In: Proceedings of IEEE International Conference on Robotics and Automation, pp. 1387–1394 (1996)
10. Ji, J., Indiveri, G., Ploeger, P., Bredenfeld, A.: An omni-vision based self-localization method for soccer robot. In: Proceedings of IEEE Intelligent Vehicles Symposium, pp. 276–281 (2003)
11. Kalman, R.E.: A New Approach to Linear Filtering and Prediction Problems. Transactions of the ASME Journal of Basic Engineering, 35–45 (1960)
12. Marques, C.F., Lima, P.U.: A localization method for a soccer robot using a vision-based omni-directional sensor. In: Stone, P., Balch, T., Kraetzschmar, G.K. (eds.) RoboCup 2000. LNCS (LNAI), vol. 2019, p. 96. Springer, Heidelberg (2001)
13. Myung, H., Lee, H.K., Choi, K., Bang, S., Kim, Y.B., Kim, S.: Mobile Robot Localization Using a Gyroscope and Constrained Kalman Filter. In: International Joint Conference on SICE-ICASE, pp. 2098–2103 (2006)
14. Ojeda, L., Borenstein, J.: Sensor fusion for mobile robot dead-reckoning with a precision-calibrated fiber optic gyroscope. In: Proceedings 2001 ICRA. IEEE International Conference on Robotics and Automation (Cat. No.01CH37164), pp. 3588–3593 (2001)
15. Shimshoni, I.: On mobile robot localization from landmark bearings. IEEE Transactions on Robotics and Automation 18(6), 971–976 (2002)
16. Solda, E., Worst, R., Hertzberg, J.: Poor-Mans Gyro-Based Localization. In: Proceedings of the 5th IFAC Symposium on Intelligent Autonomous Vehicles (IAV 2004), Citeseer (2004)
17. Sutherland, K.T., Thompson, W.B.: Localizing in unstructured environments: dealing with the errors. IEEE Transactions on Robotics and Automation 10(6), 740–754 (1994)
18. Thrun, S.: Robust Monte Carlo localization for mobile robots. Artificial Intelligence 128, 99–141 (2001)

19. Thrun, S., Burgard, W., Fox, D.: Probabilistic robotics. In: Intelligent Robotics and Autonomous Agents. MIT Press, Cambridge (2005)
20. Wan, E.a., Van Der Merwe, R.: The unscented Kalman filter for nonlinear estimation. In: Proceedings of the IEEE 2000 Adaptive Systems for Signal Processing, Communications, and Control Symposium, pp. 153–158 (2002)
21. Ward, C.C., Iagnemma, K.: Model-Based Wheel Slip Detection for Outdoor Mobile Robots. In: Proceedings 2007 IEEE International Conference on Robotics and Automation, pp. 2724–2729 (April 2007)
22. Welch, G., Bishop, G.: An introduction to the Kalman filter. University of North Carolina at Chapel Hill 7(1), 1–16 (1995)

A New Programming Interface for Educational Robotics

Javier Caccavelli, Sol Pedre, Pablo de Cristóforis,
Andrea Katz, and Diego Bendersky

Departamento de Computación,
Facultad de Ciencias Exactas y Naturales,
Universidad de Buenos Aires
Buenos Aires, Argentina
{jcaccav,spedre,pdecris,akatz,dbenders}@dc.uba.ar

Abstract. Educational Robotics uses robots as a tool for teaching a variety of subjects other than specifically robotics in undergraduate curricula. To achieve this goal is vital to have an adequate interface that allows inexperienced students to interact with robots in an easy manner. In this paper we present the current development of ERBPI (*Easy Robot Behaviour Programming Interface*), a new application that doesn't require any previous programming experience to control robots. To accomplish this, we propose to abandon the imperative programming paradigm and take a behaviour-based approach. Thus, the new application is based on the connectionist paradigm, accomplishing behaviours by establishing configurable connections between sensors and actuators. Moreover, different defined behaviours can be connected using a subsumption architecture. The new application is designed to work with different robots and simulators, and it is simple for adding new ones. Learning experiences with high school students allowed us to test its effectiveness.

Keywords: educational robotics, behaviour-based programming interface.

1 Introduction

The use of robots in undergraduate curricula has grown over the last years. The availability of low cost, easy-to-use platforms has even led to the use of robots in middle and high schools. Many teachers have an interest in introducing robots into their classrooms for teaching a variety of subjects other than specifically robotics. Thus, Educational Robotics arises, proposing the use of robotics as a teaching resource that allows inexperienced students to approach different scientific fields such as mathematics, experimental sciences, technology, information science and computing, among others. One of the aims of Educational Robotics is to aid students in building their own representations and concepts of science and technology, through the use, handling and control of robotic environments.

D. Obdržálek and A. Gottscheber (Eds.): EUROBOT 2011, CCIS 161, pp. 68–77, 2011.
© Springer-Verlag Berlin Heidelberg 2011

This approach uses the constructionist process of designing, building, programming and debugging robot's behaviours, as well as collaboration and teamwork, as powerful means of enlivening education.

Several educational robotics programming interfaces have been presented. Most are designed for university-level or late high school students and are implemented as extensions to existing programming languages. That is the case of Pyro [1], a Python-based programming framework which provides a set of abstractions that allow students to write platform-independent robot programs. Other interfaces include Not-Quite C (NQC) [2] based on C, BrickOS [3] based on C++ and leJOS [4] that is based on Java. These three interfaces are particular for Lego Mindstrom. All these interfaces require programming experience or interest in learning a particular programming language. This makes them unsuitable for middle or high school students that do not handle any imperative or procedural programming concepts, such as the idea of loops, conditions, forks or variables in a program. Microsoft also offers the commercial tool Microsoft Robotics Developer Studio [5]. This includes a visual programming interface based on a data flow approach, but again it requires knowledge of programming concepts, making it quite complex for inexperienced users.

There are also several graphical environments for simulated robots aimed at middle schools. That is the case of StartLogo [6], Squeak Etoys [7] and Scratch [8]. These are easy-to-use programming interfaces, allowing inexperienced students to make a quick start, although they maintain an imperative programming influence and are designed only for particular simulated environments. Another programming interface used in instructional settings at the K-12 level is Robo-Lab [9] for the LEGO Mindstorms robot. This is a graphical environment in which students are given palettes of icons that they can drag and drop on a canvas. The icons represent robot components like motors and sensors, as well as abstract programming structures such as loops and counter variables. This interface is particular for the Mindstrom robot, and once again uses imperative programming structures that add complexity to the robotic environment. Finally, in [10] authors present an extension to RoboLab in order to work with other robotic platforms.

Our experiences working with classroom teachers and young students have raised several issues that have motivated us to pursue the development of a behaviour-based interface, which abstracts away the imperative programming constructs and the low-level motor and sensor commands that often confuse inexperienced programmers or deter techno-phobic students. To accomplish this, we propose to abandon the imperative programming paradigm and take a behaviour-based approach. Thus, the proposed interface is based on a connectionist paradigm. The idea is that stimuli captured by the robot sensors are processed in a network of connections and result in a response for the robot actuators. To program the robot behaviours we have to establish connections between its sensors and actuators. This connections may include different mathematical functions [11]. Moreover, different defined behaviours can be connected using a subsumption architecture [12], making it possible to achieve more complex behaviours. In this way, we get a state automaton (or machine), where each state represents a behaviour and each transition a change in the environment. This state machine can be easily translated into an imperative program that the robot executes to perform the behaviour.

This paper describes the current development of ERBPI(*Easy Robot Behaviour Programming Interface*), a behaviour-based, easy to use robotic programming interface for Educational Robotics that allows to program different robotic platforms and simulators. The design of ERBPI follows the next criteria:

- *Ease of use:* The user is not supposed to have any previous programming knowledge. The interface must be intuitive and easy to learn, providing all the tools to program robot behaviours graphically, making it possible to perform drag-and-drop with robot's sensors and actuators, build sensor-actuator connections, and easily configure them.
- *Platform independence:* The application must work with a variety of robots and simulators, and be easily expandable to control new ones. The different bodies, sensors, actuators, low-level commands and protocols to communicate with high-level systems of different robots must be abstracted. Moreover, users must be able to test and run the same behaviours on multiple robots.
- *Portability:* The application must work in different operating systems and platforms to accommodate the different hardware and software available in schools or other educational institutions.
- *Flexibility:* Students from a wide range of backgrounds and teachers with a broad range of goals must be able to use the programming interface effectively, accommodating different levels, curricular needs, academic subjects and physical environments for instruction.

This paper is organized as follows. In the next section we describe ERPBI's architecture and features, and give examples of use. Afterward, we comment some experiences using ERPBI in the classroom with high school students. Finally, we draw some conclusions and discuss directions for future work.

2   The ERBPI: Easy Robot Behaviour Programming Interface

ERBPI uses a behaviour-based approach following the connectionist paradigm. It enables users to create basic behaviours, and then connect them using a subsumption architecture to create more complex ones.

To create basic behaviours, the user establishes connections between sensors and actuators, and configures them with a chain of mathematical functions. Each function can have several inputs, including sensed data and outputs from previous ones. It uses all the inputs to compute a single output, that in turn may be used to set actuators or input following functions. The user chooses functions from predefined families and configure their parameters. This schema defines an

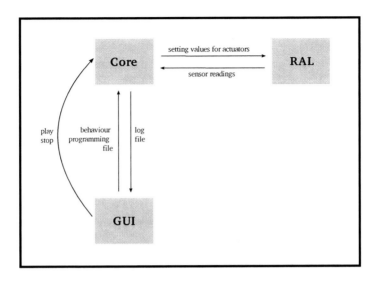

Fig. 1. ERBPI's modular architecture

execution graph that allows to infer a computation order and thus translate it to an imperative program for the robot.

All the function outputs, sensors and actuators values are normalized to the same scale $(-100, 100)$. This scale is a "percentage of activation" for each element in the schema. Normalizing all the data permits the previous schema to work properly and also that one behaviour can be used for several robots that may have different sensors or actuators.

The application has a modular design, clearly decoupling the different responsibilities in the system. The GUI (Graphical User Interface) module allows the user to graphically design the robot behaviour, and then exports this behaviour in a file. The CORE module reads this file and executes the defined behaviour. To communicate with the robotic platform (simulator or real robot), the CORE uses a particular RAL (Robot Abstraction Layer) module. There is one RAL for each robotic platform ERBPI manages. This module is in charge of normalizing all the sensor and actuator values, and also of communicating with the actual robot using its particular communication protocol. The basic architecture, including the three modules and their communication, is shown in Fig. 1. Each module is explained in the following sections.

2.1 GUI (Graphical User Interface) Module

The GUI module is in charge of interacting with the user. To start, the user selects a robot or simulator to work with. The GUI enables the user to drag and drop elements (sensors, actuators, functions) to a work canvas, and then connect them using the mouse. Different functions may be selected from a menu, dragged to the canvas, and then configured with a pop-up configuration window. Fig. 2

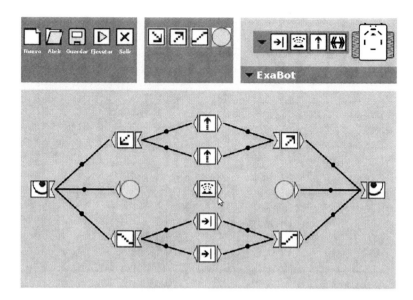

Fig. 2. A screenshot of the application. The upper panel shows the configurations and elements. The general operations (new, open, save, play, quit) are in the upper left corner. The upper-center panel has different families of functions the user can choose from (decreasing, growing, broken and constant functions in this screenshot). The upper right panel shows the selected robot with its sensors. In the canvas we can see a line following behaviour that stops when the bumpers are activated.

shows a screenshot of the GUI and Fig. 3 an example of the pop-up configuration window.

Once the behaviour is finished, the user can select a robot to execute it on. The created behaviour and the minimal sensor and actuator configuration needed for its execution are stored in a file (the behaviour-file), that will be read by the CORE. The execution of the behaviour may be started and paused at any moment from the GUI. The GUI also provides general operations to open and save files.

The GUI is implemented in Java, a good language for graphical interfaces and portable to several operating systems, only requiring the installation of the JVM (Java Virtul Machine). The behaviour-file is in XML(Extensible Markup Language), making it very simple to add new robots, sensor types, functions and other features we might add to ERBPI. A simple example of a behaviour-file is shown in table 1.

2.2   CORE Module

The CORE module is in charge of executing the behaviour. It reads the XML behaviour-file and establishes a connection with the appropriate RAL. At regular intervals, the core receives from the RAL the normalized values of the sensors,

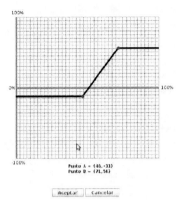

Fig. 3. The configuration pop-up window for a broken function. The change points in the function and the low and high levels can be easily configured moving them with the mouse. The scale for the normalized values $(-100, 100)$ is also observable.

executes the behaviour, and gives to the RAL the normalized values to set the actuators. The CORE stops when the GUI signals the user has stopped the execution.

To be able to execute the behaviour, the CORE has to transform the execution graph defined by the GUI in the behaviour-file to a corresponding ordered execution list, to guarantee that all the inputs for a function are ready when its turn to execute is up. For this, we used a topological sorting [13] of the execution graph. The CORE also asserts that the behaviour can be executed in the selected robot, for example that the graph is not cyclic (i.e, cannot be ordered) or that the robot has enough sensors and actuators to execute the behaviour. It also defines the communication frequency with the RAL depending on the robots working frequency. Finally, the CORE makes a log-file where all the values at a certain time are registered, including each sensor value, the output value of each function and the value of each actuator. This log file is communicated to the GUI. We plan to use it to implement a debug function in the future.

2.3   RAL (Robot Abstraction Layer) Module

The RAL modules encapsulates all the knowledge of the particular robot or simulator, providing a standard interface to the CORE module, dealing with everything necessary to communicate with the actual robot. The RAL abstracts the particular robot, its communication protocol, and normalizes the values of the particular sensors and actuators. In this way, all the specific characteristics of the robot are transparent to the CORE. A RAL must implement a standard interface that include the following methods: get the list of sensors and actuators in the robot, get the frequency the robot can work in, get the sensor values, and set the values for the actuators. To add a new robotic platform for ERBPI to

Table 1. Example of an XML behaviour-file. In this case, two sensors are needed to perform this behaviour (a sonar and an encoder). A broken function (`function1`), defined by two points, takes both sensors as inputs. The value for the motor.left actuator is set by the output of two functions

```
<behaviour>
  <sensors>
    <sensor id='sonar.0'/>
    <sensor id='encoder.motor.left'/>
  </sensors>
  <functions>
    <function id='function1'>
      <inputs>
        <input id='sonar.0'/>
        <input id='encoder.motor.left'/>
      </inputs>
      <points>
        <point x='100' y='0'/>
        <point x='150' y='255'/>
      </points>
    </function>
  </functions>
  <actuators>
    <actuator id='motor.left'>
      <inputs>
        <input id='function1'/>
        <input id='function2'/>
      </inputs>
    </actuator>
  </actuators>
</behaviour>
```

work with, a developer must only program a particular RAL for the platform implementing the general RAL interface.

All RALs are implemented as dynamic libraries. In this manner, we can add new RALs without having to recompile the CORE or the GUI. Moreover, this allows the CORE to load a different RAL on runtime, without having to restart the application. This makes ERBPI easily extendable to control different robots.

To the date, we have implemented RALs for the Khepera [14] and Exabot [15] robots, and for the YAKS (Yet another Khepera Simulator) [16] and the Player/Stage [17] simulator.

3   ERBPI in the Classroom

To explore the adequacy of the tool, a preliminary version of ERBPI was used in a special course designed for high school students during July 2010.

The class was composed of 20 students from seven high schools of Buenos Aires, Argentina. The student's programming experience varied from none to some experience with procedural languages like C, C++ or Pascal. There were also few students with some electronics background, and all mastered basic mathematical concepts such as constant, monotonous and broken functions. None of the students had experience with robots.

The course covered basic concepts of robotics and of behaviour based robotics. The preliminary version of ERBPI used for the course only had the basic conectionnist approach, lacking the subsumption feature to compose more complex behaviours. We followed a hands-on approach, programming easy behaviours from day one in groups of two or three students. Using the Braitenberg model [11], the students developed behaviours in simulators that were also tested in real robots, experiencing with the Yaks simulator [16], Khepera [14] and ExaBot [15] robots. Different behaviours were proposed for the students to solve with the robots, ranging from follow a line in the floor, go to a light spot, avoid obstacles or solve mazes. Those behaviours were developed by teaching students the scientific method, encouraging them to propose hypothesis, contrast the expected results with the ones obtained in the testing phase, and then propose explanations and changes to the original robot control. Each group also shared their findings with the rest of the class, showing different approaches and solutions to the given problems during a discussion phase. Overall, the students picked up the use of ERBPI easily and could program all the proposed behaviours quickly.

After the course, a questionnaire was given to the students in order to explore their reviews of the course and the programming interface. All students answered that they had found the interface easy to learn and use, despite they had no idea about programming robots and had not had the opportunity to control a robot before the course. All students felt that they met the objectives of the course successfully and most of them showed interest in taking more courses of robotics, computer science and engineering after the course.

In this experience we found some improvements to be made in ERBPI. For example, we plan to execute the resulting program directly in the robot when possible, instead of executing the program in the external PC with the consequent transmission of sensor data and commands back and forth. Another improvement is to increase the amount of possible functions, to broaden the tools capabilities for math teachers. We also realized how important the subsumption architecture feature is, to allow the construction of more complex behaviours from simpler ones. Students also suggested some improvements, like "cooler" or friendlier names for different objects of ERBPI.

We also tested ERBPI in shorter courses, lectures, exhibitions and others activities of popularization of science for high school students and broader public. The most important was part of a three day exhibition of the University of Buenos Aires that took place in October 2010 [18]. Many of the ideas in ERBPI were born in previous experiences with high school students, mainly two eight-week workshop on robotics we organized as a part of a program from the

Vocational Orientation Department of our Faculty during 2006 [19] and 2009 [20].

We are planning on using a full featured ERBPI in Educational Robotics courses for more high schools of Buenos Aires during the present year, as a part of a popularization of science project of our Faculty.

4 Conclusions and Ongoing Work

In this paper we presented the design and current development of ERBPI, an application to provide a simple, graphical, behaviour-based interface for Educational Robotics courses aimed at inexperienced students. To reach this goal, we propose to abandon the imperative paradigm and take a behaviour based approach. The tool is capable of controlling different robotics platforms, and it is designed to be easily expandable for new ones. It is also portable to different operating systems to accommodate the available hardware and software in schools. Experiences with high school students show that the current version of ERBPI allows inexperienced public to quickly start working with robotic environments.

We are currently working on the subsumption feature of the tool, important to allow the development of more complex behaviours. We also plan to expand the application in order to execute the behaviour directly on the robot when possible. Another improvement we are working on is to include a play-back facility to debug behaviours, using the execution log-file and a web-cam that films the robot behaviour. The idea is to use the execution log-file to show at the same time which sensors, connections and behaviours were activated when the robot took a certain action, and the play-back of the video captured with the web-cam.

During the present year we will prepare and teach educational robotics courses for more high schools in Buenos Aires, using the full featured ERBPI tool. We hope this experiences will provide extra feedback to continue and improve this project.

References

1. Blank, D.S., Kumar, D., Meeden, L., Yanco, H.: Pyro: A python-based versatile programming environment for teaching robotics. Journal on Educational Resources in Computing (JERIC), Special Issue on Robotics in Undergraduate Education. Part 2 4(3), 115 (2004)
2. Baum, D.: NQC, http://bricxcc.sourceforge.net/nqc/ (accessed March 17, 2011)
3. Markus. brickOS, http://brickos.sourceforge.net/ (accessed March 17, 2011)
4. Solorzano, J.: leJOS, http://lejos.sourceforge.net/ (accessed March 17, 2011)
5. Microsoft Robotics Developer Studio, http://www.microsoft.com/robotics/ (accessed March 17, 2011)
6. MIT's Scheller Teacher Education Program (STEP), http://education.mit.edu/drupal/starlogo-tng (accessed March 17, 2011)
7. http://www.squeakland.org/ (accessed March 17, 2011)

8. `http://scratch.mit.edu/` (accessed March 17, 2011)
9. Tufts University. RoboLab, `http://www.ceeo.tufts.edu/robolabatceeo/` (accessed March 17, 2011)
10. Azhar, M.Q.: An agent-oriented behavior-based interface framework for educationa robotics. In: Agent-Based Systems for Human Learning (ABSHL) Workshop at Autonomous Agents and MultiAgent Systems, AAMAS-2006 (2006)
11. Braitenberg, V.: Vehicles: Experiments in Synthetic Psychology. MIT Press, Cambridge (1986)
12. Arkin, R.C.: Behavior-Based Robotics. MIT Press, Cambridge (1998)
13. Cormen, H., Leiserson, C.E., Rivest, R.L., Stein, C.: Topological Sort, Introduction to Algorithms. MIT Press, Cambridge (2009)
14. K-Team, Khepera I, `http://www.k-team.com/` (accessed March 17, 2011)
15. Pedre, S., de Cristforis, P., Caccavelli, J., Stoliar, A.: A mobile mini robot architecture for research, education and popularization of science. Journal of Applied Computer Science Methods, Guest Editors: Zurada, J., Estevez, P. 2(1), 41–59, ISSN 1689-9636.
16. Yet Another Khepera Simulator, `http://freshmeat.net/projects/yaks/` (accessed March 17, 2011)
17. Player/Stage Simulator, `http://playerstage.sourceforge.net/` (accessed March 17, 2011)
18. ExpoUBA 2010, Plaza de las Ciencias, Universidad de Buenos Aires, Argentina, `http://www.uba.ar/expouba` (accessed March 17, 2010)
19. Robot programming workshop for high school students, `www.fcen.uba.ar/dov/talleres_de_ciencia/2006/computacion.htm` (accessed March 17, 2011)
20. Robot programming workshop for high school students, `www.fcen.uba.ar/dov/talleres_de_ciencia/2009/computacion.htm` (accessed March 17, 2011)

An Attempt to Teaching Programming with Robots*

Petr Čermák and Jozef Kelemen

Institute of Computer Science
Silesian University
746 01 Opava Czech Republic
petr.cermak@fpf.slu.cz,
kelemen@fpf.slu.cz

Abstract. The aim of the contribution is to present an attempt to teaching programming with robots. Two problems ad methods of their solutions are presented, namely the so called mark identification and following problem and the related method of its solution, and the alleged line following problem, and the corresponding method. The methods for solving the mentioned problems have been implemented on the robotic platform Koala. In the paper some comparisons of the two implementations by two groups of students are presented. The two versions are described, and the pros and cons are mentioned for both of two implementations.

Keywords: Robot, Programming, Education, C++, Koala robots, Computer vision.

1 Introduction

The central aim of this contribution is to sketch our ideas concerning an attempt to the development of the some of basic programming abilities of beginners in the university education level of computer programming novices. The idea is based on the use in the certain situation more attractive devices for programming than the traditional computers of the today are – using robotic hardware platforms. The earlier origins of this idea have been sketched in certain extent in some of our previous studies, e.g. in [1],[2],[3] and [4]. This contribution sketches some of the experiences with it, we have at hand up today.

It seems to be evident that from the certain perspective the robotic platforms are in certain extent similar devices as the traditional personal computers. The traditional computers have, similarly as the robotic platforms, some central processor, some input and output devices, and some possibilities to program the processor for providing the required relation between the input data and the

---

* This work is supported by CZ.1.07/2.3.00/09.0197: Strengthening of competitive advantages in research and development of information technology in Moravian-Silesian Region, Operational program Education for Competitiveness 2.3 Human resources in research and development.

D. Obdržálek and A. Gottscheber (Eds.): EUROBOT 2011, CCIS 161, pp. 78–87, 2011.
© Springer-Verlag Berlin Heidelberg 2011

output data. In the case of the traditional computers we have keyboards, mice, monitors, printers, etc., in the case of robotic platforms we have different sensors, which provide input data, and different actuators providing output performances in the robots' physical environments.

From the specificity of generation of correct input-output relations by robots' processors some qualitatively new dimensions of programming arise. A very substantial one consists in the ability of programmers to deal with in factAn real-time programming. The robots' environments are mostly dynamic, these changes are usually only hardly displayed for physically real environments. Because of the requirement to act for a robot under such conditions, it seems to be required to provide robots' processors with programs, which are able to connect the input data from the real environment very effectively with the required output data managing the robots' actuators performances. This is one among the crucial specificity of robot programming in comparison with programming usual computers having mostly, at least in the cases forming the basics of general programming training – almost nothing common with coping with programming real time processes. In the consequence of that, one among the important differences lies, for instance, in the necessity to comprehend the complexity in different ways. In the case of programming traditional problem solving procedures by common computers, the acceptable space and time measures play an important role form well known reasons.

However, in the case of programming robots working under the real time conditions, the principal requirement for having a sufficiently complex program might consist in having quick enough connection between sensed data and the output data without the necessity to pay the main attention to the computational complexity of the program behind the computation of the required output managing the actuators functioning from the input provided by sensors. To have in the mind the mentioned one and similar requirement specific for robot programming seems as important, and should be emphasized in robot programming curricula. Few information about that is e.g. in [5], where languages Lisp and C are mentioned, and in [6] which emphasized the traditional lingua franca of artificial intelligence experimentation – different dialects of the Lisp. Good inspiration might come also from [7] and from [8]. More specialized problems and their possible solutions are included in [9]. Some inspiration from programming can be found also in [10]. In the first case, the short notes follow programming reactive robots, in the second one the main emphases is put to traditional artificial intelligence programming, which is not identical with the matter of robot programming, however, Lisp could be effectively used for the purposes of robotics. Other publications are focused to general settings of problems without a special attention devoted to programming languages.

The next parts of this contribution illustrate how student face with this kind of problems in their own programming activities. The used robotic platform is the Koala fabricated by K-team. The programming language used by students is C++ The problem for solving which the robots should be programmed by students is some variants of the traditional navigation problem used on the base of input data screened by simple video cameras on Koalas' boards.

2   Problem Setting

As example two traditional navigation problems are used. The first one is the so called mark identification and following problem. The second one is declared as red line on top floor following problem. To solve these problems students must have preliminary knowledge from five areas:

- Basics of Robotics and Robotic hardware
- Embedded Programming in C/C++
- Embedded OS
- Embedded Linux platform
- Computer vision
- Theory of automata

Fig. 1. Part of the arena

The figure above shows the arena for two selected examples. The splitter between the two examples is the triangular Mark. The so called mark identification and following problem integrates the use of a number of theoretical methods and programming skills. Basically, the Koala robot platforms have pan tilt cameras for mark identification. In the course solving of the mark identification problem students must apply and program methods from the field of computer vision. First, the robot must extract the color from image, and then to provide a suitable segmentation of the sensed scene. In the case of more objects in the perceived image the process must remove a small object by measuring area, and remove them if the area is lower than a predefined value. All the objects remaining after the filtering are labeled with counting down values. Then suitable methods for mark classification are needed. Due to result of the classification we get the type of the mark and position in image given by coordinates. Type of the mark and the position is used for state the Koala robot behavior. For successful obstacle avoidance we must take into account additionally the data received by the proximity sensors. Students must implement as a finite state automaton also the well known Breitenberg algorithm. The movements of wheels are possible in both directions forward and backward by setting positive and negative integer values. The finishing of this part is defined as a stop before triangular mark. Now we define the second part of the red line following problem. The Koala robot must tilt down camera to see top of the floor, next it must extract the red color from the received image, and to provide the suitable segmentation. Filtering is provided by removing small areas and noises. To obtain the movement direction it is necessary to approximate the red line from top floor by a regression line, and to determine the angle between the regression line and the movement direction. This angle determines the setting of the left and right motors of Koala robot actuators. This task finishes two meters before the red circle mark.

3   Koalas

For experiments, we are used two autonomous Koala robots which have many additional sensors to use. The Koala robot in the configuration showed on Fig. 2 consists of the stand-alone automotive part, six boards, maximally two video cameras, and a WiFi. We describe each board in brief from the lower up to the upper parts.

Automotive autonomous part (AAP) of Koala robots contains a Motorola 68331 processor on 16MHz with a 1 MB RAM, a flash of 256 KB, and a ROM 128 KB. For movement two DC motors with incremental encoders are installed. 16 infra red proximity sensors can be used for obstacle avoidance function. The infrared proximity sensors can be used in passive mode as infrared light sensors for locating beacons. This board is also equipped by additional sensors, which can be used for monitoring the battery power, ambient temperature, motors torque, and global power consumption. To extend some of the functions or sensory inputs we can use additional analog inputs and digital I/O through Wago clamps. From software point of view the basic Koala BIOS and the so called Breitenberg algorithm are installed in the ROM.

The second board consists on four DC drivers for Pan Tilt DC motors with maximally two cameras.The protocol for driving and configuring the board is a text command based, and physically is realized by an RS232 connection. For powering of the PC/104 board a Koala PC/104 Extension Board is installed. This board converts power to 5V, and connects directly to AAP and PC/104 Main Board.

The board with micro BNC connectors on Fig. 2 is a PC/104 Frame Grabber board. This board is based on BT848 chipset well supported by Linux (V4L2) and Windows as well. The connection with PC/104 is provided trough a PCI 104 Bus. The PC/104 Main Board is the upper installed board due to passive cooling. This board is a small size PC Pentium MMX 400 MHz with a 64MB RAM. For the local programming, similarly as a standard PC it is connected with a monitor, a keyboard and contains a PC/104. This small PC board has built in standard interfaces like Onboard Video Display, Onboard Ethernet Interface, EIDE, Floppy, keyboard, and mouse . To store system and data this configuration is connected with an ultra slim ATA low power 20 GB disk (2.5").

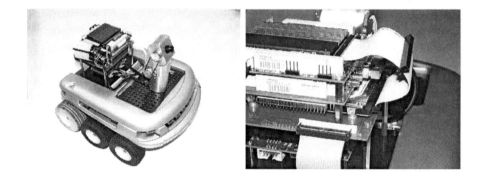

Fig. 2. The Koala and boards detail

On PC/104 board is installed Embedded Linux system. This Embedded Linux system has two variants. The first is standard Debian minimal distribution installation with V4l2. The second is based on Slax 5.1.8.1 distribution with Xfce, V4l2 and is more suitable for teaching and system recovery process. Slax Linux system is based on Slackware Linux. This Linux is able to start from flash USB or HDD. It is very simple to recover this installation to the same configuration and state in short time. No tedious installation and disk image recovery is required. We can compile and testing our software remotely with standard GNU compiler, linker and debugger. Remote connection is provided by the WiFi and ssh implementation and there is possible to start applications remotely with the XWindows interface. Thus for checking properly function of pan tilt camera we can use programs like xawtv or tvtime.

4   Problems, Solutions, Some Comparisons

We have only two Koala robots for experimentation of twenty students, which encouraged us to program library support with ability reading images from off-line source and also from pan tilt camera of the robots. This situation is shown in the Fig. 3. Student can use INSIDE KOALA preprocessor switch for off-line image analysis, in this case more precisely for the mark analysis. We assumed, that students will be spending time mainly on programming and for testing the methods of mark identification. Our practical experiences have confirmed that this assumption was correct and every student can work on project individually for more than half of all the time scheduled for the project. Programming of the Breitenberg like an algorithm, and the red line following program consumes about a third to a half of all the time. Exercises for this part of the project are organized in small groups up to four students. Students in each of groups selected the best mark following implementation for future work. As mentioned above students used library support with simple template source code in C++. Next simple example shows such a C++ template.

The template includes header part preprocessor switch INSIDE KOALA, the hardware initialization routines in case INSIDE KOALA equal to 1. Next part is a main loop where students can program the desired functionality. The last part consists of calling the stopping of all the motors and in closing of serial lines. In the following we present solutions of the two groups of students each with two tasks defined in chapter 2. Clearly that during the normal work of the mark identification and following algorithm, and if an obstacle is detected the program

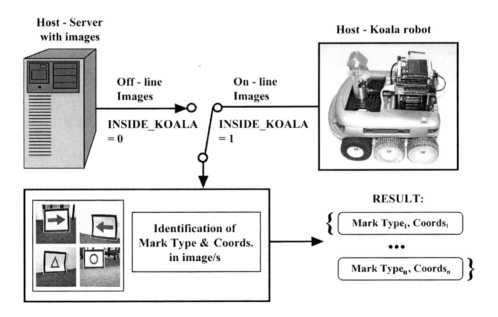

Fig. 3. Switching Image Source Off Line/On Line

Algorithm 1. Template Following markers in C++

```cpp
#include <iostream>
#include <cstdlib>
using namespace std;

#define INSIDE_KOALA 1
#include "./koala.h"

int main()
{
    unsigned char *image; int width= 768, height= 576;
    int pixels_in_image= width*height;
    Grabber_Init();

#if INSIDE_KOALA
    connectTTY();
    initPanTilt();
#endif

    /* main loop */
    do {
        /* grab a new one */
        image= Grab_One( &width , &height);
        if( image==NULL) break;

        /* *** TO DO STUDENTS *** */

    }
    while( image!= NULL && !kbhit());

#if INSIDE_KOALA
    setSpeed( 0 , 0);
    disconnectTTY();
#endif

    return 0;
}
```

flow is switched to the Breitenberg like algorithm. In the following Tables, the algorithms of two groups of students are described in a short way, because the source code is too long to present here about thousands line of C++. When the desired mark is a triangle then the mark identification and following algorithm is stopped, and the program execution is switched to red line following algorithm. For illustration Figure 4 shows the example of aplication first six steps from the algoritm on Table 1 (Group 2) on first image.

Table 1. Mark identification and following algorithm steps

Group1	Group2
Read image from on line source	Read image from on line source
Extraction mark color from image using segmentation with threshold value of channel R	Extraction mark color from image using segmentation of values $\frac{2Red}{(Green+Blue)}$ pix.
Filling areas by flood fill alg.	Filling areas by flood fill alg.
Counting number of pixels in each area	Counting number of pixels in each area
Filtering small areas and noise	Filtering small areas and noise
Labeling remained areas with countdown val.	Labeling remained areas with countdown val.
Evaluate rectangularity, roundness, compactness, topological Euler value	Load template marks for pattern matching
	Determining Weighted matrix for PM
Determining of mark types and positions by classification of attributes above and calculating center of gravity	Determining of mark types and positions by pattern matching and center of gravity
If mark COG is max 20% left or right from image center setSpeed(40, 40)	The left and right motor speed is set proportionally to difference between marks' COG and image centers
if (>20% left) setSpeed(10, 30)	
if (>20% right) setSpeed(30, 10)	

Note to Algorithm in Table 2, that the value 80 was selected as a maximum by measuring of floor tube light and direct sun shining. You can see now that Group1 has used baseline methods and algorithms, except of the mark classification. In the case of calculating the rectangularity, roundness, compactness, topological Euler value and classification could lead to better results when mark is a bit rotated. But for general result, there is no contribution. On the opposite, the Group2 has used better method for mark color extraction in different lighting conditions. Pattern matching method we can use very simply to other marks by changing templates. Proportionally driving of left and right motors lead to lower abrasion of Koala robots mechanical parts and movements are fluent. Futhermore, using the negative values can lead the Breitenberg like algorithm sneak out from gaps. A good idea with a prediction of red line course is given on Table 3. Prediction improves red line tracking in bends.

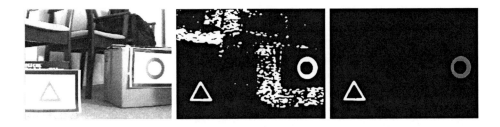

Fig. 4. Mark Identification

Table 2. Breitenberg like algorithm steps

Group1	Group2
Reading 16 values from Proximity sens.	Reading 16 values from Proximity sens.
Removing noise values if (val < 80) then val:= 0;	Removing noise values if (val < 80) then val:= 0;
Determining obstacle distance for four quadrants	Determining obstacle distance for four or eight quadrants
Determine a new direction to avoid obstacle/s and take into account last arrow mark, set speed for left and right motor with positive magnitude	Determine a new direction to avoid obstacle/s and take into account last arrow mark, set speed for left and right motor with pos./neg. magnitude

Table 3. Red line following algorithm steps

Group1	Group2
Read image from on line source	Read image from on line source
Extraction line color from image using segmentation with threshold value of chan. R	Extraction line color from image using segmentation of values $\frac{2Red}{(Green+Blue)}$ pix.
Filling areas by flood fill alg.	Filling areas by flood fill alg.
Counting number of pixels in each area	Counting number of pixels in each area
Filtering small areas and noise	Filtering small areas and noise
Determine x position of red line in 2/3 image height from bottom	Determine x1 position of red line in 4/5 image height from bottom
If red line x pos is max 10% left or right from image center setSpeed(40, 40) if (>10% left) setSpeed(10, 30) if (>10% right) setSpeed(30, 10)	Determine x2 position of red line in half image height from bottom
	Determine x3 position of red line in 1/5 image height from bottom
	From these points calculate new movement direction.
	If not found x1 use x1 from previous iteration. Calc x1 pos. prediction. Correct with predicted x1 new direction.
	setSpeed to follow mov. direction
	Store x1 for next iteration

A result of generally comparison is points for Group2. Every year we organize contests of students as a part of the exams in Computer vision. Futhermore, according to their success during the contests are students evaluated. Evaluation is using the scale from A to E, and is based on point assignment. Following lines show the criteria:

- Time from Start to Finish (sec), the best time (20 points)
- Touch obstacle/s (minus point/s)
- Mark misdetection/s (minus point/s)
- Loose on foor red line start (minus point)
- Crossing red line (minus point/s)
- Mistake on final stop distance determination (minus point/s).

5 Conclusions

Since 2007 we at the Institute of Computer Science of the Silesian University in Opava are working with Koala robots each year, and we added also some small new functionality to present the above experiments. We plane to finish the M.Sc.-level exam of Computer vision with a theoretical part, and practical part using the above described experiments, and to enlarge also the number of our robotic platforms in order to have more possibilities to personalize the examinations of the students.

References

1. Kelemen, J., Kubík, A.: Robots and agents in basic computer science curricula. In: Kozlowski, K. (ed.) Proc. 4th International Workshop on Robot Motion and Control, pp. 309–317. Poznan University of Technology, Poznan (2002)
2. Kelemen, J., Kubík, A.: RADIUS – looking for robots' help in computer science research and education. ERCIM News (15), 48–49 (2002)
3. Ačová, M., Kelemen, J., Kubík, A.: Embodied hypotheses – preliminary notes and case studies. In: Kozlowski, K. (ed.) Proc. 4th International Workshop on Robot Motion and Control, pp. 35–40. Poznan University of Technology, Poznan (2004)
4. Nemrava, M., Cermak, P.: Solving the Box – Pushing Problem by Master-Slave Robots Cooperation. JAMRIS 2(3), 32–37 (2008)
5. Arkin, R.C.: Behavior-Based Robotics. The MIT Presss, Cambridge (1998)
6. Winston, P.H.: Artificial Intelligence, 3rd edn. Addison Wesley, Reading (1992)
7. Matarić, M.J.: The Robotics Primer. The MIT Press, Cambridge (2007)
8. Braitenberg, V.: Vehicles. The MIT Press, Cambridge (1996)
9. Dudek, G., Jenkin, M.: Computational Pronciples of Mobile Robotics. Cambridge University Press, Cambridge (2000)
10. Murphy, R.R.: Introduction to AI Robotics. The MIT Press, Cambridge (2000)

Domestic Service Robots in the Real World: More on the Case of Intelligent Robots Following Humans

Jean-Daniel Dessimoz and Pierre-François Gauthey

HESSO // Western Switzerland University of Applied Sciences,
HEIG-VD // School of Management and Engineering,
CH-1400 Yverdon-les-Bains, Switzerland
{Jean-Daniel.Dessimoz,Pierre-Francois.Gauthey}@heig-vd.ch

Abstract. The international initiative "Robocup", and in particular its "@Home" league of Robocup, are excellent environments for focusing robotics research and AI as well as, more specifically, for testing the abilities of domestic service robots. Following humans has long been recognized as a basic capability in this context. It allows in our case for convenient path programming (teaching of itineraries). Although, the cognitive requirements are quite high (20 lin of knowledge, 200 lin/s of expertise), humans usually proceed in the same way. The environment is dynamic and disturbances may occur, which may cause errors. Therefore, safety measures must be devised, such as close human-robot interaction to prevent path crossing by third parties; the availability of light signals as a discrete warning; close interaction for accurate positioning in complex trajectories; coordinated, unidirectional blocking; vocally warnings and the ability to stop when people cross the path between the robot and the guide; the definition of a maximal radius of influence beyond which stopping is triggered; procedures for emergency stopping; robust vision-methods; and ultrasonic sensors and map-based obstacle avoidance. At the most abstract semantic level, about 15 bits per second of information must be acquired. For this purpose a variety of sensors are considered, each with specific advantages: a color camera, a planar laser range scanner, a 3D-ranger, ultrasonic sensors, and joint sensors. Smooth and stable real-time behavior is ensured by a 5-level hierarchical control structure and agents implemented in different technologies (computers, PLC, servo controllers, etc.), inheriting some developments resulting from research in Eurobot context.

Keywords: Standardization, knowledge, cognition, cognitics, ontology, information, model, memory, service robotics, domestic applications, following and guiding.

1 Introduction

Robotics and AI research have made significant progress to the point where many application fields are now being considered. The required functionalities of

D. Obdržálek and A. Gottscheber (Eds.): EUROBOT 2011, CCIS 161, pp. 88–101, 2011.

autonomous robots are varied and complex. To handle such varied applications, researchers and developers should develop standards and common platforms, so reasonable levels of predictability and efficiency can be achieved, and the considered applications can really materialize.

A special area of interest for the authors includes AI and more widely, cognitive sciences or "cognitics", where cognitive processes are automated. A book is now available on this topic [1]. Cognitive theory and quantitative approaches have now made evident that a prerequisite for all cognitive processing and effective developments is a clear identification of goals. The goal and area of special interest in the context of this paper is the progress of cooperative robotics and human robot interaction for the domestic environment [2,3]. The international initiative "Robocup", and in particular the "@Home" league of Robocup provide excellent environments for testing the abilities of domestic service robots. In particular, they offer the possibility of validating novel concepts in the real world and identifying the most relevant open questions and problems.

More specifically, "following humans" has been recognized for a long time as a basic and necessary capability of domestic service robots and research has already been performed for similar cases (e.g. [4,5]). In @Home competitions, among other tests, variations on the mentioned capability have been explored through the years and are presented here as "Follow and Guide" (2007), "Fast-Follow" (2008), and "Follow Me" (2009, 2010 with the new concept of "check-points").

This paper is a complementary version of a variant recently published [6], some of the previous content (in particular, a taxonomy in 5 classes of human-following capabilities) being not replicated here, while more information is given here on the need for path programming and on implementing security measures. The paper focuses on Class 1 human-following case, the main application of human-following at home: to guide a robot for training it in new grounds, without contact between guide and robot, and a typical distance of about 1 meter between them.

The theme is addressed below in details, with two main components: first a discussion about the need of path programming for mobile robots, and then the security measures to be planned, along with modes of functional implementation.

The need to teach pathways is discussed below, then successively refined into finer questions: why to follow, whom to follow, and what to follow.

2   The Need for Path Programming - Why to Follow; Whom to Follow Whom; and What to Follow

To bring domestic service robots into the real world to address the most relevant problems, one pressing requirement is the need for path programming; e.g. how to specify a robot the way from the TV set in the living room to the fridge in the kitchen. In traditional programming, trajectories can be defined textually as a set of locations in a script, or clicked with a mouse on a map. But it is far more convivial just to guide the robot once through the path.

Fig. 1. Examples of use of the human-following capability *(on the left, FastFollow; see text)*

Fig. 1 presents two examples in Suzhou (China) of Robocup 2008: 1. Fast-Follow challenge, with RH3-Y following its guide, then crossing another team, and finally successfully finishing first the walk through home; and 2. RH-Y as a cooperating caddie.

2.1 The Need for Path Programming

Robotics include many capabilities, such as AI or vision, which also make sense on their own. But from a scientific and technical point of view, robotics is most specifically motion. Robots have many joints, which require coordination. For example, Nao humanoids have more than 20 motors to control.

It is therefore no surprise that to control robots, some kind of path programming must be performed by users.

In general, the path is mostly determined by its end, and in this sense, the details of the path are not critical. Usual solutions consist of interpolating in joint space for industrial robots and limb motions and to move in straight lines for mobile robots.

In domestic applications, it is obvious that straight lines can validly be traveled only for small path increments. At medium to large scales, trajectories must be more complex, and largely unpredictable intermediary constraints must be brought into account. To some extent, robots may autonomously explore space and progressively learn what are the constraints, but for complex cases like for humans in Suntec City, Singapore, to have other humans guiding the way from @Home2010 area to ToysRUs test place is quite a necessity.

2.2 Why to Follow

In domestic applications, trajectories are relatively complex, and the current location and the desired final goal intermediary constraints must be brought into account.

It is interesting to see how the problem is handled in the case of humans. Two cases are considered. 1. The traditional and most comfortable way to define a path for a human is to have another human guiding him or her. In cognitive terms, the task is quite demanding, implying on the order of 15 bit per second of information that must be acquired (see detailed estimation in Sect. 3.1) while classical psychometric studies indicate that humans can consciously process a maximum of 30 bit/s. 2. When a path is extremely deterministic, constant for a long time, and useful for many, maps and topographic indications are usually worked out; this approach has a rather high initial cost (both for the elaboration of directions and for the training of agents using them); however, over time and as many people use the developed tools, it can become competitive with guiding.

For robots, schematically two classes of solutions may develop: in the first case, programming is performed in a more or less declarative way by programmers; and the alternate type of solutions calls for something similar to the human way. Whenever possible, the first class of solutions should apply, to load humans as little as possible; nevertheless, as for humans, the ability to learn a new path just by following potentially brings the most convenient type of solutions, especially in complex and dynamically changing home environments.

In recent years in the @Home competitions, a priority has been set on robots being able to follow humans, rather than on humans to guide robots. This priority may be useful from the perspective of fostering advances in technology. However, in the long term and for general use in society, in authors' view the final responsibility must shift again to the human guide in this context; robots should make guiding a simpler exercise by following humans as conveniently as possible, but the main responsibility for successful path following should in no way lie on their side.

2.3   Whom to Follow

In domestic applications, many tasks must be done. Yet to have a chance to master them, consideration should be focused progressively on each task. In particular, a question commonly addressed in the context of the "Follow" task refers to the ability of robots to recognize a specific human as the guide. In our approach, the tasks of human identification and of following are schematically split.

In the first case, human identification, traditional solutions for humans call for keys; in recent times and the advent of digital society, PINs, passwords and code numbers are widespread. In special contexts, ID-cards, passports, RFIDs or biometric tests provide the proper answers. Robots are machines that include computers and are more and more connected to networks; therefore, all of these solutions can similarly be envisioned for making robots capable to identify potential guides.

In the second case, following a human, it is sufficient to ensure the continuity in time and location of the perceived guide's path. With RH-Y (see Fig. 1) resources, the location of the guide can be estimated 10 times per second, with an accuracy of about 1 cm. This is sufficient to guarantee also guide's ID continuity.

2.4   What to Follow

The paradox of learning trajectories, and consequently of following humans, is that dynamic changes and long-term stationarity are assumed at the same time.

Unfortunately, there are still many other factors that behave in between and create disturbances.

Learning implies here that new trajectories are desirable, which are yet unknown for the robot. In these circumstances, it is appropriate for humans just to walk about to teach the robot by guiding.

However, learning trajectories also implies that in the future those trajectories will keep their adequacy, i.e., the domestic environment will be essentially stable.

To a large extent, the ability to follow a human can naturally lead to the ability to follow the environment; but there are also major differences, for example, in principle the human guide keeps moving, while the environment is stable.

In fact, there may be numerous other cases, e.g., doors will sometimes open or close, chairs are often moved, and humans may stand still, talk, watch television, or sleep for hours. To cope with all these phenomena requires the robot to acquire, while following a person, much more than just the trajectory; anyway, it is most probably impossible to achieve full success in all cases; occasional failures are bound to happen. Therefore, it is also important to devise appropriate security measures.

3   Implementing Security Measures and Functional Capabilities

The previous sections have shown the need for robots to follow human guides. The experience gained since the beginning of the @Home competitions, in 2006, and related research have allowed us to sketch the most appropriate security measures for the context of robots following humans , and to present how to implement them.

Some of the techniques presented below have also inherited from developments previously made for our proprietary "ARY" family, initially developed in the context of Eurobot [7] and dating for some as far back as in 1998. Some years up to 10 mobile units could cooperatively be engaged under the control of a main autonomous robotic structure [8].

Fig. 2 illustrates several of the safety measures advocated below, with our RH5-Y robot shown during the test "In the Mall" of @Home 2010 in Singapore, following one of our team members through the store: 1. The blue warning blinking light (see Sect. 3.4). 2. Coordinated blocking (Sect. 3.6). 3. Unidirectional blocking capability (Sect. 3.7). 4. The concept of the maximal radius of influence (Sect. 3.9); 5. Emergency stop mechanism (Sect. 3.10).

This section is structured with two initial paragraphs presenting the specific task, Follow-a-person, first in terms of the requirements and second in terms of the general solution. Then several security measures are successively addressed, which deal with issues, such as the possibility of close human-robot interaction to prevent crossing by third parties; the availability of light signals as a discrete warning; the benefit of close interaction for accurate positioning in complex trajectories; the necessity of coordinated, unidirectional blocking; the benefits of issuing a warning and stopping for a while if people cross the path between

Fig. 2. Overview of some security measures (*see text for more information*): 1. The blue warning blinking light reflected on the legs of the guide *(arrow on the right)*. 2. If a wheel is blocked, the other wheel gets stopped as well, in a properly coordinated way *(lower arrow)*. 3. The unidirectional blocking capability is also active *(same lower arrow)*. 4. In principle, the top circle illustrates the concept of the maximal radius of influence; in fact, the effective circle at that very moment is larger than the one drawn. It must encompass the guide, otherwise all motion would stop. 5. Emergency stop mechanism *(left arrow)*.

the robot and the guide; the definition of a maximal radius of influence beyond which stopping and staying still are triggered; and the necessity of an emergency stop procedure. Those points complement a previous publication [6], some items being shortened here and other ones expanded.

In most of the discussions below, the solutions adopted for our RH-Y robot are the ones presented. This kind of experimental validation brings a particularly concrete, validated character to the discussion and does not restrict the scope of applicability of the presented items to only this case. However, in cases where alternatives appear preferable, the latter are explicitly mentioned.

3.1 Requirements

Before attempting to implement a function, it is wise to review the main requirements. And like for deciding about the possibility of jumping over a wall, it is critical to go quantitative and know in particular the height of the wall (in "meter"). We shall focus here on the cognitive aspects. As defined in particular in [1], based on modeling (in state space and associated probabilities), time (in "second") and an information (in "bit") based calculus, key cognitive properties include knowledge (the ability to deliver the right answer, in "lin"), and expertise (the ability to deliver the right answer quickly, in "lin/s").

For a robot to follow a person and learn a new trajectory, a speed on the order of 1 m/s should be expected. Positional accuracy should be, as usual in common technical matters, on the order of 1%, e.g. of about 10 cm in a 10 m range. A trajectory can be viewed as a sequence of locations via points at intervals on the order of one location per meter considering that locations are specified in a 2-dimensional space.

This information amounts to about $n_i = 2 * \log_2(10/0.1) \cong 15[bit]$ per second, assuming equiprobability of locations of interest) and is the minimum information that the robot must acquire. Sensor configurations acquiring less information could not do the job; now if they acquire more than that, processing can in principle also be done. Considering a similar accuracy in the plane (1%, 3 coordinates, e.g. x, y, and orientation) about 21 bit of control must be elaborated. Required knowledge is consequently $K = \log_2(n_0 * 2^{n_i}) = \log_2(21 * 2^{15}) \cong 20[lin]$, and expertise $E = K/\Delta t = 20/0.1 \cong 200[lin/s]$.

In early phases, such as in Bremen and Atlanta for @Home context, the "Follow" task could be implemented in a somewhat jerky way, with start-stop increments that are similar to point-to-point motions in industrial robots. Then indirectly, with the "Fast-Follow", new specifications were elaborated for the Suzhou competition, in which "smooth" motions were required (smooth versus time, not versus trajectory in space).

3.2   Overview of Solution

For the kind of perceptive capacity estimated in the previous paragraph, and for the "Follow a person" test of @Home, vision instruments or rangers are adequate (see e.g. Fig. 3); an alternative, albeit slower mode, might rely on compliant motion, i.e. on a kind of force and torque perception. In all cases, a complex hierarchy of functions and devices are necessary.

At lower levels, depending on the considered test phase, either the position or speed controls provide the best solutions for ensuring either positional accuracy or smooth motions. During the active following phase, the speed mode is in operation, and for the previous and next navigation phases, the position mode.

From the top down, the hierarchy of controls is described here in five steps:

1. At the uppermost level (level 1), the linear and rotational robot motion commands are elaborated as speed targets based on the walker's location relative to the robot. At this point, two parallel controls are in operation. Attention is also given to possible overall mode commands, such as "sleep", "follow", or "observe and interpret remote gestures". Distance discontinuities are monitored for possible path cutting, and excessive errors are also monitored to guarantee orderly phasing out.

Perception is best done with a planar ranger (240 degree aperture, 10 Hz refresh rate, about 700 radii between 0 and 400 cm, with 1 cm accuracy; this translates into about 50 000 bit/s of raw, low-level input acquired information flow; a lot of redundancy helps to reliably cope with the complexity of the environment and noise). Nevertheless, other modes are feasible, and some have been performed in competition (e.g. color vision or ultrasonic sensors, with much

Fig. 3. General view of RH5-Y *(see text for more information)*. From top, the yellow arrows successively point at 1. a planar laser ranger; 2. an ultrasonic distance sensor; 3. a color camera; and 4. a 2-D time-of-flight ranger, i.e. a 3D camera.

less aperture though, less angular resolution and lower distance reliability). A 2D time of flight range sensor (as used in our @Home applications) is also beneficial in terms of dimensionality, but at the expense of relatively low aperture angles and signal to noise ratio. Multi-agent approaches, e.g. with our original Piaget environment (e.g. [9]), and vocal channels also act in parallel to help prevent errors and cope with them when they occur.

2. At an intermediary level (level 2), a MIMO stage performs inverse kinematics, providing the necessary joint commands (wheel 1 and 2) based on the linear and rotational speed targets naturally expressed in world, Cartesian or polar coordinates. In particular, a parameterized gain matrix is used. The functions described in points 1 and 2 are implemented on a supervisory computer (e.g. an embedded laptop).

3. Then, the motion law stage is entered (level 3), and parameterized accelerations are used for interpolating speed target values.

4. At level 4, the wheel velocity control is accomplished with two independent PID closed loop controllers with encoder management. Coordination is implicitly ensured by simultaneous commands and appropriate respective accelerations and speed targets.

Information between the laptop and servo-controllers is conveyed via Ethernet with the TCP-IP mode.

5. Finally (level 5), amplifiers manage the motor currents, ensuring that limits are not transgressed (two on/off action, closed-loop controls).

3.3   Possible Close Interaction to Prevent Crossing

Guides should adapt their walking speed to the circumstances, and, in our classical solutions, the speed evolves as the distance between guide and robot (see [6]).

3.4   Blue Blinking as a Discrete Warning Signal

It is usual for vehicles to have some warning signals, especially when visibility is poor or the risk of collisions and consequent casualties is high. In our mobile robots, we have always had a blinking signal composed of LEDs of various powers and colors that were initially meant for informing team members that operations and, in particular, parallel processes were running correctly. After the 2nd year at @Home, this signal has increased in visibility and is currently a freely programmable double blue light, which typically blinks as a discrete warning signal during following tasks.

Even though the objective risks are typically small and should remain so, laypersons are often afraid of machines (we are not aware of systemic and formal studies on this though). To communicate clearly and early about presence and activity however can reduce the possibility of surprise. This measure appears experimentally useful and may, in particular, contribute to increase awareness and confidence among laypersons. Because cooperative robots in domestic environment interact with people, such a measure should become a normal custom.

In RH-Y robots, the light management in performed in several steps: 1. Asynchronous commands can be given in Boolean mode independently on both lights (right and left) by the "strategy" agent of our proprietary, "Piaget" environment. 2. For dynamic behavior, such as blinking, the task is handed over to a parallel Piaget agent, occasionally with parameters, and is asynchronously decided by the "strategy" agent. Steps 1 and 2 occur on the supervising computer. 3. A PLC receives through Ethernet and a TCP-IP channel the instantaneous Boolean orders, and on this basis autonomously elaborates and provides robust output controls. 4. Variations are possible, whereby the PLC is ordered to modulate output signals in specified ways and R-G-B lights replace the blue lights in Fig. 3.

3.5   Close Interaction for Accuracy in Complicated Trajectories

As mentioned in Sect. 3.1, guides should adapt their walking speed to the circumstances. In particular, complicated trajectories may require a lower speed than the average. A lower speed decreases the requirements for expertise. A complex trajectory has higher requirements in terms of local perception by definition (see [6]).

For the mentioned "Follow me" test of @Home 2010 competition in Singapore (see Fig. 4), the strategy adopted by the RH5-Y robot was of the type advocated here, i.e. if and when people crossed the path between the robot and the guide, to stop for a while, to warn the guide with a vocal message of the situation and if possible, after the path cutter had gone, to restore normal operations.

3.6   Blocking in a Coordinated Way

In the real world, many disturbances occur unavoidably. Therefore, developing solutions for ideal cases is not sufficient; on the contrary, additional appropriate

Fig. 4. Example: RH-Y in @Home 2010, Singapore. *Left to right, top to bottom*: The robot starts, its light starts blinking, and it follows the official guide (1), then turns and passes the wall (2), detects a path cutter and consequently announces it will stop for 3 seconds (3); when the time is elapsed, however, the guide has gone beyond limits and the robot stands still, observing the maximum safety radius (4).

failure management procedures must be devised for situations when the main task, following the guide, cannot be achieved (see [6]).

3.7   Unidirectional Blocking

As guides drive robots, errors occur and sometimes robots collide with hard to move obstacles, such as heavy pieces of furniture (see [6]).

3.8   Coping with Path-Cutters

As a consequence of measures advocated in Sect. 3.3 and Sect. 3.4, no one should attempt to cross the path between a robot and a guide. However, people, and especially children, like to play; therefore, it is tempting for many to ignore warnings and common sense and to explore what happens when a driving path is cut. Thus, paths may be cut, and appropriate measures should be devised in anticipation (see [6]).

3.9   Maximal Radius of Influence

As the distances between the robot and the guide increase, the risk also increases that they miss each other. To prevent problems, it is wise to define a maximal radius of influence (see [6]).

3.10   Emergency Stop and Other Factors

Seven measures for security are listed above. This list is not exhaustive though and some other considerations are mentioned here, giving additional examples of ways that robots can safely follow a guide, including some approaches that have already been conducted in a @Home context.

The ultimate measure for stopping robots is to cut the power. This measure is already enforced in the @Home context. Cutting power can be viewed in several ways. In particular, the tradeoffs between a completely hard-type power breaking approach and a completely software-based emergency management approach should be considered. In most of our proprietary mobile autonomous robots ("ARY" family), the circuit-breakers only affect the power circuits of the wheel drives, and power remains in resources that do not directly affect the lowest structural stages, which ensure that the robot maintains some ability to act. For low-power elements, such as for the Katana arm, or the NAO humanoid, the question of an emergency stop is not mandatory because the risks of casualty are low. As a general guideline, a safety limit in the range of 10 W seems appropriate for this mode. More formal, international standards have come (ISO 10218-1, 2006; ISO 10218-2, 2010 and 2011).

Another trend for security is to limit as much as possible power, speed and force (for arm motions, the Katana arm of RH5-Y is already certified in this regard).

A similar feature is offered by compliant control. The latter principle may provide an alternative to the paradigm of "following". Inherently, the compliant approach ensures minimal distance and contact between the robot and the guide.

In reverse mode, a low, constant, linear speed is provided for safe and easy motions. Implementation is most simple when the ability already exists to follow humans. This is done in our case in speed servo mode, with constant acceleration speed changes.

It should be mentioned again that in as much as circumstances allow, guides should take their leading role actively and not just expect that robots are smart enough to solve all difficulties on their own; thus more is typically achievable, in results and safety.

As can be judged from professional guides of tourist groups, a special visibility feature, such as an umbrella may help to safely increase the influence radius introduced above.

Fig. 5 illustrates yet some other possible safety measures: In the context of vision-based following techniques, safety may be improved with robust vision approaches, such as the SbWCD (saturation-based, weighted intensity and hue, color differences) correlation, which is documented in a separate paper [10]

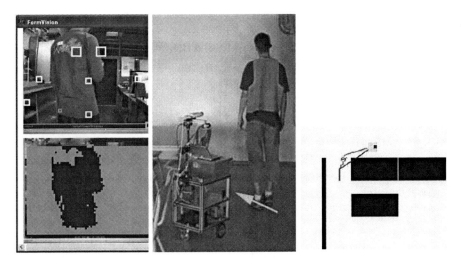

Fig. 5. Other possible safety measures: See text in Sect. 3.10. Left, vision-based, following techniques with "one of nine" optimized colors (@Home 2006); using high-visibility guide attire *(middle)*; with lateral ultrasonic sensors *(same image, arrow in the middle)*; and map-registered environment properties *(right)*

and/or by using high-visibility guide attire, such as the vests that are worn on high-speed roads.

Continuous recognition of the guide may be an advantage, even if not strictly required. In @Home 2010, in a checkpoint the guide was asked to get out of robot signt for a while. To recognize him or her, our RH-5 robot was given an original, robust, visual, saturation-based weighted color difference correlation capability [10].

Additional explored methods include the use of lateral ultrasonic sensors to avoid lateral obstacles, and map-registered environment properties for the same purpose. In the latter case, the guide position may be reached, while avoiding a table by adapting behavior to map-based constraints.

4   Conclusion

The international initiative "Robocup", and in particular the "At-Home" league of Robocup, provide an excellent environment for focusing research in robotics and AI and, more specifically, for testing the abilities of domestic service robots. Following humans has long been recognized as a basic capability in this context. Following humans allows for convenient path programming, and although the cognitive requirements are quite high, all humans usually proceed in this same way.

The environment is dynamic and disturbances occur, which may cause errors; therefore, safety measures must be devised, in particular, close human-robot interaction to prevent crossing by third parties; light signals as discrete warnings;

close interaction for accurate positioning in complex trajectories; coordinated, unidirectional blocking; vocal warnings and the ability to stop while people cross the path between the robot and the guide; the definition of a maximal radius of influence beyond which stopping is triggered; emergency stopping capabilities; and robust vision-methods ultrasonic sensors and map-based obstacle avoidance. At the most abstract semantic level, about 15 bits per second of information must be acquired; for this purpose, a variety of sensors are considered, each with specific advantages, including a color camera, a planar laser range scanner, a 3D-ranger, ultrasonic sensors, and joint sensors. Smooth and stable real-time behavior is ensured by a 5-level hierarchical control structure and agents implemented in different technologies (computers, PLC, servo controllers, etc.).

Experience in @Home context confirms a general phenomenon by which perception is crucial in mapping some of the infinitely complex reality to a much simpler, useful cognitive representation. In the typical case discussed above, it allows for an abstraction index higher than 1 000, thereby very significantly extracting the necessary application-oriented, semantic essence, as used as starting point in the quantitative cognitive assessment of Sect. 3.1. According to our opinion, above proposed methods are the best of the time and in the context of @Home the factor the most critical for success has appeared to be the ability of the guide to make use of robot capabilities.

Concerning the help at home, progress is regularly achieved, in a modest and incremental way, which can be translated in much use for society. For achieving results somehow similar or better than nowadays home helpers though, the @Home league will probably take a time similar to the soccer league in their effort. Their goal – to beat humans in world level competitions – is set in time for the year 2050.

The paper complements publication [6], each summarizing, or respectively developing different aspects.

The authors wish to acknowledge the useful suggestions of referees, numerous contributions of past RH-Y team members, as well as HESSO and HEIG-VD for their support of this research.

References

1. Dessimoz, J.-D.: Cognitics - Definitions and metrics for cognitive sciences and thinking machines (August 31,2010)(work in finalization), already accessible on http://cognitics.populus.ch ISBN 978-2-9700629-1-2
2. Wisspeintner, T., van der Zant, T., Iocchi, L., Schiffer, S.: RoboCup@Home: Scientific Competition and Benchmarking for Domestic Service Robots. Interaction Studies 10(3), 393–428 (2009)
3. Dessimoz, J.-D., Gauthey, P.-F.: RH5-Y – Toward A Cooperating Robot for Home Applications. In: Robocup-at-Home League, Proceedings Robocup 2010 Symposium and World Competition, Singapore (2010)
4. Gockley, R., Forlizzi, J., Simmons, R.: Natural person-following behavior for social robots. In: Proceedings of the ACM/IEEE International Conference on Human-Robot Interaction, HRI 2007, pp. 17–24 (2007), http://doi.acm.org/10.1145/1228716.1228720

5. Kobayashi, Y., Kuno, Y.: People tracking using integrated sensors for human robot interaction. In: 2010 IEEE International Conference on Industrial Technology (ICIT), Valparaíso, Chile, March 14-17, pp. 1617–1622 (2010) ISBN: 978-1-4244-5695-6
6. Domestic Service Robots in the Real World: the Case of Robots Following Humans. In: Domestic Service Robots in the Real World Workshop, SIMPAR 2010 Second International Conference on Simulation, Modeling and Programming for Autonomous Robots, Darmstadt, Germany (November 15-18, 2010)
7. Gottscheber, A., Obdržálek, D., Schmidt, C. (eds.) EUROBOT 2009. Communications in Computer and Information Science, vol. 82, p. 173. Springer, Heidelberg (2010) ISBN: 978-3-642-16369-2
8. Eurobot Competitions, http://www.eurobot.org, http://www.eurobot.org/conference/, http://www.planete-sciences.org/robot/video/cswis01.mpg (last visited on March 31, 2011)
9. Dessimoz, J.-D., Gauthey, P.-F.: RH3-Y – Toward A Cooperating Robot for Home Applications. In: Robocup-at-Home League, Proceedings Robocup 2008 Symposium and World Competition, Suzhou, China, July 14-20 (2008)
10. Dessimoz, J.-D., Gauthey, P.-F.: Contributions to Standards and Common Platforms in Robotics; The Role of Color and Recommended Modalities. In: Standards and Common Platform Workshop, SIMPAR 2010 Second International Conference on Simulation, Modeling and Programming for Autonomous Robots, Darmstadt, Germany, November 15-18 (2010)

Designing an Omni-Directional Infrared Sensor and Beacon System for the Eurobot Competition

Valentin Durst, Daniel Hagel, Jan Vander, Michael Blaich, and Oliver Bittel

University of Applied Sciences Konstanz, Germany
Laboratory for Mobile Robots
Brauneggerstr. 55 D-78462 Konstanz
{valdurst,hageldan,javander,mblaich,bittel}@htwg-konstanz.de
http://www.robotik.in.htwg-konstanz.de/

Abstract. In this paper the design of an omni-directional sensor which measures the angles between active infrared beacons is proposed. The aim is to develop a simple and inexpensive sensor and beacon system. Therefore an array of ten CMOS cameras with an infrared filter is used. We present the design steps and the evaluation of the sensor in detail. The systematic errors of the system are analyzed during the evaluation of the sensor's accuracy. They are compensated by a linear regression, which leads to an accuracy of less than one degree. The achieved accuracy qualifies the system for applications like landmark-based localization.

1 Introduction

The Eurobot is an international mobile robot competition where many university teams from all over Europe participate every year. One specific feature of this competition is that it is allowed to use an individual landmark detecting sensor on the top of the robot to solve the localization problem. Thus, every team has the possibility to develop an own landmark and sensor system. We decided to develop a system consisting of active infrared beacons as landmarks and an omni-directional infrared vision sensor. Using infrared light sources as beacons and a camera system with an infrared filter instead of a normal camera system has the advantage that the beacon detection does not depend on the lighting conditions. The maximal dimension of the sensor and the beacons is defined by the competition rules. These rules also specify the positions of the beacons which are placed around the playground. The developed sensor measures the angle between the beacons and the robot. Based on these measurements several localization algorithms can be adopted to localize the robot. The sensor combines ten small CMOS cameras which leads to a view angle of 360 degrees. This omni-directional design allows a continuous detection of all beacons.

The sensor system is based on the Nintendo Wii Remote camera and on several micro controllers to control and synchronize the cameras. Building the sensor with the Nintendo Wii cameras was inspired by the results of Jonny Chung Lee [11]. The advantages of using the Wii Remote cameras are the small size, the integrated I2C bus interface, the high resolution of 1024 × 768 pixel and an

D. Obdržálek and A. Gottscheber (Eds.): EUROBOT 2011, CCIS 161, pp. 102–113, 2011.
© Springer-Verlag Berlin Heidelberg 2011

included object detection. The object detection is realized by a built-in hardware blob tracking system which provides up to four points with an update rate of $100Hz$. Combining the blob tracking system of the camera with an infrared filter in front of the camera, helps to decrease distractions from other sources than the beacons.

This work starts with an overview of the related work on omni-directional sensors and project with the Nintendo Wii camera. The next section present the beacon and sensor concept. The fourth section describes the sensor hardware and software in detail. The last section present the evaluation of the sensor and the experimental results.

2   Related Work

Omni-directional camera sensors are used in many mobile robotic applications like localization [16,7,1], navigation [18,12,15,20,21], mapping [3,6] and object detection [13]. All these approaches use a single camera with a fish eye lens, a catadioptric mirror or a rotating mirror in front of the camera. An overview to omni-directional vision and the corresponding camera systems is given in [19,14]. The disadvantage of all systems that use a mirror or a fish eye lens is the image distortion caused by the mirror or the lens. Taking a 360 degree panorama image by a rotating mirror in front of a camera needs a long time of several seconds because the mirror rotation speed has to be slow enough to avoid image blurring. As mentioned before we decided to use an array of ten CMOS cameras to achieve an omni-directional camera system, in order to avoid these problems of the traditional approaches. The proof of concept of such a sensor is done in [4].

There are many different projects based on, or working with the Nintendo Wii camera. To name some of these projects: [10] use the Nintendo Wii camera for low-cost visual tracking of a landing place and a hovering flight control system. This system is based on a landing pad equipped with infrared emitters and a helicopter containing the Nintendo Wii camera. Thus, the helicopter is able to compute its position relative to the landing pad using the camera information. Jonny Chung Lee [11] used the camera for several different experiments in the area of infrared tracking. He published free software projects for finger tracking, head tracking and a low-cost multi-point interactive whiteboard. Another work with the Nintendo Wii remote controller is the simple and inexpensive robot controlling interface by Sven Olufs and Markus Vincze [17]. In this project, they use the Wii remote controller to set new targets where the robot should drive to.

3   Sensor and Beacon Concept

For the Eurobot contest the use of maximal three landmarks and a sensor to detect them is permitted. Thus, we decided to compose an inexpensive sensor which measures the angle between landmarks precisely. As landmarks, active infrared beacons with an unique ID are used. To measure the angle to these beacons, a visual sensor with an infrared filter is applied.

3.1 Unique Beacon Design

The beacons have to cover the all area of the playground. Therefore every beacon has to flood the whole area with infrared light. To achieve this, infrared emitters with a range of at least three meters and a wide transmission angle are used. To improve the transmission angle, every beacon has two infrared emitter arrays. These arrays contain four infrared emitters, placed in different angles. Another important attribute is the unique identification of each beacon by the sensor. This is realized via the two infrared emitter arrays positioned differently on each beacon, as shown in Figure 1. Due to the pinhole concept of the camera, the distance between the two blobs in the image changes depending on the range between the sensor and the beacon. Thus, for the beacons B and C the relation between the x and y value of the blobs is used to detect the beacon because this relation is distance independent. Only if this relation fits a defined range, the beacon will be recognized by the system. For the beacon A it is only checked if the two blobs are vertically aligned. By this approach, disturbing signals can be eliminated.

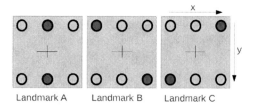

Landmark A   Landmark B   Landmark C

Fig. 1. Infrared emitter arrangement for an unique beacon code

3.2 The Sensor Concept

The rules of the Eurobot contest define the maximum size of the sensor. The space reserved for the sensor is limited to $80mm$ width, $80mm$ height and $80mm$ depth. Basically the sensor is an array of ten CMOS cameras arranged in a circle, as shown in Figure 2. These cameras are also used in the Nintendo Wii Remote Controllers. These cameras have the advantage of built-in blob tracker. Every camera can track up to four blobs at $100Hz$ in a binary image. Combining the cameras with an infrared filter, only infrared light sources are detected. With this camera array, an omni-directional sensor with a view angle of 360 degrees and a high resolution of 10240×768 pixel is available. The high resolution of the camera array leads to a theoretical angle resolution of 0.035 degree. In order to protect the adjustment of the cameras, an acrylic glass envelope is mounted around the sensor. This is important for the calibration of the sensitive cameras. Even a slight contact with the cameras could make a complete new calibration necessary.

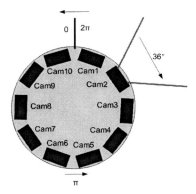

Fig. 2. The figure shows schematically the arrangement of ten Nintendo Wii Cameras to achieve a view angle of 360 degree

3.3   Hardware Design

The sensor consists of two layers as shown in Figure 3(a). The upper layer contains the cameras and a small microcontroller for each camera to start the capturing process and buffer the results. Figure 4(a) shows the top of the sensor where the ten cameras and the corresponding microcontrollers can be seen. The lower layer contains the main microcontroller and the power supply. The main microcontroller processes the measurements for each camera and provides the resulting beacon angles via USB to a standard pc. Additional to the USB connection, a trigger input is available to synchronize this sensor with other sensor systems. The complete sensor is mounted on the top of the robot as shown in Figure 3(b). It contains an USB cable, a hardware trigger cable, an acrylic glass envelope and an infrared filter for the Nintendo Wii cameras.

The power supply mounted at the lower layer is required because the microcontrollers work with a voltage of $5V$ and the cameras work with a voltage of $3.3V$. The USB port is used as power input for the sensor. It provides a voltage of $5V$ and a current of $500mA$, which is sufficient for the sensor. Thus, only a DC converter is used to provide the voltage level of $3.3V$.

A camera module on the upper layer consists of a Nintendo Wii camera and an Atmega88 microcontroller. This approach refers to the work of Udo Juerss [8]. The camera and the microcontroller are connected via I2C bus. The parts relevant for the communication with the Nintendo WII camera via the I2C bus (labeled with SCL and the SDA) and the assignment to the microcontroller is shown in Figure 4(b). The hardware which is needed to run the microcontroller consists of standard components.

3.4   Software Desing

The sensor has three different software layers. The first layer is implemented on the Atmega88 microcontrollers to control the cameras and buffer the results of

(a) Sensor without acrylic glass enve- (b) Sensor mounted on the top of the
lope.   robot with an acrylic glass envelope as
                                       sensor body.

Fig. 3. The figure shows an omni directional sensor to detect infrared emitters. The
sensor consists of 10 Nintendo Wii cameras on the upper circuit board. Each camera
is controlled by an Atmege88 microcontroller. The main microcontroller to handle the
USB connection is on the lower circuit board. An infrared filter is mounted on front of
all cameras. To protect the sensor an acrylic glass envelop is used as sensor body.

(a) Top of the sensor to show the 10   (b) The wiring diagram of a single cam-
camera modules.   era module with a detail of one Nin-
                                       tendo Wii camera and the correspond-
                                       ing microcontroller.

Fig. 4. The upper circuit board including the 10 camera modules. Each module consist
of a Nintendo Wii camera connected via I2C to an Atmega88 microcontroller. The
microcontrollers initialize the cameras and buffer there resulting data.

the camera's blob tracking algorithm. The second layer does the UART communication between the main microcontroller and the camera modules and the
synchronization of the cameras. This synchronization is required to get images
from all cameras captured at the same time. The third layer handles the USB
communication between the main microcontroller of the sensor and the controlling computer. It also manages the synchronization with other sensor systems.

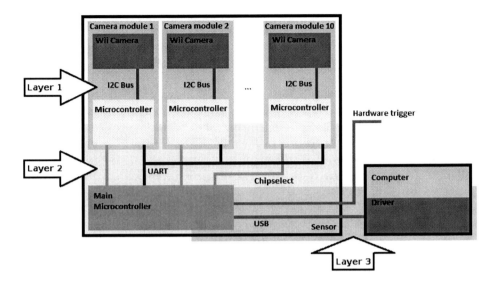

Fig. 5. Software concept of the sensor. The software is organized in three communication layers. The first layer controls the cameras and buffers the resulting data on the microcontroller. The second layer synchronizes the camera modules. The communication with the controlling computer via USB is handled in the layer 3.

A schematic of the sensor design including these layers, and the internal and external communication channels is shown in Figure 5.

Layer 1: The camera communication is based on the Nintendo Wii library by the Udo Juerss [9]. This library provides a simple usage of the camera's I2C interface. Each camera has the I2C address of 0xB0. This address can not be changed, thus every camera is controlled by its microcontroller. Before the cameras can be used for blob tracking they have to be initialized. Therefore the library provides the `wii_irs_init()` function. This initialization takes about $100ms$ on the camera, thus the microcontroller has to wait for this time before starting the capturing process. To read the blob tracking result from the camera the `wii_irs_update` from the library can be used. Each Atmega88 microcontroller stores the last blob results read from the camera. Getting the chip select signal from the main microcontroller the Atmega88 sends the blob data to the main microcontroller. This behavior is described more detailed in layer 2.

Layer 2: For the communication between the master microcontroller and the camera modules, a master and slave concept is implemented. The main microcontroller is the master and the camera modules are the slaves. If the master gets the order to provide new measurement data, it trigger the camera modules to start capturing. To support a delay free snapshot of all cameras, a broadcast mechanism is used, that causes the camera modules to take the data exactly on the same time. After this broadcast, every camera module is queried sequentially to send the resulting blob data. This mechanism is implemented with a chip select wire to every camera module.

To achieve a parallel connection for the broadcast, the chip select pins at the main microcontroller are drawn to high TTL level at the same time. This high level on the chip select wire, signal the camera modules to request and saves the actual data from the camera. After this broadcast signal every chip select wire is put back to a low TTL level sequentially, this signals the camera module to report the results back to the main microcontroller. This data transfer is realized with the UART interface of the microcontrollers. Every camera module uses the same UART bus, therefore it is important that the camera module which should send data, activates the UART interface before sending the data and deactivates it after the sending process.

Layer 3: The connection between the sensor and the controlling computer is realized with USB. Therefore the main microcontroller contains a serial to USB converter. The communication on the computer is realized with a driver, based on the player stage framework [2,5]. At the moment version 3 of the player stage framework is supported. The sensor driver provides a set of measured angles according to the player stage specification of the fiducial interface. The actual implementation, provides three angles for the three beacons, in reference to the robot orientation.

The sensor offers three different operation modes hardware trigger mode, software trigger mode and a software repeat mode. In hardware trigger mode the sensor only starts a measurement and sends the resulting data for a rising edge at the hardware trigger cable. This mode could be used in order to synchronize the sensor with other hardware modules. This is also the mode used at the Eurobot competition, in order to synchronize the sensor with the odometry module. In the software trigger mode the sensor sends one measurement set to the computer and waits for the next software trigger message from the controlling computer. In the software repeat mode the sensor sends continuous data without the need of a trigger signal.

4   Sensor Evaluation

In this section the estimation of the sensors accuracy is presented. In order to get this information, a special measuring device is developed. This measuring device is based on a table of a 3D scanning device. This table has the advantage, that the tabletop can be turned in 360 degrees by an external motor. Inside the table a rotary encoder is installed, so that the bearing of the table could be measured. There are two different systematical errors which are analyzed by these experiments: an internal camera error which is caused by the lens of the camera and an installation error, caused by the manual assembly of the sensor.

For the measurements the sensor is placed at the middle of the measuring table and the table top was turned 360 degrees. As input signal an infrared emitter is placed in three different distances as shown in Figure 6. This should

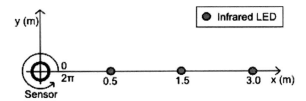

Fig. 6. Experimental setup for the evaluation process. The 3 different emitter distances simulate the conditions on the Eurobot playground. For each distance several test runs are performed.

simulate the possible ranges on an Eurobot playground. For each distance at least ten measurements are carried out.

4.1   Estimation of the Systematical Errors

The systematical errors which are analyzed are the errors generated by the camera lens and the error caused by the manual mounting of the cameras. The camera lens deform the resulting image at the camera's sensor from the center of the sensor to the boundary. The manual mounting of the cameras on the circuit board leads to an error of the camera's orientation.

All experiments show the same performance in respect to the systematical errors. The error between the measuring table and the sensor values is shown in Figure 7. The systematical error caused by the manual assembly of the sensor can be clearly identified as a different offset in the error distribution for each camera. This offset is up to four degree. The non continuous parts of the error distribution represent a camera change which leads to different offset for the next camera. The continuous parts of the error distribution are always measured on the same camera. Each camera shows a similar behavior, corresponding to the internal error caused by the camera lens, which is up to ±2 degrees. These two errors can combined to a total error of about six degree. This shows that a high optimization potential is available by correcting this systematical errors.

4.2   Compensation of the Systematical Errors

The offset is rather simple to compensate. Therefore the average offset is computed by all measurements for each camera. With this average value, the offset can nearly be removed. This offset depends on the camera. To compensate the internal camera error, the measurement values of a camera are approximated by a linear regression. The data for this example could be better approximated with a polynomial function, but in order to reduce the run-time, a linear function is used. Furthermore, by this linear regression the goal of accuracy is achieved. Due to these results a linear compensation function is estimated for each camera. This leads to a complete compensation set of functions for the sensor. Applying this compensation function set to the sensor improves the measurements as shown in Figure 8.

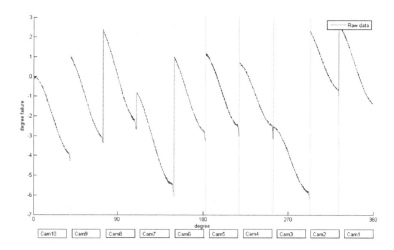

Fig. 7. Systematical error of the angle measurements for each camera. The error distribution includes an offset caused by the manual mounting of the cameras and a distortion caused by the camera lens.

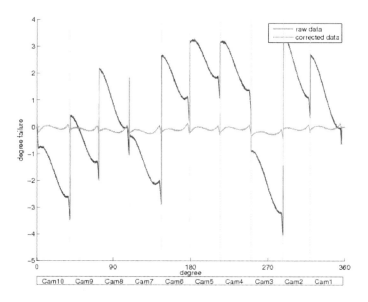

Fig. 8. Compensation of the systematical errors by a linear correction function

All compensations above are based on measurements for a emitter distance of $1.5m$. But analyzing the measurements of the other distances shows, that the systematical error depends on the distance between the sensor and the emitter. The compensation function caused by the experiments of a beacon distance from $1.5m$ can not compensate the systematical errors for other distances

Table 1. Accuracy of the uncalibrated and calibrated sensor

Description	RMSE [*degree*]	variance σ^2 [degree]
Uncalibrated sensor	4.882	2.258
Sensor with general calibration	0.6404	0.4104

measurements with the same accuracy. The different compensation results for measurements with a emitter distance of $0.5m$, $1.5m$ and $3.0m$ are shown in Figure 9. This leads to a measurement performance depending on the distance to the emitter. But in the actual sensor system the distance to the beacons is not estimated. Thus, a general compensation function which leads to the best compensation results for all distances between $0.5m$ and $3.5m$ is used. This compensation function is calculated for every camera independently. By this general compensation a distance independent accuracy with a standard deviation of the error (RMSE) of 0.6404 degree and a variance of 0.4104 degree is achieved. This leads to an improvement of about 4.3 degree for the standard deviation of the error and of about 1.8 degree for the variance. The sensor accuracy with and without the compensation is listed in Table 1.

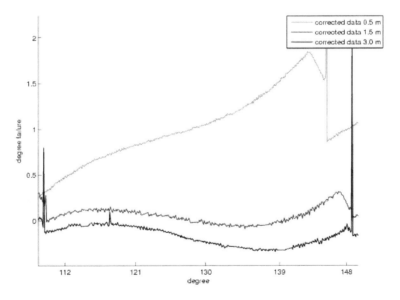

Fig. 9. Error distribution for a single camera calibrated for an emitter distance of $1.5m$. The sensor produce an offset for the error distribution by emitter distances of $0.5m$ and $3.0m$.

5   Conclusion

In this paper the development of an omni-directional infrared sensor which is used for the Eurobot competition is presented. The sensor provides angle measurements between landmarks and the current robot orientation. The main reasons for the development of an own sensor is the special requirements, a hardware device has to fulfill, so that it can be used in the Eurobot competition. The major part of this work was the hardware and software design, and the evaluation of the sensor's accuracy. Without any systematical error compensation, the developed sensor has an measurement error up to 8 degree. Due to the evaluation of the system some correction parameters to compensate the systematical errors where estimated. Applying this correction parameters to the sensor an accuracy with a standard deviation of the error from 0.6404 degree and the variance from 0.4101 degree is achieved. With this sensor which provides the measured angle to different landmarks precisely, the development of a localization approach, to improve the robot position estimation is possible.

For future work we arrange to include distance measurements to the landmarks. This distance information provides two advantages. First it can be used for a distance dependent compensation of the systematical sensor errors. This could improve the accuracy of the senor. Second the distance information can improve a localization approach for a mobile robot. Developing a beacon which can be put on the opposite robot could be another enhancement. With this beacon the position of the opposite robot can be estimated as well. Thus, an improved navigation and collision avoidance for the own robot is possible.

References

1. Aihara, N., Iwasa, H., Yokoya, N., Takemura, H.: Memory-based self-localization using omnidirectional images. In: Proceedings of Fourteenth International Conference on Pattern Recognition, 1799–1803 (1998)
2. THJ Collett and BA MacDonald. Player 2.0: Toward a practical robot programming framework. Proceedings of the Australasian (2005)
3. Delahoche, L., Pegard, C., Mouaddib, E.M., Vasseur, P.: Incremental map building for mobile robot navigation in an indoor environment. In: Proceedings of 1998 IEEE International Conference on Robotics and Automation, pp. 2560–2565 (1998)
4. Durst, V.: Construction of a wii 360 degree infrared sensor. Bachelor's thesis, University of Applied Sciences Konstanz (May 2010)
5. Gerkey, B., Vaughan, R.T.: The player/stage project: Tools for multi-robot and distributed sensor systems. In: Proceeding of the 11th International Conference (Icar), pp. 317–323 (2003)
6. Ishiguro, H., Maeda, T., Miyashita, T., Tsuji, S.: A strategy for acquiring an environmental model with panoramic sensing by a mobile robot. In: Proceedings of the 1994 IEEE International Conference on Robotics and Automation, pp. 724–729 (1994)
7. Ji, J., Indiveri, G., Ploeger, P., Bredenfeld, A.: An omni-vision based self-localization method for soccer robot. In: IEEE Intelligent Vehicles Symposium, pp. 276–281 (2003)
8. Juerss, U.: Hacking the nintendo wii remote ir sensor, http://www.cczwei-forum.de (2011-03-31)
9. Juerss, U.: The nintendo wii remote library, http://www.cczwei.de (2011-03-31)

10. Zell, A., Wenzel, K.E., Rosset, P.: Low-Cost Visual Tracking of a Landing Place and Hovering Flight Control with a Microcontroller. Journal of Intelligent & Robotic Systems (2009)
11. Lee, J.C.: Hacking the Nintendo Wii Remote. IEEE Pervasive Computing, 39–45 (July-September 2008)
12. Matsumoto, Y., Ikeda, K., Inaba, M., Inoue, H.: Visual navigation using omnidirectional view sequence. In: Proceedings 1999 IEEE/RSJ International Conference on Intelligent Robots and Systems. Human and Environment Friendly Robots with High Intelligence and Emotional Quotients, pp. 317–322 (1999)
13. Menegatti, E., Nori, F., Pagello, E., Pellizzari, C., Spagnoli, D.: Designing an omnidirectional vision system for a goalkeeper robot. In: Birk, A., Coradeschi, S., Tadokoro, S. (eds.) RoboCup 2001. LNCS (LNAI), vol. 2377, pp. 193–213. Springer, Heidelberg (2002)
14. Nayar, S.K.: Omnidirectional Vision. In: Proc. of ISRR (1998)
15. Pegard, C., Mouaddib, E.M.: A mobile robot using a panoramic view. In: Proceedings of IEEE International Conference on Robotics and Automation, pp. 89–94 (1996)
16. Song, K., Wang, C.: Self-Localization and Control of an Omni-Directional Mobile Robot Based on an Omni-Directional Camera. In: Asian Control Conference, pp. 899–904 (2009)
17. Vincze, M., Olufs, S.: A simple inexpensive interface for robots using the Nintendo Wii controlle. In: IEEE Intelligent Robots and Systems, pp. 473–479 (2009)
18. Winters, N., Gaspar, J., Lacey, G., Santos-Victor, J.: Omni-directional vision for robot navigation. In: Proceedings IEEE Workshop on Omnidirectional Vision, pp. 21–28 (2000)
19. Yagi, Y.: Omnidirectional Sensing and Its Applications. In: Technologies: Algorithms, Sensors, and Applications, pp. 568–579 (1999)
20. Yagi, Y., Nishizawa, Y., Yachida, M.: Map-based navigation for a mobile robot with omnidirectional image sensor COPIS. Transactions on Robotics (1995)
21. Zheng, J., Tsuji, S.: Panoramic representation for route recognition by a mobile robot. International Journal of Computer Vision, 55–76 (October 1992)

How to Teach Robotics to Children (12 - 16 Years Old)

Achim Gottscheber, Andreas Hochlehnert, and Lukas Mairon

SRH University Heidelberg, 69121 Heidelberg, Germany
achim.gottscheber@fh-heidelberg.de, ahochleh@t-online.de,
lukas@mairon.net

Abstract. In this paper a few methods are formulated, how to teach robotics to children and teenagers. These methods are based on the assumption that children want to learn robotics by their own choice. It is focused on the introduction of basics of robots and its programming. Lego Mindstorms NXT is used as a platform. An overview of well known competitions, using this platform, is presented. These competitions are a good way to see how effective the methods are.

Keywords: LEGO Mindstorms NXT, teaching methods, children and teenager, robotics, summer camp.

1 Introduction

Nowadays, robotics has become an important part of industry and robotics will play a bigger role in everyone's daily life soon. As an example, robots are used in the automobile industries, on planets far away from earth and they are already in everyone's home where they mow the lawn or clean the carpet. All these robots need someone, who develops them. Very often, people come in touch with the technology related to robot development during their time at University or any other form of higher education where robotic is a topic.

This is far too late. It would be better if already children and teenagers start to work with these technologies. Additionally, they could then see how 'cool' sciences could be and decide to study a subject related to this area.

Therefore, children and teenagers were taught in a one week summer course in 2010. Some methods were tested in order to see which are important points if someone works with people in this age.

Since several years, the authors have gained experience with competitions using the LEGO NXT system and experienced it with people of that age, as participants, as judges or as teachers.

1.1 First Lego League (FLL)

There are many competitions using the LEGO Mindstorm-system as a platform. Next, after some period of time a closer look on the FLL is shown, the authors have gained some experience, as participants, as judges and now as teachers.

D. Obdržálek and A. Gottscheber (Eds.): EUROBOT 2011, CCIS 161, pp. 114–122, 2011.
© Springer-Verlag Berlin Heidelberg 2011

The First Lego League is a worldwide competition which is organized by the First organization. It is designed for children and teenagers between 10-16 years of age. The only exception is in the USA, there the age-range is between 9 to 14. One takes part in this competition with a group of 5-10 participants and 2 coaches.

There are 4 main parts in which the competition is divided, robotic game, robotic design, teamwork and research presentation. In the robotic game one has to build and program a robot (the LEGO Mindstorms NXT).

The robot needs to solve tasks on a table which has a dimension of 115cm x 237cm. It is possible to get 400 points as a maximum. The robot design consists of parts like the technical design and the programming. This is evaluated by judges through a presentation of the children.

As for the teamwork, the team itself is rated. The judges would like to see how good the teammates worked together and if everybody worked or if the work was done by one or two persons only. The last part is the research presentation. Every year, the teams get a new topic. The teams have to curry out research on a subtopic and give a presentation about their results.

Children from all over the world work on the same tasks and can get the qualification for the international competition and enjoy robotics with each other. In the FLL the children learn how to work in a team, have a lot of fun and come in touch with technology.

2   Teams

In our taught course, we divided the participants into groups of 2 to 3 persons. Every group got one robot and a one PC. We noticed that the groups with 2 persons were the most efficient ones, they worked together. In the groups with 3 persons most time 2 worked together and one sat beside and did nothing. This wasn't the same person all the time and this change made these groups work slower. Another point was that in these groups the members argued much more than in groups of two persons.

We had one 'group' in which only one member worked because the second member didn't want to. Although he needn't arrange with someone else, he was slower than the groups with two members. This shows that two children, working on one robot, is the best team size for people of this age.

3   Robot

The LEGO Mindstorms NXT system was used in the presented summer camp for children. The main part of the system is the programmable NXT brick, consisting of a 32 bit ARM processor, a multiline display, 4 analogue input ports and 3 analogue output ports.

Different sensors can be plugged in into the 4 input interfaces. There are light/color sensors, touch sensors, ultrasonic sensors to measure distances and sound sensors to measure the volume. The 3 output interfaces can be used for controlling motors. These motors have inbuilt rotation sensors. All these 3 sensors were used and needed during the course and worked reliable.

We believe this system is particularly appealing for children and a good introduction to robotics. This has several reasons. The first one is that nearly everybody has already played with LEGO, so they could easily learn how to build a robot.

Second, it is easy to build a robot with this system either by using the instructions or by using own ideas. The third reason is the different possibilities how to program robots. The NXG-software is shipped with the set which is sealed by LEGO. It's a visual programming language made up with icons which are put one after the other. Therefore, it's easy to learn it and one can soon have success. The same idea is used in the "Robolab"-Software which is based on the LabView-VPE (Visual Programming Environment). Robolab is more complicated but one is able to program in a more sophistic manner.

There are several other text-based programming possibilities but for this age and the time frame of one week (typically for such courses which is usually short) the first two tools are the ones witch give the best results.

4   The Children

We thought the children and teenager for one week during summer vacation. We divided them into 2 classes one for the children from 11-13 years of age and the other one from 14-16. We did that because we thought that the younger group would be slower and need less sophisticated tasks than the older one. The impact of the first point were particularly evident during construction of the robots and in solving of the more difficult tasks.

In the 'younger' class it was easy to see who joint the course on their own choice and who was send there by their parents. The children who came by their own choice worked really hard, they wanted to learn something and always asked more and better questions.

The children who were sent by their parents either were really slow or didn't work at all. What all of them loved was playing games on the computer. It wasn't that easy to make them stop playing when they had a task. After long discussions we persuaded the children to play during the breaks and work during the lessons.

This 'agreement' wasn't accepted by all the children, some of them tried to play and believed we wouldn't see this. This became even worse, all children started to get together around the one who was playing. They argued and screamed. Of course it is important that the children have enough time to play, because otherwise they won't like the course and won't stay focused. This is nothing new. But one has to find the right balance between working and playing. In our case the children were able to do sports in the morning and then they worked about 2.5-3 hours until the lunch break. This was the time where nearly everybody was focused and did what they were told to do. After one and a half hour of break they worked another 2 hours. The lessons in the afternoon were really hard. The children either didn't want to work anymore or were not able to. In our opinion a lunch break of one hour is too long.

This may sound strange but what happened was that they started to do other things, like playing games on the computer, etc. and always wanted to go on playing instead of doing the tasks they were supposed to do.

This all sounds like we didn't have or wanted the children to have fun. This is not true. We had a lot of fun, all together, but there is a time to stop making jokes and learn (which is the reason why we were there).

One of the child said that he doesn't want to do anything. We tried hard to convince him but it was impossible so we accepted that he can not be changed. It was decided that this was the best way for him, first one needs to try to convince him but when he does not follow the instructions, then one needs to accept it. The authors were not sure if in such a situation other children would ask for the same 'rights', but most of them ignored him.

5   Methods

The course was started by building the robot. This was for the younger class a difficult task. This was a surprise because it was assumed that children in this age have already played with LEGO. In several groups was more than one person who didn't play with LEGO before.

They did need to spend one whole day to build the robot using the instructions. An interesting point was that the children loved building (and presenting) their robots (and during the rest of the course, they did improve or did a new designs of their robot). Some of them enjoyed building the robot more than writing programs for it. Nearly every day we gave them some time to improve their robot mechanically. They were much more concentrated afterwards.

The second day was the first day we used the computers. First they were confused with the program. It took a few days until all of them understood the software. To give them an easy start, their first task was to write a program which makes the robot drive a distant forward and back again.

This simple task already showed who joined the course by his/her own choice and who was sent by their parents. While some of them already finished this programming task others didn't even have started. This made teaching hard, because some of them were eager to have new more difficult tasks and others didn't even started the old one.

The first days, the fast groups were asked to wait for the others, but soon we gave the fast groups more difficult tasks. It was thought that it is unfair to slow them down just because they did what they were taught to and the others played either games or talked with others.

The second task on this day was driving a number 8 curve with the robot. Surprisingly only one of the groups solved this task and the others either gave up after a half an hour or didn't even started. We think that this was simply too much for the second day of the younger class.

The third day, we spend working with the sensors. We explained the function of each sensor and gave them tasks with every single sensor. The final task was to write a program which forced the robot to avoid crashing into walls. This task was loved by the children they presented us many different ways how to solve this problem.

The rest of the week, the younger class got similar tasks like the older ones, but they had more time. In the afternoon of the last day, it was impossible to work with them, so we allowed them to do what they want, as long as it had something to do with the robot.

Some of the groups build nice robots, other wrote more difficult programs but the major part of the groups did nothing or played computer games.

In the 'older' class, the authors didn't have that many problems as they had with the younger group. It was easy to see that all of them joined the course by their own choice and that robotics is one of their interests in which they want to learn something new.

6   Methods

The teaching in the older class was more goal-orientated. Before the actual start of the course a list of all important subjects (**key learning objectives**) they should know about programming was made (As already said in the Introduction we concentrate on the programming of a robot). Although we used a visual programming language it was important to know the basic structure of programming in order to program more complicated tasks in general.

To reach this aim, a plan for every day with it's special daily goals was prepared. Furthermore special tasks that should reinforce the learning was devised. (See the simplified Example "Daily Schedule" or the detailed schedule with all tasks in the appendix). In addition to this, every day a repetition on the day before was made as well questions were answered. This was important because the tasks of the current day was based on what was done the days before.

6.1   Example

Daily Schedule: (simplified example)

Day 1:
   Aim: The children should learn how to control the motors.
   Task: Write a program that lets the robot go straight.

Day 2:
   Aim: The children should learn how to use the sensors.
   Task: Write a program which makes the robot following a black line.

It would be a lie to say that each day's goal on the same day was reached. However, these objectives have been set deliberately high to ensure that not everyone has finished after the half of the time.

In the following a short overview which goals and tasks were set during the week and which conclusions were drawn from the results, is presented:

The first day was very hard because it was necessary to assess the knowledge and the pace of work of each participant. The main task for the day was to build the robot and after that a first look on the software was presented. While some participants had already built the robot, waiting for the introduction to the software, others were not even half finished. Because it was not expected to have a huge time difference between the participants, it became necessary to think about a slightly different teaching approach. Therefore it was decided to structure the remaining days more clearly and to prepare more tasks for the faster ones.

6.2   Our Revised Concept

First, at the beginning of the lesson a short repetition of the last day was done. After that the lesson for this day was taught. Next, the main-task for the day was explained (at the end of the day everyone should have finished this task). Everyone who completed this task earlier got additional tasks referring to the day's topic. At the end of the day one possible solution of the main task and repeated the most important things that was conveyed on this day was shown, as this was also necessary for solving the task. As further measure participants were instructed to present their solution of the main task and they explained it in detail to the others. As a result, participants were more challenged and there is the possibility that the others understand the daily topic better when the participants explain from their different point of view.

In Addition to this we tried to teach the new teaching material always in the morning, because we noticed that the participants were much more receptive at this time (same as in the younger class).

In the following days, it was very successfully taught with this new concept, reaching all the key learning objectives that were noted in the list weeks before.

(For the complete schedule see the Appendix)

6.3   Argues in the Younger Group

Unfortunately in the younger group the children argued a lot and tried to stop each other from doing whatever they did at this moment. It was impossible to stop them trying this but one can control it when one stops them as soon as one noticed it.

In the older group this was never a problem.

References

1. Berns, K., Schmidt, D.: Programmierung mit LEGO MINDSTORMS NXT. Springer, Heidelberg (2010)
2. Benedettelli, D.: LEGO MINDSTORMS NXT Thinking Robots. No starch Press (2010)
3. Siciliano, B., Khatib, O.: Springer Handbook of Robotics. Springer, Heidelberg (2010)

Appendix A: Detailed Schedule for the Week

A1 Detailed Schedule for the Week (Older Group):

Important: *The point "Task" is only a short description of the day's objective, the complete task list is under the superior point "Tasks" below.*

Day 1:

- Presentation (Short presentation about the NXT, its sensors and competitions)
- Division into groups of 2
- Construction of the robot (A NXT-Template to ensure everyone has the same robot was used)
- Teaching of the basics of NXG
  - Short description: What is NXG?
  - Explanation of the basic operations (how to open/save files etc.)
  - Explanation: How to transmit files/programs to the NXT brick?
- **Explanation:** How to drive motors with the NXT brick?
               How to use the display of the brick?

Day 2: *(Topic: Loops, switches and sensors)*

- Repetition:
  - How to use the motors?
- **Explanation:** How to use/read sensors in NXG?
- **Explanation of basic programming structure:**
  - Difference between Numbers(integer) and Text(string)
  - What are Switches (logical operations)? And how to use it?
  - How to use loops? And why?
- **Task:** (see Task 1 below under point 'Tasks')
  - Part 1: Write a program, along which the robot follows a black line (using the light sensor, switches and loops)
  - Part 2: Extend the program:
    - * If the ultrasonic sensor detects an obstacle or the touch sensor is pressed, stop all motors.
    - * If the sound sensor "hears" a loud sound, the robot should make a 180° turn.
    - * Show all sensor values on the display

Day 3: *(Topic: repetition of the day before, recognition of colors)*

- Repetition:
  - What are sensors, switches and loops?
  - What are numbers (integer) and text (string)?

- **Explanation:** What are loops and how to use them?
                   What's the difference between sensor-wait and waits?
- **Task:** Task 2 Part 1-3 (under point 'Tasks')

Day 4:

- Repetition:
  - Some time for those who hadn't finished the day before
  - Presentation of the solution
- **Short Explanation** of the "Own blocks" feature
- **Explanation:** What are boolean values (true/false) and how to use them?
                   How to use a comparison?
                   What are logical operations? (or/and/xor/...)
- **Task:** (see Task 2 Part 3-4 + Task 3 + Task 4 under point 'Tasks')
  Write a menu control using the NXT-buttons with the following functions:
  - Left arrow key: open gripper (not static: as soon as the key is released stop if it's pressed again continue opening)
  - Right arrow key: close gripper (not static)
  - Enter button: start the main program

Day 5: *(Topic: multithreading, variables, mathematics)*

- **Explanation:** What is multithreading and how to use is?
                   The usage of variables (save, read, use)
                   How to use mathematical operations?
- **Task:** Task 4 (under point 'Tasks')
- *Choose one task:* Task 3 or Task 5 or Task 6 or Task 7 (under point 'Tasks')

A2 Tasks

Task 1: *The robot should...*

... drive and follow a black line
... turn around and follow the line in opposite direction when the ultrasonic sensor detects an obstacle.
... turn around too, when the sound sensor detects a loud noise.
... stop the program when the touch sensor is pressed.

Task 2: *The robot should...*

- Part 1:
  ... start the program only when it hears a loud noise,
  ... go straight but not leave a black-bordered area.
  ... play a sound when it drives across a red dot.
- Part 2:
  ... close the grabber when it touches an item and bring it outside the black-bordered area

– Part 3:
  ... already recognize an item with the ultrasonic sensor and open the grabber.
– Part 4: Integration of a menu control (add this before the actual program)
  ... open the grabber while pressing (and holding) the right arrow key. (as soon as the key is released stop if it's pressed again continue opening).
  ... close the grabber while pressing (and holding) the left arrow key.
  ... start the main program by pressing the enter button.

Task 3: ('Compare') *The robot should...*

... go slowly straight.
... show current rotation values of both sensors on the display.
... compare the rotation values and show on the display whether the values are equal or not.

Task 4: *The robot should...*

... count a blinking light and show on the display how often it turned on/off, *Info: The light will flash at least one time and with a maximum of 3 times.*

Task 5: ('Guard robot') *The robot should...*

... give alarm when the light conditions changes very fast (when it changes slow nothing should happen)
– **Additional:** ('Radar')
  ... turn the ultrasonic sensor and measure in defined intervals the distance. if the distance is changed greatly, trigger alarm.

Task 6: ('Game console')

– Develop a game for the NXT which is either controlled by the NXT-buttons or by the motors (as a joystick, maybe with force feedback).
– Ideas:
  • Pong
  • Moorhuhn

Task 7: ('Parking') *The robot should...*

... find with the help of the ultrasonic sensors, a parking space which is large enough and automatically parking in it.
– If the robot hits something the program should be stopped.

Model-Based Nonlinear Control of 2-WMR

Gernot Grabmair

Upper Austria University of Applied Sciences,
Wels, Austria
{gernot.grabmair}@fh-wels.at
http://www.fh-ooe.at/campus-wels/

Abstract. A solid low-level movement control is essential for a successful contest robot. For two-wheeled mobile robots (WMR) numerous
control approaches can be found in literature. In this contribution it is
shown how the low-level control of a WMR can be systematically developed by model based design techniques. The resulting controller is able
to asymptotically track given motion profiles for any reference point fixed
to the robot chassis by a small extension of the well known look-ahead
control.

Keywords: wheeled mobile robot, WMR, differential drive, model based
design, nonlinear control.

1   Introduction

Numerous papers and reports on the control of two-wheeled mobile robots
(WMR) are available to the community. Besides engineering approaches (see,
e.g., [2]) the controllers are mainly based on a pure kinematic model or dynamic
effects are taken into account (see, e.g., [13]). Parameter adaptation is done in
[13], [14], [12]. More recently, some promising ones even account for tire slip
effects, see [6], [7].

From the control theoretical viewpoint approximate linearization results in
loss of controllability. Therefore, nonlinear control is indispensable. It is well
known that the kinematic model is not exact state-linearizable by static state

Fig. 1. The contest robot 2011

D. Obdržálek and A. Gottscheber (Eds.): EUROBOT 2011, CCIS 161, pp. 123–129, 2011.
© Springer-Verlag Berlin Heidelberg 2011

feedback. A detailed analysis is given in [11], [10]. The tracking control problem is tackled by a Lyapunov based approach in [4] and by exact input-to-output linearization for a virtual look-ahead reference point in [15] for the dynamic model. The internal dynamics are studied in [1]. An interesting approach is taken in [5], where the whole posture is tracked in a least square sense. A solution to the combined tracking and posture stabilization problem is presented in [9].

Most of the approaches assume full state measurements. The error due to odometry are discussed in [8], and a controller incorporating only available measurements is given in [3].

To the best belief of the authors and based on the experience from automotive applications the consideration of the WMR dynamics has to go hand in hand with tire slip. The scope of the present WMR controller is tracking control of trajectories with smooth acceleration profiles. Therefore, we may assume zero slip and consequently we neglect the plant dynamics for the tracking controller part. The tracking controller is based on the pure kinematic model, equivalent to the unicycle. Additional longitudinal and angular velocity controllers are used as inner loop control. This results in a performant controller structure stabilizing the motion of any point fixed to the WMR frame[1] that is easy to commission even for undergraduate students. Additionally, the controller allows forward and backward motion tasks.

This paper is organized as follows. First an outer loop control is developed for the unicycle type system. In the next section the inner loop velocity controllers are presented. Finally, the model based controller design process is discussed.

2   Kinematics of WMR and Posture Control

The posture $[x, y, \theta]$ of the WMR is given with the center of wheels axis (CoA) as reference point. The kinematic model of the unicycle type system is given by

$$\begin{bmatrix} \dot{x} \\ \dot{y} \\ \dot{\theta} \end{bmatrix} = \begin{bmatrix} \cos\theta & 0 \\ \sin\theta & 0 \\ 0 & 1 \end{bmatrix} \begin{bmatrix} v \\ \omega \end{bmatrix} \tag{1}$$

with control input $u^\top = [v, \omega]$. Here, we assume ideal velocity control of the inner loop and therefore, the velocities may be considered as inputs. The lateral and angular WMR velocities are related by

$$\begin{bmatrix} v \\ \omega \end{bmatrix} = \begin{bmatrix} \frac{r_l}{2} & \frac{r_r}{2} \\ -\frac{r_l}{l} & \frac{r_r}{l} \end{bmatrix} \begin{bmatrix} \omega_l \\ \omega_r \end{bmatrix}$$

to the angular velocities of the left and right wheel with radius $r_l = r_r$ and axis length l. It is well known, that even exact input-output linearization with the output $y = [x, y]$ is not possible by static state feedback due to a singularity in

---

[1] At least from the practical point of view.

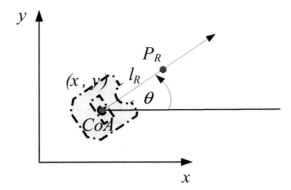

Fig. 2. The coordinate system

the resulting input decoupling matrix. Therefore, we define the look-ahead point P_R at distance l_R from CoA as output $y = [x_R, y_R]$ with

$$x_R = x + l_R \cos\theta \tag{2}$$

$$y_R = y + l_R \sin\theta . \tag{3}$$

The vector relative degree is $r = [1, 1]$. In the new coordinates the system dynamics yield

$$\begin{bmatrix} \dot{x}_R \\ \dot{y}_R \\ \dot{\theta} \end{bmatrix} = \begin{bmatrix} v_{xR} \\ v_{yR} \\ \frac{1}{l_R}(v_{yR}\cos\theta - v_{xR}\sin\theta) \end{bmatrix} \tag{4}$$

with the transformed input

$$\begin{bmatrix} v_{xR} \\ v_{yR} \end{bmatrix} = \begin{bmatrix} \cos\theta & -l_R\sin\theta \\ \sin\theta & l_R\cos\theta \end{bmatrix} \begin{bmatrix} v \\ \omega \end{bmatrix} . \tag{5}$$

The proposed control law is given by a feedforward and a PI controller part

$$\begin{bmatrix} v_{xR} \\ v_{yR} \end{bmatrix} = \begin{bmatrix} \dot{x}_{R,r} + k_P(x_{R,r} - x_R) + k_I \int (x_{R,r} - x_R)\,\mathrm{d}t \\ \dot{y}_{R,r} + k_P(y_{R,r} - y_R) + k_I \int (y_{R,r} - y_R)\,\mathrm{d}t \end{bmatrix} . \tag{6}$$

The input-to-output linearized system part is stabilized by construction. But the internal dynamics of the WMR have to be investigated further.

Case 1 $v_{xR} = v_{yR} = 0$: This is equivalent to $v = \omega = 0$ meaning the WMR is at rest. The zero dynamics

$$\dot{\theta} = 0$$

is stable but not asymptotically stable.

Case 2 $v_{xR} \neq 0$ or $v_{yR} \neq 0$: This is the technical more relevant case. A detailed analysis for general desired trajectories is best done in the Frenet frame fixed to the WMR, see [11]. For the reason of simplicity, we consider a straight movement parallel to the x-axis. The zero-dynamics corresponding to the desired movement $[x_{R,r}(t), 0, 0]$ yield

$$\dot{\theta} = -\frac{1}{l_R}\dot{x}_{R,r}\sin\theta . \tag{7}$$

In the case of forward motion, i.e. $\dot{x}_{R,r} > 0$, the look-ahead point has to be chosen in front of the WMR, i.e. $l_R > 0$, in order to achieve a locally asymptotically stable zero-dynamics. Backward motion means $\dot{x}_{R,r} < 0 \Rightarrow$ look-ahead point rear of the WMR, i.e. $l_R < 0$.

2.1   Finding a Trajectory for the Look-Ahead Reference Point

Usually, the specification of the trajectory of the CoA or of the center of the circumscribing circle seems more intuitive. Therefore, we propose to specify the desired sufficient smooth reference motion in terms of the CoA as $x_r(t), y_r(t), \theta_r(t)$, $\dot{x}_r(t), \dot{y}_r(t), \dot{\theta}_r(t)$ respecting the nonholonomic constraints. The forward or backward look-ahead motion is given with $v_r = k_{DIR}\sqrt{\dot{x}_r^2 + \dot{y}_r^2}$, $\omega_r = \dot{\theta}_r$ and

$$k_{DIR} = \begin{cases} 1 \ldots |\theta_r - \arctan2(\dot{y}_r, \dot{x}_r)| = 0 \\ -1 \ldots \text{otherwise} \end{cases} \tag{8}$$

by

$$\begin{aligned} x_{R,r} &= x_r + l_R\cos\theta_r \\ y_{R,r} &= y_r + l_R\sin\theta_r \\ \theta_R &= \theta_r \end{aligned}$$

and

$$\begin{bmatrix} \dot{x}_{R,r} \\ \dot{y}_{R,r} \end{bmatrix} = \begin{bmatrix} \cos\theta_r & -l_R\sin\theta_r \\ \sin\theta_r & l_R\cos\theta_r \end{bmatrix} \begin{bmatrix} v_r \\ \omega_r \end{bmatrix} . \tag{9}$$

It is important to mention that this modification only concerns the open loop control and not the stabilizing closed loop controller. Therefore, its stabilizing properties remain intact.

3   Velocity Dynamics and Control of WMR

Due to the mechanical construction the center of gravity (CoG) is negligibly close to the CoA. The WMR is driven by brushed DC drives with resistance R_A, machine constant k_m, and gear ratio n. The velocity dynamics can be written as

$$\begin{bmatrix} I_v & 0 \\ 0 & I_\omega \end{bmatrix} \begin{bmatrix} \dot{v} \\ \dot{\omega} \end{bmatrix} = \begin{bmatrix} d_v & 0 \\ 0 & d_\omega \end{bmatrix} \begin{bmatrix} v \\ \omega \end{bmatrix} + \beta \begin{bmatrix} 1 & 1 \\ -\frac{l}{2} & \frac{l}{2} \end{bmatrix} \begin{bmatrix} u_l \\ u_r \end{bmatrix} \tag{10}$$

with inertias I_v, I_ω, linear effective damping coefficients d_v, d_ω, and $\beta = \frac{k_m}{R_A}\frac{n}{r}$. Further, we assume that Coulomb friction is already compensated for. The longitudinal velocity controller is a simple PD-type one tuned for the equivalent plant transfer function

$$G_v\left(s\right) = \frac{\hat{v}}{\hat{u}_l + \hat{u}_r} = \frac{\beta}{J_v s + d_v} \; . \tag{11}$$

The angular velocity controller is tuned for the equivalent plant transfer function

$$G_\omega\left(s\right) = \frac{2}{l} \frac{\hat{\omega}}{-\hat{u}_l + \hat{u}_r} = \frac{\beta}{J_\omega s + d_\omega} \; . \tag{12}$$

An integral action is not necessary because the velocity controllers are always in the inner loop.

4   Model-Based Development

4.1   Parameter Identification

The models used for controller design are based on physics. Therefore, the model parameters are known or can be easily obtained from some experiments. Especially in the case of the plant transfer functions for the velocity controllers we have measured the behavior of the robot rolling down a ramp. Further we have taken some step responses.

4.2   Test Rig and Commissioning

The test rig (see Fig. 3) serves as the main tool for commissioning.

1. As soon as the controllers perform well in the simulation the prototyping is started on the test rig. The controllers are rapidly transferred from Simulink to Windows Realtime Target, that is used as realtime prototyping system. The brushed DC drives are driven by Quanser analog power amplifier modules during this development stage. The comparison of measurements with simulations have already lead to massive mechanical redesigns. E.g., screw drives have been replaced by belts and the backlash effects have been reduced.

Fig. 3. Test rig for model based controller development

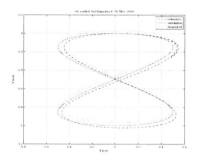
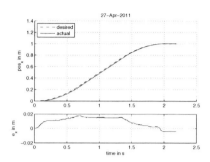

(a) Simulation results and measurements with outer pure open loop control (no position feedback, i.e. $k_P = k_I = 0$). As soon as the outer loop feedback control is tuned the error is hardly visible at the resolution of this figure.

(b) Measurements with outer closed loop control (proportional position feedback, i.e. $k_P > 0$ but small and $k_I = 0$). The test exhibits some lag error but a good final positioning behaviour.

Fig. 4. Test results

2. Afterwards the power amplifiers are replaced by the in-house developed power electronics. The controllers still remain in the prototyping system. This step resulted in some modification of the electronics in order to obtain the physically expected linear behavior of brushed DC drives.
3. Then, the controllers are transferred to the on-board microcontroller by the Realtime Workshop Embedded Coder.
4. Finally, the overall software can be applied to the contest system.

5 Conclusion

Due to the model based prototyping the controller development could be started quite soon. Therefore, it was possible to influence the design of the contest robot at an early stage. Model based development has proven as an indispensable tool that greatly simplifies the work in teams. The timelines of mechanical, control and software development can be fully parallelized.

Some measurements and comparisons of the model based design process will be presented during the talk.

Acknowledgments. The author is indebted to Michael Zauner and Raimund Edlinger for their support of the test cycles of the proposed algorithms on the mechatronic WMR platform of the Robo-Racing-Team http://rrt.fh-wels.at/ and for some of the pictures.

References

1. Eghtesad, M., Necsulescu, D.S.: Study of the internal dynamics of an autonomous mobile robot. Robotics and Autonomous Systems 54(4), 342–349 (2006)
2. Feng, L.: Cross-coupling motion controller for mobile robots. IEEE Control Systems Magazine 13(6), 35–43 (1993)
3. Jakubiak, J., Lefeber, A.A.J., Tchon, K., Nijmeijer, H.: Two observer-based tracking algorithms for a unicycle mobile robot. Int. Journal of Applied Math. and Comp. Science 12(4), 513–522 (2002)
4. Kanayama, Y.: A stable tracking control method for an autonomous mobile robot, vol. 1, pp. 384–389 (May 1990)
5. Kim, D.-H., Oh, J.-H.: Tracking control of a two-wheeled mobile robot using input-output linearization. Control Engineering Practice 7(3), 369–373 (1999)
6. Li, L., Wang, F.-Y., Zhou, Q.: Integrated longitudinal and lateral tire/road friction modeling and monitoring for vehicle motion control. IEEE Transactions on Intelligent Transportation Systems 7(1), 1–19 (2006)
7. Lin, W.-S.: Adaptive critic anti-slip control of wheeled autonomous robot. IET Control Theory & Applications 1(1), 51–57 (2007)
8. Martinelli, A.: Modeling and estimating the odometry error of a mobile robot. In: None (2001)
9. Oriolo, G.: WMR control via dynamic feedback linearization: design, implementation, and experimental validation. IEEE Transactions on Control Systems Technology 10(6), 835–852 (2002)
10. Samson, C.: Feedback control of a nonholonomic wheeled cart in cartesian space, vol. 2, pp. 1136–1141 (April 1991)
11. Samson, C., Ait-Abderrahim, K.: Mobile robot control. part 1: Feedback control of nonholonomic wheeled cart in cartesian space. Research Report RR-1288, INRIA (1990)
12. Shojaei, K.: Adaptive trajectory tracking of WMRs based on feedback linearization technique, pp. 729–734 (August 2009)
13. Soetanto, D.: Adaptive, non-singular path-following control of dynamic wheeled robots 2, 1765–1770 (2003)
14. Wang, T.-Y.: Adaptive trajectory tracking control of a wheeled mobile robot via lyapunov techniques 1, 389–394 (2004)
15. Yun, X.: Internal dynamics of a wheeled mobile robot. 2, 1288–1294 (1993)

Obstacle and Game Element Detection with the 3D-Sensor Kinect

Matthias Greuter, Michael Rosenfelder, Michael Blaich, and Oliver Bittel

University of Applied Sciences Konstanz, Germany
Laboratory for Mobile Robots
Brauneggerstr. 55 D-78462 Konstanz
{matgreut,mirosenf,mblaich,bittel}@htwg-konstanz.de
http://www.robotik.in.htwg-konstanz.de/

Abstract. Detecting objects is of fundamental importance for the Eurobot Challenge 2011. This paper presents a Kinect-based approach to detect the game elements on the game field. Using the Kinect sensor provides the advantage that elements lying behind other elements can still be detected, which is nearly impossible for a laser-based approach. The Kinect provides depth information which is projected to the 3D space, building a point cloud of the game elements. The point cloud is then analyzed for the clusters of the game elements which are passed to a classifier each. The classifier decides if the passed-in cluster is a pawn, king or the enemy robot.

Keywords: Kinect Sensor, Object Detection, 3D Classification.

1 Introduction

The Eurobot Challenge is an international open mobile robotics contest, which takes place every year. The task the amateur teams have to handle in the 2011's challenge is playing a special kind of chess. The robot has 90 seconds to make points by placing and stacking the game elements on the squares of the own team color. The robots have to play completely autonomous. Thus, a sensor and an algorithm to detect the different game elements and to distinguish them from the enemy is needed.

To detect objects on a game field like the one for the Eurobot, sensors to measure the distances to objects are needed. There are different approaches to detect such objects. One is to detect the objects in the plain of a two dimensional sensor like e. g. laser scanner. However, such systems can only detect objects in two dimensions. Furthermore, no information about the type of the object is given, e. g. no information about the object's height can be acquired. Another approach is to detect objects with a blob finder algorithm and a normal camera, where the knowledge of the camera's position and orientation is used to detect blobs of the same color and compute their position. Since all the objects of the Eurobot Challenge are lying on the floor, this approach could be used [9]. Using a 3D-sensor-based approach, the range of the possible detected objects increases.

D. Obdržálek and A. Gottscheber (Eds.): EUROBOT 2011, CCIS 161, pp. 130–143, 2011.

Here, the advantage is that objects lying behind each other can still be detected. Furthermore, the height of objects can be accessed, which is important for the Eurobot Challenge to distinguish between pawns, kings and the enemy robot.

Possible 3D camera systems are, for example, the time-of-flight cameras like swissranger [13], stereo camera systems or a 3D laser scanner [1]. However, the time-of-flight cameras and the 3D laser scanner are expensive. Stereo camera systems can be built of two cheap cameras with a satisfying accuracy. One disadvantage of such a stereo camera system, is its complexity: The system has to be calibrated and works on two pictures, where the correspondence problem has to be solved. Such a system is not robust against different light effects.

In this paper the Microsoft Kinect sensor [7] will be used as 3D sensor, published last year as a controller for the Microsoft XBox 360. The sensor with a range from 0.5 m to 8.0 m is good enough as an object detection system for the Eurobot Challenge, since the game field has a game field size of 2 × 3 meters. The sensor is not expensive compared to other 3D systems. Compared to stereo camera systems no calibration is needed and no correspondence problem needs to be solved.

This paper describes an approach to detect objects by using the depth values of the Kinect sensor. The next section covers the related work, the fourth section describes the object detection and the corresponding classification. The fifth section presents the analysis and results, the last section concludes and gives an outlook for future work.

2   Related Work

For the Eurobot Challenge the approach to avoid obstacles and detect objects is almost identical, as often for mobile robots. The detected objects are classified depending on their position on the game field as obstacle or accessible object and thus allowing the robot to plan its navigation. Collision avoidance has been successfully solved with the use of a time-of-flight camera as shown by Droeschel et al. [2]. The time-of-flight camera allows to detect objects in the 3D space instead of only one scan plane like with a laser range finder. The proposed obstacle detection method is robust about kinematic inaccuracies and noise in the range measurements.

After introducing the Kinect sensor for Microsoft's Xbox 360, many computer scientists use the Kinect as a robotic sensor. Oliver Kreylos is one of the first who successfully has used the Kinect and demonstrated a 3D reconstruction on his webpage [10]. On the webpage of the freenect library [4] various videos using the Kinect are presented, like hand detection, finger tracking or a flying device with object avoidance. The Intel Labs Seattle have presented projects using the Kinect. One of those projects is the 3D mapping of the laboratory in Seattle [5]. In this paper the freenect library is used to acquire the Kinect data and to detect objects for the Eurobot Challenge 2011. An introduction to the Kinect is given in the next section.

3   Kinect

Prime Sense's 3D-sensor Kinect[12] as shown in Figure 1(a) uses a structured light approach to compute the depth information. The in this section given Kinect information is as explained on the OpenKinect website [11]. The sensor contains, besides a normal camera, an infrared (IR) camera and an infrared emitter which provide a normal colored camera image and a depth information image, as shown in Figure 1(b) and (c). The IR-emitter is a laser diode with no modulation and a constant output level. The emitted laser ray hits an optical object, which splits the ray into a pattern of irregular infra-red light points of varying intensity. This irregularity of the pattern encodes information needed for the depth computation. The IR-camera uses a monochrome image sensor. It reconstructs the depth image out of the displacement in the IR-pattern when it is projected on the objects in the Kinect's environment. The resolution of this camera is 1200×960 at a frame-rate of 30 Hz and has an IR-pass filter at the laser's wavelength. Note that the maximal resolution of the depth image is 640×480. The IR-camera shows minimal sensitivity to both visible and 950 nm light-sources. The reconstructed depth map allows the detection of foreground objects like a person playing with the XBox 360.

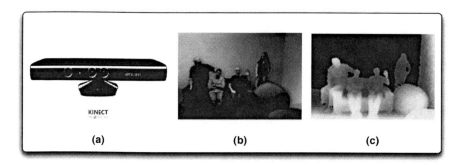

Fig. 1. (a) Prime Sense's 3D sensor Kinect. (b) A possible camera image provided by the Kinect's normal camera. (c) The corresponding depth information image to the colored image as provided by the IR-emitter and IR-camera [12].

4   Object Detection

This section describes the object detection using the Kinect and the open source library freenect [4], [11]. Figure 2 depicts an overview of the object detection algorithm. First, the processing of the Kinect's depth data is described to get the object's vertices in the three-dimensional space. The following Section 4.2 explains how each 3D object is extracted from the point cloud using a binary image. Section 4.3 presents the classification of the 3D objects to decide if the object is a pawn, king/queen, a constellation of those or the enemy robot. Since it is not exactly defined in the game's rules how a king or a queen do look like,

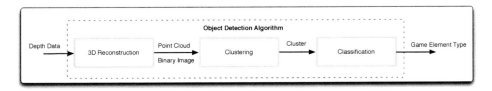

Fig. 2. Depicts a schematic overview of the object detection algorithm. The acquired depth data from the Kinect sensor is passed to a 3D reconstruction. In this step a point cloud and a binary image are constructed, which are passed to the clustering algorithm. The clustering will separate the object clusters of the point cloud and pass each object cluster to the classifier. The corresponding game element will be returned from the classifier.

the presented classifier does not distinguish between these game elements and handles both equally. Thus, these objects are referred in the following to as kings only.

4.1   3D-Reconstruction

Before the object classification can be performed, the Kinect's data containing the depth information of the robot's environment is transformed to the three-dimensional space. The freenect library provides the depth information in a periodic cycle every 33 ms in form of a 640×480 depth image. This image is manipulated to create the vertices (points with x-, y- and z-coordinates). Therefore the depth image is traversed iteratively by rows and columns and each point p_{ij} is projected sequentially to a vertex $v_k = [x_k, y_k, z_k]$, with $k = 0, .., 640*480$. Equations (1) to (4) show how the depth information for each pixel p_{ij} is projected to a 3D point with v_k. First, the depth value for each pixel d_{ij} with $i = 0, .., 639$ and $j = 0, .., 479$ is manipulated as shown in Equation (1) to d'_k. Then, the x- and y-coordinates are divided by 560.0 and then multiplied with the negative reciprocal of d', see Equation (2) and (3). Finally, the z-coordinate is projected as in Equation (4). The above presented projection with its constants is in line with the previously proposed projection matrix by Oliver Kreylos[10]. Note that the accuracy of the projection decreases with increasing distance. It is ±2 cm in a distance of 150 cm and ±10 cm for distances of about 300 cm, respectively.

$$d'_k = -\frac{d_{ij}}{34400.0} + \frac{1090.0}{34400.0} \tag{1}$$

$$x_k = \frac{1}{d'_k} \cdot \frac{p_{ij}}{560.0} \tag{2}$$

$$y_k = -\frac{1}{d'_k} \cdot \frac{p_{ij}}{560.0} \tag{3}$$

$$z_k = -\frac{1}{d'_k} \tag{4}$$

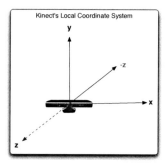

Fig. 3. The local coordinate system of the Kinect sensor. The z-coordinates (depth) are negative.

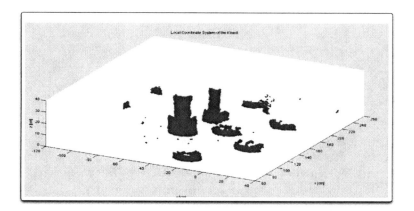

Fig. 4. An example of a point cloud containing the objects of concern. After projecting the depth information to the 3D space with the given criteria, this point cloud contains two kings and five stones. Furthermore, it contains noise from the floor and pieces of the wall of the game field. The pepper-noise (floor) will be filtered by the clustering algorithm, the pieces of wall will be dismissed by the classifier.

Since the Kinect sensor is installed with an angle of 14.5 degrees in the robot, the resulting 3D points needs to be rotated around the x-axis to prevent detecting too many floor points. Furthermore, the Kinect sensor in the robot is on a height of 25.5 cm, thus an offset of this value is added to the y-coordinate of all points. Figure 3 shows the Kinect's local coordinate system. The z-Coordinates (depth) in the coordinate system are negative (solid black z axis), thus the translated z-coordinate for each vertex is multiplied by -1 to get positive values.

A valid vertex v_k has to fulfill a set of criteria: *i)* v_k must be inside the game field. The current position of the robot is used to dismiss all v_k which lie outside the game field. This is computed from the current Kinect's position and the knowledge of the game field's dimensions. *ii)* v_k must belong to an object. Thus, floor vertices are dismissed (only a v_k with $y_k > 0$ cm is accepted) and *iii)* v_k

with $y_k > 35$ cm are dismissed, since only objects lying on the game field are of concern. The maximum height for objects inside the game area is 35 cm.

These objects could be either the enemy robot or a king stacked on two pawns. Exceeding this height should normally not occur for a v_k inside the game field.

If the set of criteria is fulfilled, v_k is added to a two-dimensional matrix, representing the field of view of the Kinect. This matrix has the same size than the depth image and if a vertex does not pass the criteria, v_k is stored with x_k, y_k and z_k equal to zero in the matrix. This matrix is further referred to as point cloud. Figure 4 depicts that with this approach, the point cloud only contains the vertices of objects on the game field instead of all the given depth information including the floor and objects outside the game. Each object is extracted out of the point cloud as described in the next section.

4.2   Clustering

For clustering in point clouds the DBSCAN algorithm as proposed in [3] is normally used to separate object clusters. However, the point cloud can contain up to approximate 50000 vertices and this approach is too slow to solve the clustering problem in an acceptable time for the Eurobot Challenge. Thus, clustering is carried out on a two-dimensional binary image, which is constructed in the 3D reconstruction step out of the Kinect's depth information. Both the point cloud and the binary image are two-dimensional matrices with $i = 640$ (rows) and $j = 480$ (columns). This image contains a 1 at position q_{ij} for a pixel p_{ij} from the depth image when a non-zero vertex was added to the point cloud, or a 0 otherwise. Thus, the 1's in the binary image correspond to the point cloud matrix with non-zero vertices. Figure 5 shows the clustering algorithm on the binary image. It contains basically three steps: *i)* The run-length (RLE) algorithm[6] is used to find horizontal lines of 1's in the image and stores its beginning and length. With this information connected areas of 1's are found, so-called blobs. Blobs smaller than 200 pixels are dismissed. *ii)* Each blob is labeled, since separated objects in the 3D space may be connected as one blob in the 2D image. The region labeling is realized with a quadripartite neighborhood as shown in Figure 6. *iii)* The clusters are classified.

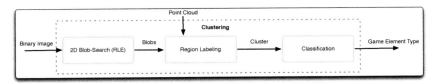

Fig. 5. Depicts a schematic overview of the clustering algorithm. First, a 2D blob search with the RLE algorithm is executed on the binary image. The detected blobs are labeled in case unconnected three-dimensional objects are connected in the 2D image. Last, the actual classification is carried out on the provided object clusters from the region labeling algorithm.

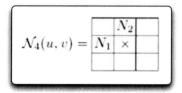

Fig. 6. Depicts the quadripartite neighborhood used for the sequentially region labeling. A pixel $N_4(u, v)$ is checked for a neighbor on the left and the upper side in the matrix.

After running the RLE algorithm the found blobs need to be labeled. Therefore each blob is traversed iteratively by rows and columns and each pixel is labeled, starting by 2. The quadripartite neighborhood checks first the left and second the upper neighbored pixels of the current blob pixel p_{ij}, with i, j representing the row and column count. The decision whether the next pixel belongs to the same 3D object relies on the euclidian distance of the vertices in the point cloud. If the euclidian distance between two neighbored pixels p_1 and p_2 is in one of the three dimensions greater than 2 cm, it cannot be the same object in the 3D space, even though it is connected in the binary image. Thus, this pixel is label with a new value incremented by one. Note that using this approach the upper part and the lower part of a king can be separately labeled. This parts are joined together if their position overlap.

The labeling algorithm mentioned above creates a graph with a vertex for each labeled region as proposed by Kraus [8]. The first pixel of a blob receives the first label and the label is added as vertex to the graph. If a collision between two labeled regions appears, the blob is inspected if both labeled regions are connected in the 3D space. If the euclidian distance of both labeled regions is under a defined threshold, the algorithm connects the two labeled regions in the graph with an edge. Thus, every blob which contains different labeled regions results in a tree in the graph, as depicted in Figure 7. The binary image acquired from the Kinect sensor contains much noise and thus, the objects have no clean horizontal and vertical edges. Due to this issue, the labeling algorithm results in many small labeled regions, which belong to the same object. The complexity to solve the created collison trees is higher on the binary image, than on an image with clean edges.

The returned tree stores the pixel p_{ij} where the collision has been detected and its corresponding label. Connected regions with different labels result in connected vertices in the graph. To resolve the collisions, these trees have to be eliminated. Therefore all child-vertices receive the label from the parent vertex, thus connected regions with different labels result in one bigger region with a unique label. The child nodes are then removed from the graph. This results in a graph with non-connected vertices, like the vertices 3 and 7 in Figure 7. After successfully resolving the collisions, the 3D object's cluster is passed to the classifier.

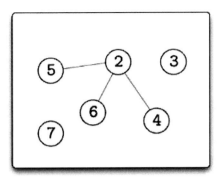

Fig. 7. Depicts a collision tree, proceeded by the labeling algorithm. This collision tree has to be solved as presented in [8].

4.3   Classification

The classification algorithm takes the 3D vertices for each detected object and tries to classify it into the following possible objects: *i)* pawn, *ii)* king, *iii)* king on one pawn, *iv)* king on two pawns or *v)* enemy robot. The passed-in vertices are analyzed for the highest point, which is the first classifier. If the height is 5 cm it may be a pawn. If the height is 25 cm it is analyzed as a king and if the height is 30 cm or 35 cm it is analyzed as a king on one or two pawns, respectively. If classification fails, the object is handled as enemy robot, since those can vary in size and shape and thus general classification cannot be defined easily.

The used classification technique for the pawns and the king is based on the Gaussian Least Mean Squares (LMS) algorithm and the computation of the center of the game elements. To uniquely compute the center coordinates of a circle, at least three or more points on its border are needed.

Figure 8 depicts the computation of the circle's center coordinates. Therefore two points at a time are connected to a line, resulting in lines $\overline{P_1P_2}$, $\overline{P_1P_3}$ and $\overline{P_2P_3}$. The intersection of the perpendicular bisector of the side lines represents the center M. The object's vertices on a height between 3 cm and 3.5 cm are used to compute M. For a valid game element these vertices should normally represent the round socket of the game element. Thus, out of the vertex' x- and y-coordinates, a linear algebraic system is constructed as in Equation (5). The values A, B, C are substituted out of the point's x- and y-components (see Equation (6)).

$$A + B(-x_1) + C(-y_1) = -(x_1^2 + y_1^2) \tag{5}$$

$$\begin{aligned} A &:= x_m^2 + y_m^2 - r^2 \\ B &:= 2x_m \\ C &:= 2y_m \end{aligned} \tag{6}$$

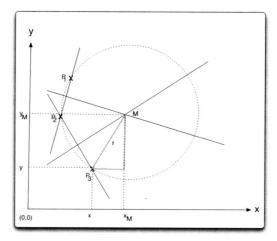

Fig. 8. Depicts the schematic approach to compute the center M of a circle from three points (P_1, P_2, P_3) on its borderline. The orange triangle depicts the theorem of Pythagoras to calculate the radius r. This is done analogous for each line connecting the given points.

The projection of the Kinect's depth data results normally in much more than only three vertices on the height between 3 cm and 3.5 cm for the object, resulting in an overdetermined equation system of the form:

$$
\begin{aligned}
\underbrace{\begin{matrix}
A + B(-x_1) + C(-y_1) = -(x_1^2 + y_1^2)\\
A + B(-x_2) + C(-y_2) = -(x_2^2 + y_2^2)\\
A + B(-x_3) + C(-y_3) = -(x_3^2 + y_3^2)\\
\vdots\\
A + B(-x_n) + C(-y_n)
\end{matrix}}_{\mathbf{Ax}} = \underbrace{-(x_n^2 + y_n^2)}_{\mathbf{b}}
\end{aligned}
\tag{7}
$$

Here, n represents the number of vertices provided by the Kinect sensor to do the computation of the circle's center. Systems of this form cannot be solved exactly, an error value $\mathbf{e}$ needs to be introduced, see Equation (8). The equation system as shown in Equation (7) is solved by using the Gaussian LMS technique.

$$
\mathbf{Ax} = \mathbf{b} + \mathbf{e} \text{ with error vector } \mathbf{e} = \begin{pmatrix} e_1 \\ e_2 \\ \vdots \\ e_n \end{pmatrix}
\tag{8}
$$

To solve an overdetermined linear algebraic system the Gaussian normal equation is computed by multiplying the transposed matrix $\mathbf{A}^T$ from the left hand side to each side of the equation:

$$
\mathbf{A}^T \cdot \mathbf{Ax} = \mathbf{A}^T \cdot \mathbf{b}
\tag{9}
$$

This equation can now be solved uniquely for $\mathbf{x} = (A, B, C)$, where $\mathbf{x}$ contains the substituted values A, B, C. $\mathbf{x}$ is needed to compute the error $\mathbf{e}$ as $\mathbf{e} = \mathbf{A}\mathbf{x} - \mathbf{b}$. $\mathbf{x}$ has now to be re-substituted as follows:

$$
\begin{aligned}
x_m &= B/2 \\
y_m &= C/2 \\
r^2 &= x_m^2 + y_m^2 - A
\end{aligned}
\tag{10}
$$

After re-substituting A, B and C, the center of the socket $M = [x_m, y_m]$ and the radius r of the object is known. The classification of the element and computation of its center is declared valid if r is between 10 cm $\pm$ 2 cm, giving a sufficient uncertainty of wrongly measured depth information due to movement of the robot and the inaccuracy of the Kinect's depth data projection. The resulting error of the LMS algorithm corresponds to $\|\mathbf{e}\|^2 = e_1^2 + e_2^2 + ... + e_m^2$.

5   Analysis and Results

This section presents the validation of the previously described object detection with the Kinect. First, the Kinect is compared to a Hokuyo laser scanner. Then three object-detection runs with different constellations of the game elements are presented. All tests are carried out on the blue start position on the game field. Tests have shown, that the object detection works as well while the robot is moving. However, due to bouncing of the robot, the Kinect provides noisier data and thus the accuracy of the object detection decreases. The results are presented in the following.

5.1   Hokuyo Laser Scanner Compared to Kinect Sensor

One main advantage of the Kinect is, that it is located on top of the robot and returns a 3D reconstruction of the game field. A laser scanner installed in the robot samples the environment on a height of approximate 2 cm, which is an obvious disadvantage, since game elements hidden behind elements nearer to the robot cannot be detected. Figure 9(a) shows the actual detected pawns; 9(b) the raw data with the object candidates as acquired from the Hokuyo laser. Another disadvantage is that the laser cannot distinguish between a pawn or a king.

Figure 10(a) shows the detected game elements on the game field; 10(b) the acquired point cloud constructed out of the depth data of the Kinect. With the Kinect the amount of detected elements is higher than with the laser-based approach. However, it can be seen in 10(a) that the elements are more inaccurate in their z-position the further they are away. This is a systematical error and is fixed by applying a linear equation to the z-positions. The Kinect-based object detection is validated in the next sections.

5.2   Object Detection Validation with the Kinect Sensor

The validation includes three different tests: $i)$ Ten pawns, $ii)$ Eight pawns and two kings and $iii)$ Four kings. Each test contains five random constellations

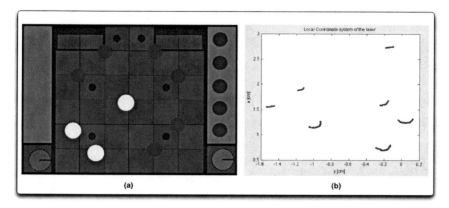

Fig. 9. (a) Depicts the detected pawns with their position on the game field for a possible start configuration. The grey circles represent the game elements, not detected with the laser, the yellow ones are detected. 9(b) Visualizes the laser data with detected pawn candidates, for the same start configuration as in 9(a).

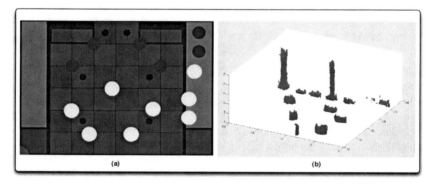

Fig. 10. (a) Presents the detected game elements with the Kinect for the same start configuration as for the laser. The grey circles represent not detected game elements, while the yellow colored are detected with the Kinect. Compared to Figure 9 more game elements are detected. (b) Visualizes the point cloud as projected from the Kinect's depth information, for the same start configuration as (a).

of the game elements and for each 100 depth images are taken into account. Figure 11(a) depicts a possible constellation of the game elements on the game field, 11(b) depicts the corresponding depth image of the objects of interest.

Table 1 shows the mean detection rates for the first test run. In the worst case, only six out of ten pawns are detected, while in the best case all pawns are detected. The average minimal detection rate 72% and the average rate over all runs is 84.4%.

The results of the second test are shown in Table 2. The mean detection rates for kings and elements of the five different runs with each 100 depth images as the test before are shown. In the worst case, seven out of ten elements are

Fig. 11. (a) Shows the camera image of the Kinect, the game elements in the field of view for the Kinect are visualized. (b) Shows the depth image corresponding to the camera image. It only contains the objects of interest. The floor and depth information outside of the game field are already filtered.

Table 1. Results for random constellations of 10 pawns, with 100 captured depth images each

Run	Min	Max	Pawns
1	8	10	8.49
2	6	10	7.97
3	7	10	8.53
4	8	10	8.75
5	7	10	8.45
Average	7.2	10	8.44

Table 2. Results for random constellations of 8 pawns and 2 kings, with 100 captured depth images each

Run	Min	Max	Elements	Kings	Pawns
		Kings and pawns			
1	7	10	8.23	0.95	7.28
2	8	10	9.24	1.75	7.49
3	8	10	8.9	1.46	7.48
4	7	9	8.32	0.94	7.38
5	7	10	9.01	1.61	7.40
Average	7.4	9.8	8.74	1.34	7.41

detected, while in the best case all elements are detected. The average minimal detection rate is 74%, the average detection over all runs is 87.4% elements. In average 1.34 kings out of two are detected. The detection rate of the pawns is 7.41 out of 8.

The results of the kings-only test are shown in Table 3. The structure of the tests is the same as the previous validations. In this test two kings, one king stacked on one pawn and one king stacked on two pawns are placed on the game

Table 3. Results for random constellations of 2 kings, 1 king on a pawn and 1 king on two pawns with 100 captured depth images each

Run	Min	Max	Average	King	King on Pawn	King on two Pawns
1	2	4	3.28	1.39	0.94	0.94
2	2	4	2.93	1.05	0.94	0.94
3	2	4	3.09	1.21	0.93	0.94
4	3	4	3.65	1.85	0.85	0.94
5	3	4	3.76	1.88	0.94	0.94
Average	2.4	4.0	3.34	1.48	0.92	0.94

field. In the worst case, two out of four elements are detected, while in the best case all elements are detected. The average minimal detection rate is 2.4 out of 4 elements, which means over 50% of the elements are detected. Since the robot moves on the game field and the object detection provides constantly the position of the objects even with only half of the elements detected a satisfying object detection is achieved. However, in the normal case, the average detection is 3.34 elements out of 4. This is a detection rate of 83.5%.

This validation suggests that the object detection works reliably with the Kinect. The reached detection rate is approximate 84.4% and thus a higher detection rate than with the Hokuyo laser is archived. However, the field of view of the Kinect is limited to only 57 degrees, compared to the Hokuyo laser with a field of view of 240 degrees.

6   Conclusions and Future Work

This paper presented a Kinect-based approach to detect the game elements for the Eurobot Challenge 2011. The depth information provided by the Kinect is translated into a 3D point cloud containing only the objects of concern in the game area. Each 3D point of a detected object cluster is passed to a classifier which categorizes the objects as either the different game elements or as the enemy robot. As primary classifier the height of the objects is used. The second classifier is the roundness of the sockets of the objects. Therefore, an overdetermined linear algebraic system is constructed and solved with the Gaussian LMS algorithm. Thus, the center of the object is computed and if the radius is 10 cm within a given tolerance and the squared error acceptable, the object is accepted as game element. Tests have shown that the object detection works reliable both in a non-moving and moving robot, with a detection rate of approximate 84%. It can be stated that the presented object detection allows the robot to autonomously detect the game elements and the enemy robot.

One flaw of the presented object detection is that it does not distinguish between a king and a queen. Future work could include the design of further classifier to distinguish between these game elements. However, since the score-points of a king or queen are almost the same, the implementation does not focus on distinguishing between them. Furthermore, classifier for the enemy robot could be introduced to distinguish between the robot and unclassified objects. Once the enemy robot is classified, a Kalman filter could be used to follow the enemy. Another area of interest is the landmark-based localization with the Kinect senor. Therefore, the landmarks could be uniquely defined shapes which would allow for the robot to measure the distance to these landmarks.

References

1. Chen, X.N., Xia, Q., Zhang, S.H., Zhou, Y., HeNan, C.N.: Province. 3D Laser Scanner System For Surveying And Engineering. In: Proc. of the ISPRS Joint Conf. of 3rd Int. Symp. Remote Sensing and Data Fusion Over Urban Areas and 5th Int. Symp. Remote Sensing of Urban Areas, Tempe, AZ, USA, pp. 14–16 (March 2005)
2. Droeschel, D., Holz, D., Stuckler, J., Behnke, S.: Using time-of-flight cameras with active gaze control for 3D collision avoidance. In: 2010 IEEE International Conference on Robotics and Automation (ICRA), pp. 4035–4040. IEEE, Los Alamitos (2010)
3. Ester, M., Kriegel, H.P., Sander, J., Xu, X.: A density-based algorithm for discovering clusters in large spatial databases with noise. In: Proceedings of the 2nd International Conference on Knowledge Discovery and Data mining, vol. 1996, pp. 226–231. AAAI Press, Portland (1996)
4. Freenect Library, http://www.freenect.com/ (visited on 2011-03-20)
5. Intellab. Intel Lab Seattle, http://ils.intel-research.net/projects/rgbd (visited on 2011-03-20)
6. Jain, R., Kasturi, R., Schunck, B.G.: Machine vision, 5th edn. McGraw-Hill, New York (1995)
7. Kinect, http://www.xbox.com/de-de/kinect/ (visited on 2011-03-20)
8. Kraus, K.: Photogrammetry: Vol. 1: Fundamentals and standard processes (1992)
9. Obdržálek, D., Basovník, S., Mach, L., Mikulík, A.: Detecting scene elements using maximally stable colour regions. In: Gottscheber, A., Obdržálek, D., Schmidt, C. (eds.) EUROBOT 2009. Communications in Computer and Information Science, vol. 82, pp. 107–115. Springer, Heidelberg (2010)
10. Kreylos, O., http://www.idav.ucdavis.edu/~okreylos/ (visited on 2011-03-20)
11. Open Kinect, http://openkinect.org/wiki/ (visited on 2011-03-20)
12. Prime Sense, http://www.primesense.com/ (visited on 2011-03-20)
13. Weingarten, J.W., Gruener, G., Siegwart, R.: A state-of-the-art 3D sensor for robot navigation. In: IEEE/RSJ International Conference on Intelligent Robots and Systems, vol. 3, pp. 2155–2160. IEEE, Los Alamitos (2004)

Identification Based Model of Ultrasonic Sensor

Jaroslav Hanzel, Marian Kĺúčik, Ladislav Jurišica, and Anton Vitko

Institute of Control and Industrial Informatics,
Faculty of Electrical Engineering and Information Technology
STU in Bratislava,
Ilkovičova 3, 81219 Bratislava, Slovakia
{jaroslav.hanzel,marian.klucik,ladislav.jurisica,anton.vitko}@stuba.sk
http://www.urpi.stuba.sk

Abstract. The contribution deals with mathematical modelling of the ultrasonic sensors. Design of the model is based on the data obtained by identification of the sensor. Novel methodology for determination of the sonar radiation cone width is presented. This procedure allows to specify the shape of the sonar radiation cone. The identification of the Polaroid sonar revealed some yet not modelled properties. The proposed mathematical sonar model is able to define the measured data. The more accurate sensor model allows the mobile robot to move in the environment more safely.

Keywords: Ultrasonic rangefinder, identification of the sonar radiation cone width, mathematical model of ultrasonic sensor.

1 Introduction

Fully autonomous performance of given tasks by mobile robots is the main goal of recent research in the field of mobile robotics. Autonomous operation of mobile robots is strongly dependent on the ability to perceive working environment provided by a sensor system, which often comprises of ultrasonic range finders. This paper deals with a design of an advanced ultrasonic sensor model capable to obtain more accurate information about the environment. Ultrasonic range finders (sonars) are characterized by a number of advantageous features such as ease of use, relatively low cost, safety, modest realisation, and thus they have a very broad possibility of exploitation in various fields of science and industry. In mobile robotics, they are used to measure distances to the obstacles in the robot neighbourhood to ensure collision-free motion and navigation in familiar as well as in unfamiliar environment. Despite all the advances, the application of ultrasonic sensors for the creation of the robot environment representation is linked with a variety of problems such as multiple reflections or extensive wide angle of the ultrasonic beam. The problems rise from the physical nature of the operating principle of these systems and resulting data from the sensing process is loaded with a variety of uncertainty. Use of an appropriate and adjusted sensory model is successful approach to minimize the amount of uncertainty in processing

D. Obdržálek and A. Gottscheber (Eds.): EUROBOT 2011, CCIS 161, pp. 144–157, 2011.

of measured data to a robot navigational map. Such advanced sensory model can be constructed on the basis of data obtained by identification of essential sonar parameters.

2   Ultrasonic Sensor

Ultrasonic systems for non-contact distance measuring are devices often used to measure the relative distances in many technical fields. The ultrasonic range finders work according to a simple principle: a packet of ultrasonic waves is generated and the resulting echo is detected. The time elapsed between a transmission and a reception is assumed to be proportional to the distance of the sensed obstacle. Sonars are often incorporated in sensory systems of mobile robots. Thereafter, this paper refers to a Polaroid ultrasonic ranging system widely used in mobile robotics [8]. The acquired range readings can be utilised by many ways. One of them is the creation of the environment representation, which in principle is a map of the environment. The occupancy grid is a popular form of the representation of the robot's workspace [6]. Occupancy grids are usually used to express the spatial arrangement of the environment as its two-dimensional projection to the plane of the robot's motion. Each cell of the grid represents definite area of space and known information about it. Main problem in map building algorithms is varied uncertainty of measured sonar data. There are several methods of handling data uncertainty and occupancy grid calculation known [5], [9].

There are basically three main sources of measurement uncertainty in the process of determination of presence of an object and its relative distance with the ultrasonic sensors. First, the measured distance r is affected by an error. In the case of the Polaroid range finder, which can detect distances from 0.15 to $10.7m$, the error of measurement is about $\pm 1\%$ of the measured distance over the entire range [8]. This uncertainty is caused by the characteristics of air such as its temperature, humidity, turbulence and pressure [10]. The second uncertainty is a phenomenon of multiple reflections, which may occur in the case that the incidence angle of signal to the obstacle is larger than a so-called *critical angle* which is strongly dependent on the surface characteristics. In this case the reflection of the signal is mainly specular and the sensor may receive the ultrasonic beam after multiple reflections, which is called a *long reading*, or it may even disappear. Therefore, in order to return a significant range reading, the angle of incidence on the object surface has to be smaller than the critical angle.

The third source of uncertainty results from the propagation of the ultrasonic signal to the space in the form of a cone with an apex in the centre of the sensor active element and an axis in the scanning direction. So the exact angular position of the object reflecting the echo might not be determined, because it may occur somewhere along the arc with the radius of the measured distance. The angle of radiation can be in fact fairly wide. The transducer can be treated as a plane circular piston in order to analyse its radiation characteristics, which is given by the *radiation directivity function* [2], [8]

$$P(\theta) = 2\frac{J_1(ka\sin(\theta))}{ka\sin(\theta)} \,, \tag{1}$$

where J_1 is the Bessel function of the first order, $k = 2\pi/l$ is the wave number dependent on the wavelength l, a is the piston radius and θ is the azimuthal angle measured with respect to the radiation cone axis. For our sensor the valid values are $a = 0.01921m$ and $l = c/f$, where c is the sound speed in air and $f = 49.410kHz$ [8].

For modelling of the uncertainty given by the wide radiation cone of the sonar sensor in angular resolution, an *angular radiation function* f_a was introduced [5], [7]. Since the intensity of the ultrasonic waves decreases to zero at the borders of the radiation cone, the degree of certainty of some area to be occupied by obstacle or to be empty, is assumed to be higher for points close to the radiation cone axis. This is realised by the angular modulation function

$$f_a(\theta) = \begin{cases} P(\theta), & 0 \le |\theta| \le \theta_k \\ 0, & |\theta| > \theta_k \end{cases} \,, \tag{2}$$

where $P(\theta)$ is the radiation directivity function (1), θ is angular distance measured with respect to the radiation cone axis and θ_k is limiting angle of the radiation cone of given sensor.

Limiting angles of the radiation cones are given by following equation [2]:

$$ka\sin(\theta_k) = 3.83 \,, \tag{3}$$

where k is the wave number and a is the piston radius.

Mathematical model of angular uncertainty of measurement requires a knowledge of the angular range in which the sensor is able to detect an obstacle. The theoretical value of limiting angle for the sensor can be calculated from an equation (3). However, if the sensor parameters are unknown, or the more precise value is needed for sensory model, the identification of the limiting angle is the only way of determining its real value.

3   Sonar Identification Method

Despite a wide variety of convenient and useful features, the frequently used ultrasonic sensors also have relatively few undesirable features. These properties significantly hinder their full and effective use, especially the uncertainty of an angular location of the object reflecting ultrasonic signal. This uncertainty causes inability to accurately determine the location of obstacles in the circular arc with an angle equal to the size of the radiation angle and the radius of the measured distance. There are not many ways to minimize this uncertainty. The options include the use of more accurate sensor with a narrower cone angle, narrowing the radiation cone by its mechanical modification or using a larger number of

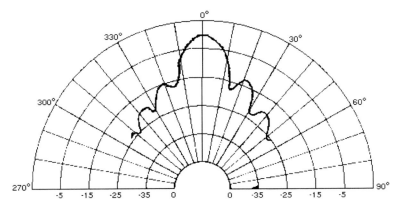

Fig. 1. Polaroid sensor radiation characteristics at sound frequency 50 kHz [8]

sensors with appropriate deployment to narrow the radiation cone using their mutual acoustic interference [1].

Mathematical modelling of ultrasound sensor uncertainties requires accurate values of certain parameters of the used sensor. It is required to know the angular range in which the sensor can detect the obstacle for the mathematical model of angular uncertainty. This value can be roughly determined from the sensor emission characteristics (Fig. 1) given by the manufacturer [8] or by its identification which is obviously more accurate. Any methods for determination of the exact radiation characteristics of ultrasonic sensors were not found in any available sources. Also measuring method for the radiation pattern depicted in Fig. 1 was not specified in the materials supplied by the manufacturer of the sensor [8]. Analysis of given radiation characteristics gives estimated size of 25° for the radiation cone angle. This value is also commonly used in robotics literature in the case of Polaroid sensor. Perhaps the only attempt to verify this value by the measurements is published in [1]. These facts leads to development of a method for determination of the size of the radiation cone angle. Identified value can be consequently used to create a precise mathematical model of the used sensor.

3.1   Identification Procedure

Development of the method was based on a detailed analysis of the sensor planar emission characteristics published by the manufacturer and shown in Fig. 1 [8]. It is clear that the characteristics consists of multiple "lobes" called the primary, secondary, etc.. The radiated acoustic signal is mainly distributed in the single primary lobe. The lobes of higher order are symmetrically duplicated by the cone axis. The primary lobe is located in the centre of the cone symmetrically divided into two parts by the axis of the radiation cone. The aim was to determine the sensor parameter, which is called the *effective angle of the radiation cone* (EARC). This parameter means the width of the radiation cone, which actually applies at the measuring distance to obstacles. After this manner the defined sensor parameter reflects practically usable ultrasonic signal cone angle and does not distinguish whether the radiation cone consists only of primary or of higher order lobes too.

Identification of the EARC size is based on the conditions close to real situations of the ultrasonic sensor utilization. Thus measured beam angle is essentially identical to angle which applies in the mapping of an unknown area occupied with a number of obstacles of various quality and character. The determined value of radiation cone angle is the one maximally possible, which in view of scanning obstacles is the worst case of the horizontal angle uncertainty. In real environments, the reflecting conditions are worse in the vast majority of cases, as compared with those in identification measurement and smaller width of the radiation cone is applied in the reflection. Yet such cases can occur, hence the determined cone width is the searched sensor parameter. EARC identification principle is as follows and is shown in Fig. 2.

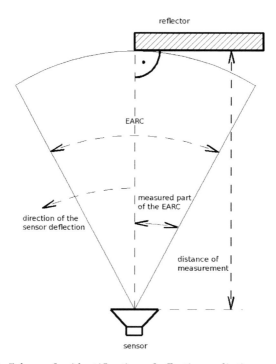

Fig. 2. Scheme for identification of effective radiation cone angle

The ultrasonic sensor is placed pointing to the free space. Essential aim of the identification procedure is to measure the size EARC at different distances. Obtained values enable to determine whether the size of the radiation cone angle varies with distance. Therefore the reflector echoing sent ultrasonic signal is placed at chosen distances. Real obstacles in robot's working environment have different sizes and shapes. Moreover, the obstacles are formed from miscellaneous materials. The reflection of the signal by the obstacle is strongly associated with the properties of its surface and it also depends on the angle at which signal hit the reflecting surface of the obstacle. The signal is reflected towards the transmitter if it hit the surface at an angle which is smaller than critical angle. Otherwise the signal is bounced away from the transmitter. It is important to consider these facts. The relative position of the sensor and the reflecting surface is chosen with the signal vertically impinging on the surface throughout the whole measurement. This selection effectively eliminates the surface properties of the reflecting object related to the critical angle. Such configuration is also ideal for a signal reflection and the maximum possible amount of energy transmitted into that direction returns back to the sensor. However, the surface properties play role even in such measuring configuration. If the surface has some absorption properties in relation to the ultrasonic signal, or if the surface has ability to distract the signal, only portion of the impinged signal returns back to the sensor. Therefore, in order to bounce maximum energy, a hard and smooth material is chosen as the reflective surface. The size of the reflector has also influence on signal reflection and it must be sufficiently large to simulate the ideal case of reflection, in which the maximum amount of acoustic energy is reflected to the receiver. The key element of the identification method is a mutual position of the sensor and reflector. The reflector is placed with its reflection surface plane being perpendicular to the axis connecting the sensor and the side edge of the reflector as shown in Fig. 2.

As mentioned above, ultrasonic signal beam spreads into the space in the form of radiation cone with spherical front part. The amount of acoustic energy gradually decreases from the cone axis to its boundaries. Determination of the radiation cone borders consists of gradually reducing amount of energy emitted towards the reflector. The requirement of vertical impingement on the reflector of gradually reduced ultrasonic signal is achieved by gradual deflection of the sensor. It is conveniently accomplished by horizontal rotation of the sensor with sufficiently small steps. The rotation begins from the base position with radiation cone axis directed perpendicularly to the reflecting plane and proceeds to one side as shown in the Fig. 2. At every step of the measurement the reflecting surface is vertically hit by diminished part of the signal and rest of the signal spread further into free space. Such gradual decrease in strength of the acoustic signal reaches the point, where the reflected signal is incapable to activate the receiver and a signal loss occurs. Thus the receiver is able to capture the echo to the particular measurement step. This sensor deflection threshold step determines a boundary of the radiation cone. This deflection step also defines so-called *limiting angle* of the radiation cone at a given distance and within that angle the sensor is able to detect the presence of obstacles. Achieving the limiting angle is indicated by the absence of echoes in successive deflection steps or by measuring distances considerably greater than the distance to the reflecting surface. This case occurs if the signal is reflected from an object situated behind the reflecting surface. Therefore the measurement should be performed in an environment large enough to safely identify the source of reflection. After this manner only the limiting angle of the radiation cone at one side of the cone axis is obtained. The second limiting angle is analogously determined with placement of the reflector on the opposite side of the axis connecting the sensor with the edge of the reflector and by deflection of the sensor to the opposite side. In this way it is possible to determine the effective angle of the radiation cone for any ultrasonic sensor with sufficient accuracy.

3.2   Experimental Results

The experiment was performed in a relatively large open room. The necessary tools were arranged as it is shown in the Fig. 2. As the reflecting surface was chosen a smooth board with dimensions $1.5 \times 0.6m$. The measuring system was placed at height of $1m$ to exclude theoretical possibility to capture the reflection from uneven floor. Reflector was placed at regular distance intervals with a step $0.5m$ in the range from 0.5 to $4.5m$. The sensor was deflected from the zero position when the cone axis is perpendicular to the reflecting surface plane (Fig. 2), to maximal deflection of $90°$ with increments by $0.9°$. Distances obtained by turning the sensor from the zero position to a maximum deflection of $90°$ and accordingly backward to the zero position, were recorded in one measurement. This procedure was repeated 10 times for each measuring. By this manner 20 distance values for each sensor deflection step were obtained. In the evaluation process of measurements, the angle of the sensor deflection presenting a loss of reflected signal was considered the angular limit of the EARC. Irregular receipt of the reflected signal was observed for deflections in the vicinity of EARC edge. It was manifested as various number of distance values corresponding to reflection as well as loss of signal. The value which appropriately represents the collected measurements for each sensor deflection angle allow to identify the boundaries of EARC. The median of the data set is such suitable representational value, because it determines the predominant number of measured distances. To verify the symmetry of EARC, the experiment was carried out also for the other side

Table 1. Measured values of the left and right limiting angle of the Polaroid sensor

Measuring distance [m]	Left limiting angle [°]	Right limiting angle [°]
0.5	22.5	19.8
1.0	21.6	12.6
1.5	20.7	12.6
2.0	20.7	12.6
2.5	20.7	12.6
3.0	20.7	12.6
3.5	19.8	12.6
4.0	18.0	12.6
4.5	11.7	11.7

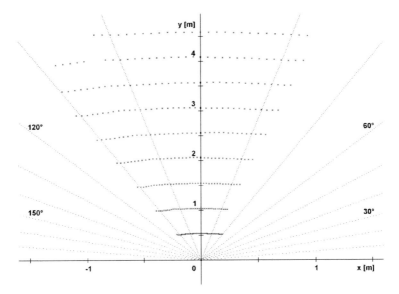

Fig. 3. Representative values of the measured data sets

of the radiation cone. Subsequently two EARC limit values for given distance from the sensor were obtained, corresponding to the left and to the right side of the cone. The Polaroid sensor limiting angles are listed in Table 1 and the medians of the measured data sets are shown in Fig. 3.

The measurement results show the properties of the used sonar. The Polaroid sensor has significantly asymmetric radiating cone, which is well documented in the Table 1 and Fig. 3. The right side of the cone is clearly wider than the left side, even though at a distance of $0.5m$ the difference is minimal and the limiting angles are approximately $20°$. This fact can be explained by the influence of secondary lobes. At short distances they have enough power to cause a reliable reflection by the obstacles. The secondary lobe becomes evident at the right side of the cone also at a longer distance, and it deforms the cone into the centrally asymmetrical shape. The left side of the cone is wide $12.6°$ at these distances, and almost exactly matches the value presented in the literature. Almost no narrowing of the EARC occurred in the measurement range. A slight decrease was observed only at a distance of $4.5m$, but gradual decline at greater distances was not possible to verify due to the room space restrictions. However a distance of $5m$ is sufficient for practical mobile robot navigation.

4   Asymmetric Sonar Model

Identification of the radiation cone angle revealed important facts relating to the measured sensor. A significant asymmetry of radiation cone with respect to the cone axis has been found. The identification also confirmed the dissipation of ultrasonic signal in the environment at the borders of the cone with increasing

Table 2. Parameters of the directivity function of the Polaroid sensor

Wave number $k[m^{-1}]$	Piston radius $a[m]$
903.791	0.01921

distance from the sensor. When designing a sensor model considering the real properties of the sensor, the above facts have to be taken into account.

The mathematical models of sonar, which were used to create robotic naviga-tional maps [5], [9], [3], model the reduction in intensity of ultrasound waves with angular distance from the cone axis by introducing the angular modulation func-tion (2). This function returns the values in the range from 1 to 0, defined by the directivity function (1) for both halves of the radiation cone. The values corre-spond to the value interval of the angular distance given by the cone axis and the limiting angle of the radiation cone. Only the projection of the cone in a plane parallel to the floor is considered. The size of the limiting angle is determined by the wave number and the radius of the active element (piston) of the sensor (Table 2). The identification of the EARC revealed a difference between the real limiting angle of the radiation cone and theoretically expected value which, for the Polaroid sensor, is 12.7°. Moreover, the size of the limiting angle varies with a distance and it is not equal for the individual halves of the cone.

The angular modulation function mentioned above (2) assumes theoretically perfectly symmetrical cone in respect to the cone axis, however the real ultrasonic radiation cone fails to satisfy these expectations. Modification of the angular modulation function enables to model the observed properties of real sensor. The essential part of angular modulation function is the directivity function associated with size of the limiting angle. So the directivity function allows to adapt the width of the radiation cone to its real size. For this reason, a *modified directivity function* given by the following formula was introduced:

$$P(\theta, \alpha) = 2\frac{J_1(\alpha ka \sin(\theta))}{\alpha ka \sin(\theta)} . \tag{4}$$

This function has two parameters. In addition to the angular distance from the cone axis θ, their values also depend on the parameter α called angular modification coefficient. By this factor the width of the directivity function can be changed, and thus the size of the limiting angle. By this way the directivity function can be adjusted to the real width of the radiation cone. The sensor iden-tification provides the dimensions of real limiting angles for various distances, thus it is necessary to calculate the corresponding values of the angular mod-ification coefficients. A functional relationship between coefficient α according to the sensor parameters and the detected limiting angle is obtained from the condition (3) and is given as follows:

$$\alpha = \frac{3.83}{ka \sin(\theta_k)} , \tag{5}$$

where θ_k is limiting angle of the radiation cone in respect to the cone axis, k is wave number and a is radius of the sensor moving element (piston).

The design of modified angular modulation function is based on analysis of measured limiting angles introduced in the Table 1 and Fig. 3. In the figure there is an apparent asymmetry of the sensor radiation cone in respect to the cone axis. This implies a different limiting angle for a given distance for both sides of the cone. Thereafter the convention introduced in the previous chapter is used. The cone side located in the Fig. 3 on the left from the cone axis (angular distance from the axis $\theta > 0$), is referred as left side of the radiation cone and side lying to the right from the axis (angular distance $\theta < 0$) is referred as right side. They are denoted as L and R in the relations and parameter names.

Since the angular modulation function is symmetrical in its original form, it cannot capture the asymmetry of radiation cone of the real sensor. This feature requires to model the real radiation cone with two different functions, left and right angular modulation function associated with left and right side of the radiation cone. This composite angular modulation function can be expressed by the following formula:

$$f_a(\theta, \rho) = \begin{cases} f_{aL}(\theta, \rho), & \theta > 0 \\ 1, & \theta = 0 \\ f_{aR}(\theta, \rho), & \theta < 0 \end{cases} . \tag{6}$$

The resulting *modified angular modulation function* is a function of angular distance θ from the axis of the cone and the radial distance ρ from the sensor surface. It consists of three parts: function $f_{aL}(\theta, \rho)$ modelling the the left side, function $f_{aR}(\theta, \rho)$ modelling the right side of the radiation cone and a constant with value of 1. This constant value for zero angular distance solves the ambiguity in assigning cone axis itself to the two functions.

Dependence of the modified angular function on radial distance is necessary for modelling EARC size change with the shift of distance from the sensor. The data analysis obtained by identifying the sensor showed the gradual uneven narrowing of the EARC. For the Polaroid sensor, the radiation cone is relatively wide for a small distance from the sensor. Though at the certain distance, the step change of its width towards its lower values was observed. This decrease of the EARC size seems to leap because the measurement was carried out with a certain step ($0.5m$). In fact, the change with distance is apparently gradual between measurement steps. As the change took place relatively quickly between two consecutive steps of measurement, it is considered as a step change. This conclusion is also confirmed by the fact that, with gradual increase of distance, the size of the EARC maintains roughly constant value in relatively large range of distances. In large measuring distance, almost at the end of scanning range, the EARC size decreased rapidly to a new value. It should be noted that these sudden changes occurred at different distances for the left and right side of the radiation cone. In conclusion, the analysed changes in the EARC size can be summarized as follows:

- Decrease of the width of the radiation cone is relatively quick at certain distance from the sensor.

- These distances are not equal for the left and right side of the radiation cone.
- The width of the radiation cone on each side is, at intervals of distance between the width changes, approximately constant.

In order to model these properties of real sensors by simple way, the sensing radial range is dissected in both halves of the radiation cone in a number of radial segments. In practice it was convenient to dissect the radiation cone to 3 radial segments. In the following text the radial segments will be designated with letters L and R in combination with the sequential index of the segment away from the sensor. The radial partition of the radiation cone results in division of the function domain of the functions $f_{aL}(\theta, \rho)$ and $f_{aR}(\theta, \rho)$ in dimension of argument ρ also in three parts. The resulting relations for these functions are given as follows:

$$f_{aL}(\theta, \rho) = \begin{cases} f_{aL1}(\theta), & 0 \le \rho < \rho_{L1} \\ f_{aL2}(\theta), & \rho_{L1} \le \rho < \rho_{L2} \\ f_{aL3}(\theta), & \rho_{L2} \le \rho \end{cases} \text{ and} \tag{7}$$

$$f_{aR}(\theta, \rho) = \begin{cases} f_{aR1}(\theta), & 0 \le \rho < \rho_{R1} \\ f_{aR2}(\theta), & \rho_{R1} \le \rho < \rho_{R2} \\ f_{aR3}(\theta), & \rho_{R2} \le \rho \end{cases}, \tag{8}$$

where $\rho_{L1}, \rho_{L2}, \rho_{R1}, \rho_{R2}$, are *radial limits* of the radial segments of left and right side of the radiation cone.

Functions $f_{aL1}(\theta), f_{aL2}(\theta), f_{aL3}(\theta), f_{aR1}(\theta), f_{aR2}(\theta), f_{aR3}(\theta)$ are angular modulation functions given by following general relation:

$$f_{ak}(\theta) = \begin{cases} P(\theta, \alpha_k), & |\theta| \le \theta_k \\ 0, & |\theta| > \theta_k \end{cases}, \text{ for } k = \{L1, L2, L3, R1, R2, R3\}, \tag{9}$$

where the $P(\theta, \alpha)$ is modified directional function (4) and θ_k are the limiting angles of particular segments. These six functions model angular uncertainty of the ultrasonic sensor for individual radial segments. Values of radial and angular boundaries of radial segments were determined from the results of identification of the EARC. However the determination of the respective values was ambiguous. Therefore the angular boundaries of the segments were chosen, so that they are either identical with the limiting angles or slightly larger to cover any fluctuations of their values. The resulting values of radial and angular boundaries are listed in Table 3 and Table 4.

Table 3. Radial limits of radial segments of the asymmetric radiation cone model

$\rho_{L1}[m]$	$\rho_{L2}[m]$	$\rho_{R1}[m]$	$\rho_{R2}[m]$
1.5	3.5	1.0	4.0

Table 4. Angular limits of radial segments of the asymmetric model of the radiation cone

$\theta_{L1}[°]$	$\theta_{L2}[°]$	$\theta_{L3}[°]$	$\theta_{R1}[°]$	$\theta_{R2}[°]$	$\theta_{R3}[°]$
22.5	20.7	11.7	19.8	12.6	11.7

Table 5. The angular modification coefficients of the radial segments

α_{L1}	α_{L2}	α_{L3}	α_{R1}	α_{R2}	α_{R3}
0.576452	0.624086	1.087834	0.651237	1.011257	1.087834

Angular modification coefficients of the modified angular modulation function for particular radial segments of the radiation cone are listed in the following table.

The resultant shape of the asymmetric radiation cone is given by determined angular and radial boundaries of the radial segments and it is depicted in Fig. 4.

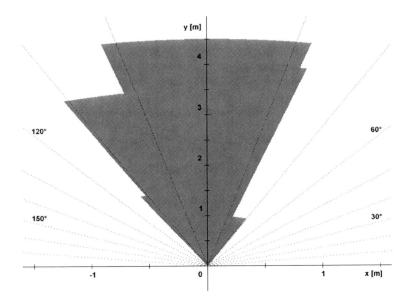

Fig. 4. Asymmetric model of radiation cone of the Polaroid sonar

5   Conclusion

Motion of the mobile robot in environment is dependent on information acquired by its sensory system. The sensory system of a common mobile robot is usually equipped with ultrasonic range-finders. These are used to measure a distance from the robot to a nearby obstacle in a given direction. The main disadvantage of the ultrasonic sensor is considerable amount of an uncertainty of various type embedded in the sensed data. Processing of the uncertain data results in inaccurate information about the environment. Thus minimisation of this uncertainty leads to the more accurate environment models and to improved robot motion in the working environment. The sensor model is a key element in the processing of gathered distance data. The mathematical models of the ultrasonic sensors used in mobile robotics are based on theoretical analysis of an ideal sonar. The proposed asymmetric model of the ultrasonic sensor is on the other hand based on data obtained by identification of the sensor really used. The identified parameter is the angular width of the sensor's radiation cone as the function of the measuring distance. Determination of this functional relation is accomplished by developed identification method. The procedure was successfully applied to identify the cone width of the Polaroid ultrasonic sensor. Acquired data revealed constriction of the radiation cone with increased measuring distance and its asymmetric shape. The proposed sensor model allows to reflect these new facts. Consequently the more accurate asymmetric sensor model simplifies the robot navigation tasks and makes them safer.

Acknowledgments. The work has been supported by VEGA grant 1/0690/09 and grant VMSP-P-0004-09. This support is very gratefully acknowledged.

References

1. Cao, A., Borenstein, J.: Experimental Characterization of Polaroid Ultrasonic Sensors in Single and Phased Array Configuration. In: Proceedings of the UGV Technology Conference at the 2002 SPIE AeroSense Symposium, Orlando, FL, April 1-5 (2002)
2. David, J., Cheeke, N.: Fundamentals and Applications of Ultrasonic Waves, April 18, p. 480. CRC Press, Boca Raton (2002) ISBN 0-8493-0130-0
3. Dekan, M., Duchoň, F.: Navigation of Autonomous Mobile Robot Using Ultrasonic and Infrared Sensors. In: Robotics in Education 2010: Proceedings of the 1st International Conference, September 16-17, pp. s.193–s.196. Slovak University of Technology, Bratislava (2010) ISBN 978-80-227-3353-3
4. Elfes, A.: Using occupancy grids for mobile robot perception and navigation. Computer Magazine, 46–57 (June 1989)
5. Gambino, F., Oriolo, G., Ulivi, G.: A comparison of three uncertainty calculus techniques for ultrasonic map building. In: 1996 SPIE International Symposium on Aerospace/Defense Sensing and Control-Applications of Fuzzy Logic Technology III, Orlando, USA, pp. 249–260 (1996)
6. Moravec, H.P., Elfes, A.E.: High Resolution Maps from Wide Angle Sonar, 1984. In: Proceedings of the 1985 IEEE International Conference on Robotics and Automation, St. Louis, USA, pp. 116–121 (March 1985)

7. Oriolo, G., Ulivi, G., Vendittelli, M.: Fuzzy maps: A new tool for mobile robot perception and planning. Journal of Robotic Systems 14(3), 179–197 (1997)
8. Polaroid ultrasonic ranging system handbook application note/technical papers (1992)
9. Ribo, M., Pinz, A.: A comparison of three uncertainty calculi for building sonar-based occupancy grids. Robotics and Autonomous Systems 35(3-4), 201–209 (2001)
10. Toman, M.: Ultrazvuk pre priestorové merania. AT&P Journal plus 2, roč. 7, s. 66–s. 75 (2001)

RoboCoP: A Protocol for Service-Oriented Robot Control Systems

Dmitry Kononchuk, Victor Kandoba, Sergey Zhigalov, Pavel Abduramanov,
and Yuri Okulovsky

Ural State University, Lenina str. 51, Yekaterinburg, Russia
yuri.okulovsky@gmail.com
http://ai.math.usu.ru

Abstract. We present RoboCoP — a new intercommunication protocol for building service-oriented robotic software. Other SOA systems
are rather straightforward applications of service-oriented approach to
robotics. The design of RoboCoP-based software exploits peculiarities
of robotics, and provides a simple and scalable way to create control
systems. RoboCoP is especially useful in scientific and educational areas, it simplifies the cooperation of developers and allows the iterative
complication of the system we create. We give a detailed description of
RoboCoP architecture; provide various examples of RoboCoP-based systems, including the control system for Eurobot competition; and adduce
comparison to other robot control systems.

Keywords: service-oriented approach, robot control system, communication protocol.

1 Introduction

Development of software for robots is known to be a difficult task. Even the
simplest control system for an autonomous robot requires knowledge of computer sciences, electronic engineering, mathematics, physics, etc. Hence, several
specialists have to work together on a robotics project. Their works have to be
then united into whole control system, parts of which use one another as subroutines. That requires certain interface for cooperation: a programming language, a
framework, or even a new operational system. Many such frameworks have been
developed [12,21]. Still, it is hard to say that any of these systems is a de-facto
standard for robotics, and some new solutions have been developed recently.

In this paper, we present our approach to robot control systems. Our primary
aim was to develop a system that suits the needs of education and science.
We wish to provide a tool that could allow people to work in their areas of
interest, and then combine their programs into one control system with a little
effort. Addition of new algorithm should not lead to revision of existing code,
nor should it demand the complete understanding of how the whole system
works. The system should therefore be *scalable*. The other important property
is *reusability*: a developer should be able to use the existing code instead of

D. Obdržálek and A. Gottscheber (Eds.): EUROBOT 2011, CCIS 161, pp. 158–171, 2011.
© Springer-Verlag Berlin Heidelberg 2011

rewriting it. The project being *open-source* is also important: we believe that only open-source solutions provide the highest efficiency of exchanging ideas and experience.

Several technical requirements have to be met so that the control system could solve real-world problems. Cooperation of subsystems inevitably leads to *overheads* that are to be *minimized*. Also, computational complexity of many robotics task demands our system to be *distributed* on several computers. Of course, that should not be the developers' concern.

There are several known approaches to software development: application public interfaces, object-oriented libraries, etc. One of the latest approaches is service-oriented architecture. Service-oriented architecture especially suits business software [11]. We talk however not about service-oriented architecture itself, but rather about the approach behind it. In this approach, a complex system is to be divided into several relatively simple applications (services), which run independently and communicate with each other via HTTP or other protocol. Internal structure of applications is not important as far as they obey their contacts.

Service-oriented approach (SOA) allows to build reusable and scalable software, including robot control systems. If we have developed a service which performs the image recognition, we can use it in any control system by sending an image to it and receiving an answer in some fixed format. SOA also helps to build distributed solutions: we run services on several computers and interconnect these computers by a network. SOA potentially eases the development, because a developer of a service does not need to know about the whole system. Therefore, SOA seems to solve many of the tasks we have set.

SOA is not well-studied in the field of robotics. Many systems demonstrate some features of SOA, like distributed run, division to subsystems, etc. Only two systems follow SOA fully. Robotic Operating System (ROS) [8,19] is built upon this approach, though SOA itself is not mentioned directly in it. Microsoft Robotics Developer Studio offers a support for SOA via Decentralized Software Services [13]. However, both implementations are very straightforward, inspired heavily by business SOA solutions. We will show that SOA can be improved to perform better in the particular case of robotics.

In section 2, we describe our modification of SOA for robotics and its implementation — RoboCoP (Robotics Communication Protocol). In section 3, we bring examples of using RoboCoP to build service-oriented control systems. In section 4, we compare RoboCoP approach to other known approaches, including ROS and MSRS.

2   Robotics Communication Protocol

RoboCoP is a protocol which allows services to communicate with each other. It performs over transport protocols, like TCP/IP or UDP. It specifies types of packages sent over network, their formats, etc. RoboCoP is divided into three layers. RoboCoP.Data is a very simple wrapping around transport protocol. It specifies *data*, one type of information inside the control system. Images from camera, commands for effector to move are data. Most services need only this layer to perform. RoboCoP.Signals is slightly more difficult, and adds another type of packages, *signals*. Signals are typically short messages that alter behavior of services. RoboCoP.Plus specifies the serialization format for data structures, configuration files format, etc.

Our implementation of RoboCoP is done on C# language. C# and .NET are powerful programming tools with many convenient features [4]. .NET is available only in Windows operating system. The open-source implementation of it, mono [14,5], allows running of .NET application on Linux and MacOS. Therefore, every .NET solution is platform-independent. Moreover, .NET compilers are developed for many programming languages (Visual Basic, Delphi [17], etc). That allows using our implementation not only with C# language, but with many other languages.

2.1 Data in RoboCoP

The model of data transmission in RoboCoP comes from Simulink [10] and Lab-View [22]. Here we build complex systems by interconnecting blocks. A block has inputs and outputs. It receives data from inputs, performs some operations and sends the result through outputs. Such a model has proven to be convenient in many areas, including robotics. In Simulink and LabView all the blocks have to be done in corresponding system. It urges developers to use these systems as primary tools and therefore limits their freedom. Our aim is to preserve the approach but to make it more available. We extend the approach so that arbitrary applications can be interconnected.

Inputs and outputs are called *data channels*. Each application has several data channels. An address is associated with each channel. For now, let us consider only TCP/IP networking addresses. In this case, output is a TCP/IP server, and input is a TCP/IP client. When the application wants to send data (an array of bytes) through an output, the data is wrapped inside a RoboCoP package. The package has a HTTP-like structure: a header that describes type of the package, its length, etc; and a body that contains the data. Then the library sends a package using associated TCP/IP address. When the application wants to receive data, it is blocked until TCP/IP client receives a package. Then the package is unwrapped and data is given to the application. It is also possible to subscribe to an input and invoke the event each time a package is received, or to receive packages asynchronously.

Aside from TCP/IP networking, other types of addresses may be used. It is possible to specify IP address for UDP communication. It is convenient when large blocks of data are being sent continuously, and loss of packages is acceptable. Another feature is a possibility to establish a RoboCoP connection with an external device via COM or USB interfaces. In that case, an address of the data channel is a string like "COM1". From the programmer side, working with the device does not differ from working with an ordinary service. The only requirement for the device is sending and receiving data in RoboCoP format. Two hardware devices may be interconnected directly via bus, without passing information to the computer. Therefore, data channels describe not only a topology of program services, but also a topology of devices' interconnection. Efficiency of hardware implementations of robotics algorithms is well-known (see, e.g., [1]). We are currently developing a set of hardware-implemented image recognition algorithms that support RoboCoP.

2.2 Signals in RoboCoP

Signals are the second way services may interoperate. A service can store an address of *a switch*. On startup, the service connects to the switch and registers itself. Registration includes sending a list of *mailslots* that the service wants to listen. When a service wants to send a signal, it sends a RoboCoP package to the switch. The package consists of a mailslot's name and a body. The switch accepts the package and retransmits it to the services that listen to the mailbox.

Some signals are standartized. For example, `GetImage` is targeted to `VideoProducer` mailbox and urges a video producer service to send a new image. `CommandComplete` service is a confirmation that a command sent to servocontroller is finished. Standard signals are also used for statistics collection. When an application sends or receives data or signal, or performs significant stage of calculations, or gets an error, it sends a signal `Debug` to a mailbox `Debugger`. The signal contains the type of the event, its time and additional information, if necessary. Services are built to visualize and help interpret this information.

2.3 RoboCoP.Plus

RoboCoP.Plus is rather not a protocol, but a set of standards for behavior of a service. It specifies the following features of services.

- All settings of a service are stored inside a section of configuration INI-file. This includes address of a switch and addresses of input and output channels. RoboCoP.Plus specifies the format of INI-file.
- The format of command line. The command line contains a path to configuration file. It can also contains settings, which override settings in configuration file. The format of representing settings in command line is specified.
- When services exchange data structures, they do it in a selected format (INI or XML), depending on settings. That does not apply to raw binary data, such as bitmaps or sounds.
- The service must provide documentation in the specified format for data channels, signals, etc.

We have developed an assembly RoboCoP.Plus. The assembly provides a template of service that matches the criteria above. The assembly uses the Thornado [3] library. This library allows to mark data structures with attributes; to perform input and output to files in several standard formats as well as to databases; check business-logic before and after input/output procedures.

2.4   Usage of RoboCoP

An example of RoboCoP-level service is shown in Listing 1. The user has to declare a class that contains settings (lines 2–5), create an instance of this class (line 9), assign its fields (line 10), and then create an instance of **Service** class (line 11). The **Service** object handles all the connections. Sending and receiving data and signals is done through its methods. In Listing 1, the program receives input data at line 13, then processes it and sends further at line 20. Signals are sent to a **Debugger** at lines 15 and 18.

On RoboCoP.Plus level, services are considerably simpler (see Listing 2). As in the RoboCoP level, we declare a settings' class (lines 3–6), and mark its fields with attributes (line 4). We can also declare a type of data package that will be processed by our service (lines 7–10), however it is redundant when the packages between services are simple (like one integer field in example) or binary (like video or sound data). Line 13 parses configuration file and creates service. Then the service accepts and parses the input data (line 16), processes it and sends further (line 20). Method **Log** sends signal to a debugger and prints the corresponded message in the console.

An example of configuration file is shown in Listing 3. Here **In[i]** and **Out[i]** specify the TCP/IP-address of *i*-th input and output respectively, **Switch** is an address of a switch, and **TestInteger** is a value of **TestInteger** field.

Listing 1. An example of a service without RoboCoP.Plus

```
1   using RoboCoP;
2   class TestSettings : IServiceSettings {
3     public Out { get { ... } }
4     ...
5   }
6
7   class TestService {
8   public static void Main(string[] args) {
9     var settings=new TestSettings();
10    ... //filling settings fields here
11    var service=new Service(settings);
12    while(true) {
13      var input=service.In[0].Receive().TextBody;
14      var integer=int.Parse(input);
15      service.Com.Send("Debugger","Computation_starts","");
16      Console.WriteLine("Computation_starts");
17      ... //computations here
18      service.Com.Send("Debugger","Computation_ends","");
19      Console.WriteLine("Computation_ends");
20      service.Out[0].Send(integer.ToString());
21   }}}
```

Listing 2. An example of a service with RoboCoP.Plus

```
1   using RoboCoP;
2   using RoboCoP.Plus;
3   class TestSettings : ServiceSettings {
4   [ThornadoField("Test_integer")]
5   public int TestInteger;
6   }
7   class TestData {
8   [ThornadoField("Test_string")]
9   public string TestString;
10  }
11  public class TestService {
12  public static void Main(string[] args) {
13    var app=new TerminalServiceApp<TestSettings>("TestService",args);
14    while(true) {
15      var data=new TestData();
16      app.Service.Receivers[0].ReceiveObject(data);
17      app.Log("Computation_starts");
18      ...//computations here
19      app.Log("Computation_done");
20      app.Service.Senders[0].SendObject(data);
21  }}}
```

Listing 3. Configuration file for the basic service

```
[Switch]
Port=1000

[TestService]
In[0]=127.0.0.1:10000
Out[0]=127.0.0.1:10010
Switch=127.0.0.1:1000
TestInteger=123
```

The differences between RoboCoP.Plus and RoboCoP are:

- Parsing of settings and creating of service is done automatically by generic-class `TerminalServiceApp`.
- Serialization and deserialization of data is also automatized by using generic-methods `ReadObject` and `SendObject`.
- Signals to `Debugger` mailbox are sent along with displaying messages on the console. Calculation of time between `Log` invocations is also performed by `TerminalServiceApp`, so basic statistics can be obtained even without `Debugger`.

Therefore, RoboCoP.Plus library resolves almost all problems with the communication itself. The only thing the developer should do is to write down the service's logic.

3   Service-Oriented Robot Control: Case Study

Let us consider an example of service-oriented control system for manipulator robot playing checkers. Its topology is drawn in Fig. 1. The features of services are as follows.

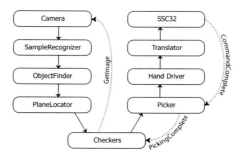

Fig. 1. Topology of services for manipulator playing checkers. Solid arrows are data channels, pointed arrows are signals.

- **Camera.** When **GetImage** signal is received, it acquires an image from web-camera and sends it in BMP or PNG formats
- **SampleRecognizer.** Analyses each pixel in received image and calculates which class it belongs to: background, white checker, black checker, etc. Sends a matrix with classes numbers.
- **ObjectFinder.** Searches connected areas of the same class. For each area, finds its center and the center's coordinates on the image. Sends a list with information about objects found.
- **PlaneLocator.** Calculates coordinates of each checkers on the board. Updates information in received list and sends it further.
- **Checkers.** By a given board, calculates the next move, gives a command to the **Picker**, waits for **PickingComplete** signal, then sends **GetImage** signal. Command for **Picker** is a list of movements, each movement is a pair of coordinates: from where a piece should be taken, and where is should be placed.
- **Picker.** Divides each movement into tasks. Each task is coordinates where the manipulator should be delivered in. Sends a list of tasks.
- **HandDriver.** For each task, calculates angles of the manipulator which brings effector in the given position. Sends a structure, where for each degree of freedom its own angle is set.
- **Translator.** Receives list, calculates signals that should be sent to each servomotor, updates list and sends it further.
- **SSC32.** Sends signals to the manipulator in controller-specified format

Let us explore some features that are provided by service-oriented approach with data channels. At first, we can easily expand the system. For example, we can add a filter that makes an image better (Fig. 2.a). There is no need to change

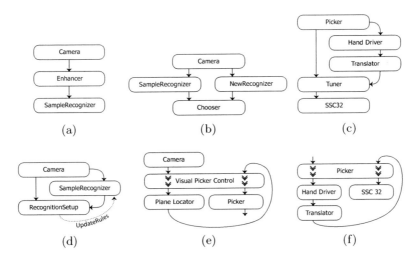

Fig. 2. Various improvements for checkers-playing robot

any other services, we only need to update configuration file. Similarly, we can develop another recognizer, which uses neural networks. If a new service follows the formats of `SampleRecognizer`, we can simply replace the old recognizer with the new one. Moreover, we can use both recognizers in our systems, as shown in Fig. 2.b. Here `Chooser` is a new service, which selects the best of offered variants. For intelligent computations, we use an open-source library GANS [16]. More complex enhancers can be developed (Fig. 2.c). `Tuner` has an experimental base with a correspondence between a request to `HandDriver`, a signal from `Translator` and an actual location of effector. It uses neural networks to interpolate this data and correct a signal from translator to improve precision (see [9] for further details).

Data channels also provide a way to setup subsystems independently. Consider a topology in Fig. 2.d. Here `RecognitionSetup` accepts both an image and a class matrix, and allows the user to see them. It also allows to assign classes to subimages and hence build a sample base. This sample base can be stored in a file. `UpdateRules` signal is used to urge recognition services to open the file and update themselves. Many services were developed for setup and debugging of different subsystems. It is possible to substitute `Camera` with `VideoPlayer` that takes images not from a camera but from files. Moreover, we can use a simulator `Board`, that stores a collection of objects and draws them as an output image. `Board` can also process `Picker`'s input by moving stored objects. Manipulator can also be tested in various ways: we can process a set of movements by `Picker`; or control hand from keyboard with `ManualControl` connected to `HandDriver`; or independently control degrees of freedom by connecting `Calibrator` to `SSC32`. Service-oriented approach with data channel simplifies the debugging greatly.

Let us consider a trickier situation. Suppose we want to see an image from a camera, choose a point in the image with the mouse and deliver the manipulator to the point. In this case, we should rearrange services as in Fig. 2.e. In `VisualPickerControl` we choose a point on the image. Then we create a list of objects in the same format that `ObjectFinder` does. The list contains only one object, coordinates of which equal the selected point. The list is sent to `PlaneLocator` to determine real coordinates of the point. The output of `PlaneLocator` is then sent back to `VisualPickerControl`, which forms a request for `Picker`. Therefore, data channels can provide a way to invoke services as subroutines.

Another example of subroutines is shown in Fig. 2.f. `Picker` produces a set of tasks. If any of these tasks cannot be achieved, the manipulator should not move. Correctness of a task cannot be determined by `Picker`. Therefore, tasks are returned in `Picker` after processing by `HandDriver` and `Translator`, and then sent to `SSC32` only if all of them are correct. In this case, `Picker` does not know which services it calls as subroutines, because the chain can be changed as in Fig. 2.c.

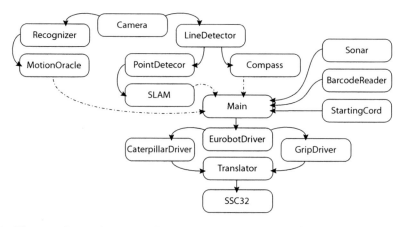

Fig. 3. The topology of services for Eurobot competitions (signals are not shown to maintain readability)

Our system is not purposed to control a manipulator. The topology for Eurobot competitions [7] is shown in Fig. 3. Note that some services are inherited from checkers-playing robot. The features of remaining services are as follows.

- `StartingCord`, `BarcodeReader` and `Sonar` adopt data from devices for RoboCoP network.
- `LineDetector`, `PointDetector`, `Compass` and `SLAM` perform a fast analysis of an image, find red-blue lines, the corners, then the position of the robot on the table. These services exploit Eurobot rules significantly and are not universal, with the exception of `SLAM`.
- `MotionOracle` analyzes the image and suggests a movement path to transfer a chess piece to the appropriate color.
- `Main` is a main control algorithm.

- `EurobotDriver`, `CaterpillarDriver` and `GripDriver` process commands, given by `Main` to moving base and grip mechanism.

`MotionOracle`, `Compass` and `SLAM` are connected to `Main` service with *oracle connections*. When `Main` wants to align the robot, or to know where it is, or to improve moving trajectory and earn scores, it sends a request to corresponding service. If the service is down, or cannot make a decision, or do not reply within the appropriate time, `Main` continues without its advice. Oracle connections allow us to perform some basic strategy even if some parts of the system are malfunctioning. Oracle connections also allow to perform real-time control, inside the limits of the personal computer architecture and the operating system: if some service `RTS` must operate within a given time limit, every service that sends to `RTS` has to be either real-time or connected with oracle connections. However, building a real-time operating systems with RoboCoP is not fully explored yet.

Additionally, we have developed `Emulator` service, which allows a robot to move on Eurobot table and manipulate objects. Depending of settings, `Emulator` produces outputs of `Camera`, `SLAM` and `Compass` services. It can also accept an input for `EurobotDriver` and perform corresponding actions.

The proposed system was implemented for Eurobot competitions in the year 2011. Usage of service-oriented approach, RoboCoP and `Emulator` allows several teams to develop and test independently following subsystems: image recognition, main algorithm, electronics (sonar, starting cord, barcode reader) and control of the robot. These subsystems were then united into one control system, distributed between two computers: image recognition on the first, and everything else on the second. Many subsystems can be reused in the next year, despite of rules changing. RoboCoP resolves many problems in development process, testing and team management exactly as intended to, and we will definitely use it in the future. Of course, there are many improvements to be made. For example, this year the late release of emulator leads to a delay in the whole project, and prevents many ideas from being implemented. Having recognized an emulator's crucial importance, next year we will develop it with a highest priority in several days after rules' publishing.

4   Comparison to Other Approaches

In this section, we will compare RoboCoP with other approaches to robot control systems. We will not consider a range of algorithms available in RoboCoP, or other technical issues, as in [12]. Our system is still in a stage of a prototype, and many important services are not developed yet, e.g. speech recognition, manipulator collision detection, many computer vision algorithms. However, such algorithms are well-studied and implemented in open libraries, like OpenCV [2], CMU Sphinx [23], etc. We only need to make bridge services to allow them acting in RoboCoP network. The development of bridges is easy with RoboCoP+ an .NET interoperation with native code.

4.1   RoboCoP as a Communication Protocol

Many standard solutions are developed for exchanging information between services. SOAP [20] is a protocol designed for service-oriented applications. WCF [18] is a novel Microsoft approach to communication. CORBA is a communication protocol originally developed for Linux, and there is a robot control system built upon it [6]. The most important difference between RoboCoP and these systems is RoboCoP's simplicity. RoboCoP does not allow doing many things: passing exceptions between services, automatically searching for required services in Internet, it does not specify a structure for messages' bodies, etc. However, we argue that these possibilities are not crucial to robot control system. A service can do nothing with an exception from other service it is unaware of. Searching for services in Internet is not required in robotics. The absence of bodies' structure is in fact an advantage that allows transmission of raw binary data. Therefore, many of standard communication requirements seem to be useless in robotics.

On the other hand, the protocol's simplicity is important. It accelerates the messages' passing and therefore minimizes the overheads that the service-oriented approach brings. It also simplifies implementation of the protocol on other languages and frameworks.

Other features of RoboCoP that distinguish it from other protocols is using hardware buses for transmission (like USB); data channels that enhance transmission in networks with a fixed topology; creation of hardware services and their interconnection by the same protocol as for software services. All of these features are unknown to be implemented in other standard SOA solutions.

4.2   RoboCoP and Non-SOA Systems

Non-SOA robot control systems differ from RoboCoP in their very foundation. We do not pretend service-oriented approach is the best paradigm for all robot control systems, since the very question of the best paradigm is rather incorrect. We believe that SOA is better for educational and scientific robotics, as it was explained in Introduction.

Many control systems developed in recent years (CARMEN, Evolution Robotics ERSP, etc) contain some service-oriented features, like dividing into subsystems that run distributed. This can be considered as an acknowledgement of SOA advantages. However, these systems are not fully service-oriented. For example, in CARMEN [15], only three layers of abstraction exist: hardware, middleware (localization and navigation) and intelligent control. These layers act like services and exchange messages, but modifications inside each layer are not service-oriented, and require another paradigm. RoboCoP steps further and states that subsystems can be divided again, and even the smallest block of a system should be writen as a service.

LabView and Simulink cannot be considered as service-oriented. They represent a program as a network of interconnecting blocks. However, a program remains a single entity, and blocks have to be written in Simulink or LabView.

RoboCoP uses Simulink and LabView approaches as a primary model of message exchange, but generalizes it to interconnection of arbitrary applications.

4.3   RoboCoP and Microsoft Robotics Studio

Differences with Microsoft Robotics Studio (MSRS, [13]) lay more in details, because both systems are fully service-oriented. Microsoft Robotics Studio offers Decentralized Software Services (DSS) as a support to service-oriented approach. DSS is very alike business service-oriented approach. Services post queries and receive replies, forming a call-stack. The queries and replies are propagated as signals, through a communication center. We believe that data channels are a more convenient model for robotics than signals. Let us list advantages of data channels.

– With data channels, the message goes through the network once. With signals, it goes twice – to the switch and then to recipient.
– Data channels do not require the center of communication. It increases robustness of the system.
– Data channels simplify creation of hardware services greatly.
– With data channels, each service has a functional form: it takes arguments and computes the result. The developer of service does not need to know names of mailboxes, where input data will be set, or how the whole system works.

We do not imply that signals should be replaced by data channels in all SOA models. Moreover, we think that data channels are convenient only in robot control system. Robot control systems differ from other areas of SOA using by the following reasons.

– The whole time the system operates, all the connections have to be set up, because information runs constantly through them. In business application, intervals between transactions depend on users and therefore are large, so connections open and close.
– In a given control system, the way of data propagation is fixed. The image from a video camera always goes to a recognition service, and never to servocontrollers. Therefore, we can assume that an input of one service is connected to an output of another. In business applications, services can invoke one another arbitrary.

Moreover, the call-stack model seems to be less convenient than the one RoboCoP uses. RoboCoP's model resembles how the information is processed by living beings. It is in fact a set of filters that transforms perception into action. MSRS model is a typical programming solution, applied for robotics straightforwardly.

Despite MSRS is costless to use, it is not free. The source code is unavailable, the DSS protocol is patented, format of data serialization is not readable by side software. It is sometimes noted that MSRS is much too powerful and much too complex for many scientific and educational tasks [21].

4.4 RoboCoP and Robotics Operating System

As MSRS, Robotics Operating System (ROS, [8,19]) is a service-oriented control system. It does not use communication center, replacing it with peer-to-peer topology and broadcasting signals. It brings all the disadvantages the signals have in comparison with data channels. RoboCoP allows more sophisticated customization of services' topology, and decreases a network's load.

.NET implementation is another important difference between RoboCoP and ROS. We believe than .NET implementation is more modern and flexible, since it allows using of convenient programming techniques (LINQ, lambda-expressions, etc.). .NET also allows using different languages for development.

Let us also note that RoboCoP and ROS are potentially compatible. We only need to construct a bridge that passes data from a RoboCoP switch to a ROS network and vice versa. We conduct further research in this area and hope that RoboCoP and ROS will be compatible in the near future.

5   Conclusion and Future Works

We have presented a new protocol RoboCoP, which allows to create a service-oriented robot control systems. The key feature of RoboCoP is data channels, which exploits peculiarities of robotics and makes service-oriented approach more elegant, easy-to-use and effective for writing robot control systems. Our solution was used in several projects, including an intelligent control of a manipulator and autonomous control system for Eurobot competitions. Our experience shows that RoboCoP successfully solves goals it was designed for, and perfectly suits needs of education and science. The release version of RoboCoP, along with documentation and various examples, will be published under GPL v.3 licence.

The most important future researches include further improvements of Robo-CoP and widening a collection of supported algorithms. Our primary area of interest is image recognition and intelligent control of robots. A special interest is a development of hardware RoboCoP services for image recognition, which are expected to significantly improve performance of video processing subsystems. We also looking forward for integration with other service-oriented frameworks, including ROS. Finally, we plan to participate in coming Eurobot competitions and use RoboCoP as a primary tool in control system development. Finally, we plan to develop an emulator for Eurobot competitions and, possibly, to grant a free access to it by a Software as a Service model.

References

1. Benedetti, A., Perona, P.: Real-Time 2-D Feature Detection on a Reconfigurable Computer. In: IEEE Computer Society Conference on Computer Vision and Pattern Recognition, p. 586. IEEE Computer Society, IEEE Press, Los Alamitos, New York (1998)
2. Bradski, G., Kaehler, A.: Learning OpenCV: Computer Vision with the OpenCV Library. O'Reilly Media, Sebastopol (2008)

3. Deyev, D.V., Okulovsky, Y.S., Chasovskikh, V.P., Popov, V.U.: Codegeneration system Thornado and its application to business software (russian). In: The Bulletin of St. Petersburg State University of IT, Mechanics and Optics, vol. 57, pp. 80–87. SPSU ITMO Press, St. Petersburg (2008)
4. Drayton, P., Albahari, B., Neward, T.: C# in a Nutshell. O'Reilly, Sebastopol (2002)
5. Dumbill, E., Bornstein, N.M.: Mono: A Developer's Notebook. O'Reilly, Sebastopol (2004)
6. Enderle, S., Utz, H., Sablatnög, S., Simon, S., Kraetzschmar, G., Palm, G.: Miro: Middleware for Autonomous Mobile Robots. In: Telematics Applications in Automation and Robotics (2001)
7. Eurobot association, `http://eurobot.org`
8. Foote, J.L., Berger, E., Wheeler, R., Ng, A.: ROS: an open-source Robot Operating System (2009),
   `http://www.robotics.stanford.edu/ang/papers/icraoss09-ROS.pdf`
9. Josin, G., Charney, D., White, D.: Robot Control using Neural Networks. In: Proceedings of the IEEE International Conference on Neural Networks, vol. II, pp. 625–631. IEEE Press, New York (1988)
10. Karris, S.T.: Introduction to Simulink with Engineering Applications, 2nd edn. Orchand Publications (2008)
11. Krafzig, D., Banke, K., Slama, D.: Enterprise SOA: Service-Oriented Architecture Best. Prentice Hall, Upper Saddle River (2005)
12. Kramer, J., Scheutz, M.: Development environments for autonomous mobile robots: A survey. Autonomous Robots 22, 132 (2007)
13. Microsoft Robotics Developer Studio,
    `http://msdn.microsoft.com/en-us/robotics/default.aspx`
14. Mono project, `http://www.mono-project.com`
15. Montemerlo, M., Roy, N., Thrun, S.: Perspectives on standardization in mobile robot programming: The Carnegie Mellon navigation (CARMEN) toolkit. In: Proc. of the IEEE/RSJ Int. Conf. on Intelligent Robots and Systems (IROS), pp. 2436–2441. IEEE Press, New York (2003)
16. Okulovsky, Y.S.: A model and implementation of universal engine for neural systems. In: Proceedings of 9th International Conference on Intelligent Systems and Computer Sciences, vol. 2, pp. 21–24. The Moscow University Press, Moscow (2006)
17. Pacheco, X.: Delphi for. NET Developer's Guide. SAMS, Indianapolis (2004)
18. Resnick, S., Crane, R., Bowen, C.: Essential Windows Communication Foundation (WCF): For. NET Framework 3. 5. Addison-Wesley, Boston (2007)
19. Robotics operating system, `http://www.ros.org`
20. Snell, J., Tidwell, D., Kulchenko, P.: Programming Web Services with SOAP. O'Reilly, Sebastopol (2001)
21. Somby, M.: Software Platforms for Service Robotics (2008),
    `http://www.linuxfordevices.com/c/a/Linux-For-Devices-Articles/`
    `Updated-review-of-robotics-software-platforms/`
22. Travis, J.: LabVIEW for Everyone. Prentice Hall, Upper Saddle River (2001)
23. Walker, W., Lamere, P., Kwok, P., Raj, B., Singh, R., Gouvea, E., Wolf, P., Woelfel, J.: Sphinx-4: A flexible open source framework for speech recognition (2004),
    `http://cmusphinx.sourceforge.net/sphinx4/doc/Sphinx4Whitepaper.pdf`

AR-Drone as a Platform for Robotic Research and Education

Tomáš Krajník, Vojtěch Vonásek, Daniel Fišer, and Jan Faigl

The Gerstner Laboratory for Intelligent Decision Making and Control
Department of Cybernetics, Faculty of Electrical Engineering
Czech Technical University in Prague
{tkrajnik,vonasek,danfis,xfaigl}@labe.felk.cvut.cz

Abstract. This paper presents the AR-Drone quadrotor helicopter as a robotic platform usable for research and education. Apart from the description of hardware and software, we discuss several issues regarding drone equipment, abilities and performance. We show, how to perform basic tasks of position stabilization, object following and autonomous navigation. Moreover, we demonstrate the drone ability to act as an external navigation system for a formation of mobile robots. To further demonstrate the drone utility for robotic research, we describe experiments in which the drone has been used. We also introduce a freely available software package, which allows researches and students to quickly overcome the initial problems and focus on more advanced issues.

1 Introduction

A quadrotor helicopter or quadcopter is an aerial vehicle propelled by four rotors. The propellers have a fixed pitch, which makes the quadcopter mechanically simpler than an ordinary helicopter. However, the quadcopter is inherently unstable, and therefore, its control is rather difficult. The progress on the field of control engineering allowed to deal with inherent instability of the quadrotors, and therefore, they have started to appear in military, security and surveillance systems.

Nowadays, the quadcopters can perform quick and complex maneuvers [1], navigate autonomously in structured [2] and unstructured [3] environments and cooperate in manipulation and transportation tasks [4]. However, the commercial quadrotor helicopters are too expensive to be used by students or small research teams. Although there exist several quadcopter toys, these are too small to carry necessary sensor equipment. In recent years, several community projects aimed to develop an affordable quadrotor helicopter have appeared [5]. However, these projects are still in progress and have not filled the gap between expensive commercial platforms and sensorless toys.

In the autumn of 2010 an affordable quadcopter, equipped with the necessary sensors and with a suitable software interface has appeared on the market. Originally intended as a high-tech toy for augmented reality games, the drone quickly caught attention of universities and research institutions, and nowadays is being

D. Obdržálek and A. Gottscheber (Eds.): EUROBOT 2011, CCIS 161, pp. 172–186, 2011.

used in several research projects. At the Cornell university, the AR-Drone has been used for experiments in UAV visual autonomous navigation in structured environments [6]. Moreover, machine learning approaches were applied to predict the position errors of the UAV following a desired flight path [7]. Other research groups used the drone as an experimental platform for autonomous surveillance tasks [8], human-machine interaction [9], and even as a sport assistant [10], which aids the athletes by providing them external imagery of their actions.

Starting to work with the drone might be time consuming, because one has to solve several implementation and 'low level' issues. Moreover, the drone itself is an unstable system and its control is not as easy as control of the ground robots. We have used the AR-Drone prototypes since March 2010, and therefore, we have gained experience with utilizing the drone as a platform for research and education. During the last year, we have been contacted by several students, who have been starting to use the AR-Drone in their projects. Most of them have similar problems with drone control, sensory data processing and usage of the provided software. Our aim is to help the AR-Drone users to quickly overcome these issues.

The hardware and firmware of the platform is described in the next section, which also provides basic information about the drone API. After that, we describe how we implemented the basic tasks of position control, object tracking, and autonomous flight. The following section briefly summarizes experiments the drone has been used for. The last section concludes benefits of the drone usage in robotic education and research.

2   The AR-Drone Platform

In this chapter, we make a brief introduction to the AR-Drone platform. We will describe not only its hardware, but also the way it can be controlled.

2.1   Hardware

The AR-Drone (see Fig. 1) is an electrically powered quadcopter intended for augmented reality games. It consists of a carbon-fiber support structure, plastic body, four high-efficiency brushless motors, sensor and control board, two cameras and indoor and outdoor removable hulls. The control board not only ensures safety by instantly locking the propellers in case of a foreign body contact, but also assists the user with difficult maneuvers such as takeoff and landing. The drone operator can set directly its yaw, pitch, roll, and vertical speed and the control board adjusts the motor speeds to stabilize the drone at the required pose. The drone can achieve speeds over 5 m.s^{-1} and its battery provides enough energy up to 13 minutes of continuous flight.

Drone control computer is based on the ARM9 processor running at 468MHz with 128 MB of DDR RAM running at 200MHz. The manufacturer provides a software interface, which allows to communicate with the drone via an ad-hoc WiFi network. The API not only allows to set drone required state, but also

Fig. 1. The AR-Drone quadcopter

provides access to preprocessed sensory measurements and images from onboard cameras.

The drone sensory equipment consists of a 6-degree-of-freedom inertial measurement unit, sonar-based altimeter, and two cameras. The first camera with approximately $75° \times 60°$ field of view is aimed forward and provides 640×480 pixel color image. The second one is mounted on the bottom, provides color image with 176×144 pixels and its field of view is approximately $45° \times 35°$.

While data from the IDG-400 2-axis gyro and 3-axis accelerometer is fused to provide accurate pitch and roll, the yaw is measured by the XB-3500CV high precision gyro. The pitch and roll precision seems to be better than $0.2°$ and the observed yaw drift is about $12°$ per minute when flying and about $4°$ per minute when in standby.

2.2   Software

The control board of the AR-Drone runs the BusyBox based GNU/Linux distribution with the 2.6.27 kernel. Internal software of the drone not only provides communication, but also takes care of the drone stabilization, and provides so-called assisted maneuvers. The bottom camera image is processed to estimate the drone speed relative to the ground, and therefore, the drone is more stable than other quadcopters.

After being switched on, an ad-hoc WiFi appears, and an external computer might connect to it using a fetched IP address from the drone DHCP server. The external computer then can start to communicate with the drone using the interface provided by the manufacturer. The interface communicates via three channels, each with a different UDP port.

Over the *command* channel, a user controls the drone, i.e., requests it to takeoff and land, change configuration of controllers, calibrate sensors, set PWM on individual motors etc. However, the most used command sets the required pitch, roll, vertical speed, and yaw rate of the internal controller. The channel receives commands at 30 Hz.

(a) Bottom camera picture in picture

(b) Bottom camera   **(c)** Frontal camera picture in picture

Fig. 2. Images provided by the drone in various modes of operation

The *navdata* channel provides the drone status and preprocessed sensory data. The status indicates, whether the drone is flying, calibrating its sensors, the current type of altitude controller, which algorithms are activated etc. The sensor data contain current yaw, pitch, roll, altitude, battery state and 3D speed estimates. Both status and sensory data are updated at 30 Hz rate. Moreover, the drone can run a simple analysis of the images from the frontal camera and search for a specially designed tags in the images. In the case the tags are detected, the navdata contains estimates of their positions.

The *stream* channel provides images from the frontal and/or bottom cameras. The frontal camera image is not provided in actual camera resolution, but it is scaled down and compressed to reduce its size and speed up its transfer over WiFi. As a result, the external computer obtains a 320×240 pixel bitmap with 16bit color depth. A slight disadvantage of the camera system is that a user cannot obtain both camera images at a time. Rather than that, the user has to choose between bottom and forward camera or go for two picture in picture modes, see Fig. 2. Switching the modes is not instant (takes ~ 300 ms) and during the transition time, the provided image contains invalid data.

Since the control board is accessible by *telnet*, the drone user can log in and change settings of the onboard operating system and adjust configuration files of the drone internal controllers. Moreover, it is possible to cross-compile an application for the ARM processor and run it directly on the AR-Drone control board. In this case, one can access the drone cameras and onboard sensors directly without a delay caused by the wireless data transfer. Thus, one can achieve faster control loops and experiment with a low level control of the drone. Even when a custom application is running on the platform control board, the internal controllers, which take care of the drone stability, can be active. However, the memory and computational limits of the control board have to be taken into account when developing an application, which should run onboard the drone.

For our purposes, we have created a simple application, which uses all three aforementioned channels to acquire data, allows drone control by a wireless joystick and performs a simple image analysis. This piece of freely available software [11] serves as a base for more complex applications, which provide the drone with various degrees of autonomy. The software does not require any nonstandard libraries and works both under GNU/Linux and Windows environments.

3   Autonomous Navigation

In this chapter, we will show how to implement several autonomous behaviours. We will start by a simple position control, continue with hovering over a moving object and traveling along a predefined path.

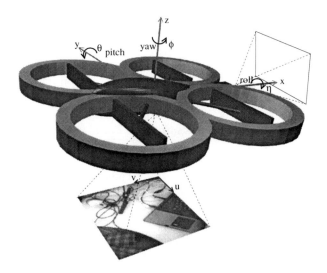

Fig. 3. Coordinate system of the drone

3.1   Dynamic Model of the Drone

In order to design controllers for the drone, it is desirable to know its dynamic model parameters. Instead of modeling the drone like a standard quadrotor helicopter, i.e., considering its propeller speeds as inputs and angles as outputs, we model the drone including its internal controller. Since the internal controller is able to set and keep the desired angles and vertical speed, we do not have to deal with complexity of the drone model [12]. Instead of it, we model the drone as a system, which has the desired pitch, roll, yaw rate, and vertical speed as its input, and its actual angles, speed, and position as its states, see Fig. 4.

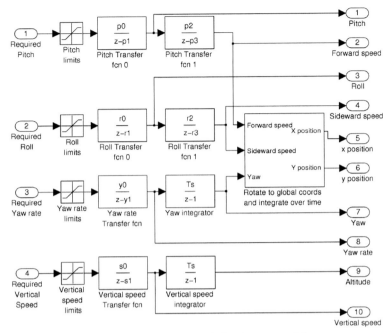

Fig. 4. A structure of the drone model

Since the position of the drone is a pure integration of its speeds, we can further simplify the model, and consider only the yaw and speeds as its state variables. Moreover, we can consider that the forward speed is given by the drone pitch, and ignore the influence of other inputs. The same can be done for the drone side speed and roll, yaw and yaw rate, and altitude and vertical velocity. Therefore, we can decompose the drone dynamic model in four first- or second-order dynamic systems and identify their parameters separately. This decoupled model allows to design separate controllers for each such aforementioned tuple of state and input variables.

To identify the parameters of the forward speed-pitch model, we have let the drone hover over a spot, then requested a -7.5° pitch and gathered the drone navdata. From the gathered data, we have extracted sequences of required pitch ϕ_i', actual pitch ϕ_i, and forward velocity v_i. Using the model in Fig. 4, we established the following linear equations

$$\begin{pmatrix} \phi_1 \\ \phi_2 \\ \vdots \\ \phi_n \end{pmatrix} = \begin{pmatrix} \phi_0 & \phi_0' \\ \phi_1 & \phi_1' \\ \vdots & \vdots \\ \phi_{n-1} & \phi_{n-1}' \end{pmatrix} \begin{pmatrix} p_1 \\ p_0 \end{pmatrix},$$

and calculated p_1 and p_0 by means of least squares. The parameters p_3 and p_2 can be calculated by a similar equation from the ϕ_i and v_i. To verify the model parameters, we compared the measured and simulated data, see Fig. 5.

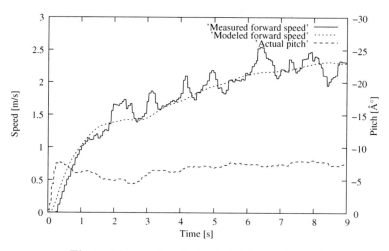

Fig. 5. Measured and simulated forward speed

To establish the remaining parameters of the dynamic model ($r_{0...3}$, $y_{0,1}$, $s_{0,1}$), a similar procedure was performed.

One has to consider that the drone model parameters differ for indoor and outdoor hulls. Moreover, the parameters vary slightly for different drones as well, and therefore, it is recommended to perform the identification procedure for each drone separately.

3.2   Position Control

Since the model parameters were calculated, we can start with controller design. Assume, that the drone is at a position (x, y, z), its yaw is ϕ, and we want to implement a controller, which moves it to a different position (x_d, y_d, z_d) with a yaw ϕ_d. In our drone model, neither the drone altitude z nor its yaw ϕ are influenced by other state variables, and therefore, their controllers can be designed independently.

The yaw subsystem has a very quick response, and therefore, a simple proportional controller is sufficient. Altitude dynamics is a bit slower because the drone inertia cannot be omitted. Therefore, we have implemented a simple PD controller for the purpose of altitude stabilization. The vertical speed (i.e., the differential channel) does not have to be estimated from height measurements, we can rather use the vertical speed from the *navdata* provided by the drone. Since both altitude and yaw subsystems contain a pure integrator, their controllers do not have to contain an integration channel for achieving zero control error. Therefore, the structure of both yaw and altitude controllers is quite simple, see Fig. 6.

When designing the position controller, we assumed, that the yaw rate (i.e., turning speed of the drone) will be small, and therefore, the pitch would influence only the forward speed and the roll only the sideward speed of the drone. To reach a desired position (x_d, y_d), we first transform it to the coordinates

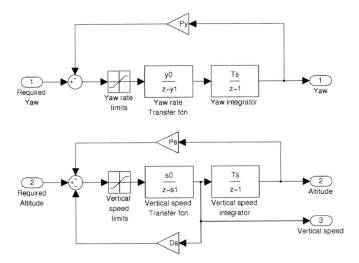

Fig. 6. Structure of the yaw and altitude controllers

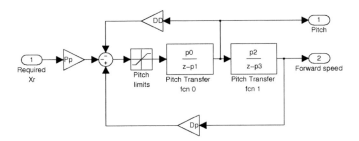

Fig. 7. Structure of the pitch (and roll) controller

relative to the drone (x_r, y_r). After that, we use the x_r as an input value of the pitch controller and y_r as an input value for the roll controller. Not only have these subsystems the same structure, but also their dynamics is similar, and therefore, their controllers will be the same. Since we know the dynamics of the system and have access to the current pitch and forward speed, we can easily implement a linear controller, see Fig. 7. Note that the proportional feedback loop is implemented in the calculation of relative coordinates (x_r, y_r) from the desired and current drone position.

Since the model parameters are known, the gains of the individual controllers can be chosen by any of the plethora methods. We have selected the controller gains using the method of pole placement [13].

With this position controller, the drone is able to quickly reach the requested position and stabilize itself without oscillations. However, there are several issues regarding the position stability. The drone position is estimated by integration of the *navdata* speeds and yaw, which are not precise. Therefore, the IMU-based position estimation is subject to drift. When flying indoors at speeds about

$1 - 2\ m.s^{-1}$, the overall precision of the position estimation is approximately
10% of the traveled distance. Moreover, the sonar-based altimeter error is higher
than 20%, and the error seems to be influenced by the type of the surface below
the drone. The yaw, which is measured by integrating a gyro signal, is also
subject to drift. Therefore, this kind of position estimation is not suitable for
long-term autonomous operation. However, the position controller works fine in
short term and is used as a base for other, more complex behaviours.

3.3   Hovering Over an Object

To keep the position estimation system stable, one needs an external reference.
One of the most simple ways is to place a distinct pattern on the ground, and
base the drone position estimation on the pattern image coordinates. This would
allow not only hovering over a fixed position, but also takeoff and landing on
a colored heliport, see Fig. 8. To do this, we just need to estimate the tracked
object coordinates and feed them to the position controller.

First of all, we have to measure the drone bottom camera field of view and
establish relation between image and real-world coordinates. Then, we have to
setup the blobfinding algorithm to search for the desired color pattern.

In autonomous operation, the bottom camera image is searched for continuous
blocks 'blobs' of a given color. The coordinates u, v of the pixel in the center
of the largest blob are calculated. These coordinates are transformed to a real
world (x_o, y_o) coordinates (we assume that the tracked object altitude is zero)
by the equation

$$\begin{pmatrix} x_o \\ y_o \end{pmatrix} = \begin{pmatrix} \cos\phi & -\sin\phi \\ \sin\phi & \cos\phi \end{pmatrix} \left[\begin{pmatrix} 0 & k_u \\ k_v & 0 \end{pmatrix} \begin{pmatrix} c_u - u \\ c_v - v \end{pmatrix} + \begin{pmatrix} \sin(\theta) \\ \sin(\eta) \end{pmatrix} \right] z + \begin{pmatrix} x \\ y \end{pmatrix}, \quad (1)$$

where $x, y, z, \phi, \theta, \eta$ are drone current position, height, yaw, pitch and roll, c_u
and c_v are image center coordinates and k_u, k_v are camera parameters, see also
Fig. 3. The k_u and k_v are approximately equal to the ratio of camera field of
view to the camera resolution. Resulting object positions x_o, y_o are sent to the
drone position controller.

This kind of position control works well at altitudes over 0.4 m. Below these
altitudes, the area viewed by the bottom camera is small and the tracked object
can be easily lost. Moreover, the air flow caused by the drone reflects from
the ground and affects drone behaviour. Therefore, it is desirable to hover in
higher altitudes and switch off the position control during takeoff and landing
maneuvers. Our experience shows that a reasonable altitude for object tracking
is over 1.5 m.

One could think that object tracking can be achieved by much simpler means
than the ones described above, e.g., the required pitch and roll can be directly
calculated from object image coordinates. Imagine such a controller in a situation, when an object is detected in the top part of the image and the drone
is requested to move forwards. To move forward, the drone is pitched down,
which causes the object to move further to the image top border, which causes
even higher forward speed. This positive feedback loop produces oscillations and

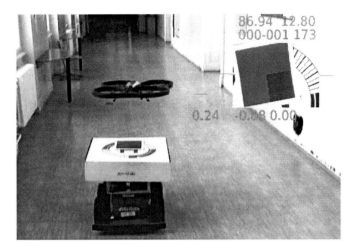

Fig. 8. AR Drone landing on a moving robot

makes the control unstable. Even when the controller would compensate for drone pitch, tilting the drone usually causes it to lose the tracked object out of sight. Due to these facts, the described position control is more reliable than simpler methods.

3.4   Visual Based Navigation

Another way to localize the drone in long term is to use the forward camera and some of the monocular-based navigation methods used for ground based robots. We have implemented a map and replay method described in [14]. The method relies on the Speeded Up Robust Features (SURF) [15] extracted from the frontal camera image. In this method, the drone is first guided by a human through an environment and creates a landmark map. After that, the map is used by the drone to repeatedly travel the taught path. The path is divided in several straight segments, each with it's own submap.

When autonomously traversing a particular segment, the currently perceived image features are matched to the mapped ones to estimate the heading relative to the segment. The distance traveled along the segment is estimated purely by dead reckoning. The navigation method is provably stable for nondegenerate polygonal paths, since the heading corrections can suppress the position uncertainty originating from the dead reckoning. The advantage of the method is its simplicity — the heading is determined by a simple histogram voting procedure — and robustness.

For the purpose of the autonomous navigation, the position control was slightly changed. When traversing a particular segment, the height control works as described in Section 3.2, the input for the yaw controller is determined from the image information, the roll position controller is disabled, and the pitch controller input equals the currently traveled segment length. Due to the low precision of

Fig. 9. Autonomous visual navigation of the drone

the IMU based distance estimation, the drone localization error is high. However, the localization error does not diverge and is kept within sufficient limits allowing the drone to autonomously navigate along the taught path.

4   Experiments

This section briefly describes two experiments performed with the drone. Videos of these experiments are available on our youtube channel[1]. In the first experiment, the drone was used as a mobile external localization system. The second experiment was concerned with performance of the AR-Drone in an autonomous surveillance task.

4.1   Mobile Localization System

Since the drone is capable to determine positions of distinct colored objects from its bottom camera image, we have used it as an external localization system. In our experiment, we tested a formation control method [16], which allows to adaptively change formation shape according to the environment constraints. Our control method is based on the leader-follower approach [17], where one of the robots (the leader) plans and executes the path, while the following robots keep a certain relative position to the leader. However, the followers might be separated from the leader by obstacles, and therefore, unable to establish their relative position accordingly. Using GPS to solve this problem would not be possible, because its accuracy is insufficient to keep a precise formation shape. To solve this, the leading robot carried the drone, which took off and provided localization when needed. Therefore, the drone was hovering above the leader and provided the followers with their positions relative to the formation leader. Using the provided and desired positions, the followers adjusted their speeds to maintain the formation.

---

[1] http://www.youtube.com/imrfel

Fig. 10. The drone taking off from the formation leader

Equation (1) shows that measurement of the drone altitude z considerably influences the results of the position estimation. Hovering over the leading robot was achieved by the method described in Section 3.3. To calculate relative follower positions, one has to measure heading of the leader. Moreover, the followers need to know their heading to compute their speed adjustments. Therefore each robot is distinguished by two rectangular areas with the same color, covering the top of it, see Fig. 10.

Since the drone altimeter is imprecise, we had to estimate the drone altitude from the leader top covering, in particular from the distance of its colored rectangles in image coordinates. This way, the altitude estimation error was about 3 % and the follower position estimation error was approximately equal to 0.05 m.

The mobile robot formation used in the experiment was composed of two followers and a leader, which carried a heliport with the drone. The following robots did not use odometry or any additional position estimation system.

4.2   Autonomous Surveillance

Consider an autonomous surveillance scenario, where the task of the drone is to monitor a set of objects of interest (OI). In particular, the drone has to fly autonomously over the objects and use its bottom camera to capture the OI images as frequently as possible. One of the possible solutions is to formulate the task as Traveling Salesman Problem [18], establish the order in which the OIs should be visited and use the navigation method described in Section 3.4 to move between the OIs.

However, the drone lacks precise position reference and might miss the desired OI. The frequency of goal visits then depends not only on the path length, but also as on the probability of arriving at a sufficient distance to the particular OI to take its photo. Therefore, one should plan a path over the OIs while considering the uncertainty of drone position estimation over the IOs.

As noted in Section 3.4, the drone position uncertainty is increasing in the direction of its movement and decreasing in the perpendicular direction [14].

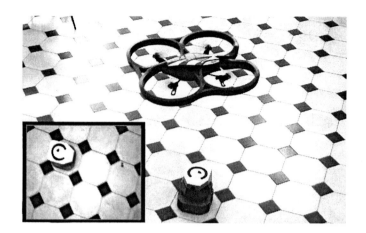

Fig. 11. The drone taking photo of the OI

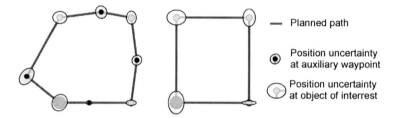

Fig. 12. Planned paths considering and not considering the position uncertainty

Therefore, we have proposed to place an auxiliary waypoint before each OI and used a SOM based approach [8] to plan the sequence of waypoints the drone should pass through.

We tested the naïve and the planning method with auxiliary waypoints for four OIs, see Fig. 12. The drone was then taught the planned paths and the success rate of goal visits was measured. The experiment showed that considering the localization uncertainty in path planning significantly increases the probability of goal visits [8].

5   Conclusion

This paper introduces the AR-Drone quadrotor helicopter as a platform utilizable in robotic research. Not only the hardware of the drone, but also its software, and communication are discussed. We described how to model this quadcopter mathematically, how to establish the model parameters, and how to use the model in position controller design. Moreover, we have shown how to implement object tracking and autonomous flight. We also presented a freely available software package, which allows to control the drone from a PC, obtain sensory data and run basic image analysis. Using this application, researchers and students can quickly overcome the initial problems and focus on more advanced issues. To further demonstrate the drone utility in robotic research, we present two experiments in which the drone has been used.

Acknowledgements. The work presented in this paper has been supported by the EU FP7-ICT project No. 216342, by the Ministry of Education of the Czech Republic grant MEB111009, and by the grants of the Czech Technical University in Prague No. SGS10/185 and No. SGS10/195.

References

1. Mellinger, D., Michael, N., Kumar, V.: Trajectory generation and control for precise aggressive maneuvers with quadrotors. In: International Symposium on Experimental Robotics, Delhi, India (2010)
2. Achtelik, M., Bachrach, A., He, R., Prentice, S., Roy, N.: Stereo vision and laser odometry for autonomous helicopters in GPS-denied indoor environments. In: SPIE Unmanned Systems Technology XI, Orlando, F, vol. 7332 (2009)
3. Blöandsch, M., Weiss, S., Scaramuzza, D., Siegwart, R.: Vision based MAV navigation in unknown and unstructured environments. In: IEEE Int. Conf. on Robotics and Automation, pp. 21–28 (2010)
4. Michael, N., Fink, J., Kumar, V.: Cooperative manipulation and transportation with aerial robots. Autonomous Robots 30, 73–86 (2011)
5. Multicopter: List of helicopter projects (2011), http://multicopter.org/wiki/
6. Bills, C., Chen, J., Saxena, A.: Autonomous MAV flight in indoor environments using single image perspective cues. In: IEEE Int. Conf. on Robotics and Automation (2011)
7. Bills, C., Yosinski, J.: MAV stabilization using machine learning and onboard sensors. Technical Report CS6780, Cornell University (2010)
8. Faigl, J., Krajník, T., Vonásek, V.: Přeučil, L.: Surveillance planning with localization uncertainty for mobile robots. In: 3rd Israeli Conference on Robotics (2010)
9. Ng, W.S., Sharlin, E.: Collocated interaction with flying robots. Technical Report 2011-998-10, Dept. of Computer Science, University of Calgary, Canada (2011)
10. Higuchi, K., Shimada, T., Rekimoto, J.: Flying sports assistant: external visual imagery representation for sports training. In: 2nd Augmented Human International Conference, pp. 7:1–7:4. ACM, New York (2011)
11. Krajník, T.: Simple 'getting started' applications for AR-drone (2011), http://labe.felk.cvut.cz/~tkrajnik/ardrone
12. Šolc, F.: Modelling and control of a quadrocopter. Advanced in Military Technology 1, 29–38 (2007)
13. Kailath, T.: Linear Systems. Prentice-Hall, Englewood Cliffs (1980)

14. Krajník, T., Faigl, J., Vonásek, V., Košnar, K., Kulich, M., Přeučil, L.: Simple yet stable bearing-only navigation. Journal of Field Robotics 27, 511–533 (2010)
15. Bay, H., Ess, A., Tuytelaars, T., Van Gool, L.: Speeded-Up Robust Features (SURF). Computer Vision and Image Understanding 110, 346–359 (2008)
16. Saska, M., Vonásek, V., Přeučil, L.: Roads sweeping by unmanned multi-vehicle formations. In: IEEE Int. Conf. on Robotics and Automation (2011)
17. Consolini, L., Morbidi, F., Prattichizzo, D., Tosques, M.: Leader-follower formation control of nonholonomic mobile robots with input constraints. Automatica 44, 1343–1349 (2008)
18. Spitz, S.N., Requicha, A.A.G.: Multiple-Goals Path Planning for Coordinate Measuring Machines. In: IEEE Int. Conf. on Robotics and Automation, pp. 2322–2327 (2000)

Team Development of an Autonomous Mobile Robot: Approaches and Results

Andrey Kuturov, Anton Yudin, Igor Pashinskiy, and Mikhail Chistyakov

Bauman Moscow State Technical University, IU4 Department,
2-nd Baumanskaya st., 5, 105005, Moscow, Russia
Lebedev Physical Institute of Russian Academy of Science,
Division of Solid State Physics
Leninskiy prospekt, 53, 119991, Moscow, Russia
kuturov@yandex.ru, {skycluster,mlazex}@gmail.com, pashinsky007@mail.ru
http://www.bearobot.org

Abstract. This article presents different approaches, used in mobile robot development by the beArobot team. The rules analysis practice is presented based on several years of the Eurobot competition participation experience. The choice of the best robot competition strategy is discussed along with a program solution for the same purpose. The article also presents several results of the team members achieved for the Eurobot 2011 project. It also gives a general idea of the mobile robot being developed. The team makes an effort to systemize its previous and current experience, thus making the article interesting for the educational purposes.

Keywords: Eurobot, mobile robot, education, analysis, modeling, motor control.

1   Introduction

Eurobot competitions [2] give an opportunity to try one's hands on a technical project, which is as close to real industrial development as possible. Such projects are even more interesting because they contain a fair share of creativity, and, moreover, because participants of the competition have to work in a team.

The beArobot team represented by the authors participated in the competitions for 3 consecutive years. Our goal is to develop a method of teaching beginners who never engaged in robots. And we make no distinction between university students and schoolchildren; on the contrary we try to find a universal approach to articulate the foundations for various levels of complexity.

This article is the consequence of positive results of the previous article [1], in which we for the first time tried to unite efforts of team members and to word our experience that includes: team work, robot development approaches, and design principles of mechanics, electronics and a mobile autonomous robot's control software. Experience in writing articles has proven to be very useful both in terms of direct training of team members (each described the work,

D. Obdržálek and A. Gottscheber (Eds.): EUROBOT 2011, CCIS 161, pp. 187–201, 2011.

he was engaged in during a project) and in terms of development of common approaches to organization of work in a team. Thus, writing an article this year was an obligatory stage in the development of a robot for the Eurobot 2011 competition.

Next we will try to clarify the approaches to team development, which we find appropriate and also present some details of the current work, which is carried out by the team members this year.

2   Analysis of the Eurobot 2011 Rules

The first action, which is mandatory for a team always includes analysis of regular rules of the competition. To save space, we do not give a description of tasks that can be found in the official competition rules[2]. The interested reader can always find this information by looking in the document.

2.1   General Rules' Task Simplifications

In order to be able to evaluate and develop a behavior of a robot on the field with the use of software, at first we introduce some rules' task simplifications.

Firstly, taking into account that the main task is two-dimensional, we assume the movement of robots in the main field and in the starting areas discrete from one cells center to the other. For greater uniformity (and simplicity) lets render the starting zone cells and supporting zone cells equal to the cells in the main gaming area. Thus, the field takes the form as in Fig. 1.

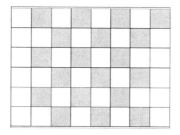

Fig. 1. The simplified gaming field for robot navigation

Secondly, we agree to develop a static model of one robot-player, i.e. for a case, when dispositions of all objects depend solely on actions of one acting subject.

Thirdly, let's select a unit for evaluation of an object's displacement then various interaction actions of a robot will be estimated in it. Initially an expert's opinion can be used for an estimation and later it can be refined by measuring the actual design solution of a robot or its part.

Fourthly, we agree to put no more than one object in each cell of the field (towers in this case are considered to be single objects). Thus, when moving objects not in order to build a tower, the cells with already placed objects can't be used for a route.

2.2   General Definitions

Before we go directly to the analysis, we must define some concepts that will be used later on. As one of the ultimate goals of the analysis can be formulated as finding alternative strategies that can win in a match, we should define a strategy in this case.

Strategy - a set of tactics in a strict sequence repetition to achieve the global goal (winning) of a robot in the competition.

Tactic - a means to select a set of alternative actions to achieve some goal.

2.3   Complexity Levels

Based on experience of participation in previous Eurobot competitions we conclude that there are several levels of robotic solutions' implementation. These levels vary in complexity of a robot's actions and its physical components. In fact, a level involves such areas of development as: mechanics, electronics, programming and project management. Each next level should include the previous, so that the levels reflect evolution of any robot's creation within a team's considered goal. In our case the goal is gradual studying, moving from less complex technical problems to more complex.

We give an expert evaluation of possible solution levels:

- Level 1 - a robot can push a pawn.
- Level 2 - a robot can move a pawn in any direction.
- Level 3 - a robot can perform the "funny configuration" action.
- Level 4 - a robot can build towers of objects.

This scheme of complexity levels can be used both for human controlled "robots", and for real autonomous robots.

2.4   Model Parameters

In competition tasks we can find the following possible parameters for a model: number of objects, number of points, complexity, and time.

On closer inspection, it appears that finally only two independent basic parameters of the model can be identified and which will be able to enter the selection criteria for alternative solutions. Those parameters are: points awarded for productive activities and time spent on all activities of a robot (productive and supportive).

"Number of elements" is a direct alternative to the "number of points" parameter, because the first can be expressed in terms of the second. We come from the assumption that the number of points in this case is a more convenient form of successful actions' evaluation due to a possibility of combining objects, leading to difficulties in determining the "number of objects" parameter. In case of the "number of points" parameter it is done a lot easier by introducing a translation table of all possible combinations of objects into points and indicating possible values for each level of solution's complexity.

A fact which confirms that there is no direct correlation between the proposed options is that actions of a robot include both productive actions which are evaluated in points, and auxiliary actions, which are not evaluated in points.

Duration of productive actions can be predicted with fair accuracy, but due to the fact that it is possible to combine objects resulting in a significant score change, this time component in this case has no direct connection with the point system.

Duration of auxiliary actions cannot be accurately evaluated due to the presence of objects that are positioned randomly on the field. It can only be predicted with a certain degree of probability for time's maximum and minimum limits.

Let's show the maximum possible limits of points per game for the previously considered levels of solution:

- Level 1 - from 0 to 180 points.
- Level 2 - from 0 to 310 points.
- Level 3 - from 0 to 350 points.
- Level 4 - from 0 to 500 points.

Maximum limits on the time parameter are from 0 to 90 seconds.

Thus, for further consideration, we have a two-parameter mathematical model with certain restrictions on the parameters.

2.5 Tactics of a Robot

Let's consider some of a robot's tasks, which it must solve on the field in order to reach its goal. These tasks may include:

1. Moving from the current point to a point of a next task selection.
2. Searching for another "free" object on the field.
3. Capturing an object for manipulation.
4. Moving an object to a desired point on the field.
5. Performing the "funny configuration" action.
6. Building a tower.

To accomplish each of the above tasks one or more tactics can be developed. The number of tactics for solving a task shows how adequate a robot can be in a situation in a match and in fact characterizes the robot's intelligence.

The minimum requirement for the number of tactics, depending on a solution complexity (note that complexity of a tactic itself depends on the level):

- Level 1 - one tactic for tasks from 1 to 4. Resulting in 4 tactics.
- Level 2 - one tactic for tasks from 1 to 4. Resulting in 4 tactics.
- Level 3 - one tactic for tasks from 1 to 5. Resulting in 5 tactics.
- Level 4 - one tactic for tasks from 1 to 6. Resulting in 6 tactics.

2.6   Tactics of a Robot

For this tactic, we assume that the scope for an algorithm that implements the tactic is a two-dimensional array of 5 by 5 items. In this case, a robot is always in the central cell of the array. Thus, while the robot is moving on the field, the array is also "moving" after it, including all new objects appearing in the scope of the array. Fig. 2 shows one of the possible situations with a disposition of objects on the field.

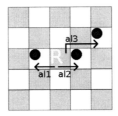

Fig. 2. Alternative actions for capturing objects in a robot's scope

The figure shows that the robot (the "owner" of white cells) has 3 alternatives for capturing objects: al1, al2, al3 (the direction of an alternative is shown with an arrow). The number of alternatives is formed by the number of objects in the array's scope.

Let's explain what lies at the heart of the search tactic for the best possible alternative. We believe that we need to minimize the total match number of a robot's cell "steps" in the field. Then it is logical to choose such an action, which minimizes further movement of a robot, such as when it finishes necessary actions and is ready to search for another object, it has to be on an adequate distance from the object.

To implement the tactic, we introduce two numerical parameters:

– an award - for reduction of future movements;
– a penalty - for distance travelled to an object.

Then the best alternative's search function has the form:

$$f_{opt} = award - penalty \ . \tag{1}$$

and the parameters are calculated as follows:

$$award = \frac{1}{dist_1} + \frac{1}{dist_2} + ... + \frac{1}{dist_{n-1}} \ . \tag{2}$$

$$penalty = \frac{dist}{n} \ . \tag{3}$$

Where: n - the number of found alternatives; dist1, dist2, distn - the distances to the relevant alternatives, but from the target cell of the calculated alternative; dist - the distance from a robot's current position to the target cell of the calculated alternative.

The alternative that has the maximum value of f_{opt} will be considered optimal.

2.7 General Ideas of a Software Based Strategy Search

Having an opportunity to consult with specialists in such areas as math and robotics, as well as having some experience in development of robotic systems, the authors were able to identify possible ways to solve the task of finding an optimal strategy for a mobile robot. Those include: methods of artificial intelligence, the method of local variations, the method of partial repetition, brute force, and the trace method.

The brute force method from all of the above methods proved to be the best to solve the problem. Since the problem is solved on a computer, the use of this method allows a solution that other methods cannot provide at our current level of engineering. The main drawback of the method is that it is necessary to perform a large number of calculations, which leads to considerable time spent on calculations.

It is worth noting that the work also raises an issue of developing a more formal mathematical solution that would expedite the further action decision making process on a robot.

2.8 A Strategy Search Algorithm

To solve the strategy search problem we further divide the field (Fig. 3, on the left) into cells, with the size of an object (a pawn). Each cell will be assumed as a point with specific coordinates (Fig. 3, on the right).

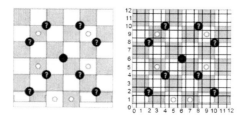

Fig. 3. The field with objects and bonus cells (on the left), a coordinate grid (on the right)

A trajectory of any movement is specified by coordinates of all individual segments of a polyline routed for a robot. Movement vectors are arranged using these coordinates. With lengths of the movement vectors and angles between them, we get the path traversed by a robot and its rotation angle.

The algorithm in Fig. 4 describes how to select an object, and then install it on a profitable cell.

To select an object we need to perform an object trace, i.e. to calculate how many times each object encountered in a robot's movement path for each destination cell of the field. And, accordingly, the most profitable object will be the one that appears more times in the way of a robot. As objects are not equal, each of them is assigned a coefficient that determines the score obtained for it on a usual no-bonus cell (Fig. 5).

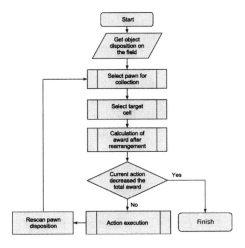

Fig. 4. The general software search algorithm

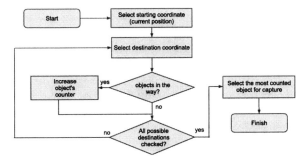

Fig. 5. The object trace algorithm

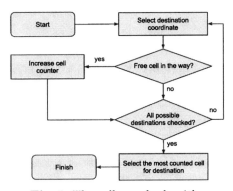

Fig. 6. The cell search algorithm

A destination cell to put the object on is selected in a similar way (Fig. 6).

In the described algorithm (Fig. 4), a robot can perform the action immediately or calculate two or more actions forward, and then choose the most profitable branch. The number of actions calculated forward we'll call the "nesting" level.

An algorithm with the infinite nesting level continues to choose a point for a subsequent calculation until the most advantageous arrangement is reached, and the subsequent displacement of objects only make the outcome worse. The field is limited, so we have a countable number of options for the location of destinations for calculation, which suggests that such an optimal solution can be found.

2.9   The Search Algorithm Implementation

The algorithm considered above was developed for needs of a mobile robot's navigation on the competition field. The base algorithm is implemented in C and is used to identify the most profitable tactics of a robot on a stationary computer. It is also used to study possible methods of solving the problem of an optimal strategy, because it gives a global solution rather than a local solution. Thus, we are able to reject various strategies that can give only a local, not an optimal solution.

In addition to a pure research usage the presented algorithm is used in a mobile robot's microcontroller based on the AVR architecture and is directly involved in the organization of the robot's action planning.

The introduced algorithm allows the robot to find the best object dispositions. Depending on the speed of a computer being used one can use different versions of the algorithm. Each increase in the nesting level directly affects the decision-making time. A margin of error of the algorithm is inversely proportional to its level of nesting, i.e. the greater the level of nesting, the more optimal the solution.

Although the proposed algorithm is developed and used for the needs of the mobile robot competitions, its use is not limited to that. For example, it can be adapted for warehouse work, where there is a need to place goods to certain places. You can also adapt it for the needs of automatic placement of electronic elements on a PCB.

3   The Automatic Control System of a Robot Motor

Motors used for a robot's movement often have no speed control of a shaft, so when load increases on the shaft the speed decreases and accordingly the speed of movement decreases also.

It is worth noting that the problem of movement on top of a flat surface has its specifics, which identifies opportunities for organization of a robot's control. This time we are introducing an intelligent system for controlling an electric motor for the needs of robot navigation on a flat surface. Having an opportunity to receive data from various independent sensors, an attempt is made to develop universal software that would ensure minimal errors in regulating drive wheels' rotation speed of a robot.

The developed control system stabilizes frequency of rotation and helps to minimize loss of speed and time, which improves efficiency of a robot. On the basis of this system, one can develop the most effective control algorithms for an electric drive.

The peculiarity of the system is an ability to optimally tune control parameters of the servo drive using the developed software. In this approach the combination of a properly configured PID algorithm incorporated in a microprocessor system, and the program debugging and diagnosis achieve optimal performance.

3.1   The System Composition

The general block diagram of the control system is shown in Fig. 7.

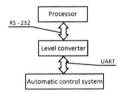

Fig. 7. The general block diagram of the system

Structurally, the system can be represented by three large blocks: the processor, level converter (LC), and the automatic control system (ACS) itself. ACS controls, regulates and stabilizes the necessary parameters. An important feature of the unit is a connection of the ACS microcontroller with the external environment via RS-232. Signals from the ACS are received by the LC unit, where they are converted, and transferred to the processor for carrying out the necessary calculations and forming commands. The processor sends commands through the LC to the ACS to setup the necessary parameters of regulation, to define the rotation frequency for stabilization or to switch the drive control algorithm.

The processor is actually a computer. The system is configured and debugged in different modes with the help of it and the developed software. After the debugging is finished, computer can be replaced with the microcontroller (MC). MC via UART receives and transmits all the necessary data, performs adjustment of the regulation parameters in accordance with the algorithms, already tested on computer in initial configuration of the system presented on Fig. 7.

For the convenience of tuning the system parameters, data visualization program was established in Object Pascal namely Delphi 7.0, which transmits, receives the data, carries out its processing and outputs in an accessible form on the computer screen. The layout of the software program is shown in Fig. 8.

UART/RS-232 level converter converts the signal levels of the microcontroller UART to RS-232 standard. Fig. 9 shows waveforms before conversion (blue line), and pulses after the conversion (red line). System design, software and algorithm

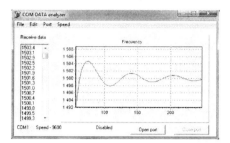

Fig. 8. The layout of the main computer program

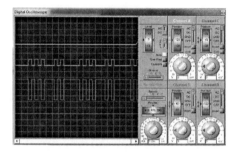

Fig. 9. Waveforms in Proteus VSM (Digital oscilloscope Tool)

of the program were developed in the Proteus VSM. Modeling and debugging were also carried out with the help of Proteus VSM.

The signals from the LC are received at the COM-port. Options of the data transmission used: 9600 baud, 6 data bits, 1 stop bit, no parity.

Let's see how the frequency is set on the drive shaft. We assume 1507.9 rpm is the needed frequency. The transfer is carried out as follows: start bit (St), 6-bit data (transmitting "1") stop bit (Sp), start bit (St), 6 bits of data (transmitting "5"), stop bit (Sp), etc.

Using RS-232 link is justified because currently RS-232-USB adapters are widespread. This allows the communication with a computer, even if it has no serial port. Computer interface greatly expands the capabilities of the motor control system, it allows you to monitor system settings, and most importantly: there is a means of diagnosing and adjusting system parameters.

3.2 The Automatic Control System

Fig. 10 shows the structure of the ACS unit.

Microcontroller (MC), using the built-in CCP (Compare-Capture-PWM), generates a signal pulse-width modulation (PWM) and submits it to the motor driver. Motor driver increases the amplitude and power of the received signal and passes it to the motor drive. The rotor of the electric motor comes into rotation, and the sensor unit reads the current value of speed.

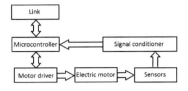

Fig. 10. The structure of the automatic control system

An array of sensors of different physical nature is called a database. In addition to the base control loop for the frequency of the motor shaft rotation (the scheme uses high-precision three-channel encoder), the database implements the control loops for current and speed of the robot relative to the field.

Additional control loops allow the regulation tailored to suit not only the mode of operation, but also features of a motor. Depending on the type of sensor it converts a certain physical value, which characterizes the speed of the motor shaft, to a corresponding electrical signal. Resulting electric impulse is transmitted to signal conditioner. It adjusts the signal: changes pulse amplitude, performs filtering, smoothing. If the signal does not require processing signal conditioner can be excluded from the system.

Processed signal is fed to a microcontroller (MC). MC, via the CCP block captures the impulse (on the rising edge for example), calculates the pulse period and finally calculates the frequency.

In the navigation tasks speed of the motor shaft rotation is not always directly connected to the current speed of the robot (slipping, skidding). In such cases, the MC uses the PID algorithm and generates a control signal, taking the external noise into account.

ACS unit using RS-232 interface as a communication channel transmits the current values of monitored parameters and accepts command signals.

3.3   The Algorithm of the Control System

Fig. 11 shows the algorithm of the microprocessor system program. The program is written in C for the AVR microcontroller.

The algorithm initializes the variables, sets up the settings of the MC, configures the interrupts, reads the frequency of the motor shaft constantly and calculates the control action applied to the motor driver.

Initially the necessary number of pulses per time unit is set, and then the time constant is set - a sampling control constant (assumed to be 10 ms). During this period of time, the MC counts pulses from the sensor and then calculates the error, defined as the difference between the number of pulses set and received from the sensor. Next, the correction term and the control action are calculated according to the PID regulator model. The calculated value of the control action is the number of rectangular pulses generated by the MC in a time period equal to the sampling control constant.

During the sampling time the calculation of all necessary parameters takes place, and on interrupt from the timer, which specifies the sampling control

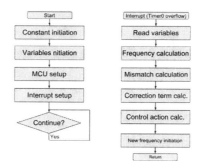

Fig. 11. Algorithm of the basic (on the left) and background (on the right) programs

constant, changes are applied to the PWM duty cycle, and as a consequence - frequency of the shaft rotation changes and thus the robot changes its speed.

3.4   Diagnostics and Setup of the System

The essence of the diagnostic system is as follows: the shaft speed and the PWM duty cycle are transmitted to a computer via RS-232 link; computer software records those parameters in a file and processes the data received. According to the file data the software program builds graphics on them, the operator can assess the applicability of the system settings for the current mode of operation. If necessary, he can run the configuration feature over the system. The essence of the setup algorithm is the selection of the optimal coefficients of regulation on the basis of the characteristics of the system in a certain mode. The program evaluates the control speed and accuracy. Fig. 12 shows the results of the system configuration program.

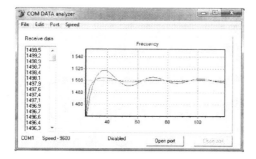

Fig. 12. Transient characteristics of the system at different settings

Before tuning the system response is represented by the green curve. In the transient characteristic the damped response is observed. The speed and accuracy of control are reduced. Configuration program passed the whole design range of coefficients, and obtained the brown chart characteristic. In this transient characteristic a small release and quickly damped oscillations (1-2 periods) are observed. This type of transient response provides good performance and fast access to the specified speed.

4   The Principles for the Mechanics Development

Rules of a next Eurobot competition are always aimed at changing the mechanical structure of a robot. It is therefore important to learn and understand a universal approach to development of mechanics rather than a specific mechanical solution.

When designing a robot's mechanics the first thing to determine is the functional requirements. They should be chosen based on a strategy of a robot. With clearly defined functional requirements, it becomes possible to determine the range of tasks for designers of mechanical assemblies.

The basic principle for mechanical design is a combination of the following requirements:

– Compactness (minimum volume occupied by mechanical assemblies);
– The minimum number of degrees of freedom while retaining full functionality;
– Reliability and durability of the construction;
– The minimum weight, the lowest center of mass possible for the robot;
– Use simple industrial drives.

The main task of designing a robot's mechanics is in satisfying all of the above requirements.

The choice of materials is also of importance to the mechanics. One of the most common and convenient material is aluminum, it can be found in a form of rods, tubes, angles and strips of different shapes, sizes and dimensions. Its convenience is in the simplicity of processing (drilling, milling, etc.), durability and reliability.

5   The Robot Mechanics for the Eurobot 2011 Competitions

This year our robot has a cylindrical shape (Fig. 13). The chassis consists of two drive wheels driven by stepper motors and 3 slippery stanchions to prevent the forward and back inclination of the robot. The drive wheels are located on the robot diameter and are as distant from each other as possible. Slippery stanchions form a triangle and are situated as distant from each other as possible for a good stability of the robot.

The seizure of objects is realized by a side cylindrical surface with a suction cup attached to a toothed belt covering the robot's perimeter. An object capture is possible because of the onboard pump working in a "vacuum" state. The pump is also able to generate pressure as well. After the capture was successful the toothed belt rotates to a position from which it is planned to put the object

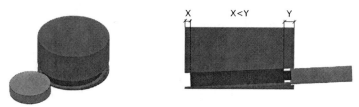

Fig. 13. The general robot idea

on the field. If building of a tower is needed, the belt is rotated from the initial position (X) for 180 degrees in a parking lot (Y), located behind the robot. The "parking" is a niche inside the robot, equipped with a mechanism for reliable clamping of an object for its retention while rising to build a tower.

The rise of an object is possible by means of lifting the whole cylindrical shell of the robot with the attached belt, sucker, and "parking". The hull rises relative to the robot's inside massive frame. Lifting is organized by means of multiple pneumatic cylinders, working from the same pump as the sucker.

Implementation of the "funny configuration" is as follows. The robot is located in an immediate vicinity of a pawn, the robot's hull is lifted to a height slightly greater than the height of the pawn, and the robot runs into a pawn so that it is in the cavity underneath. With the help of pneumatic cylinders the robot, based on the pawn, lifts itself in the air.

6   Conclusions

While preparing for the Eurobot competitions, the beArobot team has once again presented its vision of a mobile autonomous robot's development. We continue to develop approaches that in future we hope will be united in a methodology of teaching robotics to everyone.

This article presents the results of the analysis of the Eurobot 2011 competition rules, which allow us to represent the competition's tasks in a convenient form, ranged by difficulty. We believe that developing such an approach could lead to an independent method of the Eurobot rules' analysis in future, which will supply teams with an objective approach of formulation of development tasks, as well as evaluation of a robot's actions on the field.

In particular, one of the results of the analysis was the optimal moving strategy search algorithm with a robot and objects in its scope.

In the course of this work a system of automatic motor control was developed. This system has high reliability and performance, due to the use of a special diagnostics and configuration system. It is planned to improve the system further.

Separately, we want to note the experience of using Proteus VSM program in our project. It was used to simulate individual robotic systems, debugging and software configuration. In the initial stages of development, when you need to quickly simulate any electronic system of the robot, as well as for the needs of learning this package fits perfectly.

In conclusion, the basic mechanics design principles were given as the most volatile region in the competitive practice. The robot, developed for the Eurobot 2011 competitions was described.

References

1. Demidov, A., Kuturov, A., Yudin, A., et al.: Autonomous Mobile Robot Development in a Team, Summarizing Our Approaches. Technical report, 3rd International Conference on Research and Education in Robotics (2010)
2. Eurobot, international robotics contest, `http://www.eurobot.org`
3. Gerhard, S.: Beginners Introduction to the Assembly Language of ATMEL-AVR-Microprocessors (2011)
4. Thomas, B.: Embedded Robotics Mobile Robot Design and Applications with Embedded Systems. Springer, New York (2003)
5. Ted, V.S.: Programming Microcontrollers in C, 2nd edn. EMBEDDED TECHNOLOGY Series. LLH Technology Publishing (2001)

An Autonomous Robot Localization System Based on Coded Infrared Beacons

Milan Lukic, Miodrag Brkic, and Jovan Bajic

Faculty of Techhnical Sciences, University of Novi Sad,
Trg Dositeja Obradovia 6, 21000 Novi Sad, Serbia
milan_lukic@uns.ac.rs, brxnet@yahoo.com, jovanbajic@gmail.com

Abstract. One of the most important problems in autonomous robot guidance is their localization, i.e. determining their physical location within their operating area. For a wheeled autonomous robot that operates on flat rectangular surface, the mostly used localization methods are odometry and triangulation. Odometry is a method based on incremental encoders and its basic flaw is that it accumulates error. On the other hand, triangulation is a method of calculating location of robot relative to 3 landmarks (beacons) located on fixed predetermined positions. This method usually needs measurement of distances between robot and beacons, to be able to calculate robot position. In this paper we describe a different approach based on angle measurement as opposed to distance measurement, we discuss the advantages of this method and we give the details of realization.

Keywords: autonomous robot, localization, triangulation, angle measurement.

1 Introduction

Motivation for the method shown in this paper comes from years of participation of authors in EUROBOT [1] competition. As the robots are autonomous and must operate without human interfering, it is of vital importance that robot has information about its position on the playing field available during the whole duration of the match. The position is calculated by sensor measurements. Since the robot moves on the bounded flat surface, its position is fully defined by three coordinates (x, y, θ). Coordinates x and y actually signify the position of robot's central point in fixed coordinate system anchored to the playing field, and θ is the orientation, i.e. the angle between central axis of robot and x axis (Fig. 1). In this paper, we first describe some of the existing and frequently used localization methods in EUROBOT competition, and then we describe our localization method based on angle measurement.

D. Obdržálek and A. Gottscheber (Eds.): EUROBOT 2011, CCIS 161, pp. 202–209, 2011.

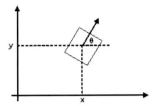

Fig. 1. Position of robot in coordinate system

2   Odometry

Odometry [2] is a robot localization method based on usage of rotary encoders. The robot has two wheels which are constantly in the contact with the surface. These wheels are mechanically coupled with encoders. The number of the pulses produced by encoders depends on the number of turns, in other words the distance traversed by wheels. Dis is an incremental method, which takes into account the assumption that the robot trajectory consists of sequence of segments that are approximately straight. The microcontroller which is processing the output signals from encoders has Quadrature Encoder Interface module (QEI) [3]. This module provides the interface to incremental encoders for obtaining mechanical position data. A typical quadrature encoder includes a slotted wheel attached to the shaft of the motor and an emitter/detector module that senses the slots in the wheel. Typically, three output channels (phase A, phase B and index) provide information on the movement of the wheel, including distance and direction. The phase A and phase B channels have a unique relationship. If phase A leads phase B, the direction of the motor is deemed positive, or forward. If phase A lags phase B, the direction of the motor is deemed negative or reverse. The Index pulse occurs once per mechanical revolution and is used as a reference to indicate an absolute position. By using QEI unit, the microcontroller always has information about direction and movement of odometry wheels, and the effective resolution is quadrupled compared to the case when only one encoder channel is used. The data coming from QEI units is processed periodically, with a period short enough that the assumption about the straightness of trajectory segments still holds (10 ms). If we assign the number of encoder increments read from respective encoders during nth period by LEFT and RIGHT, it is possible to calculate the growth for all three coordinates during given period:

$$\Delta\theta = k_1 \cdot (RIGHT - LEFT)$$
$$d = k_2 \cdot \frac{RIGHT + LEFT}{2}$$
$$\Delta x = d \cdot cos\theta$$
$$\Delta y = d \cdot sin\theta,$$

where constants k1 and k2 convert increments into real physical units. When we have these values calculated, we update robot position in n^{th} period:

$$\theta_n = \theta_{n-1} + \Delta\theta$$
$$x_n = x_{n-1} + \Delta x$$
$$y_n = y_{n-1} + \Delta y$$

The basic flaw of this method is existence of systematic error which accumulates through time. The error appears due to slipping of wheels, the assumption of straightness of trajectory between two consecutive readings, integer truncation of increment number, numerical error of calculation, etc. Having in mind the short duration of the match, if we use encoders with sufficient resolution and double-precision floating point arithmetic, by using odometry we are able to acquire information about robot position with acceptably small deviation during the whole course of the match. Still, due to accumulation of error, it is not recommended to use this method without some additional system that would allow correction of position info.

3   Triangulation Based on Distance Measurement

Triangulation is well known and frequently used localization method. The position of robot is determined by measuring distances between the robot and three fixed points on known positions. For this purpose, we use three beacon positions on the edge of the field, as defined in competition rules. In Fig. 2, these positions are designated by B_1, B_2 and B_3. One of the ways to measure distances L_1, L_2 and L_3 between robot and beacons is to put an ultrasonic transmitter in each beacon and ultrasonic receiver in robot. The controller in robot uses wireless radio link to command the beacons to start ultrasonic transmission. By measuring time between the moment of issuing the command and reception of ultrasonic signal, it is possible to calculate distances, knowing the speed of sound. Also, it is important to mention the assumption that the times of issuing and the reception of command are negligible compared to time of propagation of ultrasonic wave.

Now that we have measured distances L_1, L_2 and L_3, it is possible to calculate te position of robot. The coordinate system is perpendicular to the playing field, with origin in B_1. The unit of measure is centimeter, so the positions of the beacons are $B_2(-105, 300)$ and $B_3(105, 300)$. By applying basic trigonometric laws, we get the following equations for robot position:

$$x = \frac{L_2^2 - L_3^2}{420}$$
$$y = \sqrt{L_1^2 - x^2}$$

The advantage of this method is that it doesn't accumulate error. When it comes to realization, the biggest problem is inadequacy of measuring methods. The ultrasonic receiver we used is too sensitive to environment sounds, which leads to false distance measurement in environment that is not totally quiet. On the other hand, we are unable to use more sophisticated methods of distance

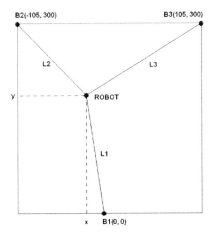

Fig. 2. Triangulation based on distance measurement

measurement such as laser sensor, due to our restricted budget. It is also important to mention that this method cannot provide the information about robot
orientation, so it would be necessary to use some other system do measure it
(i.e. electronic compass).

4   Triangulation Based on Angle Measurement

4.1   Theory

In this section, we describe our approach to localization problem based on angle
measurement. Like in previous section, we use three beacons again, but this time
we use coded infrared beacons. All of the beacons continuously and simultaneously transmit modulated infrared light signals with different codes, by which a
receiver unit on the robot can distinguish them. The receiver sensor is in the end
of the narrow cylinder which is mounted on the rotating platform. The cylinder has a narrow aperture in order to enhance directivity; the receiver is able
to receive and decode the signal only when it is watching directly towards the
transmitter. The mechanism that turns the receiver around contains a sensor
that provides the information about its orientation (i.e. rotary encoder). This
way, by turning the receiver for a full circle the robot is able to register in which
positions it sees all of the 3 beacons, in other words to measure angles between
these positions. The situation is shown in Fig. 3. If we designate the central
point of robot by R, by measurement we acquire angles $\varphi_1 = \angle\, B_1RB_3$ and φ_2
$= \angle\, B_1RB_2$, which are the input parameters for the equations that are used for
determining the position.

We get the equations for calculating the position by using the following idea.
Geometrical place of points R such that angle $\angle\, B_1RB_3 = \varphi_1$ is a circle with
center in $C_1\ (x_1, y_1)$, constructed above the chord B_1B_3, with inscribed angle
φ_1. That property comes from the theorem that all of the inscribed angles over

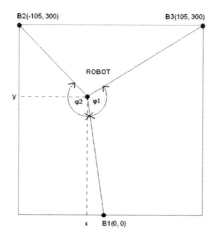

Fig. 3. Triangulation based on angle measurement

the same chord (in this case B_1B_3) are equal. The same way, we can construct a circumscribed circle with center in $C_2(x_2, y_2)$, constructed above the chord B_1B_2, with inscribed angle φ_2. These two circles intersect in two points, one of which is B_1, and the other is R. So, the first step is to determine positions of C_1 and C_2 by applying laws of trigonometry and analytical geometry. It can be shown that:

$$r_1 = \frac{\sqrt{\frac{L_1^2}{4} + L_2^2}}{2sin\varphi_1}$$

$$r_2 = \frac{\sqrt{\frac{L_1^2}{4} + L_2^2}}{2sin\varphi_2}$$

$$x_1 = \frac{L_1}{4} - \frac{L_2}{2}ctg\varphi_1$$

$$y_1 = \frac{L_2}{2} + \frac{L_1}{4}ctg\varphi_1$$

$$x_2 = -\frac{L_1}{4} + \frac{L_2}{2}ctg\varphi_2$$

$$y_2 = \frac{L_2}{2} + \frac{L_1}{4}ctg\varphi_2,$$

To make our solution more general, we have designated lengths of sides of playing field by L_1 and L_2 (in this case $L_1=210$cm and $L_2=300$cm); r_1 and r_2 are radiuses of circumscribed circles. After we have calculated coordinates of centers of both circles, we determine robot coordinates by solving the system of circle equations:

$$(x - x_1)^2 + (y - y_1)^2 = r_1^2$$
$$(x - x_2)^2 + (y - y_2)^2 = r_2^2$$

Since this is a system of two quadratic equations, there exist two solutions. One of them is, as previously explained, position of beacon $B_1(0, 0)$, and the other is the desired robot position. By solving the system, we get final equations for robot coordinates:

$$x = 2\frac{(x_1 y_2 - x_2 y_1)(y_2 - y_1)}{(y_2 - y_1)^2 + (x_1 - x_2)^2}$$

$$y = 2\frac{(x_1 y_2 - x_2 y_1)(x_1 - x_2)}{(y_2 - y_1)^2 + (x_1 - x_2)^2}$$

The above equations hold in all cases except when robot is situated on one of the lines $B_1 B_2$ or $B_1 B_3$. Let's consider the case when R is on the line $B_1 B_3$. In this case $\varphi_1 = \pi$, so geometrical place of points that are candidates for R is now a line $B_1 B_3$ instead of circle. So, we get robot position in intersection of line and the other circle, which evidently can be constructed the same way as described above, as $\varphi_1 \neq \pi$. After solving the system of one linear and one quadratic equation, we get:

$$x = 2L_1 \frac{L_1 x_2 + L_2 y_2}{L_1^2 + L_2^2}$$

$$y = 2L_2 \frac{L_1 x_2 + L_2 y_2}{L_1^2 + L_2^2}$$

In a similar fashion we get the solution that covers the case when $\varphi_2 = \pi$:

$$x = 2L_1 \frac{L_1 x_1 + L_2 y_1}{L_1^2 + L_2^2}$$

$$y = 2L_2 \frac{L_1 x_1 + L_2 y_1}{L_1^2 + L_2^2}$$

4.2   System Realization

During development of the system from its prototype version, we have made some significant adjustments that improved the accuracy and sped up its operation. The prototype had servo motor and infrared receiver SFH 5110 [4], which receives the signal modulated with carrier frequency of 36 KHz. Though functional, the prototype had significant error in calculated position due to imprecision in servo motor positioning. Besides, the carrier frequency of 36 KHz is pretty low, which leads to a long time needed for signal detection ($\sim$10ms), so the receiver head cannot turn very fast. In the first alteration we took DC motor with encoder instead of servo; this way we significantly improved the precision of angle measurement. Next, we replaced IR receiver with TSOP7000 [5], which receives the signal modulated on 455 KHz. We use the circular 10-bit code + start + stop bit. Duration of each bit is 10 periods of carrier (Fig. 4). This way we shortened the time needed for reception to $\sim$260s.

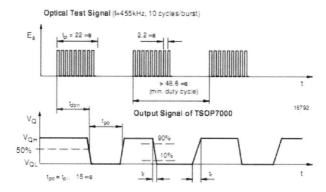

Fig. 4. Coded beacon signal and output signal from TSOP7000

These adjustments improved both the speed and precision of system, which resulted in having complete scanning and calculations done in less than 500ms. Still, there was more space for improvements. Because the receiver head was connected to the board by cable, it could not turn and scan continuously, but to rotate in one and then other direction. We overcame this problem by using a brushless DC motor from VCR. This motor has a rotary transformer which allows contactless transfer of supply voltage to the sensor, as well as transfer of signal from sensor to the microcontroller that is used for its decoding, and later for calculating the position. This improvement allowed even faster scanning. Currently the system is able to scan and calculate robot position approximately 10 times a second. Technical characteristics of the system:

- TSOP7000 infrared receiver
- Brushless DC motor with rotary transformer, for contactless power supply and signal transfer
- Rotary encoder with 1024 increments/revolution
- Atmel ATMEGA8 microcontroller which decodes the signal from sensor, measures angles and calculates the position
- XBee module for wireless communication

5   Conclusion

In this paper we showed theoretical aspects and described details of realization of a sensor system for determining position of an autonomous robot. The system has been developed by a team that has been successfully participating in EUROBOT competition for a long time, the best results being 5th place in EUROBOT 2003 and 3rd place in EUROBOT 2006. This system is relatively cheap, especially compared to a laser triangulation system. Besides, it is much more reliable than an ultrasonic system. Still, it is prone to error of angle measurement, which results in error up to 5cm in certain parts of the playing field. Still, such system is suitable for detecting the position of opponent robot, because it is allowed to put a beacon system on top of it. Then, the system uses wireless link to inform our robot about opponent's position, which is very important for collision avoidance (as it is strictly forbidden by rules). It shows that the information about opponent's position with an error no more than 5cm is suitable enough for opponent avoidance algorithm.

Acknowledgments. This work has been financed through the project III43008 of Ministery of Science, Republic of Serbia - Development of the methods, sensors and systems for monitoring quality of water, air and soil

References

1. Eurobot competition website, `http://www.eurobot.org`
2. RCVA team website,
   `http://www.rcva.fr/images/stories/site/cours/`
   `Odometrie2010/ODOMETRIE_2010.pdf`
3. Quadrature Encoder Interface technical information (from dsPIC33F Family Reference Manual), `http://ww1.microchip.com/downloads/en/DeviceDoc/70208A.pdf`
4. SFH5110 datasheet,
   `http://www.datasheetcatalog.org/datasheet/infineon/1-sfh5110.pdf`
5. TSOP7000 datasheet,
   `http://www.hobbyengineering.com/specs/Vishay-TSOP7000.pdf`

An Omnidirectional Mobile Robot for Large Object Handling

Lenka Mudrová, Václav Jahoda, Oliver Porges, and Tomáš Krajník

The Gerstner Laboratory for Intelligent Decision Making and Control,
Department of Cybernetics, Faculty of Electrical Engineering
Czech Technical University in Prague
{mudrole1,porgeoli}@fel.cvut.cz, jahoda@felaaczech.eu,
tkrajnik@labe.felk.cvut.cz

Abstract. The purpose of this paper is to introduce an autonomous mobile robot for object manipulation that is the same size as the robot. The construction has to comply with the rules of Eurobot competition. We will provide an in-detail description of the omniwheel undercart, its motion and object manipulator. This paper also provides a small insight on the robot's planned intelligence and its vision subsystem.

Keywords: Omniwheel robot, Eurobot competition, gripping manipulator.

1 Introduction

1.1 Eurobot Competion

The goal of Eurobot competition is to build an autonomous mobile robot. It has to be built by a team of students so they can present their skills and knowledge. The competition itself also helps to bring young talented students from different countries together to exchange ideas and contacts. Robots have to collect items or build objects on a well defined playground. The objective changes every year. Robots had to build a "Temples of Atlantis" using small columns and lintels in 2009. They were "Feeding the World" in 2010 by collecting red and orange balls representing tomatoes and oranges. This year challange is called "Chess up!". Robots will play a chess-like game described in Section 1.2.

The Eurobot history is quite long. It began in 1998 in France as the national robotics cup. It soon grew across Europe with national rounds established in many countries. Only the three best teams can participate in the international round that is held in a different country each year. This way students across Europe share their knowledge and ideas not only with Europeans.

1.2 Rules for "Chess Up!" Theme

The basic set of rules do not change. Robots are limited in size - with maximum height of 35 cm and their convex hull circumference must be smaller than 120 cm

D. Obdržálek and A. Gottscheber (Eds.): EUROBOT 2011, CCIS 161, pp. 210–220, 2011.
© Springer-Verlag Berlin Heidelberg 2011

in the beggining. Robot can deploy some of its devices and extend its perimeter up to 140 cm. The playground is a rectangle of 210 cm by 300 cm. There are stands for beacons 2 in every corner and in the middle of the shorter sides. Each team can use only three of them. Two robots play against each other. One match is 90 seconds long.

As mentioned above this year's challenge is a chess-like game. The playground is an oversized chessboard with red and blue areas, fig. 1. Items (chessmen) are two kings, two queens and fifteen pawns. The pawn is a disk of 5 cm in height and 20 cm in diameter. The king and queen can be 23 cm high and have the same diameter. The pool of items is common for both players, therefore, robots can steal competitor's figures. Also towers can be built using one king or queen and putting pawns underneath. There are bonus areas marked with a black stain so that more strategies could be put in action.

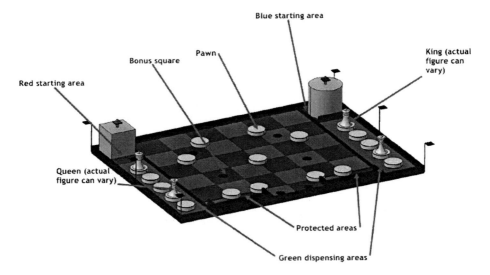

Fig. 1. Playground with play items (take from Eurobot rules)

1.3   Project Goal

Participating in this competition allows us to use and exchange our knowledge, meet interesting people and learn about state of the art technology. We have focused our abilities on creating a custom undercart of the robot using three omnidirectional wheels this year. This calls for more complicated movement control and position estimation. In order to save time we had to go beyound the conventional capabilities of pick and place strategy. We designed the robot so that it can collect and store a king, a queen and three pawns. We could theoretically store a king, a queen and eleven pawns. The problem is that the items are also heavy. A normal load would be 2.9 kg and a theoretical load could be 5.9 kg. This is a challenge for our mechanical construction.

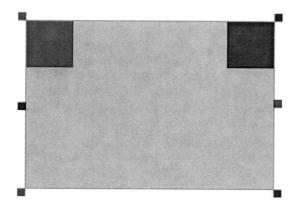

Fig. 2. The beacon's stands (take from Eurobot rules)

We focused on the artificial intelligence too. We designed a system of cameras recording the playground. We are using computer vision to get the positions of play items and opponent. The planning algorithm takes the inputs as position of the robot, trajectory of the opponent, opponent strategy (if they steal items or not) and the position of items on the playground throughout the whole match.

1.4 Paper Structure

The rest of the paper is organized as follows. It starts with an introduction, next chapter is an overview of robot concept. After that parts of robot are described in more detailly, sections describing the robot mechanics, manipulator and motion can be found. The conclusion is followed by acknowledgments and references.

2   Overview

Our robot is built from dural and all parts are custom made for our robot (we don't use any ready made brick-box). It is based on three omni wheels which also creates three storage bins for the items. We have placed a system for collecting the items in the storage bins. This system consists of two plastic hands. Each hand is controlled using a servo. Those servos are placed on a plastic base, which can go up and down, powered by one DC motor.

One micro-controller unit is used to control the motion. Each wheel has one DC motor and a rotary encoder so we are able to measure the rotations very precisely. Collecting data from the three rotary encoders allows us to calculate a rough estimation of our position in the field. An emergency stop button is connected directly to these modules just in case. The modules are written in

C programming language. We are using an ultrasonic bumper as a basic opponent detection which is also connected to the modules. They are all connected to the main board to be able to communicate with other parts. This subsystem takes in the desired location (x, y, φ) and outputs the current one.

Robot localization will be based on three subsystems. The rotary encoders give us the rough estimation. We will equippe the robot with infrared beacons to improve the precision. Finally the third one will be a visual subsystem. Last year, we designed localization system based on laser optical mouses [5], but we have mechanical problems to mount it on the undercart. The most probable position will be counted using Kalman filter.

Three bins are used to collect and carry the items. The collecting system is controlled by a micro-controller and is written in C. We are estimating a load of one king, one queen and four pawns although it could hold up to eleven pawns at once.

We are using a sbRIO-9642 by National Instruments [7] as the main board. It handles all the planning and higher level control. The board is equipped with FPGA (110 inputs/outputs) and a processor with real-time operating system VxWorks. It is designed to be programmed in the LabView software. It can also handle custom C or Matlab code. This boards collects all the data from all the sensors and make the decision that is passed back to the subsystems that perform the operation.

The vision system consists of two small cameras and a Toradex Robin board. It is placed on the beacons available on the playground, 2. The computer vision

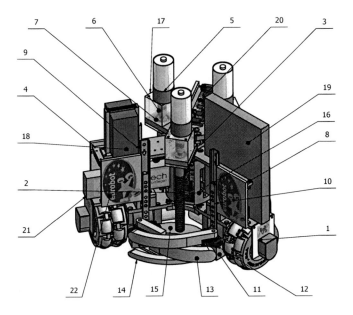

Fig. 3. Robot overview

Table 1. Description of robot overview

Number	Description	Number	Description
1	Omniwheel	12	Servo
2	Central tubular	13	Plastic hand - left
3	Motor anchorage	14	Plastic hand - right
4	Holder	15	Plastic screw-thread
5	Motor	16	H-bridge
6	Flexible conjunction	17	Plexiglass
7	Bearing	18	Microcontroller
8	Holder	19	Central planning board
9	Vertical rail	20	H-bridge
10	Vertical rail	21	Battery
11	Plastic board with servos	22	Sponsor's advertisement

software is written in C as well and uses OpenCV. The cameras are connected through a USB interface so that we can handle relatively large data flow. The software will recognize the competitor's robot, our robot and the items on the playground. It calculates their positions and sends the data wirelessly to the robot using an Xbee module.

Each beacon is equipped with infrared diodes placed in circles too. Each beacon blinks with different frequency. The robots are equipped with an infrared transistor to receive this signal. These transistors have a small receiving angle to receive data from only one of the beacons. It is driven by a stepper motor to be able to receive information more precisely. The system knows three angles to the beacons and is able to triangulate its position. It allows us to know the position of the opponent's robot and the planning algorithm makes decisions based on the opponent's strategy.

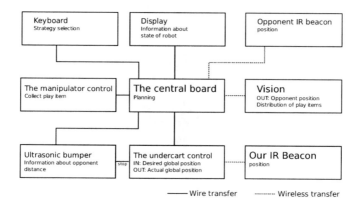

Fig. 4. Module structure

3 Mechanics

3.1 Omnidirectional Undercart

An omni wheel is a special type of wheel, see fig.5. It has a small rollers around the main body of the wheel. The wheel can rotate as any conventional one and it can move perpendiculary to the direction of regular motion. Whe have used an omniwheel with two lines of side rollers, this type is more powerful than the one lined one and the side rollers never loose touch with the ground and it does not create any unwanted vibrations.

Fig. 5. The omniwheel

Undercart with three or four omniwheels can be constructed [4]. The advantages of three wheels are lower price (no need a wheel, motor, controlling circuitry), smaller construction. The main disadvantages are the forces acting on the motors and a harder position calculation. The disadvantage of four wheels is price, of course, the advantages are a little easier math, "classic" shape of undercart - the square. But in our case, the square undercart isn't good because no space is left for the storage bins for play items. So we decided to built omnidirectional undercart using three wheels because three storage bins can be built.

Fig. 6 shows the concept and construction of undercart.

We had to solve several problems that are crucial to the operation of the robot. First of all the wheels need to be strictly perpendicular to the ground. And then the rotary encoder has to be connected to the wheel somehow.

We designed a system, see fig. 7. The wheel has a main axis, from the side where the motor is connected, from other side rotary encoder is connected. The axis is placed in the bearing and it is connected to the undercart using a U shaped part. The axis and undercart are made from dural material (we don't use any brick-box), undercart can accept a selection of gripping motors and construction holes for wires.

The undercart is designed to be more versatile and hopefully suitable for consequent years of the competition. It can be refitted for a different objective.

3.2 Robot Body

Despite the universal design of the undercart, robot body, fig. 3, is built to fit this year's mission. The main part of the construction is a massive dural frame. It

216   L. Mudrová et al.

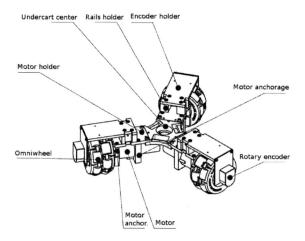

Fig. 6. The robot undercart

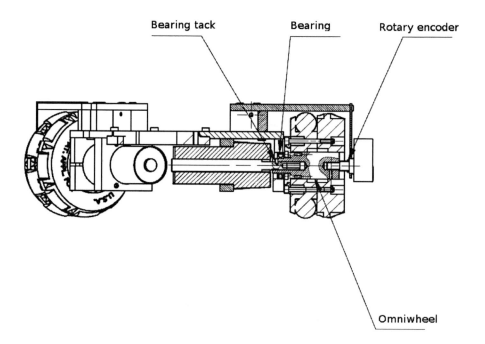

Fig. 7. Detail of gripping the wheel

has a tubular shape to be able to hold the wireing connecting undercart and the control board. It also provides some space for the batteries, the micro-controller board and the main control board.

Each storage bin, fig. 8 is equipped with two plastic hands, each controlled by a servo. Servos are mounted to the plastic board. The platform can go up and down and is powered by an extra motor placed under the roof. We placed the emergency stop button on the roof along with a diagnostic display and a keyboard as a main input. There is a platform for the opponet's beacon and an ultrasonic bumper and infrared receiver.

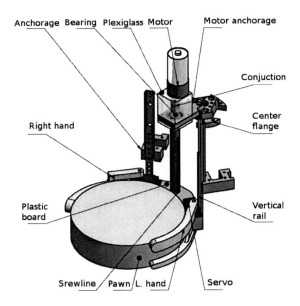

Fig. 8. Detail of mechanics for collecting play items

4   Manipulator

Fig. 8 desribes the detail of one manipulator. There are three identical collectors. Two plastic parts - hands are designed to hold the items. Each hand is equipped with a strong servo motor. It can hold 12 kg per centimeter, its gearwheels and lever are made of metal. The microcontroller module connected to the servo also measures the input current to detect servo loading. We discussed if servo loading won't be a problem (servo isn't designed for this purpose, but only for switching), but we counted that it shouldn't be a problem (with overheating etc.) We have placed microswitches on the hands for better feedback information in order to ensure maximum dependability of the system.

Our strategy is built towers too, so manipulator can raise play items. For this purpose hands with servos are placed on plastic board that has screw-thread and it is connected to the screwline. For better force distribution, the plastic board is connected to two more vertical rails. The screwline is actuated by a DC motor, between the motor and the screwline a flexible junction is mounted.

The plastic hands and the board with a screw thread are manufactured using 3D printing technology.

5   Motion and Controlling

The undercart has three DC motors, these motor are from small handy drilling machines. We decided to use them because they have a very good rotary speed (about 200 rotations per minute), they are mechanically strong and against normal modelling motors with same parameters are more than 20 times cheaper. It is a good challenge to controll them.

Each wheel has a rotary encoder with 2000 pulses per rotation, H-bridge and a microprocessor to control it. We use a STM32 - VL Discovery board. Operating code is written in C, rotary encoder is read and it allows to control rotary speed of motor, changing PWM parametres and counting absolute position on the playground.

Motion module gets inctructions from the main board, it receives the desired global position X, Y, ϕ and sends the actual global positions and confirmation about reaching desired position.

From absolute desired and actual position relative position $p = [x, y, \varphi]^T$ is counted, the three distances of wheels $d = [d_1, d_2, d_3]^T$ can calculated:

$$d = A \cdot p, \tag{1}$$

where

$$A = \begin{bmatrix} cos(0) & sin(0) & r \\ cos(\frac{2 \cdot \pi}{3}) & sin(\frac{2 \cdot \pi}{3}) & r \\ cos(\frac{-2 \cdot \pi}{3}) & sin(\frac{-2 \cdot \pi}{3}) & r \end{bmatrix},$$

where r is robot radius.

We defined absolute coordinate system, position $(0,0)$ is in the corner of blue start area on the playground. The problem of self localization is an inverse problem to equation 1. Matrix A is regular, so relative position can be calculated using measured distances from rotary encoders:

$$p = A^{-1} \cdot d$$

6   Conclusion

This year we wanted to concentrate on perfect mechanical design. We constructed an omniwheel undercart because it doesn't have to move a lot which allows the robot to save time that could be used to collect play items. The undercart was designed to be more versatile and hopefully suitable for the coming years of the competition. We wanted to be able to collect one king, one queen and three pawns at a time, so three storage bins were designed. The classic square robot can't hold such a number of play items. The robot undercart and body are built from dural and all parts are custom made.

At the finalization time of this paper, robot is built but it will be tested duting the following days. For the czech national round, we would like to have precise robot control and localization using rotary encoders. Our strategy is based only on finite state machines among the four strategies adopted the basic one is to build two towers in the bonus areas. From previous experiences, we suppose that it will be enough to proceed to the international round.

At first one part of the team will be testing "dummy" robot for national round, other team members will improve some parts of the robot, etc: computer vision. Last year, we designed a camera system that is placed in the beacons so could have "global" view of playground. Code for detecting play items will be modified and use the known distribution variants of play items, opponent position will be observed too.

We would like to have a second localization module too. On the playground are three stands for beacons, beacon system based on infrared signal was designed. In the beacons are infrared diodes placed around the beacon. Infrared diodes are powered by square signal, each beacon has different signal frequency. On the roof of our robot is placed a receiver. This receiver is built from one infrared transistor, it has a very small receiving area and it is conected to the stepper motor. transistor rotates and receives signals from the beacons, angles are known and distance is counted from light intensity. This method has a problem with asynchrounous data and it will have to be solved. From this and rotary encoders position, the most probable position will be counted using Kalman Filter.

We supposed that our strategy will be modified too because we would like to use information about global opponent position and play items position from the camera system. We will use state machines too (during previous competitions we observed that robots based on artificial intelligence were very slow), but it will be more sophisticated.

Acknowledgements. Construction of this robot would not be possible without support of companies RobZone [9], National Instruments [6], Hackers models [3], Secondary school of Engineering at Prosek, Prague [8] and Center for Machine Perception [1]. Our university - Czech Technical University in Prague support us too.

We thank all members of team FELaaCZech [2]:

- Jan Baxa (programming engineer)
- David Cifera (designing engineer)
- Jan Černý (programming engineer)
- Tomáš Drábek (assistant engineer)
- Václav Jahoda (designing engineer)
- Jaroslav Halgašík (designing and programming engineer)
- Vladimír Horyna (programming engineer)

- Karel Lenc (computer vision)
- Lenka Mudrová (designing and programming engineer)
- Aleš Ondrá ček (computer vision)
- Oliver Porges (programming engineer)
- Jan Vakula (computer vision).

We thank Eurobot organizers and volunteers for their efforts in contest organization.

References

1. Center for Machine Perception, http://cmp.felk.cvut.cz/
2. FELaaCZech - Team Web Pages, http://www.felaaczech.eu
3. Hacker model - rapid prototyping, http://www.hacker-model.com
4. van Haendel, R.: Design of an omnidirectional universal mobile platform (2005)
5. Mudrová, L., Faigl, J., Halgašík, J., Krajník, T.: Estimation of Mobile Robot Pose from Optical Mouses. In: International Conference on Research and Education in Robotics, Eurobot Conference 2010, pp. 10–15 (2010)
6. National Instruments, http://www.ni.com
7. Singleboard - sbRIO-9642, http://www.ni.com/singleboard/
8. Secondary School of Engineering at Prosek, Prague, http://www.sps-prosek.cz
9. RobZone - Robotic vacuum cleaner, http://www.robzone.cz

A Practical Mobile Robotics Engineering Course Using LEGO Mindstorms

Ana C. Murillo, Alejandro R. Mosteo, Jose A. Castellanos, and Luis Montano

Department of Informatics and Systems Engineering
I3A, University of Zaragoza, Spain
{acm,mosteo,jacaste,montano}@unizar.es

Abstract. Mobile robotics and autonomous systems are subjects of increasing interest in the curricula of engineering studies, being application domains of growing importance in leading research and industry trends. In order to fulfill this demand, we have designed a robotics course for students from different engineering degrees and backgrounds. The course includes basic ideas from main topics in mobile robotics, with an important practical component. During the course, each student team is provided with a LEGO Mindstorms kit to freely build a robot and develop several modules demonstrating the specific competences being taught. Complete integration of all modules is the last step towards participation in a final obstacle-race competition, which has been shown to be a very successful and motivating activity for the students. This paper summarizes the course content, goals and methodology and details the results obtained in the student contest performed in the recent years.

Keywords: Mobile robotics course, student contest, LEGO Mindstorms.

1 Introduction

Robotics applications have become widespread in recent years, moving from confined industrial environments to daily life situations. Increasingly automated cars, rescue vehicles for distress situations, home robots that aid in housekeeping tasks, envisioned assistants for the elderly are a few examples of present and eagerly anticipated robotic presence in our lives.

In particular, our research group has strong expertise in the fields of autonomous and service robotics, a core competence in this kind of applications. Therefore, we have designed different activities related to engineering and service robotics, to push and promote both the engineering studies and the robotics field among current and prospective students. The focus of this paper is an undergraduate course, whose main goal is to provide students with basic concepts and skills about mobile and autonomous robotics. We teach well-known algorithms used to solve basic tasks in these systems and to provide students with a robotic platform where they can practice and test all these ideas.

D. Obdržálek and A. Gottscheber (Eds.): EUROBOT 2011, CCIS 161, pp. 221–235, 2011.

In educational frameworks, the typically high cost of robotic hardware can be an obstacle in the way of designing practical activities for students, that could otherwise be addressed by means of simulations. However, the use of real robots provides a richer challenge for students, that have thus to tackle the varied problems that appear in complex systems involving sensors, actuators, embedded computers and software; besides this offers them a more fulfilling and engaging experience. In recent years, some toy-like products have reduced this entry gap enormously, providing most of the characteristics that exist in standard research robots in packages more suitable and affordable for education. In particular, we have focused our activities on the LEGO Mindstorms platform. The Mindstorms robots have already been used in didactic activities at a broad range of academic levels: from school kids [2] to multi-robot research projects [1]. We have leveraged this platform as a key resource to build upon in our Service Robotics course, which is taught at the several engineering degrees described next.

1.1 Framework of Our Robotics Course: Engineering School and Related Degrees

Our engineering school at the University of Zaragoza has 2900 students enrolled in five major engineering degrees. Besides, there are 300 postgraduate and PhD students. The robotic field is of great interest for many engineering degrees; therefore, our robotics course is offered as a common course for students from the different degrees detailed next.

The engineering degrees offered in our school are currently in transition from the older structure to the new European Bologna education plans. Currently, engineering studies consist of 5 academic years, 300 ECTS, with a level of competences equivalent to the new Master level, according to the European Higher Education Area. The robotics course presented here is currently offered at the following engineering degrees at the CPS: *Industrial Engineering, Telecommunications Engineering and Computer Science Engineering.*

As mentioned above, current degrees are being adapted to the European Higher Education Area. In this new framework, our university is offering several bachelor degrees (4 years, 240 ECTS), and the robotics course is planned to be part of last years courses in many of them: *Electrical Engineering, Mechanical Engineering, Electronics and Automation Engineering, Industrial Technologies Engineering, Telecommunication Technologies and Services Engineering and Computer Engineering.*

2 Mobile Robotics with LEGO Mindstorms

The LEGO Mindstorms platform has already been used at a broad range of activities regarding not only robotics learning and dissemination but other engineering topics. There are from robotics research results based on this platform

[1],[5] to multiple teaching experiences in different academic levels and different subjects (control, mobile robotics or programming) [9],[7],[3],[6],[13]. Recent studies are dedicated to evaluate up to which level this kind of platforms are an effective motivation [10]. This is a fact that we can easily guess and check when we propose students to work with them, not only for specific robotics, but to learn other related subjects [8].

2.1 LEGO Mindstorms Platform

We use the LEGO Mindstorms, version NXT 2.0, as robotic platform to run the experimental part of our course. This robotic platform is composed by its core part, the NXT brick that contains an ARM microprocessor, and a set of sensors and servo-motors that can be connected to the main block. We can connect up to 3 motors and 4 sensors from a wide range of possibilities, e.g., we work with reflected light, sonar, sound, touch, gyro, compass and camera sensors. Fig. 1 shows the NXT brick with the standard components connected to it and details of some additional sensors we use in the course projects. The NXT brick contains a small display to edit, control and launch programs and to allow the running program to display information. The programming can be done both directly at this console or, more often, from a computer. Once the program is compiled in the computer, it can be transferred to the NXT through USB or Bluetooth.

There are plenty of possibilities to program the Mindstorms, but as main development platform in our practical sessions, we use RobotC [12]. This programming environment also provides access to the NXT brick file system and allows uploading and debugging programs on the brick (shown in Fig. 2). This framework uses the industry standard C-programming language and additional language extensions specifically designed for sensors and motor usage.

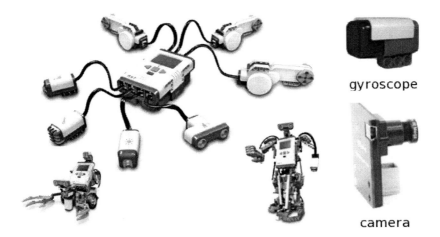

gyroscope

camera

Fig. 1. Mindstorms standard components connected to the NXT brick and sample robot models (left) and details of some non standard used sensors (right)

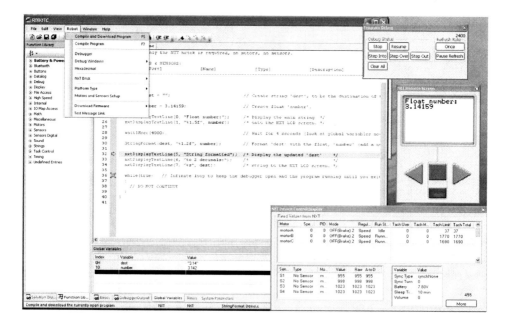

Fig. 2. Robot C programming environment

3   Our Course: Service Robotics

The course aim is to explain and develop different aspects and technologies of the so-called Service Robotics, which is an increasingly popular field with many new applications. The Service Robotics field is devoted to most robotic applications out of typical Industrial Robotics, where traditional robotic arms or manipulators are applied in automated industrial processes.

As previously mentioned, this course is offered to different engineering studies, such as Telecommunication, Computer Science, Electronic and Automation and Industrial Engineering. Therefore, the multidisciplinary orientation is inherent to this course.

The course has a strong practical orientation and the student is encouraged from the beginning to freely propose solutions and alternatives in mechanical aspects, programming techniques, sensors to be used, and so on. However, there is another important objective: the students should learn the basic theoretical foundations of robotics, in such a way that they are able to apply them. More detailed goals, methodology and course components are described in the following subsections.

3.1   Course Goals and Methodology

This section describes first the goals of the course, regarding the competences that will be developed and the results that we expect from the students after passing the course. Secondly, the methodology and activities developed through the course are summarized.

Competencies developed and expected results. This course aims to make the student develop some general skills related to engineering and robotics and acquire some specific capabilities in robotics. The specific capabilities are directly related to the contents learned in the course, while the general competencies developed are the following:

- Capability to combine general and specific knowledge in order to propose innovative solutions to technological problems.
- Problem-solving skills, with initiative, creativity and criticism.
- Oral and written knowledge communication.
- Capability of continuous and autonomous learning.
- Team work.

The learning results of the course, i.e., what every student who passes the evaluation should achieve, are the following:

- Knowing the basics and typical applications of intelligent robotic systems.
- Understanding perception techniques in robotics and how to apply them.
- Being able to implement algorithms to model the environment and localize the robots on it.
- Being able to apply path planning and navigation techniques in simple environments.
- Being able to select the most suitable robotic framework for a particular application.
- Being able to understand a research paper on the topics included in the course and explain the content to other students.

Methodology. The methodology applied is based on three completely integrated pillars: classroom sessions, tutored laboratory sessions and group project. In the first one, the basic concepts and technologies are described in such a way that the students learn the solid scientific and technical foundations of robotics to be applied in the practical sessions and in the group project. In the second one some tutored practical sessions are developed in the laboratory using the real robot and sensors. These sessions are associated to the classroom sessions and developed after each group of conceptual blocks. The results of each practical session are used by the students in the third pillar, the group project, as pieces to build and integrate in the robots the methods learned. In the laboratory sessions and the practical work the students are organized in pairs, preferably coming from different engineering backgrounds to be complementary. Both the results of tutored sessions and the group project are evaluated. Finally, a part of the evaluation is based on a competition or contest between groups. We think this additional part of the evaluation acts as an incentive for improving the resulting autonomous robot capabilities. This way, the students feel more involved in the learning process, try to understand better the theoretical concepts transmitted, and their creativity is encouraged. So far, the experience confirms these expectations.

3.2   Course Program - Classroom sessions

The classroom sessions are devoted to introduce the basic concepts and techniques in robotics in order that the students are able to develop a complete autonomous robot. Diverse aspects are developed in this multidisciplinary course: mechanics, control, programming, perception systems, trajectory generation, specific robotic techniques, and a general vision about the state of the art of Service Robotics. The course aims to simultaneously transmit solid scientific and technological foundations and practical methods to apply them. Many of the studied techniques are complemented with exercises which are oriented to reinforce the theoretical parts and to prepare the practical sessions in the laboratory in a rigorous way. The exercises are solved and presented by the students, and discussed with the professor and the rest of the students.

An important characteristic we seek in the course is to design a program that students with different backgrounds (electric, automation, computer science, communications engineering) are able to follow. The course will provide the students with the concepts and techniques to be applied in the laboratory sessions. Besides, when designing the program, it was very important to synchronize properly the classroom sessions with the practical sessions, to make sure the theoretical basis have been previously analyzed in the classroom sessions. Following these criteria, we have developed the course program into the following blocks:

1. *Introduction.* A general perspective about the state of the art in Robotics is described. A historical evolution of robots, techniques, and applications is presented, and the most relevant results in the last years are shown.

2. *Service Robotics.* The major questions to be solved in autonomous robots are presented and justified. The closed loops perception-localization and mapping-task and motion planning-motion control-locomotion and actuation are described in a general way, providing some hints about how each of these problems can be tackled.

3. *Spatial representation, locomotion and kinematics.* The mathematical tools to manage the object and robot absolute and relative localization, transformation equations, and motion computation, both in 3D and 2D, using these tools are developed. The different types of robots from the point of view of locomotion mechanisms are described and the involved geometric and kinematic models are presented.
   (a) Homogeneous representation.
   (b) Translation and rotation in the space.
   (c) Reference systems and transformations.
   (d) Types of robots. Motion and drive mechanisms and models.

4. *Concurrent Processes* The basic notions about programming of parallel processes, mutual exclusion and semaphores are explained. The objective is that

the students are able to model and program tasks in the language used in the next practical sessions, such as continuous odometry computation or range sensors testing for collisions.
(a) Task execution and parallel processes.
(b) Exclusive access and semaphores.

5. *Perception.* A description of the main internal and external sensors used in robotics to compute the motion and the localization in the environment is presented. A special focus on visual sensor is given, since one of the practical sessions is devoted to the use of a camera on the robot.
(a) Odometry and inertial sensors.
(b) Range sensors.
(c) Computer Vision in Robotics.
(d) Other sensors.

6. *Autonomous Navigation.* Methods for trajectory generation, control of the motion, and moving object tracking are described. The basic path planning and reactive navigation techniques are discussed, maintaining the focus on the ones that can be implemented in the robots used in the laboratory sessions.
(a) Automatic motion generation and tracking of trajectories.
(b) Path planning.
(c) Reactive navigation.

7. *Localization and environment modeling.* Localization, map building and basic SLAM techniques from the information of the sensors presented in previous blocks are described. The techniques are also adapted to the specific hardware used in the laboratory sessions.
(a) Localization.
(b) Map building.
(c) Self-localization and map building with different sensors.

8. *Types of Mobile Robotics architectures.* The different software architectures proposed and used in mobile robotics are described and related.
(a) Deliberation systems.
(b) Reactive systems.
(c) Hybrid systems.
(d) Behaviour-based systems.

The temporal distribution of these chapters/blocks and the practical sessions, detailed in next subsection, is summarized in Table 1.

3.3 Course Program - Practical sessions

This course has a large practical component, including four guided sessions and a robotics group project summarized next. As described, we chose the Robot C framework [12] for the development of these practical sessions with the LEGO Mindstorms robots.

Table 1. Temporal distribution of classroom and laboratory sessions in the course

weeks	classroom (3h/week)	laboratory (3h/week)
1st	Chapters 1&2	
$2^{nd} - 3^{rd}$	Chapter 3	P1
4th	Chapter 4	Hours to finish designing the robots
$5^{th} - 6^{th}$	Chapter 5	P2
7th	Chapter 6	P3
$8^{th} - 9^{th}$	Chapter 7	P4
$10^{th} - 14^{th}$	Chapter 8 & invited seminars	Autonomous work and tutoring hours to integrate the final group project
15_{th}	Student results presentations	Competition event

P1 - Initial practical session. This session consists of designing and building a mobile robot from a Mindstorms kit and getting used to the development environment and programming language that will be used in the course, Robot C. Every group will be provided with a Mindstorms kit and should design and build a free-design robot that should just fit a few requirements to be able to perform the compulsory tasks of the rest of practical sessions. Besides, a few simple exercises should be done to get to know the Robot C programing environment and the range, quality and way of accessing the robot sensors.

P2 - Motion generation and odometry estimation. This session aims to practice the advanced motion generation and estimation (from chapters 5a and 6a) and the design of concurrent processes (chapter 4). Each group has to program a module for their robot that estimates the odometry of the robot as it moves. This task must be launched in parallel with the main program of the robot. In this case, the main task of the robot will be performing a pre-defined trajectory, including some curved paths, such as an 8-like trajectory.

P3 - Vision based object tracking. This session has been designed as an introduction to vision based tasks, such as tracking, in robotics (from chapter 5c). In particular, a simple object tracking will be implemented and tested, augmenting the modules of the robot with object recognition and object tracking functions.

P4 - Autonomous navigation. This last practical guided session consists of implementing basic autonomous navigation tasks (chapter 6b and 6c). Building on the motion module built on previous sessions, the students will implement necessary algorithms for autonomous robots: path planning given a map of the environment and reactive behaviours to avoid unknown obstacles.

Group project - Student robotic contest. Each group will develop a project based on their designed robot and implemented modules during the guided sessions. First they need to integrate all previous modules, and then augment the system with new algorithms proposed by each group to achieve a series of tasks to be performed in a common scenario. Besides, the students are provided with a

Table 2. Details of student working hours distribution in the course

Activity	Hours
Classroom sessions (including discussions and presentations)	30
Guided practical sessions in the laboratory	12
Attendance to seminars from guest robotics researchers	4
Autonomous work in the laboratory or office hours (including discussions with the supervisor)	15/20
Work out of the laboratory (preparation of reports, exercises, studying)	15/20

Table 3. Details of the grading criteria at the different student evaluation activities

Activity	Grade	Description - criteria
Practical sessions	30%	Demonstration and oral discussion with the instructor about the modules developed in practical sessions P2, P3 and P4. Besides, student should hand in reports of preparation work for the practical session and brief post-session report explaining the implemented module.
Group Project	30%	Demonstration of the team project developed functionalities, i.e., demonstrate how many tasks from the contest the robot is able to achieve (each team individually, still out of the contest execution).
Competition results	10%	Contest results achieved by each team as explained in Section 4.
Classroom discussion	10%	Oral presentation and discussions in the classroom sessions, including a final presentation of the team contest achievements.
Classroom exercises	10%	Exercises and problems solved from the proposed exercises in the classroom sessions. These are related to demonstrate the understanding of the concepts explained in the classes or from research papers proposed to be read.
Robot design	10%	Originality and/or quality of the robot designed by each team.
Optional tasks	10%	This additional part can be obtained in the final grade by implementing additional and innovative tasks in the project team, different from the required ones (for example integrating different available sensors, such as a gyro, or implementing new modules for additional skills to demonstrate in the given scenario or out of it).

scenario where to implement and test optional tasks from the more advanced concepts at the course (chapter 7). The details of this contest (scenario, tasks,...), which is being currently developed by our students, are given in the following section 4. The performance of each team will be evaluated individually and in a contest among all the teams, as an additional motivation for innovative and efficient solutions.

3.4   Course Evaluation

The course is designed with the idea that each student should approximately invest the hours detailed in Table 2 in each activity, and each of these activities will be evaluated along the quarter.

Students are required to hand in some exercises before each laboratory session, and perform a demonstration or report after it. Besides, each student will be evaluated during the classroom sessions, through participation in discussions and exercises proposed and through the oral presentations of the modules developed in the practical sessions. Finally the group project contest will be the main evaluation activity, where all modules developed in the practical sessions and project should be demonstrated. The students should prove their project functionality in the contest and also make a presentation describing the interesting or key ingredients in their design. A more detailed distribution of the grading evaluation is shown next in Table 3. Due to the sometimes random component in the contest results, we provide the students with additional ways to obtain the maximum grade with optional activities. This helps to avoid the fact that only the winners of the race achieve the maximum final grades.

4   Results of the Course and Student Robotic Contest

This section describes the results after deploying this course during the last three academic years, paying special attention to the final robotic contest run among the students at the end of the course.

4.1   Results from the Course

Results after running this course for the last three years are very satisfactory: students get very involved in the course, they obtain good results and grades and their interest on robotics activities is also increased after the course, with many of them performing following courses and master thesis in related topics. We have around 15 or 20 students in a class, working in teams of two or three students. Average grade obtained in two previous years (current year is still to be evaluated) is 8 (10 is the maximum grade). Most of the 15 teams that had taken part in the course during previous years were able to execute most of the tasks in the final competition.

4.2   Robotic Competition: Scenario, Tasks and Results

The basic idea of the competition is to integrate all the modules developed in the practical sessions. Then, students should program some additional skills for each robot to take part in the contest-race among all teams: robots should perform as fast as possible, and as accurate as possible, all the required tasks. Each year, we adapt or slightly change the required tasks to be performed during the competition but the basic ideas are similar. The scenario built for last year competition and a detailed scheme of its different areas are shown in Fig. 3.

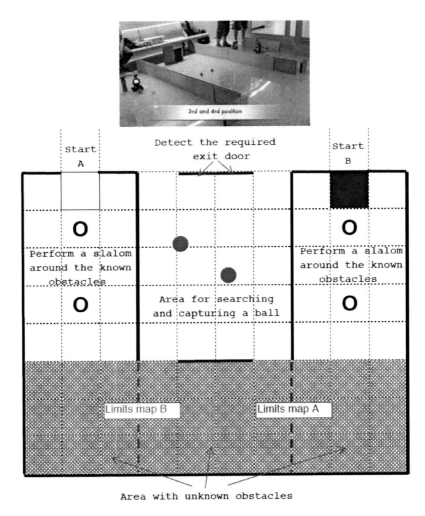

Fig. 3. An image of the real scenario built during the competition (top) and a scheme of the contest scenario (bottom), pointing in which parts of the scenario the robot should perform each of the tasks

Required tasks. Given a map of the environment, each team has to be able to perform the following tasks in specific areas of the scenario:

- Detect the starting location from the ground color. This would allow the robot to initialize its starting location coordinates, its goal location coordinates and the goal-color.

- Perform a "slalom" through known obstacles in part A of the scenario.

- Traverse the maze in part B of the scenario. The map only provides the out-limits, but unknown obstacles can appear, therefore the robot should be able to avoid them and re-plan its way out of the maze.

- Find and catch a ball, using the camera and some kind of clamp or grasping mechanism, in part C of the scenario.

- While carrying the ball, the robot should identify using the camera which is the exit-door of its given color and get out through it.

Designed robots. Students are told to build a robot with these requirements:

- The motion should be based on wheels, fitting approximately the differential drive kinematics model.

- The third motor should be used to close a grasping mechanism, and the camera should be placed pointing towards it.

- The robot should include as well a reflected light sensor pointing to the floor to detect signs in the ground, and a sonar sensor pointing to the front to avoid obstacles.

Figure 4 shows some examples of the different robot constructions built by the students of this course. Most of these robots were able to perform all tasks. Initially, every robot has to demonstrate individually all the activities that it is able to perform properly. Then, sorting the participants according to the time needed to perform all the tasks, all the teams take part in a kind of play-off: pairs of robots compete against each other, and the winner of each round qualifies for the next. Figure 5 shows two robots searching and capturing the ball, in the scenario built for the competition. A more detailed summary of the achievements can be observed in the videos available in the course website[1]. The competition evaluation considers not only the fastest participant on getting out of the scenario, but also how good the tasks were achieved on the way.

Fig. 4. Examples of the robots built by the students and podiums of two previous years with winners of the race

---

[1] http://webdiis.unizar.es/~anacris/carrera10/index.html

Fig. 5. Video frames of a contest round with two participants in the scenario during searching phase (left) and trying to catch the ball (right)

5   Advanced Robotics Experimentation

For students interested in robotic, we offer them to perform projects/thesis on advanced robotics topics and solve more complicated tasks. The growing popularity of the Mindstorms platform makes possible the use of research- and industry-grade tools as a transitional step, by using the same software suites that are deployed in more powerful robots. Two approaches are possible: on the one hand, the use of regular software in small laptops on-board the robot or nearly located using Bluetooth; on the other, the replacement of the stock NXT firmware with an embedded controller. From the most extended ones in the robotics community, two of each of these options are available to enthusiast alumni:

1. Player robotic library [4]. This library provides an abstract layer (via so-called interfaces) over a large variety of robotic platforms. It is widely used in the research community for both simulation and real experimentation. A driver (nxt) developed by the authors and available right now in the project SVN enables control of the NXT actuators via direct USB connection.

2. ROS – Robot Operating System [11]. This newer robotic framework is well-suited for complex robots, with many degrees of freedom, and possibly using a cluster of embedded machines instead of a single computer for control. Software modules in ROS are structured in *stacks*, such as NXT-ROS which enables full interaction with a NXT brick.

3. LejOS – Java for LEGO Mindstorms.[2] Moving into the embedded domain, this project delivers a tiny Java virtual machine that replaces the stock firmware and a suite of accompanying tools. Thus, it enables the use of Java and its modern characteristics on-board the robot. A class library is also provided that gives access to the NXT sensors and actuators.

4. GNAT GPL Ravenscar edition for Mindstorms.[3]. Advanced topics arising in high-reliability and safety embedded systems can be approached by means of the software suite made available under GPL license by AdaCore. This tool, which also replaces the stock NXT firmware, enables usage of Ada, a language

---

[2] Available at `http://lejos.sourceforge.net`
[3] Available at `http://libre.adacore.com/libre/tools/mindstorms/`

well-suited for high-integrity systems; SPARK, an Ada subset aimed at automatic code validation; and the Ravenscar profile, designed for safety-critical real-time software that has to undergo certification.

As initial results regarding these advanced topics, the following activities have been finished:

- One student designed during his Master thesis an environment to remotely monitor and control Mindstorms robots with LejOS, including algorithms from the course and additional motion models and algorithms regarding planning and avoidance.
- The authors working in multi-robot cooperation have prepared a LEGO model which houses a regular nettop and a small Hokuyo laser rangefinder. With this setup, localization and communication can be easily achieved in indoor setups, offering the possibility of Master-level research projects using the mentioned tools, under the guidance and expertise of the researchers in the department.

6 Conclusions

This paper summarizes framework, goals and contents of our service robotics course. This course is offered in our engineering degrees, since mobile robotics and autonomous systems are subjects of increasing interest in the curricula of engineering studies, being application domains of growing importance in leading research and industry trends. The course is given in a multi-disciplinary class environment and has a strong practical component. The practical part of the course is based on LEGO Mindstorms, which the students use to freely build a robot to perform the learned and required tasks and take part in the final course contest. This strong practical component has been shown in our experience to be a highly motivating factor for the students, specially the final course contest. The results have been really interesting, with very good final gradings both for the students (average of 8.5 out of 10) and the course (the students highly value this course).

Acknowledgments. We gratefully acknowledge our department (Informática e Ing. de Sistemas) and school (Escuela de Ingeniería y Arquitectura) for their financial support to get the materials and the colleagues that helped setting them up.

References

1. Benedettelli, D., Casini, M., Garulli, A., Giannitrapani, A., Vicino, A.: A LEGO Mindstorms experimental setup for multi-agent systems. In: 3rd IEEE Multi-Conference on Systems and Control, pp. 1230–1235 (2009)
2. Druin, A., Hendler, J. (eds.): Robots for kids: exploring new technologies for learning. Morgan Kaufmann Publishers Inc., San Francisco (2000)

3. Gawthrop, P., McGookin, E.: Using LEGO in control education. In: Dormido, S., Morilla, F., Sanchez, J. (eds.) 7th IFAC Symposium on Advances in Control Education. IFAC, Madrid (2006)
4. Gerkey, B.P., Vaughan, R.T., Howard, A.: The player/stage project: Tools for multi-robot and distributed sensor systems. In: Int. Conf. on Advanced Robotics, pp. 317–323 (2003)
5. Goncales, J., Lima, J., Malheiros, P., Costa, P.: Realistic simulation of a LEGO Mindstorms NXT based robot. In: Control Applications (CCA) Intelligent Control (ISIC), pp. 1242–1247. IEEE, Los Alamitos (2009)
6. Grega, W., Pilat, A.: Real-time control teaching using LEGO® Mindstorms®. In: IMCSIT, pp. 625–628 (2008)
7. Kim, S.H., Jeon, J.W.: Educating C language using LEGO Mindstorms robotic invention system 2.0. In: Proc. of IEEE International Conference on Robotics and Automation, pp. 715–720 (2006)
8. Klassner, F., Continanza, C.: Mindstorms without robotics: an alternative to simulations in systems courses. SIGCSE Bull. 39, 175–179 (2007)
9. Leitão, P., Gonçalves, J., Barbosa, J.: Learning mobile robotics using LEGO Mindstorms. In: 9th Spanish-Portuguese Congress on Electrical Engineering (2005)
10. McWhorter, W.I., O'Connor, B.C.: Do LEGO® Mindstorms® motivate students in CS1? SIGCSE Bull. 41, 438–442 (2009), http://doi.acm.org/10.1145/1539024.1509019
11. Quigley, M., Gerkey, B., Conley, K., Faust, J., Foote, T., Leibs, J., Berger, E., Wheeler, R., Ng, A.: ROS: an open-source robot operating system. In: IEEE/RSJ Int. Conf. on Robotics and Automation (ICRA 2009): Workshop on Open Source Software (2009)
12. RobotC, http://www.robotc.net, carnegie Mellon University - Robotics Academy
13. Talaga, P., Oh, J.C.: Combining AIMA and LEGO Mindstorms in an artificial intelligence course to build real world robots. J. Comput. Small Coll. 24, 56–64 (2009)

An 8 Year Old Educational Robotics Program – Structure, Methodology and Goals

Othon da Rocha Neves Jr.[1], João Bosco da Mota Alves[2],
and Josué J.G. Ramos[3]

[1] SESI Industry Social Service, Florianopolis, Brazil
[2] UFSC/EGC - Knowledge Engineering and Management, Florianopolis, Brazil
[3] CTI, Renato Archer IT Center, Campinas, Brazil
othonrnj@sesisc.org.br, jbosco@inf.ufsc.br, josue.ramos@cti.gov.br

Abstract. The "Talents For the Industry Program", is an 8 year educational robotics program that has been running in Brazil since 2002. The program was created with the goal of developing talents with the ability to deal with technology using robotic activities as a tool to reach this goal. The program was implemented in a set of four hour weekly activities that lasts 18 months. The main objective of this paper is to show how these goals are mapped in the structure, methodology and classes of this program.

Keywords: Robotics, program, methodology, goals.

1 Introduction

There is a growing use of robotics as tool for learning and education [1,2]. There has also been a growing the number of conferences and publications addressing this theme. Considering the importance of this subject, this paper presents an educational robotics program that started its planning phase in 2001 and has been running since 2002, and it is nearly nine years old.

The report to UNESCO from the International Commission on Education for the Twenty-first Century [3] has inspired some educational programs in Brazil and has also been discussed within industrial associations including FIESC (Santa Catarina State federation industry association)[4]. The main conclusions of this report were: i) it compares the state of development in Brazil with other countries and compares Brazil's development with the development of its educational system; ii) it stress the relation between the rate of technical progress of a country and the quality of human action, making evident the need to train people capable of using new technologies innovatively; iii) it shows the need for new skills in industry; iv) it stresses the need that the educational system must answer to these needs, not only giving the necessary training, but also in preparing senior staff for this task.

Considering the limitation of these entities in regular schools, FIESC decided to implement a project outside the regular schools as a more immediate option. More importantly, the results could help in designing new models and new projects. It was decided that it would develop a technology education program.

D. Obdržálek and A. Gottscheber (Eds.): EUROBOT 2011, CCIS 161, pp. 236–247, 2011.

In 2001 the planning and preparation process began and the result was the creation of a program that started in 2002. This pedagogical work resulted in a course called Educational Technology Journey wich was applied in three semesters or units. These courses have been applied in several cities of the state of Santa Catarina, since the first semester of 2002.

This introductory section has presented the motivations of Educational Technology Journey; Section 2 presents the Mode of the operation of the program; Section 3 presents how the classes are conducted; Section 4 discusses how the goals of the program are reached and Section 5 presents the conclusions.

2 Talents for the Industry - Mode of Operation

The Education Program called Talents for the Industry [5] aims to identify, develop and promote talent in among children and youth. The Education Program was established by the Federation of Industries of the State of Santa Catarina. The program includes educational sites, educational materials with a physical structure, staff development and the management of teachers. This structure was replicated in four sites of application of the course in different cities of the state.

The course is taught by an instructor with a technical-technological background and a complete high school education and there is an instructor per teaching site. The work of the instructors is guided and supervised by an educator. Now, after a didactic and operational adjustment the classes are composed of a maximum of 24 students divided into groups of four students.

In designing an educational robotics program, it is necessary to define a set of operational aspects such as timing, the training of instructors, group size and age, the characteristics of classrooms and materials, and educational materials. The next section presents how these aspects are implemented and the factors that led to each decision.

2.1 Frequency and Characteristics of the Groups

Groups have a single weekly meeting from 3:30 to 4 hours. This duration is relatively long for a young person but it allows for the projects to be completed in a single meeting. The classes are composed of a maximum of 24 students divided into groups of four. In general, activities with robotics materials are performed in groups. Based on the experiences of the supplier of educational material, wich recommend that a group should not be less than three and no more than four, we adopted this criterion. The number of groups was initially set to eight, as it was noticed that a group with this size complicated the implementation of complex projects. The class was reduced to six teams after the second year of the project. In the definition of the age range (11 to 17) the decision was that a project of this nature would have greater impact if applied to students in the early stages of the elementary and secondary education. The educational program aims to lay the foundations of a technological culture and extent their abilities

and cognitive development. Thereby, the student will can act as a creative agent
of technological solutions for their problems and within their communities.

2.2   Instructors and Pedagogical Support

In the beginning, the question was what would be more effective: an educator
with an interest in technology or a techie with a taste and interest in pedagogy?
Experience had shown that both solutions are feasible, though, since the beginning the program has made the choice of a full-time technician, with the close
supervision of a educator interacting with the class in part-time. In the case of a
teacher with Educator background there is a need for a deep technical training.
Thus, the course currently is taught by an instructor with technical-technological
and complete high school education, with one instructor per site with the work
constantly guided and supervised by an educator.

2.3   Classrooms and Materials Available in the Classrooms

The classroom for project activities should provide space for all workbenches,
each equipped with a computer and enough space for mounting and assembly
experiments. It should also include the teacher's desk with a structure similar
to the student's benches. Also necessary are a desk to house the boxes of the
robotics kits and a space for the installation of arenas for the realization of
the challenges, where everyone can watch the performance of projects. Since
2002 three rooms were set up in different cities of the state of Santa Catarina,
currently there are four rooms.

The basic kit for robotics is sufficient to conduct many educational activities.
There are plastic blocks of varying sizes and fittings, gears, pulleys, wheels, axles,
motors, touch sensors, light sensors, and a programmable logic controller. This
equipment comprises a basic set of about 750 pieces, which serves a group of
four students. But some sites, of course, have other additional themed kits. It
is possible to perform the entire process with one kit per group and accomplish
educational goals. However, there are sites dealing with different themed kits and
other technologies that provide reserves of spare parts and long-term projects,
which remain mounted after the end of class. Complementary kits help teachers
manage events outside conventional classrooms.

2.4   Relation Between Age and Teaching Material

The Characteristics of the equipment helped identify the age range of the educational program. We defined the minimum age from aspects related to student motivation and interest at the activities feasible with the equipment. The
equipment incorporates educational activities with mechanical components and
dynamic logic programming. Especially this last mobilizes a small number of children under the age of 10 years. We found that from 11 years old the percentage of
students with this interest grows significantly. Although this finding was made in

rapid experiments with a relatively small group, it has supported the definition of the minimum age of 11 years for participation in the educational program. Years of experience confirmed this definition. Over the subsequent eight years the program only accept two students under the age of 11 in the subsequent eigth years: these children were accpet because parental request. The child's interest contributed to the success of this procedure in such cases. The upper age limit was not determined by strong pedagogical reasons, it was decided that the program was applicable to high school students under 18. It is also important to report that since 2006 the activities were extended to the adult public due to the demand. Some sites case they originate specific adults class. Then, in 2008, the classes were redesigned specifically for the adult public.

2.5   External Actions

They include participation in external events, fairs and exhibitions of projects. During the first seven years, a number of students and projects were selected for participation in national scientific fairs aimed to elementary and middle schools, and inventors fairs sponsored by various organizations. To extend participation in external events, a larger group of students showed projects within the sponsoring industrial companies, where students had the opportunity to present their work and their ideas to industry workers. These external events stimulated the creation of more complex projects, and creates the need to managing the project plan and schedule, and also created the need for the development of oral and written language. This is an important strategy since the activities in the classroom are intensely practical and constructive. The consolidation of knowledge organization of thought are encouraged and strengthened by these strategies.

3   Talents for the Industry - The Classes

The dynamics of the classes consists mainly in solving problem situations whose solutions can be found in technological possibilities of the material. This happens in the creation and construction of a prototype, which can be a machine, vehicle, robot or other mechanical system. Optionally the system can be powered and controlled by a programmed logic on a personal computer and uploaded to the robot controller. For example, building a conveyor that carries spare parts and recognizes the parts by color or a vehicle following a black line on the floor. Besides the technological material, other pedagogical resources are available on the website of the educational program, where there is content in the form of text, images and videos, personal pages of students and teachers and blogs. Among other pedagogical resources, can be included demonstrations and technical visits to industry, participation in events as scientifc and inventor fairs and tournaments.

3.1   Handout and Motivation Materials

A set of basic texst was produced to generate motivation for the robotics theme. This basic text is a required reading for the teacher, and optional for the student, and it is seen as the main way of assuring the program's uniformity despite the program's geographical dispersion. This text is composed of three units: i) Introduction to Robotics: Concepts, History and Technology. Deals with the history of robotics and technology while introducing basic concepts of mechanics and production, transmission and transformation of the movement; ii) Robotics and Industry: Applications and News: This is the current state of robotics development and deployment of the robot industry while introducing concepts of control, and programming logic; iii) Robotics and Research. Technology and Science: Presents what scientists are preparing for the future of robotics, while introducing advanced concepts and programming techniques applicable to mobile robotics.

3.2   Curricula Content

The availability of teaching materials (robotic kits) also interfere in the content of the educational program of this study, which consist in a situation-problem-oriented, dealing with robotics, in particular, and industrial automation, in general. This is a worthwhile approach since this knowledge is of strategic interest to the industry association, that is the main sponsor of the program.

The course consists of three full semesters, each composed of 20 meetings. Usually, these meetings have the structure of a workshop where one creates a project that addresses one or more situations-problems. There are different meetings when students are building larger projects to participate in external events. There are free themed workshops, where students define what will be done. In the first 20 workshops the students work with mechanisms, in the other 40 they must also work with programming and logic. But regardless of these variations, there is a standard structure that can be called a typical workshop, which is repeated throughout the process.

3.3   A Typical Class

In a typical workshop, the group is divided into teams of four students. This team can remain constant throughout the educational program, but this is not necessary. Each member of a team can have a different role in a class as: assembling the objects or mechanisms, separation and organization of parts, program coding, presenting the project, etc. It is appropriate to the teacher to identify the roles and promote the rotation between the students in every new workshop.

A typical workshop has four stages: **context, challenge, solution and discussion**. Invariably this process leads to the construction of a mechanical prototype and control software, whose performance is shared with the entire class. The role of the context phase is to give meaning to the problem situation that will be created. For this, the instructor may consult the program texts themselves or any other material available on the web. He can also, through interaction with the students, bring to the context the knowledge they possess on the subject. Once the scene is set, a problem situation is presented as a challenge or a series of challenges.

Different combinations of problem situation and solutions can be explored. In more complex workshops before presenting the challenge, it can be proposed a step by step assembly of a basic project, that doesn't solve the problem in the original form, but it asks for changes or some compliment or extension to solve it.

This extension enables the use of complex situations in the time frame available and additionally provides the opportunity for interaction and appropriation of knowledge available on this project. Sometimes this basic design of a complete mechanism of a machine as a vehicle or a robot is offered, and the student has to create the program that controls the machine. Sometimes an incomplete version of the software is also made available, requiring reading, comprehension, application and test to identify the changes needed to tackle the challenge.

The **discussion** starts with the presentation of projects. In general, the first team makes a more complete presentation and the subsequent teams focuses on the differences between their solution. The teacher also promotes an interaction with students through a series of questions with the meaning and purpose to encourage and direct to reflection and verbalization of issues associated with the goals of that workshop. There are questions of a technical-technological and of attitudinal nature. It is assumed that the success of teams pass through the knowledge and also the skills and attitudes required in group activities. At the end of the discussion, students are encouraged to make a written account of the lived experience: a short text where he can put personal impressions of subjective or technical nature, including images of the project or team working. In the first year of the project this report took place in a paper logbook. Then these accounts were made on the web in the form of blogs. The bloggers in principle were public, and since 2006, the blogs were hosted on the educational program's own site.

In addition to this educational role of blogs in the primary education program, its implementation has brought side benefits. For example, the general supervision of the program had a good sense of what happened in classrooms spread across different cities of the state. Another example, once that ideas and solutions created on a class are discovered, they are applied or enhanced in a different class. As teachers were also blogging, new teachers had access to everything that was done in previous editions by other teachers, and the results of the actions reflected in the blogs of students. The set of blogs that is being built is a picture of the culture produced in the program.

3.4   An Overview of the Challenges

The educational program allows application of variations by the teacher, so he or she has the freedom to introduce new topics, share the results with other teachers through blogs, creating sections with free themes for giving space for students expressing their creativity in proposing their own challenges, see Figure 1. But there is a common well-defined route to be applied by all. The course consists of a series of challenges that using two mechanisms that are sufficiently simple: a conveyor belt and a mobile robot, Figure 2.

Fig. 1. This picture shows a typical challenge of cooperative robotics on using Robelius variants configured a forklift

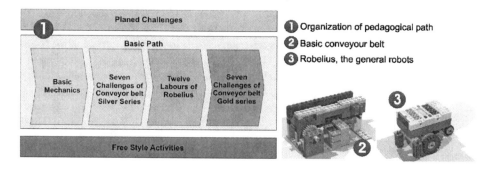

Fig. 2. This picture shows in the left the infogram for the activities development and in the right the two basic mechanisms used for challenge: a conveyor belt and Robelius

The conveyor belt is used to start the programming activities. Since it has only one motor and it works fixed on the assembly table its assembly and operation is simple. There are three sets of proposals, identified as challenges with names associated with their increasing complexity: Silver Series, Gold Series, Super Series.

The first challenge of the silver series is to move the belt without any control. The solution is the minimum program. Each challenge adds functions: a start button, that runs for a specified time, stop button, reverse button, detecting the presence of parts, lack of parts, alarms, detection and disposal of different pieces by color, count lots of parts, etc.

The Silver and Gold Series have seven challenges each one, and the teacher provides optimal solutions for each one of them. The Super Challenge series is not scheduled to be held in actual classroom, solutions are not even available. But propositions of associations of conveyors or devices that manipulate the pieces that come off the conveyors. The goal is to encourage the emergence of unusual ideas that can be exploited free classes, serve as student insights to the creation of new projects that might contribute to the collection of solutions naturally arranged inside the blogs in the theme related to the conveyor belt.

3.5   Mobile Robot Challenge, and the Twelve Labors of Robelius

The other series of the challenges is called "The Twelve Labours of Robelius" in reference to the Twelve Labors of Hercules in Greek mythic literature. Robelius is the name given to a mobile robot with two motors, two light sensors pointed at the ground for the identification of ground tracks and marks on the area of navigation. This robot does not contain any type of effector that acts over the world. This is a generic platform in order to make navigation experiments. In the first "Work of Robelius" the student is asked to solve some primitives navigation problems that can be solved with the resources of the educational material. This means moving the robot forward, backward, left and right, identify the limits of the demarcated area, following a black trail on the ground space, identify lateral markings close to the trail and identify the track end tags, identify crossings, and take the street on the right or in the left. These initial challenges are resolved using the commands of the programming language that act at the level of the motors To achieve the later more complex challenges, the teacher provides a library of macros that correspond to the challenges addressed above, now transformed into a compound statement. We can then say that the challenges are programmed into the subsequent level of the robot. Here the student has contact with the notion of modularity of the software.

The infograms shown in the Figure 2 shows the two basic mechanical assemblies for the completion of the series. It also shows the regular flow path of the challenges along with other resulting from the freedom given by the creativity of the teacher and students, which are the programmed challenges and the free themes.. The series of conveyor challenges "Silver Series" and "Gold Series" can be mixed with the series "The Twelve Labours of Robelius" to give more dynamic to the classes with the variation of the mechanical assemblies. What matters here is that it is good start with simple mechanics with a single motor, and that it is fixed on the table. A simple project free the student to diagnose errors and correct programs. The Gold series brings challenges logically more complex that stimulates the development of the capacity to use the combinations of flow control structures in programming.

It must be understood that what was described here corresponds to the regular program, that is what is the common background of the Educational Program, distributed by the cities. It is necessary to remark that there are also variations due to the freedom for creation given to the teacher and students.

4   Discussion: Evaluation the Program's Tangible Goals

This session discusses how the methodology helps to achieve the tangible goals of the program, which are i) Technological Fluency, ii) Development of Cooperation Capacity, iii) Ability to Solve Problems, iv) Ability to Contribute Creatively, v) capacity of expression and preservation and dissemination of knowledge.

4.1   Development of Technological Fluency

Technological fluency in this context means the capacity of dealing with technological gadgets as gears, sensors and the integration of a controller to operates this gadget. It also means the capacity to associate the knowledge developed in a simulator of the reality to the real life.

In the environment of the classes students have the opportunity to interact intensively with technological content objects. There are moments that favor interaction through challenges on a pre-defined incomplete or in an insufficient, but contextualized and meaningful project. There are times when the students is defied to solve problems based on the shortcomings and incompleteness of previous projects, creating opportunities to the incorporation and growth of knowledge based on previous concepts and solutions. And finally, there are moments that emphasize the production of new solutions for problems identified by the students.

In the development of the program a set of tools are used as computers with development and projects tools, search for information tools, programmable logic controllers and program development software; mechanical assemblies with motors, transmission and processing of motion using mechanical components as gears, pulleys, wheels, axes. These set of tools if properly used by the students and teachers promotes a significant development of technological fluency for the teenagers. Also the type of Technological Fluency developed acquires a character of complexity and sophistication characterized by the ability of synthesis with very different technologies related to computer and control of movement and physical acting upon the world.

Although the Education Program does not create opportunities to transfer this acquired fluency out of the robotics kit material universe used, it creates a more general opportunities for verbal expression about the experience either within the team, class, shows, fairs and exhibitions. In this case the fluency goes beyond the limited sphere of material used.

4.2   Development of Cooperation Capacity

The mere fact of organizing a group of four people to achieve the common goal of building a project or overcoming a challenge requires the development of the ability to work cooperatively and at the same time they are threatened by the failure of not completing the project on schedule, this is a very serious issue that teaches people to work cooperatively.

There are other factors that contribute to making the process more effective. Very often the solution of the proposed situations is outside the visible range of students. It was not taught a method that solves a situation. They are extremely young. No past experience that definitely contributes. So in these cases, the solution has a character of a random search.

This solution of the problem as a random search has two softening factors: the first is that the solution space has its dimension reduced by the fact that the student knows the material solution is in the robotics kit Lego, its components and its fittings. The second is that there are several teams working together searching the solution in the solution limited space. As in the search process there is, of course, interaction between the teams, there is a tendency of convergence to the better solution of the moment and carry out a search for the optimization of variations around that solution.

This process works as a ritual that reinforces the maxim of the cooperation: "No one of us is stronger and powerful than all of us" [6]. The workshops were designed to demonstrate and to give awareness of the power and strength of a group, considering that this is a foundation of the ability to cooperate. The teacher has to identify opportunities to make the mediation of positive and negative attitudes towards cooperation, helping the group to identify its relations with successes and failures, the advantages and difficulties. Outside the context of the teaching material, the search spaces are more complex but the experience of cooperation and team spirit can prevail.

4.3 Development the Ability to Solve Problems

What we call problem may have very different nature in different situations. The competence discussed here, is the ability to solve problems is a general form. There are problems that can be solved with logic. Sometimes combines logical thinking with the use of a knowledge we have about the problem domain. The knowledge that "we have" can be directly applicable in solving the problem. Sometimes one has no knowledge directly applicable, but through some kind of analogy another knowledge can be transferred to the situation. When it is possible to materialize, or transfer the necessary knowledge, one has to build it.

In all of these resources it is compounded by the possibility to try, try, evaluate, and try again. It's not a question of method, but the attitude before the defiance, and the possible failure in an attempt.

The workshops do not present methods for solving problems, but they works for building attitudes in front of a problem. The first key point is to see the problem as a challenge. And the fun side of the problem that lead to appreciate the problem or would like to be called for help in solving a problem. Starting from the structure of a created situation, the team work leads to the awareness of the need of a clear definition and identification of a problem by the application of knowledge and the materialization of knowledge for the benefit of the solution in a process of decision making. The teacher has to observe the shortcomings of the process and conduct the mediation of the results as they are success or failure are they easy or difficult.

4.4 Development of the Ability to Contribute Creatively

The Education Program Workshops does not promote a method or especific activities with defined objectives for the development of creativity. Instead, the workshops are responsible for maintaining a climate favorable to creativity. Creativity is a very human characteristic and indeed people who do not consider themselves creative, maybe they have some barriers that blocked ones creativity in many different orders. The most obvious is the fear of making mistakes. There is no reason not to try and learn from mistakes. The material allows for immediate testing of ideas. There is no reason to turn ideas into action immediately. Naturally the simple observation of several attempts is an insight to another. The teacher has to observe the balance between the process of divergence and convergence, and identify the successes and failures, difficulties and opportunities for facilities to mediate the factors that favor the creation of an environment conducive to creativity.

4.5 Evaluation of the Global Goals

As it was stated in introductory section the Program is sponsored by a Industry association that wanted to contribute in building alternatives or at least proposing alternatives for the regular school. As it was stated in UNESCO report conclusion it is stressed the relation between the rate of the technical progress of a country and the quality of the human action, **making evident the need to train people capable of using new technologies innovatively**. Based on a qualitative evaluation of the Program's Tangible Goals, presented previously, it can be said that a program as it was presented is capable of giving to teenagers the capability of dealing with the new technologies and having innovative behavior in the a field that is important to industry, that is the automation technology associate to robotics.

5 Conclusion

This paper presented the various aspects of a Educational Robotics program in operation for nine years, among them it is included the operational aspects including student age, class size, materials used, frequency and duration of meetings, type of experiments. It is also an assessment of what tangible results were achieved with the development of activities.

It is hoped that the presentation of an experience with such an extension be contributing to the development of the educational use of robotics.

References

1. Young, G.O.: Kids' Club as na ICT-Based Learning Laboratory. Informatics on Education 1, 61–72 (2002)
2. Resnick, M., Rusk, N., Cooke, S.: The Computer Clubhouse: Technological Fluency in the Inner City. In: Schon, D., Sanyal, B., Mitchell, W. (eds.) High Technology and Low-Income Communities. MIT Press, Cambridge (2011) (online version [1], retrieved on March 20)
3. Delors, J.: Learning: The Treasure Within. UNESCO (1996)
4. FIESC - Industry Federation of Santa Catarina, http://www.fiesc.org.br/
5. SESI - Talents For the Industry Program Site, http://jet.sesisc.org.br
6. Brotto, F.O.: Jogos Cooperativos: Se o Importante Competir, o Fundamental Co-operar. Projeto Cooperacão (in Portuguese) (2002)

A New Three Object Triangulation Algorithm Based on the Power Center of Three Circles

Vincent Pierlot, Maxime Urbin-Choffray, and Marc Van Droogenbroeck

INTELSIG Laboratory, Montefiore Institute, University of Liège, Belgium
{vpierlot,M.VanDroogenbroeck}@ulg.ac.be

Abstract. Positioning is a fundamental issue in mobile robot applications that can be achieved in multiple ways. Among these methods, triangulation is a proven technique. As it exists for a long time, many variants of triangulation have been proposed. Which variant is most appropriate depends on the application because some methods ignore the beacon ordering while other have blind spots. Some methods are reliable but at a price of increasing complexity or special cases study. In this paper, we present a simple and new three object triangulation algorithm. Our algorithm works in the whole plane (except when the beacons and the robot are concyclic or colinear), and for any beacon ordering. Moreover, it does not need special cases study and has a strong geometrical meaning. Benchmarks show that our algorithm is faster than existing and comparable algorithms. Finally, a quality measure is intrinsically derived for the triangulation result in the whole plane, which can be used to identify the pathological cases, or as a validation gate in Kalman filters.

Keywords: mobile robots, positioning, triangulation.

1 Introduction

Positioning is a fundamental issue in mobile robot applications. Indeed, in most cases, a mobile robot that moves in its environment has to position itself before it can execute its actions correctly. Therefore the robot has to be equipped with some hardware and software capable to provide a sensory feedback related to its environment [1]. Positioning methods can be classified into two main groups [3]: (1) *relative* positioning, and (2) *global* or *absolute* positioning. The first group (also called *dead-reckoning*) achieves positioning by odometry which consists to count the number of wheel revolutions to compute the offset relative to a known position. Odometry is very accurate for small offsets but is not sufficient because of the unbounded accumulation of errors over time (due to wheel slippage, imprecision in the wheel circumference, or wheel inter axis) [3]. Furthermore odometry needs an initial position and fails when the robot is "waken-up" (after a forced reset for example) or is raised and dropped somewhere, since the reference position is unknown or modified. A global positioning system is thus required to recalibrate the robot position periodically.

D. Obdržálek and A. Gottscheber (Eds.): EUROBOT 2011, CCIS 161, pp. 248–262, 2011.

Relative and global positioning are complementary to each other [1,4] and are typically merged together by using a Kalman filter [12,14]. In many cases, global positioning is ensured by beacon-based triangulation or trilateration. Triangulation is the process of determining the location of a point by measuring angles to it from known points, while trilateration methods involve the determination of absolute or relative locations of points by measurement of distances. Because of the large variety of angle measurement systems, triangulation has emerged as a widely used, robust, accurate, and flexible technique [10]. Another advantage of triangulation versus trilateration is that the robot can compute its orientation (or heading) in addition to its position, so that the complete *pose* of the robot can be found. The process of determining the robot *pose* from three beacon angle measurements is termed *Three Object Triangulation* [7]. Fig. 1 illustrates the process of triangulation. In the remainder of this paper, we concentrate on three object triangulation methods.

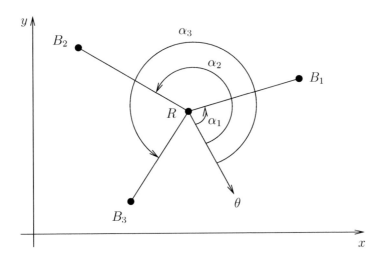

Fig. 1. Triangulation setup in the 2D plane. R denotes the robot. B_1, B_2, and B_3 are the beacons. α_1, α_2, and α_3 are the angle measurements respectively for B_1, B_2, and B_3, relatively to the robot reference orientation θ.

1.1   Related Works

Various triangulation algorithms may be found in [1,5,6,7,8,10,11,12,13,14,15,16]. These algorithms can be classified into four groups: (1) *Geometric Triangulation*, (2) *Geometric Circle Intersection*, (3) *Iterative methods* (Iterative Search, Newton-Raphson, etc), and (4) *Multiple Beacons Triangulation*. The first group could be named *Trigonometric Triangulation* because it makes an intensive use of trigonometric computations. The second group computes the parameters (radius and center) of two (of the three) circles passing through the beacons and the

robot, then it computes the intersection between these two circles. The first and
second groups are typically used as a solution of the three object triangulation
problem. The third group linearizes the trigonometric relations to converge to
the robot position after some iterations, from a starting point (usually the last
known robot position). The fourth group addresses the more general problem of
finding the robot pose from multiple angle measurements (usually corrupted by
errors). It appears that the second group (*Geometric Circle Intersection*) is the
most popular for solving the three object triangulation problem [13,16].

These algorithms all have advantages and drawbacks, and the method has to
take the requirements of a particular application into account, which leads to
make some compromises. For example, if the setup contains three beacons only
or if the robot platform has a low computing power, methods of the first and
second groups are the best candidates. Methods of the third and fourth groups
are appropriate if the application must handle multiple beacons and if it can
accommodate to a higher computational cost. The main drawback of the third
group is the convergence issue (existence or uniqueness of the solution) [7]. The
main drawback of the fourth group is the computational cost [1,5].

The drawbacks of the first and second group are usually a lack of precision
in the following points: (1) the beacon ordering needed to get the correct solution, (2) the consistency of the methods when the robot is located outside
the triangle defined by the three beacons, (3) the strategy to follow when falling
into some particular geometrical cases (typically mathematical undeterminations
when solving trigonometric equations with an argument equal to 0 or π, division
by 0, etc), and (4) the quality measure of the computed position. Simple methods of the first and second groups usually fail to propose an answer to all these
raised issues. To work in the whole plane and for any beacon ordering (for instance [11]), they have to consider a set of special geometrical cases, resulting in
a lack of clarity in the method. Finally, none of these algorithms gives a realistic
quality measure of the computed position.

1.2   Overview

Our paper presents a new three object triangulation algorithm that works in the
whole plane (except when the beacons and the robot are concyclic or colinear),
and for any beacon ordering. Moreover it uses a minimal number of trigonometric
computations and, finally, it leads to a natural and quantitative quality measure
of the computed position.

The paper is organized as follows. Our triangulation algorithm is described in
Section 2. Section 3 presents simulation results. Then, we conclude the paper in
Section 4.

2   Description of a New Three Object Triangulation Algorithm

Our algorithm belongs to the second group, that is: *Geometric Circle Intersection*. It first computes the parameters of the three circles passing through the

robot and the three pairs of beacons. Then it computes the intersection of these three circles, by using all the three circles, not only two of them.

Our algorithm relies on two assumptions: (1) the beacons are distinguishable (a measured angle can be associated to a given beacon), and (2) the angle measurements from the beacons are taken separately, and relatively to some reference angle θ, usually the robot heading (see Fig. 1). Note that the second hypothesis simply states that angles are given by a rotating angular sensor (goniometer). Such sensors are common in mobile robot positioning using triangulation [2,3,6,15,16,17]. By convention, in the following, we consider that angles are measured counterclockwise (CCW), like angles on the trigonometric circle. Changing the rotating direction to clockwise (CW) requires a minimal changes of our algorithm.

2.1   First Part of the Algorithm: The Circle Parameters

In a first step, we have to find the locus of points R that *see* two fixed points B_1 and B_2 with a constant angle α_{12}, in the 2D plane. It is a well-known result that this locus is an arc of the circle passing through B_1 and B_2, whose radius depends on the distance between B_1 and B_2, and α_{12} (Proposition 21 of Book III of EUCLID's Elements). More precisely, this locus is composed of two arcs of circle, which are the reflection of each other through the line joining B_1 and B_2 (see the left drawing of Fig. 2).

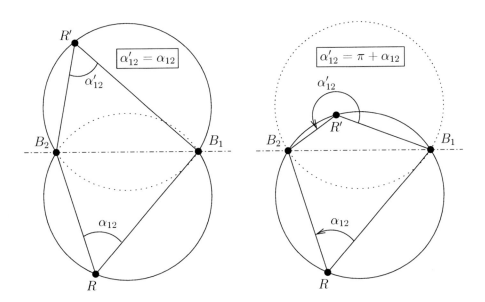

Fig. 2. Left-hand side drawing: the locus of points R that *see* two fixed points B_1 and B_2 with a constant angle α_{12}, in the 2D plane, is formed by two arcs of circle. Right-hand side drawing: the ambiguity about the locus is removed by taking the following convention: $\alpha_{12} = \alpha_2 - \alpha_1$.

A robot that measures an angle α_{12} between two beacons without any caution can stand on either of these two arcs. It would be the case if the beacons were not distinguishable or if the angular sensor was not capable to measure angles larger than π. To avoid this ambiguity, we impose that, as shown in the right-hand drawing of Fig. 2, the measured angle between two beacons B_1 and B_2, denoted α_{12}, is always computed as $\alpha_{12} = \alpha_2 - \alpha_1$ (this choice is natural for a CCW rotating sensor). This is consistent with our measurement considerations and it removes the ambiguity about the locus. For now the locus is a single circle passing through R, B_1, and B_2. But it requires that beacons are indexed and that the robot is capable to guess the index of any beacon.

The circle equation may be derived by using the complex representation of 2D points (ARGAND diagram). The idea consists to express that the complex argument of $(B_2 - R)$ is equal to the complex argument of $(B_1 - R)$, plus α, or:

$$\arg \left\{ \frac{B_2 - R}{B_1 - R} \right\} = \alpha$$
$$\Rightarrow \arg \left\{ (B_2 - R) \overline{(B_1 - R)} \right\} = \alpha$$

Then replacing R by $(x + iy)$, B_1 by $(x_1 + iy_1)$, and B_2 by $(x_2 + iy_2)$, we have that

$$\arg \left\{ (x_2 + iy_2 - x - iy)(x_1 - iy_1 - x + iy) e^{-i\alpha} \right\} = 0$$
$$\Rightarrow Im \left\{ [(x_2 - x) + i(y_2 - y)][(x_1 - x) + i(y - y_1)][\cos\alpha - i\sin\alpha] \right\} = 0$$
$$\Rightarrow -\sin\alpha (x_2 - x)(x_1 - x) + \sin\alpha (y_2 - y)(y - y_1)$$
$$+ \cos\alpha (x_2 - x)(y - y_1) + \cos\alpha (y_2 - y)(x_1 - x) = 0$$

where $i = \sqrt{-1}$. After many simplifications, we find the locus

$$(x - x_{12})^2 + (y - y_{12})^2 = R_{12}^2$$

which is a circle whose center $\{x_{12}, y_{12}\}$ is located at

$$x_{12} = \frac{(x_1 + x_2) + \cot\alpha (y_1 - y_2)}{2}, \qquad y_{12} = \frac{(y_1 + y_2) - \cot\alpha (x_1 - x_2)}{2}$$

and whose squared radius equals

$$R_{12}^2 = \frac{(x_1 - x_2)^2 + (y_1 - y_2)^2}{4 \sin^2 \alpha}$$

These equations may also be found in [13]. The replacement of α by $\pi + \alpha$ in the above equations yields the same circle parameters (Fig. 2, right), which is consistent with our measurement considerations. For an angular sensor turning in CW direction, one have to change the sign of $\cot\alpha$ in the center coordinates equations. In the following, we use these notations:

- B_i is the beacon #i, with coordinates $\{x_i, y_i\}$,
- R is the robot position, with coordinates $\{x_R, y_R\}$,
- α_i is the measured angle for beacon B_i with respect to the robot orientation,
- $\alpha_{ij} = \alpha_j - \alpha_i$ is the bearing angle between beacons B_i and B_j,
- $T_{ij} = \cot(\alpha_{ij})$,
- $\mathcal{C}_{ij}$ is the circle passing through B_i, B_j, and R,
- c_{ij} is the center of $\mathcal{C}_{ij}$, with coordinates $\{x_{ij}, y_{ij}\}$:

$$x_{ij} = \frac{(x_i + x_j) + T_{ij}(y_i - y_j)}{2}, \qquad y_{ij} = \frac{(y_i + y_j) - T_{ij}(x_i - x_j)}{2} \qquad (1)$$

- R_{ij} is the radius of $\mathcal{C}_{ij}$, derived from:

$$R_{ij}^2 = \frac{(x_i - x_j)^2 + (y_i - y_j)^2}{4\sin^2\alpha_{ij}} \qquad (2)$$

All the previous quantities are valid for $i = 1, 2, 3$ and $j = (i)\,mod\,3 + 1$. The special cases ($\alpha_{ij} = 0$ or $\alpha_{ij} = \pi$) are discussed later.

2.2   Second Part of the Algorithm: The Circles Intersection

From the previous section, each bearing angle α_{ij} between beacons B_i and B_j constraints the robot to be on a circle $\mathcal{C}_{ij}$, passing through B_i, B_j, and R (Fig. 3). The parameters of the circles are given by Equ. 1 and 2. Note that we are in the case of a trilateration problem with virtual beacons (the circle centers) and virtual range measurements (the circle radii). Common methods use two of the three circles to compute the intersections (when they exist), one of which is the robot position, the second being the common beacon of the two circles. This requires to solve a quadratic system and to choose the correct solution for the robot position [13]. Moreover the choice of the two circles is arbitrary and usually static, whereas this choice should depend on the measured angles and beacons configuration.

Hereafter, we propose a novel method to compute this intersection, by using all the three circles, and reducing the problem to a linear problem. To understand this simple method, we first have to remind the notion of the *power center* (or *radical center*) of three circles. The *power center* of three circles is the unique point of equal *power* with respect to these circles [9]. The *power* of a point p relative to a circle $\mathcal{C}$ is defined as:

$$\mathcal{P}_{\mathcal{C},p} = (x - x_c)^2 + (y - y_c)^2 - R^2 \qquad (3)$$

where $\{x, y\}$ are the coordinates of point p, $\{x_c, y_c\}$ are the circle center coordinates and R is the circle radius. The power of a point is null onto the circle, negative inside the circle and positive outside the circle. It defines a sort of distance of a point relative to a circle. The *power line* (or *radical axis*) of two circles is the locus of points having the same power with respect to each circle [9]. It is perpendicular to the line joining the circle centers and passes through the

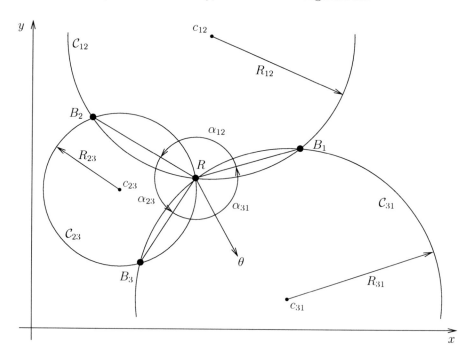

Fig. 3. Triangulation setup in the 2D plane, using the geometric circle intersection. R is the robot. B_1, B_2, and B_3 are the beacons. α_{ij} are the angles between B_i, R, and B_j. $\mathcal{C}_{ij}$ are the circles passing through B_i, R, and B_j. R_{ij} and c_{ij} are respectively the radii and center coordinates of $\mathcal{C}_{ij}$. θ is the robot orientation in the world coordinate.

circle intersections, when they exist. When considering three circles, the three power lines, defined by the three pairs of circles are concurring in the power center [9]. Fig. 4 shows the power center of three circles for various configurations. The power center is always defined, except when at least two of the three circle centers are equal, or when the circle centers are colinear (parallel power lines).

The third case of Fig. 4 (right-hand drawing) is remarkable as it perfectly matches to our triangulation problem (Fig. 3). Indeed, the power center of three concurring circles corresponds to their unique intersection. In our case, we are sure that the circles are concurring since $\alpha_{31} = -(\alpha_{12} + \alpha_{23})$ by construction (only two of the three bearing angles are independent). It has the advantage that this intersection may be computed by intersecting the power lines, which is a linear problem. The power line of two circles is obtained by equating the power of the points relatively to each circle (Equ. 3). In our problem, the power line of $\mathcal{C}_{12}$ and $\mathcal{C}_{23}$ is given by:

$$(x - x_{12})^2 + (y - y_{12})^2 - R_{12}^2 = (x - x_{23})^2 + (y - y_{23})^2 - R_{23}^2$$

$$\Rightarrow x\,(x_{12} - x_{23}) + y\,(y_{12} - y_{23}) = \frac{x_{12}^2 + y_{12}^2 - R_{12}^2}{2} - \frac{x_{23}^2 + y_{23}^2 - R_{23}^2}{2}$$

$$\Rightarrow x\,(x_{12} - x_{23}) + y\,(y_{12} - y_{23}) = k_{12} - k_{23}$$

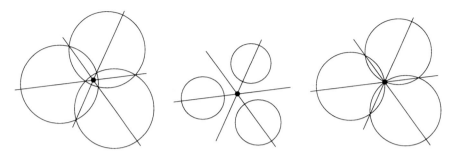

Fig. 4. The black point is the power center of three circles for various configurations. It is the unique point having the same power with respect to the three circles. It is the intersection of the three power lines.

where we introduce a new quantity k_{ij} which only depends on $\mathcal{C}_{ij}$ parameters (k_{ij} is the power of the origin relatively to $\mathcal{C}_{ij}$, divided by two):

$$k_{ij} = \frac{x_{ij}^2 + y_{ij}^2 - R_{ij}^2}{2} \tag{4}$$

In our triangulation problem, we have to intersect the three power lines, that is to solve this linear system:

$$x\,(x_{12} - x_{23}) + y\,(y_{12} - y_{23}) = k_{12} - k_{23}$$
$$x\,(x_{23} - x_{31}) + y\,(y_{23} - y_{31}) = k_{23} - k_{31}$$
$$x\,(x_{31} - x_{12}) + y\,(y_{31} - y_{12}) = k_{31} - k_{12}$$

As can be seen, any of these equations may be obtained by adding the two others, which is way to prove that the three power lines coincide in a unique point: the power center. The coordinates of the power center, that is the robot position is given by:

$$x_R = \frac{\begin{vmatrix} k_{12} - k_{23} & y_{12} - y_{23} \\ k_{23} - k_{31} & y_{23} - y_{31} \end{vmatrix}}{\begin{vmatrix} x_{12} - x_{23} & y_{12} - y_{23} \\ x_{23} - x_{31} & y_{23} - y_{31} \end{vmatrix}}, \qquad y_R = \frac{\begin{vmatrix} x_{12} - x_{23} & k_{12} - k_{23} \\ x_{23} - x_{31} & k_{23} - k_{31} \end{vmatrix}}{\begin{vmatrix} x_{12} - x_{23} & y_{12} - y_{23} \\ x_{23} - x_{31} & y_{23} - y_{31} \end{vmatrix}} \tag{5}$$

The denominator D, common to x_R and y_R is equal to:

$$D = \begin{vmatrix} x_{12} - x_{23} & y_{12} - y_{23} \\ x_{23} - x_{31} & y_{23} - y_{31} \end{vmatrix} = \begin{vmatrix} x_{12} & y_{12} & 1 \\ x_{23} & y_{23} & 1 \\ x_{31} & y_{31} & 1 \end{vmatrix} \tag{6}$$

which is the signed area between the circle centers, multiplied by 2. This result confirms that the power center exists, that is $D \neq 0$, if the circle centers are not colinear. The special case $(D = 0)$ is discussed later.

2.3   First (Naive) Version of the Algorithm

A first, but naive version of our algorithm is described by Algorithm 1.

Algorithm 1. First version of the algorithm.

1. compute the three cot(.): $T_{ij} = \cot(\alpha_{ij})$,
2. compute the six circle centers coordinates $\{x_{ij}, y_{ij}\}$ by Equ. 1,
3. compute the three squared radii R_{ij}^2 by Equ. 2,
4. compute the three parameters k_{ij} by Equ. 4,
5. compute the denominator D by Equ. 6. Return with an error if $D = 0$.
6. compute the robot position $\{x_R, y_R\}$ by Equ. 5 and return.

This method is correct but it is possible to simplify it with some considerations about the involved equations. First, note that the squared radii R_{ij}^2 only appear in the parameters k_{ij}. If we replace the expression of R_{ij}^2 (Equ. 2) in the expression of k_{ij} (Equ. 4), we find, after many simplifications that:

$$k_{ij} = \frac{x_i x_j + y_i y_j + T_{ij}(x_j y_i - x_i y_j)}{2} \tag{7}$$

which is much simpler than Equ. 2 and 4 (no squared terms anymore). In addition, the $1/2$ factor involved in the circle centers coordinates (Equ. 1) as well as in the parameters k_{ij} (Equ. 4) disappears in the robot position coordinates (Equ. 5). This factor can thus be omitted. For now, we use these modified circle center coordinates $\{x'_{ij}, y'_{ij}\}$:

$$x'_{ij} = (x_i + x_j) + T_{ij}(y_i - y_j), \qquad y'_{ij} = (y_i + y_j) - T_{ij}(x_i - x_j) \tag{8}$$

and parameters k'_{ij}:

$$k'_{ij} = x_i x_j + y_i y_j + T_{ij}(x_j y_i - x_i y_j) \tag{9}$$

The second version of our algorithm is given in Algorithm 2.

2.4   Final Version of the Algorithm

The most important simplification consists in translating the world coordinate frame into one of the beacons, that is solving the problem relatively to one beacon and then add the beacon coordinates to the computed robot position. In the following, we arbitrarily choose B_2 as the origin ($B_2 = \{0, 0\}$). The other beacon coordinates become: $B_1 = \{x_1 - x_2, y_1 - y_2\} = \{x'_1, y'_1\}$ and

Algorithm 2. Second version of the algorithm.

1. compute the three $\cot(.)$: $T_{ij} = \cot(\alpha_{ij})$,
2. compute the modified circle centers coordinates $\{x'_{ij}, y'_{ij}\}$ by Equ. 8,
3. compute the modified parameters k'_{ij} by Equ. 9,
4. compute the denominator D by Equ. 6. Return with an error if $D = 0$.
5. compute the robot position $\{x_R, y_R\}$ by Equ. 5 and return.

$B_3 = \{x_3 - x_2, y_3 - y_2\} = \{x'_3, y'_3\}$. Since $x'_2 = 0$ and $y'_2 = 0$, we have $k'_{12} = 0$, $k'_{23} = 0$. Also, we can compute the value of one $\cot(.)$ by referring to the two other $\cot(.)$ because the three angles are not independent ($\alpha_{31} = -(\alpha_{12} + \alpha_{23})$):

$$T_{31} = \frac{1 - T_{12}T_{23}}{T_{12} + T_{23}} \tag{10}$$

The final algorithm is given in Algorithm 3.

Algorithm 3. Final version of the algorithm.

Given the three beacon coordinates $\{x_i, y_i\}$ and the three angle measurements α_i:

1. compute the modified beacon coordinates:

$$x'_1 = x_1 - x_2, \qquad y'_1 = y_1 - y_2, \qquad x'_3 = x_3 - x_2, \qquad y'_3 = y_3 - y_2$$

2. compute the three $\cot(.)$:

$$T_{12} = \cot(\alpha_2 - \alpha_1), \qquad T_{23} = \cot(\alpha_3 - \alpha_2), \qquad T_{31} = \frac{1 - T_{12}T_{23}}{T_{12} + T_{23}}$$

3. compute the modified circle center coordinates $\{x'_{ij}, y'_{ij}\}$:

$$x'_{12} = x'_1 + T_{12}\, y'_1, \qquad y'_{12} = y'_1 - T_{12}\, x'_1$$

$$x'_{23} = x'_3 - T_{23}\, y'_3, \qquad y'_{23} = y'_3 + T_{23}\, x'_3$$

$$x'_{31} = (x'_3 + x'_1) + T_{31}\, (y'_3 - y'_1), \qquad y'_{31} = (y'_3 + y'_1) - T_{31}\, (x'_3 - x'_1)$$

4. compute k'_{31}:

$$k'_{31} = x'_1 x'_3 + y'_1 y'_3 + T_{31}(x'_1 y'_3 - x'_3 y'_1)$$

5. compute the denominator D (if $D = 0$, return with an error):

$$D = (x'_{12} - x'_{23})(y'_{23} - y'_{31}) - (y'_{12} - y'_{23})(x'_{23} - x'_{31})$$

6. compute the robot position $\{x_R, y_R\}$ and return:

$$x_R = x_2 + \frac{k'_{31}(y'_{12} - y'_{23})}{D}, \qquad y_R = y_2 + \frac{k'_{31}(x'_{23} - x'_{12})}{D}$$

2.5 Discussion

This algorithm is very simple, while keeping a strong geometrical meaning (each involved quantity has a physical meaning). Moreover, the number of conditional statements is reduced (there are two tests related to the argument of cot(.) and one conditional test to check if $D = 0$), which increases its readability and eases its implementation. Furthermore, computations are limited to basic arithmetic computations and two cot(.) computations. Among these computations, we have to take care of the cot(.) and the division by D. If a bearing angle α_{ij} between two beacons is equal to 0 or π, that is the robot stands on the line B_iB_j, the $\cot(\alpha_{ij})$ is infinite. The corresponding circle degenerates as the line B_iB_j (infinite radius and center coordinates). The robot position is the intersection of the remaining power line and the line B_iB_j. It can be shown that the mathematical limit $\lim_{T_{ij} \to \pm\infty} \{x_R, y_R\}$ exists and corresponds to this situation. The algorithm could deal with these special cases but it is not necessary. In practice, we have to avoid *Inf* or *NaN* values in floating point computations. This can be done by limiting the cot(.) value to a minimum or maximum value, corresponding to a small angle that is far below the measurement precision. In practice, we limit the value of the cot(.) to $\pm 10^8$, which corresponds to an angle of about $\pm 10^{-8}$ [*rad*]; this is indeed far below the existing angular sensor precisions.

The denominator D is equal to 0 when the circle centers are colinear. For non colinear beacons, this situation occurs when the beacons and the robot are concyclic (they all stand on the same circumference, termed the *critic circumference*). In that case, the three circles are equal as well as their centers, which causes $D = 0$. For colinear beacons, this situation is encountered when the beacons and the robot all stand on this line. For these cases, it is impossible to compute the robot position. This is referred as *the restrictions common to all three object triangulation*, whatever the algorithm used [10,13,16]. The value of D, computed in the final algorithm, is the signed area delimited by the circle centers, multiplied by 8. It is quiet natural to use the absolute value of D as a quality measure of the computed position. Indeed $|D|$ decreases to 0 when approaching the critic circumference (almost colinear circle center, almost parallel power lines). In the next section, we show that $1/|D|$ is a good approximation of the position error. In practice, $|D|$ can be used as a validation gate after the triangulation algorithm or when using a Kalman filter with triangulation. Finally, it should be noted that the robot orientation may be determined by using any beacon B_i and its corresponding angle measurement α_i, once the robot position is known.

3 Simulations

In order to validate our algorithm, we have performed some simulations in a square shaped area (4×4 [m^2]), with three non colinear beacons. For each point in this area, we compute the exact angles α_i seen by the robot (the robot orientation is arbitrary set to 0 degree). Then we add Gaussian noise to these angles, with zero mean, and with two different standard deviations ($\sigma = 0.1°$ and $\sigma = 1°$). The

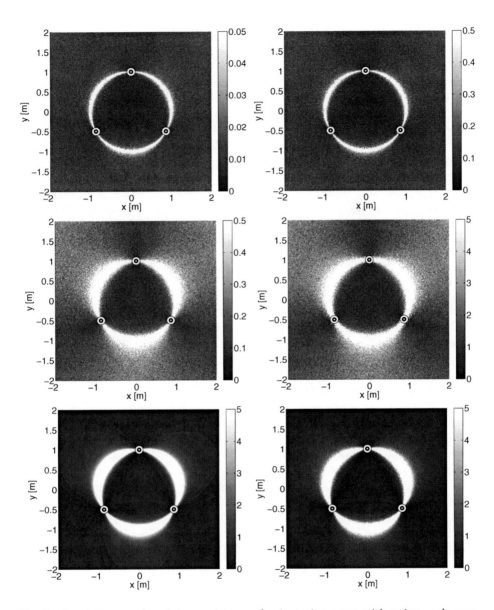

Fig. 5. Simulation results giving position and orientation error with noisy angle measurements. The beacon positions are represented by black and white circles. The left column is the result for $\sigma = 0.1°$, the right column is the result for $\sigma = 1°$. The first, second and third rows show the position error (expressed in $[m]$), the orientation error (expressed in $[degree]$), and the quality measure $1/|D|$ (D being expressed in $[m^2]$) respectively.

noisy angles are then used as inputs of our algorithm to compute the estimated position. The position error Δd_R is the Euclidean distance between the exact and estimated position. The orientation error $\Delta \theta_R$ is the difference between the exact and estimated orientation. The experiment is repeated several times to compute the mean of the position error $E\{\Delta d_R\}$ and the mean of the orientation error $E\{\Delta \theta_R\}$. The means of the position and orientation error are drawn in Fig. 5. The beacon positions are represented by black and white circles. The left column is the result for $\sigma = 0.1°$, the right column is the result for $\sigma = 1°$. The first, second and third rows show the position error, the orientation error, and the quality measure $1/|D|$ respectively.

Our simulation results are consistent with common three object triangulation algorithms [11,13]. In particular, we can easily spot the critic circumference where errors are large. From these graphics, one can see that $1/|D|$ has a similar shape than the position or orientation error, up to a constant multiplicative factor. It can be proven (but this beyond the scope of this paper), by a detailed sensitivity analysis of the robot position error with respect to angles, that

$$\Delta d_R \simeq \frac{1}{|D|} \Delta \alpha \, f(.)$$

where Δd_R is the position error, $\Delta \alpha$ is the angle error, and $f(.)$ is some function of all the other parameters. This explain why $1/|D|$ can be used as an approximation of the position error, up to a constant multiplicative factor.

In this paper, we do not provide results obtained with a real sensor. An absolute comparison between simulation results and real data is at least difficult if not impossible to produce because many unknown or uncontrolled parameters impact on results. The precision of the sensor is one of these critical parameters but the absolute position of beacons and the sensor position onto the robot are very difficult to measure with a high accuracy. These difficulties did not prevented us to implement the algorithm and run it on our platform with success during the qualification of the Eurobot competition.

We have also compared the computational time of our algorithm against two other algorithms. The first algorithm is the *Generalized Geometric Triangulation* from Esteves *et al.* [11]. The second is the *Geometric Circle Intersection* from Font-Llagunes *et al.* [13]. We chose these algorithms because they work in the whole plane and for any beacon ordering, like ours. The simulations were performed in the same square shaped area, with a resolution of 0.5 [mm]. It appears that our algorithm is about 40 % faster than Esteves *et al.* [11], and 20 % faster than Font-Llagunes *et al.* [13], for exactly the same precision.

4   Conclusions

This paper presents a new and simple three object triangulation algorithm based on the power center of three circles. As it exists for a long time, many variants of triangulation have been proposed. Which variant is most appropriate depends on the application because some methods ignore the beacon ordering while other have blind spots. Some methods are reliable but at a price of increasing complexity or special cases study. Our algorithm works in the whole plane (except when the beacons and the robot are concyclic or colinear), and for any beacon ordering. It does not need special cases study, which makes it clear. Moreover it has a strong geometrical meaning (each involved quantity has a physical meaning), while keeping simple. Furthermore it uses only basic arithmetic computations, and two cot(.) computations. Benchmarks show that our algorithm is faster than existing and comparable algorithms. Finally it naturally gives a quality measure of the triangulation result in the whole plane. Simulation intuitively show that $\frac{1}{|D|}$ is a natural and efficient criterion to estimate the precision of the positioning. To our knowledge, algorithms of the same family do not provide such a criterion. This quality measure can be used to identify the pathological cases (critic circumference), or as a validation gate in Kalman filters based on triangulation.

References

1. Betke, M., Gurvits, L.: Mobile robot localization using landmarks. IEEE Transactions on Robotics and Automation 13(2), 251–263 (1997)
2. Borenstein, J., Everett, H., Feng, L.: Where am I? Systems and methods for mobile robot positioning. Tech. rep., University of Michigan (March 1996)
3. Borenstein, J., Everett, H., Feng, L., Wehe, D.: Mobile robot positioning - sensors and techniques. Journal of Robotic Systems 14(4), 231–249 (1997)
4. Borenstein, J., Feng, L.: Umbmark: A benchmark test for measuring odometry errors in mobile robots. SPIE, Philadelphia (1995)
5. Briechle, K., Hanebeck, U.: Localization of a mobile robot using relative bearing measurements. IEEE Transactions on Robotics and Automation 20(1), 36–44 (2004)
6. Casanova, E., Quijada, S., Garcia-Bermejo, J., González, J.: A new beacon-based system for the localization of moving objects. In: IEEE International Conference on Mechatronics and Machine Vision in Practice. Chiang Mai, Tailand (2002)
7. Cohen, C., Koss, F.: A comprehensive study of three object triangulation. In: Mobile Robots VII, vol. 1831, pp. 95–106. SPIE, San Jose (1993)
8. Demaine, E.D., López-Ortiz, A., Munro, J.I.J.: Robot localization without depth perception. In: Penttonen, M., Schmidt, E.M. (eds.) SWAT 2002. LNCS, vol. 2368, pp. 177–194. Springer, Heidelberg (2002)
9. Eiden, J.D.: Géometrie analytique classique. Calvage & Mounet, Paris (2009)
10. Esteves, J., Carvalho, A., Couto, C.: Generalized geometric triangulation algorithm for mobile robot absolute self-localization. In: International Symposium on Industrial Electronics (ISIE), vol. 1, pp. 346–351. Rio de Janeiro, Brazil (2003)
11. Esteves, J., Carvalho, A., Couto, C.: Position and orientation errors in mobile robot absolute self-localization using an improved version of the generalized geometric triangulation algorithm. In: IEEE International Conference on Industrial Technology (ICIT), Mumbai, India, pp. 830–835 (December 2006)
12. Font-Llagunes, J., Batlle, J.: Mobile robot localization. Revisiting the triangulation methods. In: International Federation of Automatic Control (IFAC), Bologna, Italy. Symposium on Robot Control, vol. 8 (September 2006)

13. Font-Llagunes, J., Batlle, J.: Consistent triangulation for mobile robot localization using discontinuous angular measurements. Robotics and Autonomous Systems 57(9), 931–942 (2009)
14. Hu, H., Gu, D.: Landmark-based navigation of industrial mobile robots. International Journal of Industry Robot 27(6), 458–467 (2000)
15. Lee, C., Chang, Y., Park, G., Ryu, J., Jeong, S.G., Park, S., Park, J., Lee, H., Hong, K.S., Lee, M.: Indoor positioning system based on incident angles of infrared emitters. In: Conference of the IEEE Industrial Electronics Society (IECON), vol. 3, pp. 2218–2222 (November 2004)
16. McGillem, C., Rappaport, T.: A beacon navigation method for autonomous vehicles. IEEE Transactions on Vehicular Technology 38(3), 132–139 (1989)
17. Pierlot, V., Van Droogenbroeck, M.: A simple and low cost angle measurement system for mobile robot positioning. In: Workshop on Circuits, Systems and Signal Processing (ProRISC), pp. 251–254. Veldhoven, The Netherlands (November 2009)

Humanoid Robot Reaching Task Using Support Vector Machine

Mirko Raković, Milutin Nikolić, and Branislav Borovac

Faculty of Technical Sciences, University of Novi Sad
Trg Dositeja Obradovića 6, 21000 Novi Sad, Serbia
{rakovicm,milutinn,borovac}@uns.ac.rs
http://www.iim.ftn.uns.ac.rs

Abstract. A novel approach for the realization of the humanoid robot's reaching task using Support Vector Machine (SVM) is proposed. The main difficulty is how to ensure an appropriate SVM training data set. Control law is firstly devised, and SVM is trained to calculate driving torques according to control law. For purpose of training SVM, sufficiently dense training data set was generated using designed controller. However, dynamic parameters of the system change when grasping is performed, so SVM coefficients were altered in order to adapt to changes that have occurred. In the stage of verification, the target point to be reached by the robot's hand is assigned. The trained SVM determines the necessary torques in a very efficient way, which has been demonstrated by several simulation examples.

Keywords: Humanoid Robots, Reaching, SVM.

1 Introduction

Bearing in mind that we can expect soon the "living and working coexistence of robots and humans", one of the very important tasks that will be imposed on humanoid robots is to manipulate the objects in their environment. In doing this, they will have to be ready to reach the objects with the aim of their grasping, and this is expected to be realized in a way involving the trajectory shape and realization efficiency that are very similar to those of humans. Reaching is always supervised by a visual system which estimates the relative mutual position of the object and hand, since the exact positions of either the robot's hand or the object to be grasped are not known in advance. Investigations have shown [1,2] that the trajectory of the man's hand in the reaching task in a free space is approximately a straight line. The same principle is to be also applied in the realization of the robot's hand reach, and the efficiency of the realized motion is expected to be close to that of human [3,4,5,6]. There are several ways in which such reference motion can be realized, and the main problem is how to execute the motion in a sufficiently effective way. Trajectory generation can be computationally intensive, and relies heavily on model accuracy. Also, dynamical properties of object that robot is grasping is rarely known, so motion has to be adaptable to changing dynamics of whole system.

D. Obdržálek and A. Gottscheber (Eds.): EUROBOT 2011, CCIS 161, pp. 263–276, 2011.

In this paper we present a method for developing control system for robotic arm reaching movement, which to a large extent corresponds to human's behavior. One of the basic characteristic of human reaching is that it is realized quickly (without hesitating) and that exact position of the object to be grasped is not known (it can be estimated only visually). Also, neither exact hand trajectory is specified nor driving torques at joints are known. We adopted, as humans do, a straight line hand path during reaching, moving hand faster at beginning, slower when it is closer to target position. When hand picks up an object of unknown mass to place it on a different location dynamics of system change, and control system has to adapt accordingly. The way how to realize motion of such characteristics is in the focus of this study.

2   Control Law

We will model the robot's hand motion as a point mass m connected to the target point by a spring K and a damper C (Fig. 1).

If it is supposed that the position of the target point is fixed, the motion of the system can be described by the following second-order differential equation:

$$m\ddot{\mathbf{r}} = -K(\mathbf{r} - \mathbf{r_d}) - C\dot{\mathbf{r}} . \tag{1}$$

Vectors $\mathbf{r}$ and $\mathbf{r_d}$ define current and target point position, while m, C and K are mass, dumping coefficient and spring stiffness, respectively. It is known that the response of the second order system will not have an overshoot if the following condition is satisfied:

$$C \geqslant 2\sqrt{mK} . \tag{2}$$

If the equality in (2) is satisfied, the system is critically damped, which means that it has the fastest possible response without overshoot. If the damping coefficient is increased, the system will still have no overshoot, but the approach of the point mass to the desired position will last longer. Therefore, it comes out that by changing the damping coefficient C we can modify the time of the movement realization. It is well known, that with the robots, the overshoots of the desired position must not be allowed under any circumstances. For instance, if the desired hand position is close to obstacle, and if the robot overshoots the desired position, collision may occur.

In order for the humanoid robot's arm to move in the way shown on Fig. 1, it is necessary to determine the corresponding driving torques at all the joints. To this end, a mathematical model of the robot's hand is formed, with three degrees of freedom (DOFs) (two at the shoulder and one at the elbow), as sketched in Fig. 1.

The motion of multi-body system can be described by the following differential equation:

$$\mathbf{H\ddot{q}} + \mathbf{h_0} = \boldsymbol{\tau} \tag{3}$$

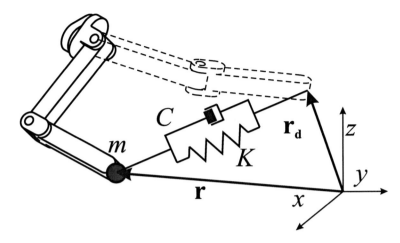

Fig. 1. Robot's arm with three DOFs

where $\mathbf{H}$ is the inertia matrix of the system; $\mathbf{h_0}$ is the vector that includes the velocity and gravitation effects; $\ddot{\mathbf{q}}$ is the vector of joint accelerations, and τ is the vector of driving torques.

Based on the relations of direct kinematics, it is possible to find the relationship between the robot's tip and joint coordinates:

$$\mathbf{r} = f(\mathbf{q}) . \tag{4}$$

By differentiating equation (4) one obtains the relation between the joint velocities of the robot's hand, as well as the relation between the joint accelerations and linear acceleration of the robot's hand:

$$\dot{\mathbf{r}} = \mathbf{J}\dot{\mathbf{q}} \tag{5}$$

$$\ddot{\mathbf{r}} = \mathbf{J}\ddot{\mathbf{q}} + \mathbf{A} \tag{6}$$

where the matrix $\mathbf{J} = \partial\mathbf{r}/\partial\mathbf{q}$ represents the system's Jacobian and the vector $\mathbf{A} = \left(\partial^2\mathbf{r}/\partial^2\mathbf{q}\right)\dot{\mathbf{q}}^2$ is the adjoint vector-column. The combination of equations (1), (3), (4), (5) and (6) gives an expression that allows us to calculate the corresponding driving torques at the joints:

$$\tau = -\mathbf{H}\left(m\mathbf{J}\right)^{-1}\left(K\left(\mathbf{r} - \mathbf{r_d}\right) + C\mathbf{J}\dot{\mathbf{q}} + m\mathbf{A}\right) + \mathbf{h_0} . \tag{7}$$

Thus, it is important to point out the driving torques can be calculated only if $\mathbf{J}$ is a square matrix (i.e. when the system has no redundancy), which is fulfilled in the case considered. However, if the system is redundant, the Jacobi matrix is not square, so the inverse matrix $\mathbf{J}^{-1}$ does not exist. Such case is not considered here, but it is necessary to remind that the addition of certain conditions can allow the determination of a pseudo-Jaciobian that could be used in expression (7).

2.1   Generating the Training Set

Our aim is to use the presented model to form an appropriate training set. Based on equations above, training data set for SVM training is calculated.

As evident from (7), the driving torques τ depend on the joint coordinates $\mathbf{q}$, and velocities $\dot{\mathbf{q}}$, and distance between the current and target positions, $(\mathbf{r} - \mathbf{r_d})$. If we want to change the movement duration (the rate of hand motion), it suffices to change only the coefficient C. Hence, we will adopt the angles $\mathbf{q}$ and angular velocities $\dot{\mathbf{q}}$ at all hand joints, position vector of the hand from the target position $(\mathbf{r} - \mathbf{r_d})$, as well as the damping C as inputs, and the driving torques τ at the joints corresponding to such motion as the outputs. The procedure of determining the input and output quantities is as follows:

1. An arbitrary point in the robot's workspace is selected as the starting position of the robot's hand
2. For the selected point, the inverse kinematics problem is solved.
3. An arbitrary point is then selected in the robot workspace to serve as the desired (target) position.
4. The damping coefficient is also arbitrarily selected from the predefined range.
5. The system's motion is simulated, and the driving torques in each iteration are calculated from equation (7).
6. When the distance between the current and target positions is sufficiently small, the simulation is stopped and the steps 3-6 are repeated, the last state serving as the starting one for the subsequent simulation.
7. After generating a sufficient number of movements, the procedure is stopped.

In this way the hand's motion is simulated from the point at which the previous movement terminated to the next (arbitrarily chosen) target point. For each time instant, the values of all input and output quantities are obtained. The input vector thus formed for the training set $\left[\mathbf{q}^T \ \dot{\mathbf{q}}^T \ (\mathbf{r} - \mathbf{r_d})^T \ C\right]^T$ is of dimension 10, whereas the dimension of the output vector τ is 3.

3   Basics of Machine Learning

Since, we are using SVMs to generate movement of robot hand it is necessary to briefly describe what SVM represents and how it works. We will be using error backpropagation (EBP) algorithm to adapt learned weights, so we are also giving a brief insight into RBF networks and EBP algorithm itself.

3.1   SVM Regression

There are a number of algorithms for approximating the function for establishing the unknown interdependence between the input and output data, but an ever-arising question is, how good is the approximation of the function $y = f(x)$. In determining the approximating function, it is necessary to minimize some of the error functions. The majority of the algorithms for the function approximation minimize the empirical error.

With the function approximation algorithms that minimize only the empirical error, there arises the problem of a large generalization error. The problem appears when the training set is small compared to the number of different data that can appear at the input. Structural Risk Minimization (SRM) [7] is a new technique of the statistical learning theory, which apart from minimizing the empirical errors, also minimizes the generalization errors (elements of the weight matrix $\mathbf{w}$). Hence, it follows that the structural error will be minimized by minimizing function of the form:

$$R = \frac{1}{2} \|\mathbf{w}\|^2 + C \sum_{i=1}^{l} |y_i - f_a(\mathbf{x}_i, \mathbf{w})|_\epsilon . \tag{8}$$

In (8), the error function with the ϵ insensitivity zone was used as the norm. The parameter C is the penalty parameter which determines the extent to which the empirical error is penalized relatively to the penalization of the large values in the weighting matrix. Network input is denoted by $\mathbf{x}$, and desired output is denoted by y. Approximating function is denoted by $f_a(\mathbf{x}, \mathbf{w})$ and it has to be chosen in advance. Since case considered is highly nonlinear, for approximating function we have chosen radial basis function (RBF) network with Gaussian kernel, which is basic constituent of the feedforward artificial neural networks. For RBF network output is calculated by:

$$f_a(\mathbf{x}, \mathbf{w}) = \sum_{i=1}^{N} w_i \exp\left(-\gamma \|\mathbf{x} - \mathbf{c}_i\|^2\right) + \rho . \tag{9}$$

The nonlinear SVM regressions (minimization of (8)) determines the elements of the weight matrix $\mathbf{w}$) and bias ρ. During the SVM training, support vectors ($\mathbf{c}_i$) are chosen from set of training data. Design parameter ρ defines the shape of RBFs, and it is experimentally chosen to minimize VC-dimension, which provides good generalization [8].

3.2   RBF Network Adaptation

As a result of SVM regression we acquire RBF network with Gaussian function as kernel. Since model always contains some inaccuracies and during grasping dynamics of whole system changes it is necessary to adapt network parameters on-line. For that purpose EBP algorithm is used, which minimizes standard cost function [8]:

$$E(\mathbf{w}, \mathbf{c}, \gamma, \rho) = \sum_{i=1}^{l} (y_i - f_a(\mathbf{x}_i, \mathbf{w}, \mathbf{c}, \gamma, \rho))^2 . \tag{10}$$

This problem is nonlinear and nonconvex, therefore, many local minima can be expected, and EPB merely guarantees convergence to closest local minima. As a starting point for optimization we are using weights and coefficients obtained by SVM regression. Since SVM regression finds global minimum of error function (8) it is safe to assume that initial guess will be close to global minimum of EPBs cost function (10). Therefore, we can assume that EPB will find global minimum of error function (10).

For adapting coefficients and weights we have used following equations:

$$w_i^{t+1} = w_i^t + 2\eta \left(y^t - f_a \left(\mathbf{x}^t \right) \right) \exp \left(-\gamma^t \left\| \mathbf{x}^t - \mathbf{c}_i^t \right\|^2 \right) \tag{11}$$

$$\mathbf{c}_i^{t+1} = \mathbf{c}_i^t - 4\eta \left(y^t - f_a \left(\mathbf{x}^t \right) \right) w_i^t \gamma \exp \left(-\gamma^t \left\| \mathbf{x}^t - \mathbf{c}_i^t \right\|^2 \right) \left(\mathbf{c}_i^t - \mathbf{x}^t \right) \tag{12}$$

$$\gamma^{t+1} = \gamma^t - 2\eta \left(y^t - f_a \left(\mathbf{x}^t \right) \right) \sum_{i=1}^{N} w_i^t \exp \left(-\gamma^t \left\| \mathbf{x}^t - \mathbf{c}_i^t \right\|^2 \right) \left\| \mathbf{x}^t - \mathbf{c}_i^t \right\| \tag{13}$$

$$\rho^{t+1} = \rho^t - 2\eta \left(y^t - f_a \left(\mathbf{x}^t \right) \right) \tag{14}$$

where t stands for iteration step and η represents experimentally chosen learning rate.

4   Simulation Results

In this section we describe the procedure of the SVM training for the task of the robot's hand reaching the object. The simulations of the robot's hand were carried out on the humanoid robot model [9]. Verification of the SVM control for the robot's hand motion is realized by assigning random points in the workspace to be reached by the robot's hand. Subsequently, RBF network adaptation is described, and verification of control is performed on two different cases.

4.1   Model of the Robotic Hand

The humanoid robot was modeled using the software that allowed the formation of a multi-body dynamics system with branched, open or closed, kinematic chains whose links are interconnected with the joints having only one DOF [9]. Since only hand motion is simulated, Fig. 2 shows only the part of the humanoid robot that represents its right arm. The shoulder joint is modeled by two DOFs, whereas the elbow has only one DOF, with the humerus and radius being $0.4\,m$ long, and weighing $5\,kg$ each.

4.2   The SVM Training

Let us remind that the inputs to the SVM training set are the joint coordinates $\mathbf{q}$, velocities $\dot{\mathbf{q}}$, the remaining distance to the target position $(\mathbf{r} - \mathbf{r_d})$, and the damping coefficient C, by which the hand motion speed is indirectly assigned, whereas the outputs are the joint driving torques $\boldsymbol{\tau}$. The hand's target position in the workspace is randomly assigned under the constraint that the x-coordinate

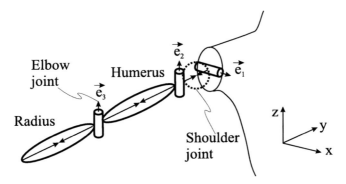

Fig. 2. Robot's arm with three DOFs

of the given position is positive. In this way, the workspace is defined by the hemisphere of a radius of 0.8 m.

In order to obtain an SVM with good generalization properties it is necessary to prepare a sufficiently dense training set, i.e. training data has to be equally distributed throughout whole input space. To do so, we have used procedure described in section 2.1. In order to calculate joint driving torques from equation (7) we adopted mass m to be $m = 26\ kg$ and elasticity coefficient to be $K = 1000 N/m$. That means that robot's hand will be moving as a point mass weighing $26\ kg$ connected to target position with spring of elasticity coefficient $1000\ N/m$ and dashpot, whose damping coefficient C is randomly chosen in the span from 450 to $850 N s/m$. That selection of parameters ensures hand's movement without overshoot. This Driving torque (at each joint) is limited to be between -80 and $80\ Nm$.

Approximately one million noisefree data pairs were generated, which span whole input space. Because SVM training is very time consuming we have randomly chosen 10000 input-output data pairs to use for SVM training. Input and output data obtained this way were first normalized, and then SVM was trained by minimizing empirical risk (8) with ϵ−insensitivity zone of 0.01 and penalty parameter $C = 100$.

4.3   Validation of the Robot's Hand Motion for the Object Reaching Task Using SVM

To validate the control of the robot's hand motion using the trained SVM model, it was necessary to assign unseen input data. The simulation was carried out in the following way. In the beginning, the starting position of the robot's hand is assigned in the world coordinate frame. Based on the relations of the inverse kinematics, the values of joint coordinates $\mathbf{q}$ corresponding to this position were calculated. Since we assumed that the hand moves from the rest, the values of joint velocities in the beginning of the simulation are 0. Then, the target position in the workspace is selected in a random way, as well as the damping coefficient C, which remained constant during the realization of one movement.

Based on these data, using the trained SVM, three driving torques at the arm's joints were determined and then applied in the simulation of the motion. The action of the joint driving torques causes the movement of the hand and values of the joint coordinates, joint velocities, as well as the distance to the target position changes. In each sampling period, using the information about the instantaneous state of the robot (distance from target position, joint angles and joint velocities) the trained SVM determines new driving torques to be applied at all joints, which produces further hand movement. If a driving torque exceeds predetermined maximum/minimum of $\pm 80\ Nm$, maximum/minimum driving torque is applied at corresponding joint The process is repeated until the hand tip stops. After that a new target point is randomly selected, and the process is repeated.

Fig. 3 shows two different simulated movements, which differ only in respect of the damping coefficient. Starting and target positions of the hand in both cases are the same. The values of damping coefficients are $C = 450\ Ns/m$ (first case Fig. 3a) and $C = 850\ Ns/m$ (second case, Fig. 3b). It is evident that in both cases the hand's trajectory almost coincides with the linear path, and that there are no overshoots on the way to the target position. Also, hand's speed is much greater at the beginning of the motion than at it's end which coincides with desired movement. Positioning error in cases considered is less than $2.5\,mm$, and no overshoot occurred.

As stated above, damping coefficient C is used to indirectly assign movement speed. When C is $450\,Ns/m$ rise time (time from 10% to 90% percent of distance

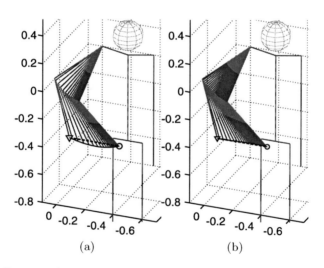

(a)   (b)

Fig. 3. Stick diagrams showing the hand's motion for the two different cases. Damping coefficients are a) $C = 450\ Ns/m$; b) $C = 850\ Ns/m$. Hand's position is plotted every $75\,ms$. Trajectory of hand's tip *(full line)*, desired trajectory *(dashed line)*, target position *(circle)* and start position *(triangle)* are shown.

traveled) is $0.86\,s$, but when C is $850\,Ns/m$ rise time is $1.8\,s$. Hence, rise time (and total movement time) increases as the damping coefficient C increases. It should also be noted that movements with smaller damping coefficient C produce greater deviations from desired linear path.

Since we have used model of robotic arm to create training set for SVM, it would be interesting to present what would happen if model of the system changes. In order to do so, we have simulated case where robot is carrying an object of $1\,kg$ mass, which directly impacts dynamic of robotic arm. For the sake of comparison we have simulated case with same starting and end position, but robot is not carrying any weight. Starting position is low in front of the robot, and target position is $1.2\,m$ above starting positions. Damping coefficient is selected to be $C = 850\,Ns/m$. In both cases we will be using SVM to calculate driving torques as in previous cases. Results are displayed in Fig. 4.

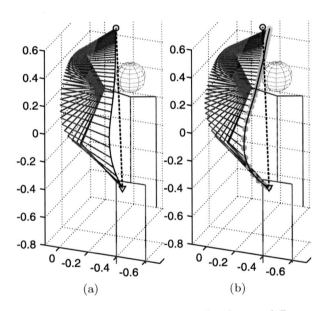

(a)   (b)

Fig. 4. Stick diagrams showing the hand's motion for the two different cases: a) movement without weight b) movement with weight. Hand's position is plotted every $75\,ms$. Trajectory of hand's tip *(full line)*, desired trajectory *(dashed line)*, target position *(circle)* and start position *(triangle)* are shown.

In case depicted on Fig. 4a, positioning error is less than $1\,mm$. Rise time is $1.82\,s$, which is approximately equal to rise time in case from Fig 3b. This means that rise time (and total movement time) is not distance dependant, but only depends on damping parameter. When robot is holding point mass, robot's tip misses target by $55\,mm$, which is substantially larger than in previous case. Also it is clearly noticeable that trajectory of hand's tip considerably deviates from desired linear path. This difference is due to change in dynamics of whole system, while procedure for driving torque calculation remains the same. That's why, this method is unsuitable for grasping task, and tasks during which system parameters change.

4.4   On-Line RBF Network Adaptation

To compensate for changes we have to constantly adapt our control system. After SVM training we acquire RBF network, which is used to calculate driving torques, thus it controls our robotic hand. As stated before, for adapting RBF network we will use EBP algorithm, which is briefly described in section 3.2.

If we take a closer look into equations (11 - 14) it can be noted that in order to perform EBP adaptation, input and corresponding output data pairs are needed. In our case input vector is $\left[\mathbf{q}^T \ \dot{\mathbf{q}}^T \ (\mathbf{r} - \mathbf{r_d})^T \ C\right]^T$ and output vector is $\boldsymbol{\tau}$. For basic SVM training we have calculated (using equation (7). That is no longer possible since we have assumed that model has changed and it is unknown to robot, so other way of calculating desired output is needed.

Suppose that, at each time sample values of joint coordinates and velocities ($\mathbf{q}^t$ and $\dot{\mathbf{q}}^t$) are known. Damping coefficient for whole movement C is determined in advance, and stereo vision can be used to calculate distance to target position ($\mathbf{r}^t - \mathbf{r_d}$). At each sampling time we are calculating new driving torques $\boldsymbol{\tau}^t$. When that torque is applied certain linear acceleration of robot's tip arises. Lets assume than we can measure that acceleration by using accelerometers that measured value is $\ddot{\mathbf{q}}^t_m$). We can also calculate speed of robot' tip $\dot{\mathbf{q}}^t_m$) by integrating measured acceleration. Since dynamics of the system have changed, calculated values of driving torques are not same as desired values. But it is desired that robot's tip moves in accordance with equation (1). Since we have calculated hand's speed, and measured acceleration we can calculate new distance to target position, for which measured movement is in accordance with equation:

$$\left(\mathbf{r}^t - \mathbf{r_{d}}_{new}\right) = -\frac{1}{K}\left(C\dot{\mathbf{r}}^t_m + m\ddot{\mathbf{r}}^t_m\right) . \tag{15}$$

Now, for input data $\left[(\mathbf{q}^t)^T \ (\dot{\mathbf{q}}^t)^T \ (\mathbf{r}^t - \mathbf{r_{d}}_{new})^T \ C\right]^T$ desired output is exactly $\boldsymbol{\tau}^t$. We are using data pairs calculated this way to adapt RBF. We were unable to determine desired output for certain input (since model is unknown), so we have determined input that fits known output.

4.5   Verification of RBF Network Adaptation

Verification of control system adaptation process is similar to process verification described in section 4.3. We assign arbitrary chosen start and target positions and damping coefficient. Also, in some parts of simulation we add point mass to robot's tip. At each sampling instant, using state of the system (joint coordinates, join velocities, distance to target position and damping coefficient) driving torques are calculated. Those torques are applied at appropriate joints, resulting in acceleration of hand's tip. Using that acceleration, we calculate (equation (15)) input-output data pair for RBF network adaptation, which is adapted in each time instant with learning rate $\eta = 5 \cdot 10^{-8}$.

Firstly, last two simulated cases (rising of hand with and without carrying weight (Fig. 4)) were repeated, but this time control system was adapted on-line. Results of simulations are shown on Fig. 5. When robot's arm is not carrying any weight, dynamics of robot are same as one used to train SVM, so it is expected that movements with and without adaptation are the same. It is evident from figures 4a and 5a, that those two motions are almost identical. When control system was adapted on-line positioning error has slightly decreased to 0.8 mm. Rise time has slightly increased form 1.8 s to 1.82 s.

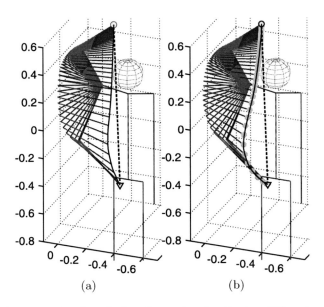

(a)   (b)

Fig. 5. Stick diagrams showing the hand's motion for the two different cases: a) movement without weight b) movement with weight. Hand's position is plotted every 75 ms. Trajectory of hand's tip *(full line)*, desired trajectory *(dashed line)*, target position *(circle)* and start position *(triangle)* are shown.

On the contrary, when robot is carrying weight, differences between movements (Figs. 4b and 4b) are significant. At the beginning motions look the same, since adaptation has not yet taken hold. After certain amount of time, when enough data pairs for RBF network adaptation were acquired, motions begin to differ. When there was no adaptation, tip of the hand veered off course and missed desired target position by 55 mm (Fig. 4b). In contrast to that, when adaptation was performed robot's tip stopped within 1 mm from desired position, which is same as in case when no mass was carried. As expected, rise time is higher $(1.95\,s)$ than in case when there was no weight, because the control system was not sufficiently altered at the beginning of motion, and during that time hand's tip does not travel in direction of target position. It should be noted that already during first hand movement RBF network has fully adapted to change that occurred.

In last case considered, we have simulated pick-and-place task performed by humanoid robot. Firstly, humanoid's hand moves without any weight to the pick-up position. Then, robot picks up object weighing $1\,kg$ and moves it to desired 'place' position. After reaching that position hand will move to arbitrary position. This case is especially interesting since dynamics of the system changes two times, first time when robot picks up an object, and second time when robot puts down the object, and continues to move freely. Each phase is displayed separately in Fig. 6.

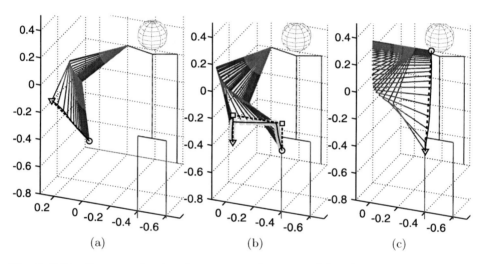

(a)   (b)   (c)

Fig. 6. Stick diagrams showing three stages of motion: a) hand movement to pick up location b)hand pick-and-place movement c) hand movement from drop off to arbitrary position. Hand's position is plotted every 150 ms. Trajectory of hand's tip *(full line)*, desired trajectory *(dashed line)*, target position *(circle)*, intermediate positions *(squares)* and start position *(triangle)* are shown.

During first phase (Fig. 6a), robot moves without any mass attached to it, and it reaches desired position with accuracy of $1\,mm$ and no overshoot. Then robot picks up an object and starts moving upwards to intermediate position depicted by square on Fig. 6b. Since, positioning at this point is not of great significance, when hand's tip reaches within $50\,mm$ of first intermediate position, it starts moving towards second intermediate position. When hand's tip reaches within $50\,mm$ of second intermediate point, it starts moving towards 'drop off' position.

During whole movement control system is constantly adapting to change that occurred. The adaptation is carried out successfully, and positioning error at place where robot should place object is less than $1\ mm$, also hand positioned itself without overshoot. At this point robot releases object that it carried, and dynamics changes once again. Robot starts moving to arbitrary position constantly adapting RBF coefficients. It reaches its final position (Fig. 6c) with accuracy of $1\ mm$, what tells us that adaptation was successful once again.

5   Conclusion

The work considers the use the SVM for the realization of humanoid reaching task. It is assumed that the human hand moves in a same manner as a point mass m connected to the target position via a spring and a damper. The mass, the stiffness and the damping are selected so as to obtain a critically or overcritically damped rectilinear motion of the point mass. For an identical motion of the humanoid's hand, based on the known motion of the point mass, it is possible to calculate the joint driving torques. In this way, the input and output data of the training set are formed.

Since the relation between the input and output data is nonlinear, the SVM was trained using the kernel trick, the RBF serving as a kernel function. After completed training, the obtained SVM was validated.

Several examples demonstrated that the application of the driving torques obtained using the SVM produced hand motion close to linear. Also, the presented examples have unequivocally shown that no overshoots arisen in the realization of the movement to the target position.

Using SVM obtained from model of humanoid arm, has some serious drawbacks if dynamics of system changes. Movement is vastly nonlinear, and robot's hand misses its target substantially. To address this issue we have employed EBP algorithm to alter existing control system in order to compensate it. This approach was validated on several examples. Examples have shown, that adaptation to changes in system mass is performed successfully, during just one grasping motion. After adaptation final positioning is even slightly improved. All the presented examples are related to the task of the object's reaching by one hand. The humanoid robots, in a dynamic environment of humans, will be forced to realize two-handed manipulation in real time, so this will be one of the focuses of our future work. It should also be pointed out that the target position in the presented examples was related to stationary goal position. Since the objects in the human environment are mobile, it is important to realize the tasks of reaching objects that are movable. Therefore, the future investigations have to be concerned with the task of reaching mobile objects, as well as with the realization of two-handed manipulations using SVM and EBP.

Acknowledgments. This work was supported by the Ministry of Technology and Development of the Republic of Serbia under contract No. 44008.

References

1. Konczak, J., Dichgans, J.: The development toward stereotypic arm kinematics during reaching in the first 3 years of life. Exp. Brain. Res. 117, 346–354 (1997)
2. Konczak, J., Borutta, M., Dichgans, J.: The development of goal-directed reaching in infants, II. Learning to produce task-adequate patterns of joint torque. Exp. Brain. Res. 113, 465–474 (1997)
3. Grosso, E., Metta, G., Oddera, A., Sandini, G.: Robust Visual Servoing in 3-D Reaching Tasks. IEEE Tran. on Robotics and Automation 12(5), 732–742 (1996)
4. Coelho, J., Pater, J., Grupen, R.: Developing haptic and visual perceptual categories for reaching and grasping with a humanoid robot. Robotics and Autonomous Systems 37, 195–218 (2006)
5. Gaskett, C., Cheng, G.: Online Learning of a Motor Map for Humanoid Robot Reaching. In: Proc.of 2nd Int. Conf. Computational Intelligence, Robotics and Autonomous Systems, Singapore (2003)
6. Blackburn, M., Nygen, H.: Learning in robot vision directed reaching: A comparison of methods. In: Proc. of the ARPA Image Understanding Workshop, Moterey, CA (1994)
7. Vapnik, V.: The nature of statistical learning theory. Springer, Heidelberg (2000)
8. Kecman, V.: Learning and Soft Computing: Support Vector Machines, Neural Networks, and Fuzzy Logic Models. The MIT Press, Cambridge (2001)
9. Potkonjak, V., Vukobratović, M., Babković, K., Borovac, B.: General Model of Dynamics of Human and Humanoid Motion: Feasibility, Potentials and Verification. Int. Jour. of Humanoid Robotics 3(2), 21–48 (2006)

Development of a High Speed 3D Laser Measurement System for Outdoor Robotics

Jens Schlemper, Lars Kuhnert, Markus Ax, and Klaus-Dieter Kuhnert

University of Siegen, Faculty IV - Science and Technology,
Institute for Real-Time Learning Systems
Hoelderlinstr. 3, 57068 Siegen, Germany
{schlemper,lars.kuhnert,kuhnert}@fb12.uni-siegen.de,
markus.ax@uni-siegen.de

Abstract. This paper describes the development of a 3D laser measurement system for application in outdoor robotics. Over the last few years several approaches have been examined concerning this issue. In the majority of cases, a 2D laser scanner, including its whole weight, is used by a rotating motion to obtain a three dimensional model of the near and far environment. To prevent the disadvantages, like particularly the loss of velocity during the scanning process due to the high mass to be accelerated, a novel approach is illustrated within this paper. By mounting a light weight mirror directly in front of the 2D laser scanner, a higher velocity can be achieved while capturing the environment. In addition, further improvements in the minimization of power consumption and also in the reduction considering the complexity of hardware can be reached. The achievement of a 6 Hz frame rate represents the result of this research.

Keywords: 3D laser scanner, outdoor mobile robotics, high speed, dynamic objects.

1 Introduction

During recent years, the application of obstacle detection and path planning for autonomous navigation of mobile robots has been a big challenge. In order to attain autonomous navigation and collision avoidance it is very important to know as much as possible about the near and far environment. Therefore, the acquisition of the surroundings as a three dimensional model is inevitable.

So far, there are two major approaches of capturing the environment in 3D, image-processing based systems and time-of-flight based systems. Both have deficits in various ways. Image-processing based systems are considerable dependent on computer power and also suffer from external influences of the environment like rapid changes in light conditions. This affects mainly the robustness of such systems. Time-of-flight systems like laser range finders are almost independent of environmental influences. Another big advantage is that laser scanners can measure distances in high ranges. Ranges of over 100 meters are not uncommon.

D. Obdržálek and A. Gottscheber (Eds.): EUROBOT 2011, CCIS 161, pp. 277–287, 2011.

However, especially the use of 2D laser scanners in the field of navigation and obstacle detection is often unsuitable in outdoor robotic applications. A case in a point is the detection of objects which are either above or below the detection line (compare[1] p. 13). For these reasons the deployment of 3D laser scanners on mobile robotic platforms becomes more and more preferable. Concerning this issue, several approaches have been examined [6][7][8][9]. Most of these implementations have one thing in common. They almost always use a 2D scanner, which is assembled on a rotating mechanical device. In fact, the results of such systems are good but however considering the complexity of the hardware, the increased accelerated mass and power consumption by moving the entire laser scanner, including all of its weight, is the other side of the coin.

In the presented paper a different approach is described. To prevent the already mentioned disadvantages of rotating an entire scanner system, we use a rotating mirror mounted in front of the 2D laser measurement system. What we have gained in contrast is a high speed 3D laser scanner system, which can reach a frame rate up to 6 Hz and a usable field of view up to 120° in horizontal direction and 90° in vertical direction.

But first of all, in the next chapter, systems are presented, which have already dealt with this issue. Afterwards, chapter three sets the focus on the individual hardware components in detail as well as considering the whole system. The fourth and fifth chapter describe the results of implementation and calibration, while the final chapter draws a conclusion and points out future work.

2 Previous Work

In the range of commercial 3D laser measurement systems there are a few products that will be mentioned in the further course. For example the 3D laser scanner, which the company *Velodyne*[13] has developed, is very useful for applications in the field of mobile robotics. Accordingly, this scanner delivers excellent results. There are used 64 laser beams, which provide a lateral resolution of 0.4°. The field of view has an amount of 360° in horizontal direction as well as 27° in vertical direction. The decisive advantage of this system is that the 64 laser beams can be rotated up to 900 revolutions per minute. Resulting therefrom, a scanning frequency of up to 15 frames per seconds is possible. The resulting point clouds consist of over 1.8 million points, which are transmitted via an Ethernet interface for further processing. For these reasons such types of laser measurement systems are, besides from a few exceptional cases, highly suitable for mobile robotic applications like collision avoidance or path planning.

In the area of terrestrial laser scanning, which focuses on the surveying of buildings or landscapes for three dimensional models, the *ILRIS-HD* developed by the company *Optech*[14], is presented. With a minimal stepping size of 0.000745° the environment can be captured very precisely.

This yields to the conclusion, that commercial 3D laser measurement systems have mostly two things in common. On the one hand most of the systems follow the same technical approach by rotating a 2D laser scanner without the consideration of mass acceleration and power consumption. The second commonality is that the devices are very expensive in acquirement. For these reasons we have tried to develop a similar system which meets the requirements for applications of mobile robotics, as mentioned above, and also tries to keep the overall costs as low as possible.

The basic approach, to use a rotating mirror mounted in front of a 2D laser scanner, has already been implemented with success. For example T. C. Ng [1] or J. Ryde et al. [2] have developed a similar 3D laser measurement system. Both use different methods for mounting the mirror in front of the laser scanning device and they use a various number of faces with also different arrangements. For further information, we refer to the corresponding papers [1] and [2].

3 Hardware

The heart of our 3D laser measurement system forms the 2D line scanner *LMS221*, which the company *SICK* [15] has developed (see Figure 3a). The scanner is very appropriate for outdoor robotic applications because of its robustness and protection class convention. It operates with a constant update rate of 75 Hz and uses a serial interface for data transmission. In addition, the laser scanner can be actuated in different modes. For example the range can be restricted to a maximum (8 m, 16 m, 32 m, 80 m) and there is also the possibility to select the resolution (0.25°, 0.5°, 1°) depending on the used application. The scanner operates with the usual transmitter-receiver technique called time-of-flight principle. This means that a laser diode (transmitter) is used to emit a pulse of light in its direction of view and afterwards an optical lens gathers the returning light, which is received by a photo detector (receiver). Since the speed of light c is known, the driver electronic is able to measure the amount of time which the light needs to travel twice the distance between the detector and the surface of an object (round-trip time t_r). If the round-trip time is determined correctly the distance is equal to $c\frac{t_r}{2}$. The accuracy of the measurements depends on the precise determination of the round-trip time. To get the distance of more than one point the laser beam is usually deflected by a rotating mirror. Thereby, the viewing angle is enlarged by 180° in a single revolution.

Another integral component of our 3D laser measurement system is the mirror device which is mounted in front of the 2D laser scanner (see Figure 1c). This mirror assembly consists of an incremental rotary encoder, a stepping motor and an off-the-shelf surface mirror. As shown in Figure 3b the rotary encoder and the stepping motor are mounted face to face connected and fixed by an axle. In between a mirror forms the center of the whole construction. There are several opportunities to position the surface mirror. One possibility is to place the intended rotation axis through the center of gravity to keep the torque of inertia as low as possible. And on the other hand the rotation axis can be placed as far to the back as possible. Due to the fact that the laser spot moves vertically along the surface of the rotating mirror, the last method is the better choice. As seen in Figure 1c the surface of the mirror is divided in two areas. One area has a normal mirrored surface, whereas the other area has a black matted surface.

(a) 3D laser scanner mounted on $AMOR^1$[11]

(b) 3D laser scanner model

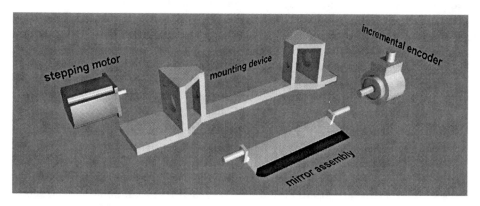

(c) Exploded assembly drawing of the mirror device

Fig. 1. Hardware of the 3D laser scanner

The reason of such an arrangement is that in some cases the approximately one centimeter big laser spot goes partially beyond the reflecting side of the mirror, which produces an ambiguous result. The clue is that the black part absorbs the trespassing light to make the distance measurement unambiguous. The disadvantage of such an arrangement is that the horizontal field of view of 180° cannot completely be used. The horizontal and also the vertical field of view angle depend on some factors. In this case, the length and width of the mirror play a major role. These variables primarily determine the horizontal field of view and the spatial position of the whole mirror device in relation to the emission point of the laser beam. Thus, the closer the mirror device is mounted to the laser points output, the better is the optimal usable horizontal field of view. The vertical angular field of view is limited to the maximum of 90° by the

---

[1] AMOR (Autonomous Mobile Outdoor Robot).

body of the laser scanner. In the presented system the mirror has a length of 180 mm and a width of 20 mm.

To ensure a synchronization of the laser scanner data with the position of the mirror, the combination of a stepping motor and an incremental encoder is used, which form a closed loop control. The stepping motor has an incremental size of 1.8° per step by exerting a maximum torsional moment of 105 Ncm with a current consumption of 2.48 A per phase. In consideration of the fact that the load on the stepping motor is not very high, the dimensioning is more than sufficient. A special designed micro-controller board provides the operation of the motor in micro stepping mode. In conjunction with the encoder the stepping motor can be positioned with an accuracy of 0.018°. The synchronized data is then processed and provided by a network controller board which is specifically designed for this system.

Since, within this chapter we have talked extensively about the hardware design, the next chapter focuses on the implementation and calibration of the system.

4   Implementation

One of the biggest challenges within this approach is the synchronization of the laser scanner data with the encoder position. This makes it generally possible to perform an accurate data analysis. For that purpose we need a deeper understanding of the used SICK laser scanner. As already mentioned, the laser scanner creates 75 scan lines per second, that are transmitted via serial port with a baud rate of 500 kbps. The communication between host and the laser measurement system is possible in both directions. This is affected by a telegram frame structure which includes either the sending commands or the receiving data. In contrast the incremental encoder delivers values with an exact update rate of 27 kHz by using a polling technique, which enables the allocation of each tilt value to a associated distance value in a whole scan line. This creates the precondition of a fast scanning process. Several methods to synchronize the laser scanner data with the position of the mirror device are studied by O. Wulf [8]. In contrast to that approach, we do not use any time stamp technique, but we use a synchronization impulse generated by the laser scanner emitted at every starting/ending point of a new scan line. The emitting signal triggers the process of buffering the laser scanner data and the encoder readings in a circular buffer. Now we are able to output the cached synchronized data simultaneously and we are also able to receive new data from the laser scanner and the encoder. The whole synchronization process is clarified in a block diagram, shown on Figure 2. After the synchronization of the laser scanner data with the encoder readings has been executed, we need an appropriate method to provide the synchronized data. As mentioned above we use an Ethernet interface controller board for data transmission. Since we want to use the 3D laser scanner for several applications at the same time, a server-/client-architecture is utilized to make this possible. Therefore, we use the User Datagram Protocol (UDP) for transmission purpose.

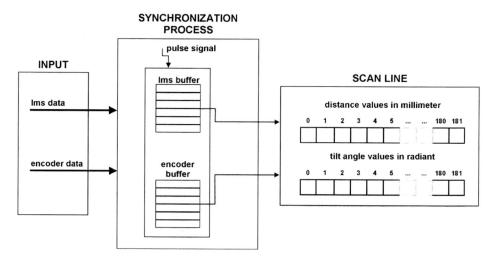

Fig. 2. Synchronization process as block diagram

Each client is now able to receive the raw synchronized data from the controller board with an update rate of 75 scan lines per second. The raw data comprises two arrays, each one consists of 181 values. The first array includes the distance values in millimeter and the second array the belonging calculated angle positions of the mirror assembly in radiant. Furthermore, these two values in combination with the horizontal angle, given by the laser scanner resolution, represent the spherical coordinates, which can be transformed to Cartesian coordinates with the help of the following equations:

$$x = r \cdot \sin\theta \cdot \cos\varphi$$
$$y = r \cdot \sin\theta \cdot \sin\varphi$$
$$z = r \cdot \cos\theta$$

The variable θ (polar angle) determines the angle between the z-axis and the position vector r. In contrast, φ (azimuth angle) describes the angle between x-axis and the vertical projection of r into the x-y-plane. After having created the raw point cloud we have to calibrate the whole system, which is described in the next chapter.

5   Calibration

For calibration purpose we need to define the transformation between the 3D point cloud coordinate system and the 3D world coordinate system. Accordingly, we need to calculate the correct orientation and location of the 3D laser scanner within the 3D world coordinate system. Due to the fact that the mirror can be positioned at an exactly defined angle, the internal calibration is already accomplished. Initially, the resulting point cloud is rotated around the three axes x, y and z in a wrong way. The degree of the rotation around the x-axis (pitch angle) is very noticeable, which is caused by the tilted position of the 2D laser scanner. As against the other two axes are not really affected. To calculate the rotational matrices to retransform the point cloud, we use a plane fitting algorithm which is introduced in the work of D. Eberly [3]. In our case we need a point cloud, which describes a defined plane object similar to a floor or a wall. With the algorithm of D. Eberly, we are now able to calculate the normal vector of that given plane by doing a singular-value decomposition of the following 3x3 covariance matrix:

$$\begin{pmatrix} \sum_{i=1}^{m}(x_i - a)^2 & \sum_{i=1}^{m}(x_i - a)(y_i - b) & \sum_{i=1}^{m}(x_i - a)(z_i - c) \\ \sum_{i=1}^{m}(x_i - a)(y_i - b) & \sum_{i=1}^{m}(y_i - b)^2 & \sum_{i=1}^{m}(y_i - b)(z_i - c) \\ \sum_{i=1}^{m}(x_i - a)(z_i - c) & \sum_{i=1}^{m}(y_i - b)(y_i - c) & \sum_{i=1}^{m}(z_i - c)^2 \end{pmatrix}$$

The variables x_i, y_i and z_i are the components of the given measured 3D points. The resulting eigenvector with the smallest eigenvalue represents the normal vector of the desired plane. With this information it is possible to calculate the rotational matrices of the roll, pitch and yaw angle of the laser scanner coordinate system in relation to the world coordinate system. While the determination of the point cloud translation is negligible because the origin of the coordinate system is positioned directly in center of the mirror.

6   Results

In this chapter we want to show some results, which have been achieved by using the described 3D laser scanner. The attention is focused on two different types of capturing the environment. The first case describes captured 3D models during a static scanning process without dynamical influences. The second case on the other hand deals with the detection of dynamical objects. Due to the fact that every scene has been taken outdoors, the ability for applications considering autonomous outdoor robotic platforms can be confirmed.

Beginning with the static case, the figures 3a and 3b show a facade of a building captured with a distance of about 12 m and a scanning time of 3 s. On another scan (see figure 3c) you can see a person with outstretched arms standing 6 m away from the laser scanner in front of a wall. Regarding the 3D images in detail you can see some irregularities. Especially, on figure 3a there seems to be a pincushion distortion of the scanned data. This is significantly seen when looking at the vertically aligned window frames. But what looks like a pincushion distortion is actually the correct sampling of the environment. However, this behavior can be justified by the fact that the laser scanner captures the environment by a rotating movement. Thereby, the trajectories of the laser beams, which are deflected during the tilting movement of the mirror, run on curved paths (see figure 3d). This occurs because of different measured distances at a constant horizontal angle. This means, that the higher the angle relatively to the coordinates' origin, the greater the impact on the curvature is.

(a) A facade of a house as 3D model   (b) A facade of a house in reality

(c) A person as 3D model   (d) Pointcloud: Trajectories of the points

Fig. 3. Static scanning

In the further course, this affects consequently the triangulation of the result-ing point cloud. The whole mentioned effect can be compensated by increasing the horizontal resolution.

Furthermore, the accuracy of the 3D meshes can be evaluated by looking at the different possible disturbing sources. We distinguish between two types of disturbances. On the one hand there are factors which can be compensated by using a specified calibration procedure like explained in chapter 5 (calibration). On the other hand there are disturbances given by the sensors characteristic properties like for example random noise. Finally, there is one decisive factor which influences the accuracy of the resulting data. In this context the accuracy of the used 2D laser scanner has to be mentioned. Looking at the *SICK LMS 221* technical description (see [17], pp. 29-30) the accuracy of the scanner is about $\pm 15mm$ with a statistical error of *1 sigma* standard deviation. Other possible disturbing factors like the absolute incremental encoder do not need to be considered because of its noiseless characteristics.

In contrast to the static scanning process, in the second case, the focus is not on the high resolution of 3D meshes, but the possibility of high speed scanning opens up further opportunities in the field of autonomous robotics. The detection of dynamic objects is possible With a frame rate of up to 6 Hz. Figure 4 shows

Fig. 4. Dynamic object detection

a sequence of scans to illustrate the possibility of dynamic object detection with a frame rate of 5 Hz to 6 Hz. On the resulting scans you can see a person is passing the robot with walking speed. For better illustration we combine four scans captured sequentially in a row, in order to merge all in one frame. We have also removed shadows, which have been cast by the person as polygonal volumes. Beyond, to set the focus on the walking person we have also colored the polygonal area of interest.

This yields to the conclusion, that in both cases the resulting data is useful for further 3D processing, especially for applications in the field of mobile robotics. Actually, many algorithms have been examined over the last few years. In this context, we would like to introduce an initiative, which arised in order to focus on the 3D perception. It is developed and supported by an international community of robotics and perception researchers (see R. B. Rusus and S. Cousins [12]). This approach pursues the merging of various state-of-the-art algorithms for filtering, model fitting and segmentation, feature estimation, surface reconstruction and registration in one software library called *PCL (Point Cloud Library)* [16]. These preprocessing algorithms form principally the basis for solving different high level operations like navigation or collision avoidance for example.

7   Conclusion and Future Work

The development of a 3D laser scanner system is presented in this paper. As improvement we use a rotating mirror device to prevent high accelerated mass movements, high power consumption and high costs of hardware complexity in terms of providing high speed measuring of the near and far environment. During our research, we figured out that some further improvements need to be done. For example, the projection of color information on meshes given by a imaging device is also a topic which already has been done by our research group [10] in the context of a previous version of our 3D laser scanner, but not yet applied to the described 3D laser measurement system within this paper. Summing up the resulting 3D information of the environment captured by the described 3D laser scanner can be used in various applications in the field of mobile outdoor robotics, especially concerning applications in which high speed scans are intended.

References

1. Ng, T.C.: Development of a 3D LIDAR system for autonomous vehicle guidance. SIMTech Technical Reports 6(1), 13–18 (2005)
2. Ryde, J., Hu, H.: 3D laser Range Scanner with Hemispherical Field of View for Robot Navigation. In: Prceedings of the IEEE/ASME International Conference on Advanced Intelligent Mechatronics, July 2-5, pp. 891–896. Xi'an, China (2008)
3. Eberly, D.: Least Squares Fitting of Data. Geometric Tools, LLC (2008), http://www.geometrictools.com/
4. Schroeter, D., Newman, P.: On the Cross-Calibration of a Camera and 3D-Laser Range Finder. In: Proceedings of the 2nd SEAS DTC Technical Conference, Edinburgh (2007)
5. Zhang, Z.: A Flexible New Technique for Camera Calibration. IEEE Transactions Pattern Analysis and Machine Intelligence 22(11), 1330–1334 (2000)
6. Cole, D., Newman, P.: Using laser range data for 3D slam in outdoor environments. In: ICRA 2006, Proceedings IEEE International Conference on Robotics and Automation, Orlando, USA, May 15-19, pp. 1556–1563 (2006)
7. Nüchter, A., Lingemann, K., Hertberg, J., Surmann, H.: Heuristic based laser scan matching for outdoor 6D SLAM. In: Proceedings 28th Annual German Conference on Artificial Intelligence, Koblenz, Germany (2005)
8. Wulf, O., Wagner, B.: Fast 3D Scanning Methods for Laser Measurement Systems. In: Proceedings International Conference on Control Systems and Computer Science, Bucharest, Romania (July 2003)
9. Steinhaus, P., Dillmann, R.: Aufbau und Modellierung des RoSi Scanners zur 3D-Tiefenbildakquisition. Institut für Rechnerentwurf und Fehlertoleranz, University of Karlsruhe, Germany
10. Kuhnert, L., Kuhnert, K.-D.: Sensor-fusion based real-time 3D outdoor scene reconstruction and analysis on a moving mobile outdoor robot. KI-Künstliche Intelligenz Special Issue: Off-road robotics, 1–7 (2011)
11. Kuhnert, K.-D., Seemann, W.: Design and realisation of the highly modular and robust autonomous mobile outdoor robot AMOR. In: Proceedings of the 13th IASTED International Conference on Robotics and Applications, pp. 464–469. ACTA Press (2007)

12. Rusu, R.B., Cousins, S.: 3D is here: Point Cloud Library (PCL). In: Proceedings of the 2011 IEEE International Conference on Robotics and Automation, Shanghai, China (2011)
13. Velodyne High Definition LIDAR, `http://www.velodyne.com/lidar/lidar.aspx` (accessed March 15, 2011)
14. Optech Incorporated, `http://www.optech.ca` (accessed March 15, 2011)
15. Sick Sensor Intelligence, `http://www.sick.com` (accessed March 15, 2011)
16. Point Cloud Library, `http://www.pointclouds.org`, (accessed April 26, 2011)
17. Sick LMS200/211/221/291 Technical Description,
    `http://www.sicktoolbox.sourceforge.net/docs/`
    `sick-lms-technical-description.pdf` (accessed March 15, 2011)

A Robot Competition to Encourage First-Year Students in Mechatronic Sciences

Johannes Stier, Gero Zechel, and Michael Beitelschmidt

Chair of Dynamics and Mechanisms, Department of Continuum Mechanics,
Faculty of Mechanical Engineering,
Technische Universitaet Dresden, Germany
{johannes.Stier,gero.zechel,michael.beitelschmidt}@tu-dresden.de

Abstract. In 2010, for the first time, a robot competition was organized at the Technische Universitaet Dresden for first-year students of
mechatronics. The competition was supposed to give the students a push
of motivation for their studies. Four different challenges were developed
and combined to a relay competition. The robots were built with LEGO
MINDSTORMS NXT 2.0 and programmed with NATIONAL INSTRUMENTS
LABVIEW. In this article the project's organization and implementation
as well as the gained experiences are described.

Keywords: robot, challenge, course, relay competition, LEGO
MINDSTORMS NXT 2.0, LABVIEW, stairwalker, labyrinth, crane, ball
transporter, mechatronics, education.

1 Introduction

The first two semesters for students being at the beginning of their mechatronics
studies are called orientation year, including a guided study start and only general basic modules like mathematics or fundamentals of electrical engineering.
Starting in 2010, a project week themed "Mechatronics Self-Made" was introduced into the first term. It was established by the dean of mechatronics Prof.
Dr.-Ing. Michael Beitelschmidt and the studies committee mechatronics. The
project is a mandatory module because credit points can be gained. During the
project week, the participating students have to build robots to solve different
kinds of tasks. To increase the students' motivation, there is a relay competition
at the end of the project. Building robots gives the students a playful opportunity to "feel" what mechatronics is really about and to determine whether
mechatronics is the right study if they are uncertain.

The main goals of the project are to convey the following basic skills to the
students:

- handling actuators and sensors, and programming a microcontroller,
- signal processing with self-developed algorithms,
- constructing simple mechatronic systems to satisfy defined tasks.

D. Obdržálek and A. Gottscheber (Eds.): EUROBOT 2011, CCIS 161, pp. 288–299, 2011.
© Springer-Verlag Berlin Heidelberg 2011

Hence the following project topics can be obtained:

- getting to know actuators and sensors,
- developing a simple motion control and implementing it on a microcontroller,
- developing strategies within a team to build mechatronic systems,
- reflecting gained competences in the project and somebody's own strength and failings.

2 The Project's Structure

2.1 The Hardware and Software

The project is based on the LEGO MINDSTORMS NXT 2.0 robot building system. It is easy to use, easy to get familiar with and offers manifold possibilities to build robots solving a specified task. Originally, the robots can be programmed with the LEGO MINDSTORMS NXT 2.0 SOFTWARE. It was developed by NATIONAL INSTRUMENTS and is based on LABVIEW. Like LabVIEW, it uses the concept of graphical programming, offering a simple way to program the NXT device. The NXT-Software is quite easy to understand and to use, but a more complex program with sophisticated control strategies is beyond the software's horizon. Another way to program the NXT is to use NXC, a special programming language based on C [2]. Additionally, the platform LEJOS offers the possibility to program the NXT in JAVA [3]. Using those two programming languages to implement a motion control would in fact not limit its complexity, but it could be too difficult for first-year students. As a consequence of those facts, LABVIEW itself was used for the robot programming, offering a special NXT library (NXT Toolkit). It is a good compromise between LEGO MINDSTORMS NXT 2.0 SOFTWARE and NXC respectively LEJOS, and gives the students an easy way to understand and program the robots. The students get also an introduction into graphical signal-flow oriented programming.

2.2 The Concept

All participating students are divided into teams of four participants. When subscribing to the project, the students can choose a team. One of four different challenges is assigned to every team. The four challenges together compose a course that must be passed on time. Therefore, relays are formed consisting of four teams, one team of each challenge. At the end of the project, all existing relays are taking part in a competition with the aim of being the fastest relay passing the course. This gives the students a further push of motivation.

2.3 The Course/The Four Challenges

As mentioned in the section above, the course to be passed by each relay consists of four challenges. An illustration of the whole course is shown in Fig. 1. The challenges are of different kind each, with different difficulties in three fields: control,

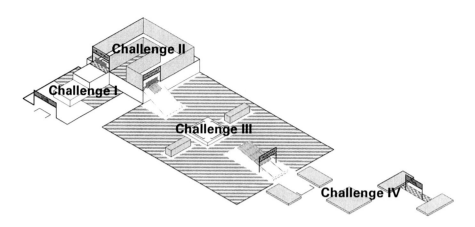

Fig. 1. The whole relay competition course

construction and programming. Defined handovers connect the challenges, with which the token is passed from one team to the next one. To prevent the relay run to be interrupted by a robot failure, each challenge has a certain time limit. If this limit is exceeded by a team, the team gets a time penalty, and the team of the following challenge may start manually.

Challenge I: *Stairwalker.* In Challenge I, the students have to create a robot that is able to climb two steps of certain dimensions, as the course's illustration in Fig. 2 shows. The main aspect of this challenge is construction, representing the mechanical part of mechatronics. Consequently, in addition to the standard LEGO MINDSTORMS EDUCATION NXT BASE SET the students get the LEGO MINDSTORMS EDUCATION RESOURCE SET, offering more parts to build a robot and thus making it easier to construct. Control and programming are less important though, but may not be disregarded. When reaching the top level of the stair, the token will be passed to the following team of Challenge II by contacting a flap gate at the checkpoint between the two challenges. To allow a fair competition at the end of the project, certain rules have to be followed:

- The robot must be set to the scratch line and may be aligned manually.
- The robot must start autonomously after an acoustic signal.
- The robot may be reset to the scratch line by the team's decision at any time and may restart. The time measurement continues in the meanwhile.

Challenge II: *Labyrinth.* Fig. 3 shows the course of Challenge II. In this challenge, a robot has to be developed that is able to move autonomously through a corridor of known dimensions, but of unknown shape. The labyrinth consists of a square plate with an equally spaced grid. Every field in the grid represents a labyrinth segment. The labyrinth's final construction is illustrated in Fig. 7 and Fig. 11. Walls of different length can be combined and put on the square plate to shape a labyrinth. Hence, there is a great variety of possible labyrinth

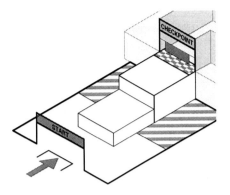
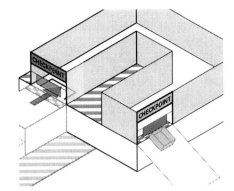

Fig. 2. The course of Challenge I   **Fig. 3.** The course of Challenge II

designs. In contrast to Challenge I, the robot's construction is less important. The main focus is the control and the programming of the robot. Challenge II is supposed to point up the interaction of sensors and actors. The token is passed to the following challenge, Challenge III, by hitting a mechanism, which forces a basket to slide down a chute. As described in the challenge before, there are several rules that need to be followed:

- The final labyrinth's shape will be published prior to the competition.
- The maximum length of a straight corridor is restricted. All corridors are perpendicular to each other, and there are neither junctions nor dead ends.
- The robot may only start after the flap gate was contacted by the team of Challenge I.
- The corridor walls may only be contacted by the touch sensors. If another part of the robot gets in contact with the walls, there will be a penalty of five seconds for every applied labyrinth segment.
- The robot may be positioned backwards three labyrinth segments by the team's decision at any time. The time measurement continues in the meanwhile.

Challenge III: *Crane.* The course of the third challenge is shown in Fig. 4. A robot has to be constructed, which is able to detect a basket's position, lifting it afterwards, turning around with regard to two obstacles and putting the basket into one of four boxes. After leaving the chute, the basket's position is random. Similar to Challenge I, construction is the main aspect of Challenge III. Thus, the students get the LEGO MINDSTORMS EDUCATION RESOURCE SET in addition to the LEGO MINDSTORMS EDUCATION NXT BASE SET. Moreover, control and programming are less important. The main difficulty of this challenge is to build a crane with an arm as large as possible, with respect to the construction's stability and the given parts. By putting the basket into one of the four boxes, a teeter-totter is activated, and the token is passed to the following team of Challenge IV. Certain rules are specified to allow a fair competition:

- The built robot (crane) has to be mounted on a given platform.
- The challenge is finished when the basket has been put into one of the four boxes.
- Putting the basket into box two, three or four gives a time bonus.

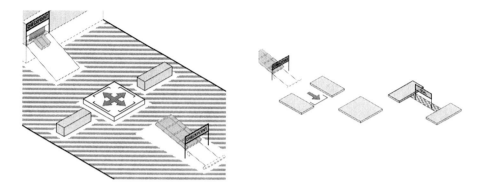

Fig. 4. The course of Challenge III   **Fig. 5.** The course of Challenge IV

Challenge IV: *Ball Transporter* The last and final challenge is the *Ball Transporter*. Fig. 5 shows a basic illustration of the challenge's course. A robot has to be built that can transport a given ball from a scratch line to the finish line, passing known obstacles without touching them. The ball must be placed on a given LEGO brick and may not be dropped while moving. Besides the brick, the ball may not touch any other part of the robot. Hence, touching an obstacle or accelerating and braking with discontinuous jolt means losing the ball and leads to a restart. Planning a smooth trajectory and implementing it is the main aspect of this challenge, requiring control and programming skills rather than construction skills. Similar to all other challenges, there are several rules that need to be followed:

- The robot must be positioned at the scratch line with the whole ball being in front of the line.
- The robot's start is triggered by the teeter-totter. In its initial state, the teeter-totter touches the floor at the side of Challenge IV. When the basket is put into on of the boxes by the team of Challenge III, the teeter-totter is lifting. This one change must be detected to start the run.
- After passing the finish line, an acoustic signal has to be emitted, denoting the end of the transport and the whole relay.
- The ball is considered to be dropped if it touches any other part rather than the brick on which it lies. When dropping the ball, the robot must be reset to the scratch line and must restart. The time measurement continues in the meanwhile.

3 Preparing the Project/The Planned Time Schedule

The organization of the project was mainly done by employees of three chairs from different faculties. Additionally, six students of the third and fifth term mechatronics were hired as student assistants to support the organization and implementation. Their main part was the challenges' brainstorming as well as development and planning in the preface of the project. For each challenge, one sample solution was built by the students to proof whether the devised tasks are solvable. Two trails were used to test if the prepared challenges and their sample solutions are working in the way they were supposed to, and to determine the rules that will be applied for each challenge during the relay competition.

The project's whole organization – concerning the students' registration into the teams, the download of the topics with the challenge descriptions and the propagation of news – was realized with the Saxon E-Learning system OPAL [1].

Because the project is a module in the first term, credit points can be gained. Thus there needs to be some kind of exam. For that reason, two presentations were established, which the students will have to give. The content of the first presentation – called team presentation – has to be a summary of possible solutions for their challenge and must be given to all other teams of the same challenge. The detailed description of the students' favorite solution, which they are going to implement, will be a topic as well. This presentation has the aim to encourage the students to analyze a given task, to develop strategies to solve it and to prepare a presentation. All teams of one relay are participating in the second presentation – called relay presentation – to present the solution for their challenge. Because the teams of every relay are randomly chosen by lot, this is the first time the relay's robots are presented to all relay members. It is supposed to help the relays to optimize their run in the competition, especially the pass of the token. A knowledge transfer between all teams of a relay is intended to be a further outcome. To gain the credit points, every student has to participate in all presentations.

As mentioned before, the composition of the relays is chosen by lot one day before the competition. By this mean, the students are helped to focus on their own challenge without prescinding from it. In addition, an unequal workload within a relay shall be prevented. But to give the relays the chance to test their run, especially the pass of the token, there are two training sessions. The first session is scheduled one day before the competition, immediately after the chose by lot, and the second session – a kind of "warmup" – is scheduled a few hours prior to the competition at the competition day.

The project was planned to take place in 2010 from the 15th of November to the 19th of November. To have enough space for all teams, the university's festival room could be reserved, offering a lot of tables, chairs and a video projector. All of the research and student assistants involved in the project's planning are supposed to assist the participating students during the project week. The students have the opportunity to work from 9am to 10pm, giving them sufficient time to solve their challenges.

4   The Project Week

The project began on November 15th in 2010, as laid down in the time schedule. Up to this date, the students' registration and the project's whole organization have almost been completed. Eighty students divided into twenty teams were expected to participate in the project. Thus there were five teams for each challenge resulting in five relays in the end. After a brief introduction to the project, its aims and the time schedule, an a brief introduction to LABVIEW followed, and the LEGO MINDSTORMS KITS were handed out to the students. The students used the remaining time of the day to get familiar with LEGO MINDSTORMS, LABVIEW as well as their challenges and began to work out possible solutions.

On day number two, the students could use almost the whole time to work on their solutions. Their working time has been interrupted only by the team presentations. Taking part at these presentations was quite interesting for the assistants. Particularly, the concepts developed by the students to solve their challenge differed a lot from each other and can be described as unusual in some cases.

The third day was a public holiday in Germany. But the students got the offer to work on this day as well, but without technical assistance and with a reduced working time.

On Thursday, the fourth day of the project, the students were supposed to be almost done with their robots. In the morning, the relays were chosen by lot, and in the evening, the relay presentations were given. The relay presentations did not have the effect of a knowledge transfer as they were intended to be. But they were a helpful opportunity for all teams to get to know the partners of their relay. Immediately after the presentation, a photo of every team and relay was taken. Simultaneously, the first relay training sessions took place. There were two relay courses for these sessions the students could use, but without unveiling the labyrinth's final shape. A photo of the whole course is shown in Fig. 11. The training sessions offered a good possibility for the students to test their solutions and to practice and optimize the relay run for the competition.

Friday was the project's last day. The day began with the second training sessions in the morning. Afterwards, there was just a little time to the relay competition in the early afternoon. Thus the teams did not have much time to change their robots, they could only adjust them. The relay competition was the highlight of the project. All students gathered around the competition course and cheered on the teams of their relay. To avoid having teams with a non-working robot, the day before the assistance team increased the support for teams struggling with their solution. Thus all teams had a robot to take part in the competition. Many robots had to restart their run, but completed their part of the relay course within the time limit. Only a few robots had to cancel their run because of the time limit. Astonishingly, there were no robot failures due to hardware problems. An example robot for each challenge show Fig. 6, 7, 8 and 9. After the relay competition, there was a presentation ceremony to honor the winners. First of all, the fastest relay and the fastest team of the winning relay in comparison to the teams of the other relays in the same challenge were

Fig. 6. Example robot for Challenge I

Fig. 7. Example robot for Challenge II

honored. Furthermore, there were three special prices: the best construction, the best show and the best design. These prices were assigned by independent juries consisting of students and research assistants not being involved in the

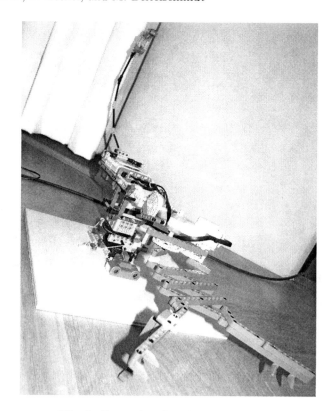

Fig. 8. Example robot for Challenge III

Fig. 9. Example robot for Challenge IV

project. In the end, every student successfully participated in the project and got a certificate.

5 Evaluation and Further Enhancements

To evaluate the project and to get the participating students' opinions, OPAL was used again. With its survey function, a survey was prepared and the students were asked to take part in. Thus they had the opportunity to contribute to the improvement of the project. There were mainly questions about the project's organization and the relay competition with its challenges. The students could also give their comments to special topics. Unfortunately, only one fourth of the students took part. Almost all opinions were positive, and, in some cases, the answers revealed problems the organization team did not expect.

The main problems the students had to face in the first days were the handling of LABVIEW and the programming task at all, with which every team had to deal. The more the teams advanced with their solutions, other problems became more significant. For example, some teams realized that their original solution did not work as they expected and they had to change large parts of their construction. Especially one team, working on Challenge I and building the robot "hulk" (see Fig. 6), had to fight with the stability of the LEGO parts. The teams of Challenge II and Challenge IV mainly dealt with problems in optimizing their robot to reduce the time the robot needs to pass the course and to increase its reliability.

The LEGO MINDSTORMS NXT 2.0 exposed to be a good mean to build robots in an easy way. Because of its structure, imaginable nearly every robot can be implemented. Using LABVIEW instead of NXC or the original LEGO Software

Fig. 10. Festival room DUELFER-Saal at the TECHNISCHE UNIVERSITAET DRESDEN with the team tables

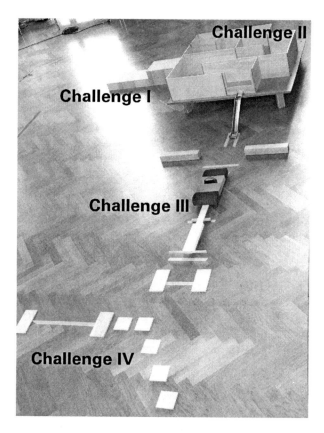

Fig. 11. Photo of the final and complete course used for the relay competition

for programming was a good choice. Assuming that the majority of the students did not program yet, LABVIEW offered an easy way to understand the field of programming. But to avoid difficulties in the very beginning of the project, there has to be a more detailed introduction into LABVIEW, and maybe some kind of notepad with fundamental facts could be created for the next run of the project.

The media center of the TECHNISCHE UNIVERSITAET DRESDEN documented the project and produced a short movie. This clip can be found on the university's YOUTUBE channel (http://www.youtube.com/user/TUDresdenTV#p/u). To get a brief insight into the project week, a picture of the festival room with the team tables is shown in Fig. 11.

This year, there will be a project week too. Students participating in the project in 2010 will be engaged as student assistants for organization and assistance. All experiences gained in 2010 will be used for the project's improvement.

6 Summary

There were four different challenges and it was the participating students' task to build robots to solve them. LEGO MINDSTORMS NXT 2.0 and LABVIEW were used to develop those robots, offering a variety of possible solutions. The challenges' courses composed a relay course the teams had to pass on time at the end of the project. This competition encouraged the students to improve and adjust their robots as best as possible.

To summarize, the project was a success. It was a great experience for everyone: The students participating, the student and research assistants and all other people taking part. Although it was stressful in some cases, the effort was worth it. Using a robot competition to give first-year students of mechatronics a push of motivation for their studies pointed out to be an appropriate mean.

References

1. Bildungsportal Sachsen: Online Platform fuer Akademisches Lehren und Lernen (OPAL) (2011), `https://bildungsportal.sachsen.de/opal/dmz/`
2. Hansen, J.: Next Byte Codes & Not eXactly C (2011), `http://bricxcc.sourceforge.net/nbc/`
3. Andrews, P., Stuber, J.: leJOS - Java for LEGO Mindstorms (2011), `http://lejos.sourceforge.net/`

Engineering Education Program at Kanazawa Institute of Technology: A Case Study in Department of Robotics

Ryoichi Suzuki and Nobuaki Kobayashi

Kanazawa Institute of Technology, Department of Robotics,
7-1 Nonoichi, Ishikawa 921-8501, Japan
{r-suzuki,kobayasi}@neptune.kanazawa-it.ac.jp
http://www.kanazawa-it.ac.jp

Abstract. Engineering design is the process of devising a system, component, or process to meet desired needs. It is well known that a decision making process and an integrated learning are important. The paper focuses on the robot engineering program of the Department of Robotics at Kanazawa Institute of Technology in Japan. The goal of the program is to integrate core / advanced knowledge and practical skills for making mechanical systems or robotic systems. After the introductory course in first three years the curriculum offers an integrated learning course called Design Project III. Students are able to get competence for designing, implementing and operating in robotic field. An outcome of Design Project III is also introduced in the paper.

Keywords: Engineering design, project based learning, design-implemented learning, integrated learning.

1 Introduction

Kanazawa Institute of Technology (KIT) was established in 1965. It is a nationally famous private university which offers a good engineering education. KIT has 14 departments, e.g. Mechanical Engineering, Aeronautics, Electrical and Electronic Engineering, Information and Communication Engineering, Information and Computer Science, at the present. The Department of Robotics at KIT started in 2004. The robot engineering program is accredited by Japan Accreditation Board for Engineering Education (JABEE) since 2008.

In the robot engineering program for undergraduates of the Department of Robotics, knowledge of underlying science and engineering, core fundamental knowledge, advanced fundamental knowledge, personal / interpersonal skills, practical skills and attitudes are integrated into several courses in the first three years of the curriculum. First year students take the introductory course of Basic Robot Design and Design Project I. Second year students take the course of Design Project II. Third year students take a design-implement project course of Design and Exercise for Robotics and they build a robotic car. During the first

D. Obdržálek and A. Gottscheber (Eds.): EUROBOT 2011, CCIS 161, pp. 300–309, 2011.
© Springer-Verlag Berlin Heidelberg 2011

three years, students learn also communication and presentation skills. Fourth year students have one more integrated learning experience as a course called Design Project III that lead to the acquisition of disciplinary knowledge and professional skills, product and system building skills by demonstrating a project.

The paper describes the engineering education program of the Department of Robotics at KIT. An outcome of the integrated learning is introduced also as a case study.

2   Introductory Courses in the First Three Years

The introductory course at KIT consists of three main parts; lecture-based learning, project-based learning, and design-implemented experience. Students learn various important knowledge and skills in fields of robotics.

Robotics is an interdisciplinary field including mechanical, electrical, computer, and control systems engineering. It offers a good basis for different engineering subjects. The introductory course of the Department of Robotics in first three years is summarized in Fig. 1. Students get knowledge of underlying science and engineering, core / advanced fundamental knowledge for robotics, and personal / interpersonal / practical skills and attitudes step by step. These courses are connected into an integrated learning course of Design Project III. The goal of the introductory course is to get knowledge and skills for making a robotic car or a robotic system.

Students learn basic knowledge and skills for robotics in the lecture-based course. They also learn how to combine these knowledge and skills in the project-based course. Furthermore the design-implemented exercise is provided to develop interpersonal / practical skills such as communication, teamwork, creativity, design, problem solving, and implementation. The characteristic of the curriculum is described in the following section.

2.1   Lecture-Based Course

The course will introduce the basic science and technology in robotics. The various subjects are provided to students in the lecture based course. The representative subjects are shown in Fig. 1.

In the lecture of Engineering Practice, students acquire practical skill to design and implement control program for the robotic car. The lecture offers exercise for sensor fusion, data acquisition, integrating electrical circuits, understanding actuators, and manipulation of industrial robots. Students are able to integrate knowledge and skills that they have learned in the previous semester.

2.2   Project-Based Course: Design Project I and II

Design Project I and II carry out a project-based learning. The students are able to gain engineering design experience through an engineering design process. They choose open-ended problems relating to robotics, and then they identify

	First year	Second year	Third year	Fourth year
Lecture-based learning	Mathematics Physics Mechanics and Dynamics (Knowledge of underlying science and engineering)	Electronics Computer Programming Systems and Control	**Engineering Practice** Mechatronics Robot Control Artificial Intelligence Machine Learning	**Design Project III**
Project-based learning	**Design Project I**	**Design Project II**		
Design-implemented experience	**Basic Robot Design**		**Design and Exercise for Robotics**	

Fig. 1. Introductory course in the first three years and Design Project III at KIT

theme of project, characterize design projects, generate design concepts, evaluate design concepts, select the most promising concept, and design in detail. The engineering process covered in Design Project I and Design Project II are:

- To identify theme of project
- To characterize design projects
- To generate design concepts
- To evaluate design concepts and to select the optimal concept
- To design in detail
- To present results.

Students may comprehend necessity and importance of engineering design process in order to challenge open-ended problems. These project-based courses are utilized for the following course of Design and Exercise for Robotics and Design Project III.

2.3   Design-Implemented Experience: Basic Robot Design and Design and Exercise for Robotics

"Basic Robot Design" will introduce basic robotics topics including mechanical structures, sensors, effectors, actuators, and algorithm. LEGO Mindstorms is employed for understanding these topics. The course is important to cultivate self-learning motivation for freshman.

Students have a design-implemented experience by making a robotic car in the course of "Design and Exercise for Robotics". An example is shown in

Fig. 2. Scene in Basic Robot Design

Fig. 3. A robotic car developed by students

Fig. 3. They design the body of the car, steerages, reduction gears, mechanical structures, and sensors in team composed 5 or 6 persons, and they implement the control program for system integrating sensor, actuator and electrical circuit to a microcomputer. The control performance of the robotic car is evaluated by comparative experiments. Our department holds a speed contest for robotic cars in the end of the introductory course.

3   Workspace "YUMEKOBO" for Extracurricular

KIT supports individual students in their extracurricular activities. KIT established an innovative facility named YUMEKOBO: Factory for Dreams and Ideas. It is a workspace for creative activities equipped with machine tools, devices to make electronic circuit boards, and is staffed with technicians to support

Fig. 4. Challenge to robot competition: ABU Asia Pacific Robot Contest

Fig. 5. Challenge to international competition: RoboCup

students. Students are able to have experience making mechanical models and robotic prototypes at this facility.

KIT also promotes the following team projects, which gives financial support to teams working on product making. About 30% students of the department of robotics join such kind of projects. They have good experience for integration their knowledge and practical skills in extracurricular.

- **Robot design project:** *Making a robot that can coexist with people*
- **Challenge to RoboCup:** *Fusion of robot engineering and artificial intelligence*
- **Development of assistive devices:** *Realization of self-independence and rehabilitation*
- **Mechanical support project:** *Lifesaving in a large-scale disaster*
- **Autonomous vehicle design project:** *Building an unmanned automatic transport vehicle*
- **Solar car project**, **Formula car project**, and others

4 Integrated Learning

4.1 Purpose of Integrated Learning

Integrated learning is defied that students practice and learn personal and inter-personal skills, and practical skills such as product, process and system building skills, simultaneously with disciplinary knowledge. It is important that integrated learning experiences that lead to the acquisition of disciplinary knowledge, as well as practical skills.

After the introductory course the Department of Robotics offers the integrated learning course called Design Project III. Fourth year students carry out again engineering design process themselves. They are able to get competence for designing, implementing and operating in robotic fields.

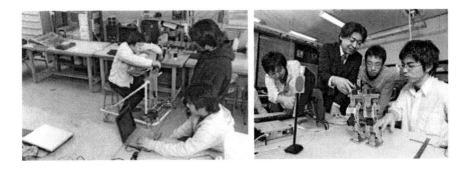

Fig. 6. Scene in Design Project III

4.2 A Case Study of Design Project III

The outcomes of Design Project III are briefly introduced in this section. The project title is "Robotic assistive devices for persons with upper extremity disabilities." The poster material for oral presentation is attached below.

$\Diamond$ $\Diamond$

**Robotic assistive devices for persons
with upper extremity disabilities**

Motivation and purpose
Robotic assistive devices are increasingly used to improve quality of life of persons with disabilities. The purpose of the design project is to propose robotic meal-eating devices for people with upper extremity disabilities. Two prototypes are designed and developed for experimental validation and performance evaluations.

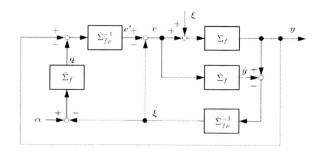

Fig. 7. Internal model control scheme for force detection

Target users and requirements

Persons with upper extremity disabilities (e.g. paraplegia, quadriplegia, and dystrophy)

- They want to eat and drink independently at their own pace.
- They want to select various foods and beverages.
- They want to take assistive devices anywhere.

Problems

- The potential market for robotic assistive devices to aid the disabled and elderly is extremely large in Japan. However, the commercial products are still few and expensive.
- Control technology for assistive devices is not well researched and verified to improve performance.

Applied Techniques

- The internal model control (IMC) based controller shown in Fig. 7 is implemented on controllers to improve performance for grasping control and contact force detection. The controller is able to estimate contact force as by setting a set point.
- The face recognition program for path planning is developed and implemented on the host PC (see in Fig. 8).
- Eye / voice typing systems will be integrated to the prototypes.

Prototype A: *Drinking*

The robotic assistive device for drinking is shown in Fig. 9. The prototype consists of five servo motors. The motors are used for manipulations. A controllable gripper and a small camera are mounted on the end of the link. After detecting the position of the lips, the robotic device generates appropriate path, and provides drinks for the user. Grasping force is controlled by using IMC scheme.

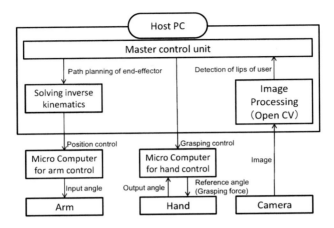

Fig. 8. System configuration

Fig. 9. Robotic assistive device for drinking

Specifications
Size(W*D*H): 0.50*0.25*0.48-0.66[m]
Arm length: 0.60[m]
Weight: 6.2[kg]
Power: 12[V]
Controller: M16C/Tiny, H8/3052F
Actuator: Servo motor, DC motor(12[V], 4.5[W])
Camera: 2.0Mpixel, 30fps

Prototype B: *Eating*

The robotic assistive device for eating is shown in Fig. 10. The prototype consists of two DC motors and one rotary damper. An adjustable spoon is attached at the end of the link. The spoon dips into bowls, scoops up various foods, and presents foods near the lips of the user. The contact force detection system by using IMC is implemented without a touch sensor. If the spoon touches the lips or another part, then the spoon stops automatically.

Fig. 10. Robotic assistive device for eating

Specifications
Size(W*D*H): 0.20*0.17*0.26[m]
Arm length: 0.32[m]
Weight: 3.2[kg]
Power: 12[V], 15[V]
Controller: PC with MATLAB, SIMULINK, xPC Target
Actuator: DC motor

Expectation and future works
The portable robotic device will be useful for eating and drinking anywhere anytime without any assistance. Caregivers will be able to reduce efforts needed for providing meals. Further experiments and assessments are required to improve the control performance of the prototypes.

5   Conclusion

The paper was introduced the robot engineering program for undergraduates of the Department of Robotics at KIT. The outcomes that integrate skills with

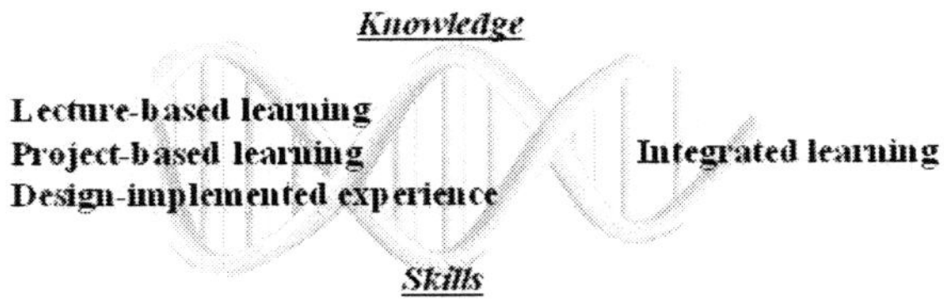

Knowledge

Lecture-based learning
Project-based learning   **Integrated learning**
Design-implemented experience

Skills

Fig. 11. Complex helix structure of curriculum

disciplinary knowledge were also introduced as a case study of Design Project III. It seems that students are able to get competence for designing, implementing and operating in robotic fields from other outcomes. The provided curriculum both the introductory course during the first three years and the integrated course in the fourth year perform very well like a complex helix shown in Fig. 11. More than 95% students of the department of robotics find full-time employment before graduation every year. In further step KIT will adopt and implement the CDIO approach for the engineering education program. Learning assessment and program evaluation will be carried out more strongly.

References

1. Kanazawa Institute of Technology,
   http://www.kanazawa-it.ac.jp/ekit/index.html
2. Matsuishi, M., et al.: International Collaborative Project in Engineering Design Education between Kanazawa Institute of Technology and Singapore Polytechnic. In: Proc. International Conference on Engineering Education, ICEE 2004, Florida, USA (2004)
3. Crawley, E., Malmqvist, J., Ostlund, S., Brodeur, D.: Rethinking Engineering Education. Springer, Heidelberg (2007)

Autonomous Robot Navigation Based on Clustering across Images

Tomas Vintr, Lukas Pastorek, and Hana Rezankova

Department of Statistics and Probability, University of Economics,
Prague, nam. W. Churchilla 4, 130 67 Prague 3, Czech Republic
{tomas.vintr,lukas.pastorek,hana.rezankova}@vse.cz

Abstract. The aim of this paper is to present a novel approach to the autonomous robot navigation based on clustering of image descriptors. The descriptor called Speeded-Up Robust Features (SURF) is a scale- and rotation-invariant detector, which can visually navigate a robot in a large outdoor and indoor environment. By incorporating several clustering methods, which are derived from fuzzy set theory and inspired with biological background, such as Fuzzy C-mean (FCM), Kohonen's Self-Organizing Map (SOM) and Neural Gas algorithm (NG), we detect center positions of natural clusters crosswise the recorded images. Center positions represented by vector prototypes are used as reference points in the decision making of the robot navigation.

Keywords: SURF, Autonomous robot navigation, Two layers classification, Feature descriptor clustering, Neural gas, SOM, FCM.

1 Introduction

The navigation algorithm implemented in the research of the autonomous robot navigation, described in [6],[7], consists of two parts – training and testing phases.

In the training phase, a robot is manually driven in outdoor conditions and it creates, using the Speeded-Up Robust Features (SURF) algorithm, see [1], a high dimensional map of its surrounding environment. In the autonomous navigation mode (testing phase), the recorded map, consisting of ten-thousands feature vectors (SURF descriptors), is used as a basis for navigation.

Each recorded feature descriptor (64-dimensional vector) includes information about the surroundings of the detected distinctive interest points in the image (corners, T-junctions, borders, see Fig. 1).

The current navigation uses SURF, which matches detected feature descriptors between different images, based on Euclidean distance. The algorithm can classify the same interest point under different viewing conditions. The difference in image coordinates between the matched descriptors (learned landmarks and detected new interest points) is computed and the modus estimated by a histogram is used as correction value for the robot movement.

The aim of this paper is to prove the working clustering concept for the robot navigation through finding the sets of SURF descriptors, where each feature

D. Obdržálek and A. Gottscheber (Eds.): EUROBOT 2011, CCIS 161, pp. 310–320, 2011.

Fig. 1. SURF descriptors (the white points) in a sample image

vector describes the same landmark crosswise all the images and to describe the surrounding area of the interest points (prototypes) learned in the training phase.

The methods, used in this paper, derived from well-known fuzzy c-mean, see [8], and self-organizing neural networks, see [5],[9], are described in Section 2. In Section 3, the map of SURF descriptors, consisting of 64-dimensional mean vectors (prototypes) and a covariance matrix of positions of feature descriptors in the images, was tested by the robot and the results were compared with performance of the actual algorithm.

2 Clustering Algorithms

The paper deals with dataset of feature descriptors, generated by the navigation algorithm is spread over surface of 64-dimensional hyper-sphere. Because of this fact, the clustering, as a well-known statistical multidimensional tool, is chosen with its classificatory and dimension-reductive capabilities, which are suitable for exploring and recognition of hidden patterns in data. The paper focuses on the possibilities of using and implementing clustering algorithms to the robot navigation in the autonomous mode from two different "clustering" points of view.

2.1 Self-Organizing Maps and Neural Gas

Kohonen's self-organizing maps (SOM), described in [5], are used for transformation of nonlinear relations in the training dataset through a set of nodes (neurons) to a low dimensional (1- or 2-dimensional) manifold in the feature space ($\mathbf{R}^n \rightarrow \mathbf{R}^2$). Through an iterative training and simple geometric relations among neurons, SOM preserve relations in the input space. Similar patterns in the data input space evoke a similar feedback in the close neurons on the mapping grid in the output space. This principle is a crucial and efective solution to represent important parameters of the input data.

Each neuron, from the set of neurons C_i, $i \in \{1, \ldots, c\}$ is represented by a d-dimensional weight vector (called the prototype or reference vector):

$$\mathbf{c}_i = [c_1, \ldots, c_d],$$

where d is the dimension of the input space ($\mathbf{R}^d$) and i is the neuron index. Relations among the neurons are characterized by the environment which forms the map structure (topology and shape).

Kohonen's maps consist of two layers (the input and output layer). The Input layer is considered as the distribution layer, where input vectors are presented to all nodes of the mapping grid (the output layer) for the competition. The output layer is represented by the above mentioned weight vectors.

The structure of the neuron map (grid) can be arranged on a rectangular or hexagonal lattice. A hexagonal grid is prefered because it keeps constant distances between neurons.

Prior to a competition of every neuron for the closest position to the input vector, an initialization of weight vectors of the neurons has to be done. First *random* or *linear* initialization, which computes eigenvalues and eigenvectors of input dataset, is applied and then weight vectors are initialized along the first two principal eigenvectors, which specify the principal tendencies in the training dataset. and *batch* training algorithm.

In every training step of the sequential algorithm, one vector $\mathbf{x}_i$ is randomly chosen from the input dataset, $\mathbf{X} = \{\mathbf{x}_1, \ldots, \mathbf{x}_n | \forall \mathbf{x}_i \in \mathbf{R}^d\}$, where n is the length of the training dataset, is presented to the map and the distances between the sample vector and all reference weight vectors are calculated. A neuron, whose position is the closest to the input vector, is considered as a winner ($\mathbf{c}_k$). Distances are computed according to the Euclidean metric.

$$\|\mathbf{x} - \mathbf{c}_k\| = argmin_i \|\mathbf{x} - \mathbf{c}_i\|. \tag{1}$$

The winning neuron, called *Best Matching Unit* (BMU), and his topological neighbours, adapt his weight vector according to the formula

$$\mathbf{c}_i(t+1) = \mathbf{c}_i(t) + \alpha(t)h_{ki}(t)[\mathbf{x}(t) - \mathbf{c}_i(t)], \tag{2}$$

where t represents the time (an iteration step), $\alpha(t)$ is the learning rate at time t, $h_{ki}(t)$ is neighborhood kernel around BMU k and $\mathbf{x}(t)$ input vector.

In the batch algorithm, the whole training set is presented to a mapping grid, the dataset is partitioned into subregions called Voronoi polygon or polyhedra, according to the closest neuron rule. Then, new weight vectors are calculated as weighted average, where neighborhood function values are considered as weights

$$\mathbf{c}_i\left(t+1\right) = \frac{\sum_{j=1}^{n} h_{ki}\left(t\right) \mathbf{x}_j}{\sum_{j=1}^{n} h_{ki}\left(t\right)}. \tag{3}$$

Commonly used learning rates in the SOM toolbox, as time-depending functions ($0 < \alpha_t < 1$), are *linear* $\alpha\left(t\right) = \alpha_0 \left(1 - t/T\right)$, *inversely proportional to time* $\alpha\left(t\right) = \alpha_0 / \left(1 + 100t/T\right)$ and *power series* $\alpha\left(t\right) = \alpha_0 \left(0.005/\alpha_0\right)^{t/T}$ where T is the maximum number of iteration steps and α_0 is the initial learning rate.

Neighborhood functions, which are functions of connection proximity between the neuron i and winning neuron $\mathbf{c}$ on the mapping grid, are taken *gaussian* neighborhood $h_{ki}\left(t\right) = e^{-d_{ki}^2/2\sigma_t^2}$, *bubble* $h_{ki}\left(t\right) = m(\sigma_t - d_{ki})$, *cutgauss* $h_{ki}\left(t\right) = e^{-d_{ki}^2/2\sigma_t^2} m(\sigma_t - d_{ki})$, and *epanechicov* $h_{ki}\left(t\right) = max\left\{0.1 - (\sigma_t - d_{ki})^2\right\}$ where σ_t is the neighborhood radius at time t, $d_{ki} = \|r_k - r_i\|$ is the distance between winning neuron k and neuron i and $m(x)$ is the step function: $m(x) = 0$ if $x < 0$ and $m(x) = 1$ if $x \geq 0$, see [11].

The neural gas (NG) algorithm, see [9], is a similar vector quantization procedure to the self-organizing map, but leads to lower distortion errors than from K-mean, Maximum entropy clustering and SOM, converge faster to a lower distortion error and obeys gradient descent on an energy surface, as it is proved in [9]. In comparison to SOM, NG doesn't incorporate a fixed grid topology, but involves a "neighborhood ranking" list.

During the training phase, weight vectors are ranked according to their euclidean distance from an input vector $\mathbf{x}_i$, $(\mathbf{c}_{i_0}, \mathbf{c}_{i_1}, ..., \mathbf{c}_{i_{c-1}})$, where $\mathbf{c}_{i_0}$ is the closest reference vector to $\mathbf{x}_i$ and with $\mathbf{c}_{i_1}$ being the second closest, and $\mathbf{c}_{i_l}$, ($l = 0, ..., c - 1$), being the reference weight vector, for which there are k vectors:

$$\|\mathbf{x} - \mathbf{c}_j\| < \|\mathbf{x} - \mathbf{c}_{i_l}\|. \tag{4}$$

The index l, associated with each vector $\mathbf{c}_i$, is denoted by $l_i(\mathbf{x}, \mathbf{c})$ depending on $\mathbf{x}$ and $\mathbf{c} = (\mathbf{c}_1, ..., \mathbf{c}_c)$. The adaptation formula is given by:

$$\Delta\mathbf{w}_i = \epsilon(t).h_\lambda(k_i(\mathbf{x}, \mathbf{c})).(\mathbf{x} - \mathbf{c}_i). \tag{5}$$

Commonly used learning rate $\epsilon(t) \in [0, 1]$ is usually $\epsilon(t) = \epsilon_i(\epsilon_f/\epsilon_i)^{t/T}$, where t and T represent an iteration step t and T is the length of the training phase. Martinetz chose exponential form of neighborhood function $h_\lambda(l_i(x, c)) = e^{(-l/\lambda(t))}$. The parameter $\lambda(t)$ determines the number of prototype vectors updating their position and is given by gradually decreasing function: $\lambda(t) = (\lambda_f/\lambda_i)^{(t/T)}$.

In the application part, in the case of training dataset, the data normalization (inevitable step of data preparation), which is usually necessary for suppressing the variable's influence on the training data, turned out as meaningless. As mentioned above, the dataset did not require further normalization. Despite the normalized character of the input dataset $\mathbf{X}$, we examined the effect of standardization functions (logarithmic and histogram equalization) on the performance of SOM and NG clustering algorithms. The dataset $\mathbf{X}$ was partitioned, in case of both methods, into a few clusters, from the set of clusters $\mathbf{C}$, defined with cluster prototypes in $\mathbf{R}^{64}$(*log* function – less then 9 percent, *histD* – less then 2

Table 1. Error measurements

Method	Initialization	Training	Quantization error	Topographic error
SOM	Linear	Batch	0.2693	0.0795
		Seq	0.2684	0.0287
	Random	Batch	0.3114	0.0969
		Seq	0.2908	0.0243
NG	Random	Seq (10 epochs)	0.1698	X
		Seq (5 epochs)	0.2539	X

percent, the rest of the predefined number of clusters remained empty), which was the undesirable situation, considered as a proof of the normalized character of the input dataset.

The next step in the SOM algorithm is a prototype vector initialization. We used *random* and also *linear* initialization for reference vectors, which where consequently trained with *sequential* and *batch* training algorithm on the first traveled segment (batch algorithm is considered as successful as sequential training). The NG map was trained using only a sequential algorithm, but with the different predefined number of epochs (five and ten epochs were chosen). After the map training, we applied the quality functions (SOM toolbox uses two measures of clustering performance): A average quantization error and a topographic error (for results see Table 1).

2.2 Fuzzy C-Mean

The second approach is to use the clustering method based on the fuzzy c-mean algorithm (FCM), see [2]. Hereinafter we use notation from [8] with one exception: for number of columns and rows of covariance matrix we use s instead of p.

The objective function we want to minimize is given by

$$J_f\left(\mathbf{X}, \mathbf{U}_f, \mathbf{C}\right) = \sum_{i=1}^{c} \sum_{j=1}^{n} u_{ij}^m d_{ij}^2, \tag{6}$$

where $\mathbf{X} = \{\mathbf{x}_1, \ldots, \mathbf{x}_n\}$, $\mathbf{X} \subset \mathbf{R}^d$, is data set, and $\mathbf{C} = \{C_1, \ldots, C_c\}$ is the set of cluster prototypes, $\mathbf{U}_f = (u_{ij})$ denotes fuzzy partition matrix with the conditions

$$\sum_{j=1}^{n} u_{ij} > 0, \forall i \in \{1, \ldots, c\}, \tag{7}$$

$$\sum_{i=1}^{c} u_{ij} = 1, \forall j \in \{1, \ldots, n\}, \tag{8}$$

and $d_{ij} = \|\mathbf{x}_j - \mathbf{c}_i\|$ in the chosen metrics, where $\mathbf{c}_i$ is the cluster prototype vector of C_i.

We set the weighting exponent to $m = 2$ and we estimated a number of clusters for FCM $c = 1000$. The number of 64-dimensional input vectors in data sets, we analyzed, was about $n \approx 50000$, so we met the condition $1 < c < n$.

We tested two algorithms. The basic FCM, where $d_{ij} = |\mathbf{x}_j - \mathbf{c}_i|$ is Euclidean distance and the Gustafson-Kessel algorithm, see [3], which uses the cluster-specific Mahalanobis distance instead of the Euclidean distance, where the distance is defined for every cluster as

$$d^2 (\mathbf{x}_j, C_i) = (\mathbf{x}_j - \mathbf{c}_i)^T \Sigma_i^{-1} (\mathbf{x}_j - \mathbf{c}_i), \tag{9}$$

where Σ_i is the $s \times s$ covariance matrix of the cluster C_i. Covariance matrices are assumed to be of equal size setting $\det \Sigma_i = 1$ and therefore the update equations for the covariance matrices are

$$\Sigma_i = \frac{\Sigma_i^*}{\sqrt[s]{\det \Sigma_i^*}}, \tag{10}$$

where

$$\Sigma_i^* = \frac{\sum_{j=1}^n u_{ij} (\mathbf{x}_j - \mathbf{c}_i)(\mathbf{x}_j - \mathbf{c}_i)^T}{\sum_{j=1}^n u_{ij}}. \tag{11}$$

It was not possible to implement any of these algorithms. The basic FCM algorithm found such a minimum of J_f that all centers were placed to or very close to the average point of the data set independently on initialization. The problem of the Gustafson-Kessel algorithm was in solving Σ_i because $\sqrt[64]{\det \Sigma_i^*}$ was often very close to zero. We found the implementation of this algorithm quite difficult on usual personal computer.

To overcome the problem of finding minimum at the average point we set the condition

$$\forall i \in \{1, \ldots, c\}: \quad \text{if } u_{ij} < \tilde{u}_{pi} \text{ than } u_{ij} = 0, \tag{12}$$

where $\tilde{u}_{pi}$ is p-quantile of i-th row of matrix $\mathbf{U}_f$, and we set $p = 1 - \frac{20}{n}$, under the conditions (7, 8).

Due to the condition (12), we computed the position of the new prototype vectors only out of the 20 nearest points of the input dataset in the Euclidean metrics. The algorithm with this condition (FCM20) generates proper clusters.

3   Clusters in the Image Plane

The outcomes of the methods described in the previous chapter were sets of clusters described by their prototype vectors in $\mathbf{R}^{64}$. It is necessary to represent the clusters in the image plane, so that we can implement the results into the navigation algorithm. It is possible to do so as we know the positions of SURF descriptors in every image. As there does not exist any trivial projection of SURF descriptor prototypes on the image plane $\mathbf{R}^{64} \to \mathbf{R}^2$, it is not possible to use a weighting function obtained by clustering algorithms. We solved this problem by assigning all the nearest SURF descriptors to every found cluster prototype vector in $\mathbf{R}^{64}$:

$$\forall \mathbf{x}_j \in \mathbf{X}, \exists_1 C_k \in \mathbf{C} : \quad |\mathbf{x}_j - \mathbf{c}_k| = \min \left\{ |\mathbf{x}_j - \mathbf{c}_i| \, | i \in \{1, \dots, c\} \right\}. \qquad (13)$$

By the assignation based on (13) we generated sets $\mathbf{X}_i$ of nearest descriptors for every cluster C_i, $i \in \{1, \dots, c\}$.

By the projection of sets $\mathbf{X}_i$ on the image plane, we obtained an information about the position of the clusters crosswise the images. We found out these:

1. Most of $\mathbf{X}_i$ describe more than one object in an image (Figs. 3, 4 and 5). These objects are very similar to each other but it is possible to distinguish them according to their position in an image. There are between 1 and 4 clusters in every $\mathbf{X}_i$ projected to $\mathbf{R}^2$.

2. There are different clusters in $\mathbf{R}^{64}$ which describe an identical object in an image. It means that there are clusters in $\mathbf{R}^2$ described by more than one cluster in $\mathbf{R}^{64}$.

3. 20 "nearest" points of every cluster in $\mathbf{R}^{64}$, which were generated by the algorithm FCM20 and which we used as the only members of sets $\mathbf{X}_i$, describe in $70-80\%$ cases one object (Fig. 2) and in another cases two or more objects in an image, while one of the clusters in $\mathbf{R}^2$ was significantly dominant in 90% cases.

Finding 2 has no significant effect on the navigation, because there is no problem to navigate according to one object on the basis of two descriptions. On the other hand Finding 1 has very serious impact on the navigation, so it was necessary to separate the clusters obtained in $\mathbf{R}^{64}$ into several clusters according to their position in $\mathbf{R}^2$.

Fig. 2. 20 "nearest" points from FCM20 in the image plane (1024×768pt). We can see that 20 "nearest" points in this case describe only one object.

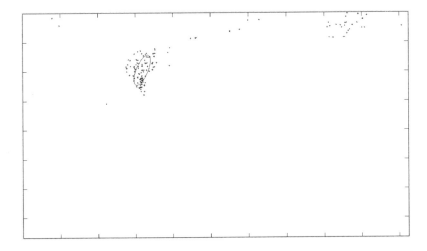

Fig. 3. FCM20 – randomly chosen $\mathbf{X}_i$ in the image plane ($1024 \times 768\text{pt}$) generated by FCM20. In this case $\mathbf{X}_i$ describes 2 objects. One in a left upper corner of an image and partly another object in a right upper corner. There are also some outliers.

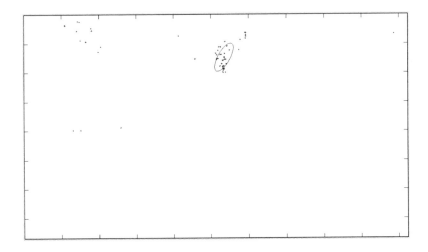

Fig. 4. SOM-Linear-Batch – randomly chosen $\mathbf{X}_i$ in the image plane ($1024 \times 768\text{pt}$) generated by SOM. There is 1 dominant cluster describing 1 object in the upper center and also 1 object in left upper corner of an image. There are only a few outliers.

Fig. 5. NG - 10 epochs – randomly chosen $\mathbf{X}_i$ in the image plane (1024×768pt) generated by Neural Gas. $\mathbf{X}_i$ describes 2 objects. Nicer one chosen as dominant.

We decided to separate $\mathbf{X}_i$ in $\mathbf{R}^2$ using E-GK algorithm, see [4]. There is an additional user–defined parameter, called merging threshold α, $\alpha \in [0, 1]$. The authors claim that the algorithm should work with built in adaptive merging threshold for clustering the datasets, which contain fewer than 10 clusters. That was attained because $\mathbf{X}_i$ was composed of 4 or fewer clusters. But we realized that the algorithm struggles with detecting fewer than 3 clusters. We were unable to set the parameters of the algorithm to overcome this problem.

Finally, we decided not to separate $\mathbf{X}_i$ into several clusters, but to use modus of frequencies of $\mathbf{X}_i$ projected to $\mathbf{R}^2$ to find a dominant cluster in every $\mathbf{X}_i$ in $\mathbf{R}^2$ and to describe this cluster by its prototype vector $\mathbf{c}_i$ from $\mathbf{R}^{64}$ and its covariance matrix Σ_i in $\mathbf{R}^2$.

In Figs. 2, 3, 4 and 5 we can see covariance matrix Σ_i projected on the image plane as an ellipse. The major axis of the ellipse could be interpreted as the estimation of the trend in the movement of one SURF descriptor across the images.

The matrix adjusted in the manner described above was implemented as a map in the navigation algorithm of the robot.

4   Conclusions

In this paper, we have presented the image-crosswise, a two-level clustering approach to the autonomous robot navigation. The principal difference from the current navigation algorithm, proposed in [6], was not the simple finding of the close descriptors from the learning-phase dataset (in terms of Euclidean distance), whose locations were specified with their x y coordinates in the associated image, but the finding of the best matching reference descriptors, denoted with cluster prototypes.

The basic fuzzy algorithms (FCM and Gustafson-Kessel algorithm) were not able to identify sufficiently the prototype feature descriptors, so they needed to be modified. We used unsupervised clustering algorithms, such as adjusted FCM20, SOM, NG, which generated the map of prototypes (cluster centers) through the iterative training. These vector prototypes, with their feature description, were used as map patterns, according to which the dataset was partitioned into subregions (clusters).

In the second level, every subregion was explored in $\mathbf{R}^2$. We were unable to use E-GK algorithm to divide subregion into the correct number of clusters, so the modus of frequencies was used for finding the dominant cluster in the subregion and the covariance matrix for its description.

In the testing phase, the map of centers of the environment was used in the experimental trail. Despite the seasonal changes of the environment (learning phase – December; testing phase – March) the closed-path performance of the robot navigation verified the working concept based on the clustering across images. It can be used as a basis for the next research.

In the future work, we would like to focus on the robust clustering methods suitable for a high dimensional clustering, and a low dimensional clustering whose advantages are in the estimation of the number of clusters. We would like to find an one-layer algorithm to sort such data. Also adjustment of FCM20 algorithm could be promising.

Acknowledgements. We would like to express deep thanks to Tomas Krajnik from Czech Technical University in Prague, who was helpful in our research and was willing to provide the robot in the learning and testing phase.

We obtained E-FCM Matlab code from professor Kaymak, for what we are also very grateful.

This work was supported by project IGA VSE F4/5/2011.

References

1. Bay, H., Tuytelaars, T., Van Gool, L.: SURF: Speeded up robust features. In: Proceedings of the Ninth European Conference on Computer Vision, Graz, pp. 404–417 (2006)
2. Bezdek, J.C.: Pattern Recognition with Fuzzy Objective Function Algorithms. Plenum Press, New York (1981)
3. Gustafson, E.E., Kessel, W.C.: Fuzzy clustering with fuzzy covariance matrix. In: Proceedings of the IEEE Conference on Decision and Control, pp. 761–766. IEEE Press, San Diego (1979)
4. Kaymak, U., Setnes, M.: Fuzzy clustering with volume prototypes and adaptive cluster merging. IEEE Transactions on Fuzzy Systems 10(6), 705–712 (2002)
5. Kohonen, T.: Self-organizing maps, 3rd edn. Springer, Berlin (2001)
6. Krajnik, T., Faigl, J., Vonasek, V., Kosnar, K., Kulich, M., Preucil, L.: Simple, yet stable bearing-only navigation. Journal of Field Robotics 27, 511–533 (2010)
7. Krajnik, T., Preucil, L.: A Simple Visual Navigation System with Convergence Property. In: European Robotics Symposium 2008, pp. 283–292. Springer, Heidelberg (2008)

8. Kruse, R., Doring, C., Lesot, M.J.: Fundamentals of Fuzzy Clustering. In: Advances in Fuzzy Clustering and its application, pp. 3–29. John Wiley and Sons, Chichester (2007)

9. Martinetz, T.M., Berkovich, S.G., Schulten, K.J.: "Neural-gas" network for vector quantization and its application to time-series prediction. IEEE Transactions on Neural Networks 4, 558–569 (1993)

10. Rezankova, H., Husek, D., Snasel, V.: Cluster Analysis of the Data (in Czech). Professional Publishing, Prague (2009)

11. Vesanto, J., Alhoniemi, E., Himberg, J., Kiviluoto, K., Parviainen, J.: SOM Toolbox for Matlab 5 (2000), http://www.cis.hut.fi/somtoolbox/

Distributed Control System for a Mobile Robot: Tasks and Software Architecture

Anton Yudin and Mikhail Semyonov

Bauman Moscow State Technical University, IU4 Department,
2-nd Baumanskaya st., 5, 105005, Moscow, Russia
{skycluster,m7onov}@gmail.com
http://www.bearobot.org

Abstract. This article discusses several aspects of the distributed control system being developed for a mobile robot. The aim for the system is ease of use for educational purposes and flexibility for easier and faster robot development for new projects. Movement tasks are formulated for better understanding of the distributed program architecture. The network protocols necessary for the system's operation are discussed. The higher level protocol's concept being developed by the authors is provided and an example of the protocol use is presented.

Keywords: Eurobot, mobile robot, distributed control system, modular systems, network protocol, education.

1 Introduction

The practice of developing mobile robots for the Eurobot competitions [2] includes all the main stages of the production cycle of any modern high-tech device. In addition to project management participants of the team's development process are faced with research, design and development of mechanics, electronics, control programs, and finally with integration of individual system components into a single robotic solution. Bearing in mind that most of the competitors are students, the question of learning and acquiring new knowledge and skills is one of the most important.

Year after year, the competition offers developer teams a new task, which in turn leads to a complete revision of the mechanical structure of the previous robot. Mechanics when being changed influences electronics and control programs. A few years of robot developing is enough to notice that each of these areas may provide basic building blocks which will facilitate development of future systems. And if universality for the mechanics can be achieved only at the level of individual system components (e.g. motors, wheels, and fasteners), the electronics and the software can both be involved in a core of unchanged structure.

In this article, the authors attempted to summarize the experience of creating such a core system, while continuing to carry out one of the goals of the beArobot team they belong to: find and develop basic solutions for teaching and for use

D. Obdržálek and A. Gottscheber (Eds.): EUROBOT 2011, CCIS 161, pp. 321–334, 2011.

in the competition. In the previous article [1] the purpose and the relevance of
a distributed control system were justified, general structure of the system was
represented, the principle of configuring and using the system was given, and
the hardware implementation of the system was described.

2   The Problem Statement

To start with, let's present the hardware devices which will be used later on when
describing the core of the distributed control system. In this case, we consider
one of subsystems of a mobile robot, namely - a subsystem of relative navigation
(Fig. 1)

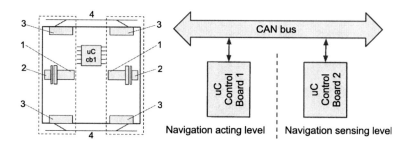

Fig. 1. The composition of the relative navigation subsystem. To the left: the structure
of mechanical devices (1 - engine, 2 - sensing encoder, 3 - button, 4 - bumper). To the
right: the configuration of the electronics on various control levels.

The figure shows relative navigation subsystem's two parts, which represent it
physically. The mechanical structure in this case is sketchy on the location of the
mechanisms, but nevertheless all the subsystem's necessary devices are present.
The configuration of control electronics is reduced to two printed boards with
microcontrollers that use the 8-bit AVR architecture. One of the boards is shown
in the mechanical sketch of Fig. 1. Its functions include direct motion control of
a robot's chassis for point to point movement tasks (in the figure: uC Control
Board 1, uC cb1; further on cb1). The second board (in the figure: uC Control
Board 2; further on cb2) coordinates a robot's navigation system: processes data
from additional sensors, identifies obstacles, builds movement routes and sends
commands to the first board.

The complete control system can be represented with 4 to 7 control boards,
but in this case, for simplicity of the proposed approach's description, we confine
ourselves to the two outlined above.

Now let's consider the actions that are available to the cb1 control board
(Fig. 2). By its example, we hope to show the idea of how the proposed control
system will be organized and how it will operate.

As can be seen in the figure, the cb1 board, in addition to liaison functions
with the cb2 board, provides such functions as: indication of a bumper's state,

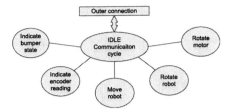

Fig. 2. The available actions of the cb1 control board

indication of encoder sensors' meter readings, activation of the robot's linear motion, activation of the robot's rotation, activation of a single motor's rotation.

Next, we will consider the three figures (Fig. 4, Fig. 5, and Fig. 6) which demonstrate processes that occur on the cb1 board, as well as their interactions. For this purpose we introduce the following notation (Fig. 3).

Fig. 3. The description of the graphical notation

Fig. 4 shows[1] processes that the cb2 board can initiate on the cb1 board, and that are assigned to work with sensors onboard of the robot's chassis.

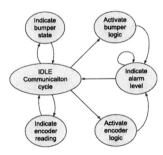

Fig. 4. The processes machine for the sensors on the chassis

When activated, the processes can monitor the sensor's status automatically according to some local control logic (algorithm). In case a necessary change is recognized the board can reveal it by increasing the level of the network's alarm in a certain way. Also on request, the processes can indicate the current status of sensors on the chassis.

---

[1] Fig. 5 and Fig. 6 also show the processes which can be initiated by the cb2 board.

Fig. 5 shows the processes that allow individual rotation of each motor's shaft. There are two possible control algorithms: the first rotates a motor's shaft at a certain angle, the other rotates a motor's shaft at a certain speed. According to the algorithms' start commands the board's microcontroller automatically begins monitoring bc1's sensor readings and using them in the algorithm. Also an algorithm that processes the state of a robot's bumper works in parallel with the basic algorithm and in case of a collision the level of the network's alarm is raised, resulting in immediate and automatic motor stop.

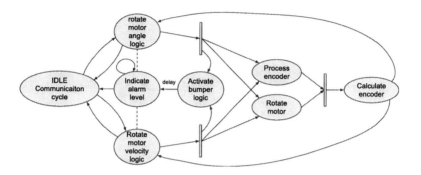

Fig. 5. The process machine for manual control of a motor

Finally, Fig. 6 shows the processes involved in managing movement of the robot on a flat surface. In this case, the two motors are controlled organically to achieve a common goal: move the robot with constant velocity or move it within a certain distance. By analogy with the previous example, in this case, a separate, simultaneously executable algorithm allows the motors to stop automatically and raises an alarm on dangerous states of the bumper.

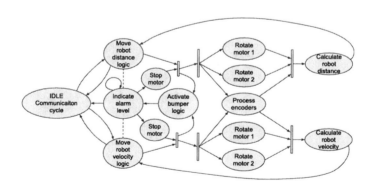

Fig. 6. The process machine for automatic control of the robot's movement

Thus, we formulated both the composition of the system to automate and the content of the processes which are to be automated. Next, let's consider the way these requirements are to be implemented in a distributed control system.

3   The Program Architecture

As it was briefly mentioned before the distributed control system's core being developed consists of hardware and software parts. The hardware part was described in detail in the previous article [1] and the considered control hardware's configuration was described earlier in this article (cb1 and cb2 boards). From now on we will concentrate on the software part.

Architecture of the software core focuses on such characteristics as:

1. Simplicity and speed of a firmware upgrade for all microcontrollers in a network;
2. Efficiency of the network hardware resources' utilization;
3. Reliability of individual functions through decentralization of the network.

As long as we consider network operation for the core parts an industry networking standard was selected for the low level needs of communication between individual nodes in the system with possible real-time operation. The standard is called CAN (Controller Area Network). This standard [3] does not include the entire stack of the necessary protocols, so it was supplemented by the CAN Kingdom protocol [4], which appeared to be the most flexible implementation of available higher layer protocols for CAN. This protocol allows a system designer to easily specify data flows in an arbitrary way (change software network topology), and also allows a developer to use the whole range of CAN-addresses at his discretion.

To describe the developed approach let's refer to Fig. 7, which shows the levels of interaction in the network in comparison with the standard OSI model of network interactions.

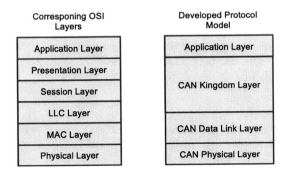

Fig. 7. A comparison of the developed protocol stack and the OSI model

Generally speaking, CAN Kingdom is not a top-level protocol for the CAN bus, unlike its counterparts - CAN Open, Smart Distributed System, DeviceNet. It does not limit a system developer neither in a field of available CAN-addresses, nor in a logical structure of software parts of a system. However, it introduces some restrictions on the format of packets sent over the network. The key difference of CAN Kingdom from similar protocols is that it defines logical entities with which it is possible in an arbitrary way to organize data streams from one node to another, also allowing distribution of CAN-addresses so as to ensure effective node communication. It is important to note the following CAN Kingdom concept, which in future the authors will expand - "a single point of configuration". This means that all nodes in a system but one should be programmed directly just once and then be able to be integrated into a network, allowing them to read current configuration of it. As a result a system designer has to deal with only one node. That significantly reduces the complexity of the system setup.

Primitive types used in the CAN Kingdom protocol are divided into:

1. Applied types - entities that contain information to be transmitted:
   - Bit - the smallest data cell;
   - Line - a data string of one/several primitive Bits. Maximum size - 8 Bits;
   - Page - a collection of Lines. Maximum size - 8 Lines;
   - Envelope - message IDs (CANID);
   - Letter - a CAN-bus message, a combination of one Page and one Envelope.

   The applied primitives constitute a hierarchy: Letter consists of Envelope and Page, Page consists of several Lines, and Line consists of several Bits.
2. Service types - metadata primitives which are needed for proper transmission/reception of the applied primitives:
   - Form - information describing Page's content;
   - Document - a collection of Forms;
   - List - array of primitives (Bits list, Lines list, Forms list, Documents list ...);
   - Folder - a primitive container that is tied up with one or more Envelopes and one Document.
   - Letter - a CAN-bus message, a combination of one Page and one Envelope.

   The Folder primitive can be compared to a gate through which a node communicates with the network. And associated Document - with rules of entry and exit through these "gates". See Fig. 8 for relations between the primitives.

The CAN Kingdom specification determines a central node in a network, it is called King. This node is responsible for initial setup of other nodes, but before

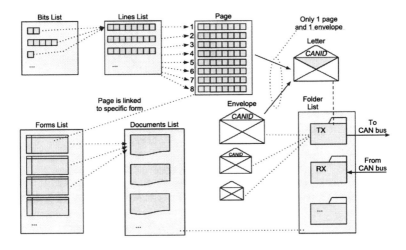

Fig. 8. CAN Kingdom's primitives and relations

that is possible it is needed to program (a controller's memory or a separate memory chip) all the nodes with the following information:

- A physical address of the node (CANID);
- Data's transfer rate;
- An identification number of the configuration message.

The process of designing a system based on the CAN Kingdom protocol is generally carried out as follows:

1. A system developer is studying modules' documentation. The documentation includes - lists of entities and their descriptions, and algorithms (functions) of the module.
2. A program of a network setup is being developed. The setup is done using 21 predefined configuration messages. During the setup the King node sends a freeze-message to all nodes, after which all of them must stop working on the network and get ready to change the configuration. Next, according to the setup King creates primitives for each node, combining those that are lower in the hierarchy described before in more general entities. Finally it assigns the Folder primitives on each node with identifiers (CANID). Two nodes can communicate with each other only if the Folder primitive on each node has the same CANID and the format of the Document primitive is the same (done in order for nodes with the appropriate Form primitive to be able to recognize received information). After finishing the setup a run message is sent to all nodes, after which they resume normal operation in the new configuration.
3. The resulting network is tested and debugged.

The authors have already begun to implement the CAN Kingdom protocol in the C language. Some of the structures, reflecting the CAN Kingdom primitives are listed below.

```
typedef struct Bits_t { // -- BIT --
  Direction tr; // direction of transfer ( tx | rx )
  uint8 raw;     // raw data
  uint8 sz; // number of meaningful bits in raw data
  uint8 fmt;     // format identifier (e.g. m, sm, mm)
} Bits;

typedef struct List_t { // -- LIST --
  Direction tr;        // (tx | rx)
  ListContent content;  // bits, lines, forms etc.
  ListId id;           // list identifier
  ListCell startCell;   // pointer to the list start
} List;

typedef struct Line_t { // -- LINE --
  Direction tr;        // ( tx | rx )
  ListCell bitsChain;   //    bit
} Line;

typedef struct Form_t { // -- FORM --
  Direction tr;        // (tx | rx)
  uint8 numlines;    // number of lines
  ListCell linesChain;
} Form;

typedef struct Doc_t { // -- DOCUMENT --
  Direction tr;        // (tx | rx)
  uint8 numForms;    // number of associated forms
  ListCell formsChain;  // array of forms
} Doc;

typedef struct Envelope_t { // -- ENVELOPE --
  uint8 msb;     // most significant byte
  uint8 lsb;     // less significant byte
  Tumbler enable; // envelope activation
} Envelope;

typedef struct Folder_t { // -- FOLDER --
  uint8 id;       // folder identifier
  ListCell doc;      // pointer to document
  Direction tr;      // (tx | rx)
  Tumbler enable;    // folder activation
  uint8 numEnvs;     // number of associated envelopes
  Envelope* envs;    // array of envelopes
} Folder;
```

The Page primitive is combined with the Form primitive, and the Letter primitive has no data type, as it is formed only when sending messages and is not intended for storage.

CAN Kingdom's main task is to organize flows of information in a network and to determine the format of transmitted messages. That is not enough for arranging full interaction of distributed nodes of the system. For an efficient and flexible system it is also important to ensure for each node: possibility of algorithms' configuration and possibility of parallel tasks' execution (calculative and applied). The solution to this problem would be the next level of protocol stack that runs on top of the CAN Kingdom protocol.

3.1   The Higher Level Protocol Jet Jerboa

Developing of a high-level application protocol is one of the key tasks in the authors' approach. At this point the protocol is not fully developed, but the basic concept is introduced for its further clarification. The working title of the protocol is "Jet Jerboa". According to this concept a node has several atomic functions. The atomic function is indivisible and runs on a single node. There are also complex functions, which constitute a chain of atomic functions that can run on different nodes. Complex function is the oriented graph in Fig. 9.

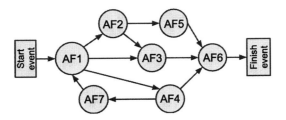

Fig. 9. A complex distributed function

As one can see, it is possible to form an algorithm of a complex function defining relations between atomic functions, and where possible - execution can be parallelized as atomic functions can run on different nodes. If we introduce the atomic function "iterator" it is also possible to arrange a cyclic operation of some areas of the graph. It will return control to a certain point until some condition is met; otherwise the cycle will be endless.

It is useful to divide atomic functions into two categories:

1. General atomic functions which can be run on any node in a network;
2. Specific atomic functions which can be run only on certain nodes.

All atomic functions have unique identifiers no matter which node they belong to. Start and finish of an atomic function's execution are accompanied by events, which also have unique identifiers within a network. For example, an atomic function starts execution by the event "at_func_1_req", which was received by a network and finishes with the event "at_func_2_ind", which, depending on configuration, can be transmitted over the network or be a node's purely internal event.

A modifier can be transmitted together with an event. It sets an operation mode for a function. Identifiers of a function's input parameters are defined when configuring a network and are stored in a node's internal table. Before a start of execution it is determined whether a node has needed information, if so, the information is recorded in an appropriate memory cell that then will be used by the function - if not, the node sends a "data request" message over the network.

Finish of a function also constitutes one or more events that can serve as start of other functions' execution. The means to deliver events over a network is the subject of further development.

Memory, as well as computational resources, has distributed nature - each node stores information that can be used by it or by other nodes. Thus it is necessary to distinguish between nodes of information providers and nodes of information consumers. Information providers are usually represented by a variety of sensors. Any node can be an information consumer. In a sensor's measurement a node determines by its internal configurable metadata tables whether it owns the data. It is then stored locally or broadcasted over a network.

It is important to note one feature of the developed architecture - active use of broadcast messages, i.e. messages that are accepted and processed simultaneously by multiple nodes. In some cases this allows to reduce overall network traffic, as well as to increase overall speed of information processing.

3.2   The Jet Jerboa Protocol Example

To illustrate the Jet Jerboa protocol, let's consider a robot's movement on some route. As before our system consists of 2 components:

– Motion controller (N1)
– Route coordinator (N2)

Table 1. Functions of the N1, N2 nodes

Function	gId	lId	inParamList	preEvents	postEvents
N1					
Relative linear movement	1	1	d7,d9	e8	e1
Rotation at angle	2	2	d8,d10	e9	e2
N2					
Route guidance	3	1	out1,out2	e3..e7,out3	e8,e9
Get the next destination point	4	2	d5..d7	e1,e2	e7..e9

Table 2. Events of the N1, N2 nodes

Event	gId	lId
N1		
Finish relative movement	1	1
Finish rotation	2	2
Front collision	3	3
No front collision	4	4
Rear collision	5	5
No rear collision	6	4
N2		
Final destination reached	7	1
Start of relative movement	8	2
Start of rotation	9	3

Table 3. Data of the N1, N2 nodes

Data	gId	lId	data
N1			
Current coordinate increase	1	1	$(\Delta 1, \Delta 2)$
Current angle increase	2	2	$\Delta 15$
Current movement state	3	3	moving
Current bumper state	4	4	front bumping
N2			
Array of route points	5	1	$(\Delta 1, \Delta 2; \Delta 0)$-$(\Delta 3, \Delta 4; \Delta 30)$-$(\Delta 5, \Delta 6; \Delta 45)$
Current point of movement start	6	2	(3,4)
Current destination point	7	3	(5,6)
Current rotate angle	8	4	30
Current movement velocity	9	5	10
Current rotate velocity	10	6	2

Where:

- gId - a global function identifier, is assigned when configuring a system;
- lId - a local identifier of a function, indicated in module documentation;
- inParamList - an array of input datas identifiers, is initialized on configuration;
- preEvents - an array of identifiers of events causing start of functions;
- postEvents - an array of identifiers of events caused by finish of functions;
- data - data contents;
- out1 .. out3 - external influences and data.

Initially, hardware modules are documented with tables for functions, data and events, but without being tied to a global identifier. Visually a function can be represented as a junction with incoming and outgoing arrows (Fig. 10); where the arrows represent data and events (input or output). Binding of local identifiers (lId) to global (gId) ones occurs during configuration of a system.

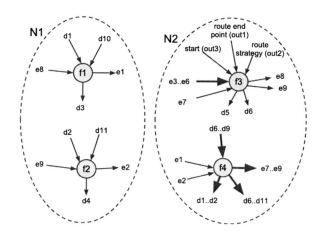

Fig. 10. A graphical representation of functions' binding to data and events

Arrows with "e_" prefixes represent events and appear in the network as broadcast packets with the event's global id information. Arrows with "d_" prefixes represent data and can appear in a form of broadcast messages, if the producer of this data is not its user.

When an event message arrives, software modules browse their internal tables of functions searching whether the event is a beginning of a function. If yes, then before starting the function the input data is prepared. The module's local (inner) data table is searched and the identifiers of required data are compared to those stored in the table. If the data is in the inner table - it is written to a startup parameters table of the function without any query on the CAN bus. If the data with the specified identifier is not found in the local data table - a network broadcast request message is dispatched for the data. A node that owns this data will answer. And finally the obtained data is recorded in the startup parameters table of the function.

Once all parameters are obtained, a function begins execution. The result of it is changed data, which also corresponds to global identifiers that are unique to the entire system. Further on, this data can be written in a local data table if the current node is the owner of the data, or sent over a network with a broadcast message and a data user has to accept it and write it in its data table.

A function execution also results in a list of events which as well as the changed data correspond to global identifiers. When a function finishes operation a network message is sent as an event. All nodes receiving this message check their internal table of functions for required actions and then a process of starting a new function repeats.

Fig. 11 represents a fully connected system of functions.

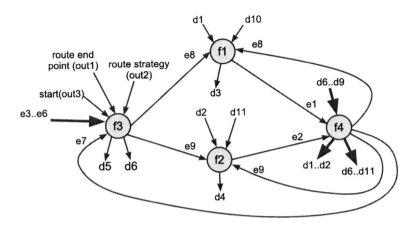

Fig. 11. A system of connected functions

From the figure one can see that the path e8-e1-e8 and e9-e2-e9 will be repeated for as long as the functions f3 will generate output data d5 different from zero. It should be noted that the proposed architecture solution does not apply for a final decision, but merely illustrates the concept.

4   Conclusions

In this article, the authors tried to summarize the current state of the distributed control system for an autonomous mobile robot. This system was previously presented in a more general form [1].

Detailed examination of tasks put for one of the levels of the system is a good way to better understand the approach being developed. Since the discussed problems of the navigation level are very common in practice of development of mobile robots, this material could be used as a base for future development of guidelines for the course on competition robotics, read by one of the authors among the first-year students[2].

Developing the previously described approach the authors presented a network model of the system, and also discussed in detail the nuances of the CAN Kingdom protocol used for needs of the system, partly including the software code implementing the protocol for better presentation.

---

[2] An optional course on basics in robotics for first year students in Bauman Moscow State Technical University, IU4 department.

The main point of future development is the Jet Jerboa upper level protocol. This protocol actually has to implement special requirements reasonable for the whole system, which were formulated as follows:

1. Simplicity and speed of a firmware upgrade for all microcontrollers in a network;
2. Efficiency of the network hardware resources' utilization;
3. Reliability of individual functions through decentralization of the network.

An example of the network implementation based on a simple 2 node configuration showed how the network is meant to operate.

In future, the described approach and concept are supposed to form a complete real-time system, the main application of which will be in the field of teaching robotics.

References

1. Vlasov, A., Yudin, A.: Distributed Control System in Mobile Robot Application: General Approach, Realization and Usage. Technical report, 3rd International Conference on Research and Education in Robotics (2010)
2. Eurobot, international robotics contest, http://www.eurobot.org
3. CAN Specification, version 2.0. Robert Bosch GmbH, Stuttgart (1991)
4. Fredriksson, L.-B.: CAN Kingdom specification, rev. 3.01. Kvaser AB, Kinnahult, Sweden (1995)
5. Clinger, W.D.: Foundations of Actor Semantics. Technical report, MIT (1981)
6. Robin, M.: Communication and Concurrency. International Series in Computer Science. Prentice Hall, Englewood Cliffs (1989)

University Education in Robotics and Advanced Automation: A Certified Lectures Perspective and Strategy for Development of Didactical and Technical Course Model

Duško Lukač[1] and Werner Schollenberger[2]

[1] Rheinische Fachhochschule Köln gGmbH, University of Applied Science,
Department of Mechatronics and Robotics, Vogelsanger Strasse 295,
50825 Köln, Germany
lukac@rfh-koeln.de
[2] Head of Department of Education and Training at FANUC Robotics Deutschland GmbH,
Bernhäuser Straße 36, 73765 Neuhausen a.d.F., Germany
schollenbergerw@fanuc-robotics.de

Abstract. This paper examines the development of the so called certified university courses in robotics and advanced automation at German universities, based on cooperation between the industry and universities. It looks in detail at the conceptual development of the certified university course and gives a solution for the didactical-technical part of the concept. As an example, the cooperation between Rheinische Fachhochschule Köln gGmbH – University of Applied Sciences with FANUC Robotics Deutschland GmbH is analyzed in detail. It states that the legal and didactical-technical part of the concept has been essential for the viability of the course. It concludes that the higher education politics and company politics are missing well designed joint concepts but that the future is bright for these certified courses so long as they are conceptually well designed and industrial sector remain committed.

Keywords: Robotics, Certified University Courses, Education, Training, Automation, University- Industry Cooperation.

1 Introduction

Robotics as the subject of study today, is a regular component of the curriculum at the most universities and advanced technical colleges in Germany and worldwide. During the 80's discussions have been hold [1] about the suitability of the integration of the robotics in the curriculum at the universities and advanced technical colleges. It has been discussed at the time does it makes sense or not. Today such discussions do not exist anymore; because robotics as a scientific discipline has found the place in the universities' and colleges' curriculums which has been adjusted to the requirements of the industry. Consequently also the curriculums in engineering studies in Germany, especially at the advanced technical colleges, has been adjusted and developed in such

D. Obdr\v{z}\'alek and A. Gottscheber (Eds.): EUROBOT 2011, CCIS 161, pp. 335–347, 2011.
© Springer-Verlag Berlin Heidelberg 2011

way that they enable the graduates, with the knowledge and skills, to respond to the knowledge and skills requirements expected in the industry. Such process of the curricula adaptation is very dynamic, because the technical progress in the field of mechatronics and robotics is regarded to be remarkably dynamic. Bearing this in mind, universities, colleges and schools have a permanent task of adaptation and improving of the existing curricula. In the usual case professors, as responsible persons for their lecture, have to adapt their lessons to the technical progress and to renew their lecture. This task is in the practical case not always satisfactory, neither for the professor nor for students, because very often professors are lacking the time and also equipment for sufficient improvement of the lectures and appropriate self-preparation to the new topics. Such preparation, in order to be satisfactory in terms of the quality-focused and high-quality lectures, includes not only acquisition of the new theoretical knowledge but also the acquisition of the practical skills oriented to the theoretical knowledge. Within these considerations some universities and academics came to conceptual cognition and conclusion that such tasks can only efficiently be carried out, if sufficient, contemporary know-how as well as equipment is available and can be offered for use to the students and teaching staff. Thus, one way out, is collaboration between universities and the experts on the market. Those collaborations have behind the directly positive effects on the quality and contemporary aspects of the lectures, also further side-effects. Those effects, behind the financial benefits, are enhancing the reputation of the universities and awareness level of the industrial partners and their products. It can be referred to as circuitously, joint marketing strategy. Furthermore improving of the basic research, possibilities of the additional qualification of the students by offering the certified courses and lectures as well as new potential business opportunities for students and graduates are further positive side-effects.

2   Concept of Certified Lectures Perspective in Robotics

In Germany basic research is a key mission of the universities, while applied research is the key mission of the universities of the applied sciences as well as some institutes and associations. Applied research is also a common matter of the industry whereby, research and development tasks are carried out in industrial laboratories with the exclusion of the experimental, medical trials that are usually positioned at educational medical centers. Research unions with universities and higher education centers complement industries' fundamental research requirements when business research and development financial plans are diminished by further competitive demands and pressures. In addition, partnership with higher education institutions is a possibility of monitoring innovative progresses in science and know-how and the chance to work on issues with a practical relevance. Partnership with industrial companies develops the consideration of the industrial challenges by revealing higher education institutions ability to industrial problems and industrial methods to follow a line of analysis. On the other hand, partnership with universities assists the scientists in the industry to stay in progress with the newest progresses in broad fields of fundamental disciplines that are of planned, long-term interest to the corporation. Industry supported research and education at higher education institutions and internships improve basic and graduate education by giving universities and students' information for better recognizing of industrial problems, thus inspiring the preparation of researchers and graduates for an industrial condition. These interactions also make available to the industrial associates a pool of contenders for job staffing. Cost-effective expansion resulting from higher education institutions spinoff businesses and innovative product introductions rooted in higher education institutions innovations is considerable and growing. Thus, industrial human resources practice and the numerous examples show that, today it is beneficial to have a knowledge proof in certain field of studies not only issued by the higher education institutions but also in the same time from the industrial experts in this certain field of study. Moreover some human resources departments quite often expect from the applicant to give evidence about the expert or advanced knowledge. It is result of the certain degree of the mistrust to the single university education, because of the initial described problems with the obtaining and imparting of the contemporary knowledge. The expert or advanced knowledge presupposes long-standing experience in the field or it can be to great part verified with the proofed involvement and methodical examination of the specific industrial problems. Thus, assuming the industrial partners are due to daily business, aware of the practical application problems, than it is expected that those are introducing their practical experience into the product trainings and certified courses. So, in one university-industry collaboration, the experiences obtained from the industrial partners imparted during their product trainings and certified courses, is an ideal channel for effective and time constrained possibility to impart the new knowledge and know-how to the students and their lecturers. So, adjustment and supplement of the current lecturers with the in the industries carried out special product trainings is a possible way of holding the university lectures at the newest level regarding the application part of the lessons. In order to ensure the quality of such lecturers, those must be developed in such ways, that the expert knowledge, can only be obtained if the student, proofs his/her knowledge by taking part on time constrained practical and theoretical trainings finished with the certification. Such certification procedures but may not stay in conflict with the regular university assessments defined by the specific regulations and acts governing higher education. Therefore, two-tier assessment procedures have to be developed which supplement each other in regard of the imparted content and time. Detailed analysis of such kind of course model is described in the next chapter.

3   Example of University-Industry Collaboration in Robotics

In the following one example of the realization of so called certified university lectures, under consideration the requirements for the legal, didactical and ethical realization, is described. The idea about the educational collaboration between the universities and industries is old, but indeed in Germany there are not as many universities, who are in the field of the robotics actively, and didactically collaborating with the known, market leader robotics companies like KUKA Robotics

GmbH or FANUC Robotics Deutschland GmbH. For example with the KUKA Robotics GmbH company – a market leader in the automotive segment worldwide [2] – only two universities are actively collaborating in the field of the joint developed university lectures, which enable the students not only to obtain the university certificate of performance but also to get the industrial certificate of performance during the same lecture. Some of those universities are RWTH Aachen; German Aerospace Center (DLR), Fachhochschule Augsburg – University of Applied Sciences and Rheinische Fachhochschule Köln gGmbH – University of Applied Sciences. With the FANUC Robotics Deutschland - a market leader in the general industry segment worldwide [3] – the case is quite similar. University of Stuttgart and Rheinische Fachhochschule Köln gGmbH – University of Applied Sciences (RFH) are collaborating actively with the company. But the kind of the collaboration with the mentioned universities is quite dissimilar, regarding the concepts and fields of collaboration. While some collaboration is targeting scientific subjects, the others are of the educational character. In order to focus at one such detailed concept, this paper will present a development of the educational concept, with focus on didactical and technical issues, developed with the cooperation between Rheinische Fachhochschule Köln gGmbH – University of Applied Sciences and the company FANUC Robotics Deutschland GmbH. Such concepts must be detailed analyzed while taking into consideration financial aspects, time and educational outcomes related to the current application-oriented education but in the same time saving the impartment of broad and basic knowledge. First, looking on the financial aspects, those are important factors to enable covering of the costs but in the same time also to support the motivating factors to take part in the certified courses and to make efforts to successful finishing them. The certified university lectures, which are regarding the content, high-qualitative as similar training courses offered by the FANUC Robotics Deutschland GmbH, company costs only 100 Euro. Those costs are so defined to be at acceptable level for the students, but in the same time to be of motivating nature. It means those "symbolic" fees are the part of the didactical concept. The similar robotic courses which are offered by the FANUC Robotics Deutschland GmbH cost much more if directly booked at the company. The costs of those are at the moment 1700 Euro. This information has very stimulating character for the students, especially because of the fact that students just need to pay comparatively low fees for the same benefits. This amount is not the source of revenues for the company; they just cover the general running expenses. Also, the fees which students have to pay have a motivating character because the student which has paid the fee is in this way strongly committing him-/herself to learn about the subject if they want acquire the certificate of performance [4]. Certification procedure offered by the company takes place in Stuttgart (400km far way from Cologne), where the FANUC Robotics Deutschland GmbH has its training classrooms. It means the student becomes prepared at RFH the in Cologne and becomes in Stuttgart assessed in practice and theory. According to the concept, during and after visiting the robotics lectures at the university students have the possibility in the same or separately, in the running or following semester to take a part in the certification procedure. If student is not interested to take part at certification, he/she needs to pass standard exam at the university. The whole procedure is simplified explained in the following figure.

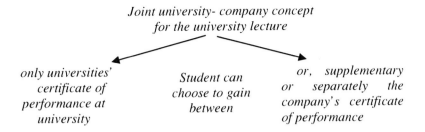

*Joint university- company concept
for the university lecture*

*only universities'
certificate of
performance at
university*

*Student can
choose to gain
between*

*or, supplementary
or separately the
company's certificate
of performance*

Fig. 1. Certification procedure

To assure the quality of the assessment, the topics of the practical and theoretical assessment are chosen by the FANUC Robotics Deutschland GmbH and are not obtainable for the students because in order to keep the objectivity of the concept save and to keep the high-quality of the training on the adequate level. The topic of the assessment is but known to the lecturer, which has itself to pass the same exam, in order to be able to convey the knowledge in the appropriate way and to prepare the students for the certification procedure. Lecturers are regarding the application-oriented know-how constantly educated by the company in order to be topical in the field of study. Second, regarding the time component of the procedure, as usual at German university, students can resit the examination and therewith certification exam 3 times [5]. Regarding the time scheduling, the course which is offered as a component of the university lecture, must fulfill time requirements for the university lectures on the one hand, as well as the requirements about the duration of the company courses on the other hand. From universities' view, behind the international acts, national regulation defined in the University Law North Rhine-Westphalia (HRWG) have to be taken into consideration and to be realized. From the company's view the training framework, shaped by didactic department of the company, is to be taken into the consideration while shaping universities lecture. It is necessary because FANUC Robotics Deutschland GmbH with issuing of the company certificate gives a quality proof of the knowledge, which only can be issued if person really can verify imparted knowledge needed to assure quality standards. The project outlay of a course at a university in Germany is defined by the so called "semester week hours" (SWH). Additionally is to be taken into consideration that the achievements of the exams in the Bachelor and Master studies are valued by 4 + 2 SWH courses with 10 so called "achievement points" (according to European Credit Transfer System (ECTS) points used, to describe the student work load. ECTS was "developed by the European Commission in order to provide generally valid and accepted procedures for the recognition of study qualifications gained by students on courses outside their home country. It is also intended to provide more binding conditions, more flexibility and a greater degree of clarity in the organizing and running of courses for foreign students. ECTS gives students the opportunity to clarify definitively with their home university how many courses or classes they should attend while they are abroad and under what conditions the qualifications they obtain will be recognized by the home university on their return" [6]. Besides, one ECTS point corresponds to an amount of work involved of approx. 30 hours per semester (student workload). Therefore 14-16 working weeks for courses and the exam preparations are usually needed, so that calculation of the university lecture must include an average weekly amount of work of about 20 to 30 hours. This corresponds to 1 achievement point (AP). Obligingly according to ECTS 60 APs per academic year are to be achieved. SWH are also used for the calculation of the fees. Analogously to school hours, one university hour lasts 45 minutes. In order to keep the defaults of the ECTS achievement point system including the legal restraints about for the university lecture, for the planning of the joint company-university lecture it must be set the time frame of 16 SWH. From the point of view of the FANUC Robotics Deutschland GmbH, the course must include minimum 26 course hours, in order to keep the requirements for certification fulfilled. Bearing this in mind the course has been developed. The content of the lecture is developed in that way that the knowledge transferred to the students is not banded only with one product or company, but that comprises general practical and theoretical information about the robotics. Knowledge-specialization is supplemental part of the lecture and is oriented to the company specific solutions. Similar concept exists also with the company KUKA Robotics GmbH, so that basic knowledge transferred is the same. In regard of the practical part of the university-industry lecture a complex problem, directly related to the practice, has been developed and used as a basis for the preparation on the certification procedure. The concept must fulfill the technical requirement in terms of the technical quality of the assessment system in order to keep the quality of the application oriented part of the lecture on the adequate level. In the following chapter technical and practical part of the concept is presented. At the moment we are certifying in each semester max. 8 examinees by the KUKA company and in this semester we are certifying 7 examinees by the FANUC company. The assessment by FANUC comapny is scheduled for the 22 calendar week. Problems with the certification at the beginning are organization of the preparation courses for the students parallel to lectures, because students and lecturers (trainer) have further daily obligations, so that courses needs to be prepared by consulting the central planning office of the university. The program is realised since 2009. For the next years further stuff must be trained in order to be prepared to carry out the preparation courses so that the organizational flexibility of the courses can be enhanced.

4 Practical and Technical Realization of the Certified Lectures

To find an appropriate way of the course design, a draft which intends a theoretical and practical test has been compiled. A didactical method therewith refers to the practice of the teaching and learning, their theoretical imbedding and reflection. It is the basis for the description, explanation, realization and evaluation of teaching learning situations. It delivers models for the planning, structuralisation and analysis of the lessons [7]. While the didactics should provide an action orientation and a leading idea for the teaching, the methodology serves to their concrete realization. The purpose of the methodology is the organization of the learning processes. Methodically in our case, we are dealing with a practical solution for the problem on account of the problem description. The time constrained assessment at university is developed in that way, that the named criteria for the APs to ECTS on the one side and for the optional certification supplement on the other side, are fulfilled.

Theoretical part of the lecture covers topics as the kinematics, national and European security matters for secure work with industrial robots and in robot cells, programming of the robots and visualization. For the practical part, the common industrial systems and devices has been analysed to find the "cut-set" of the usual used devices needed to accomplish standards industrial process. The problem definition should serve on the one hand the practical realization of the in theory provided substance, and on the other hand to prepare students for the certification procedure at the FANUC Robotics Deutschland GmbH company. Thus, behind the named theoretical subjects of study, following practical subjects need to be assessed:

- Basics and advanced knowledge about the fieldbus systems including the programming and conceptualization of the currently often used field bus systems in the industry, as e.g. Profibus, Profinet, DeviceNet or CANopen.
- Basics and advanced knowledge about the programming of the industrial robots, with reference to the certain industrial product, as e.g. FANUC robots
- Basics and advanced knowledge about the programming of PLC devices including the Visualization with WinCC and WIN AC
- Methodical possibilities for the solution of a complicated automation problem on basis of the problem description. The solution of the task includes the work with the modern quick Gripper-Change-System for 2-Finger pneumatic and electric gripper.

The listed topics above are dynamic, meaning that adjustment needs to take a place to the industrial development. For it, close consultations with the industrial partner are to be hold in regular time steps. To impart the knowledge related to the listed practical subjects, the system presented in Figure 2. has been developed. The presented system connects all relevant mechatronic components one sophisticated industrial application has to have. The robot is programmed by using the FANUC R-30iA control unit [8], which again actuate the 2-Finger-Pneumatic-Gripper PGN plus 80 [9] via a quick Gripper-Change-System SWS21 [10]. Both components are the products of the Schunk Company, which is specialized producer of the gripper systems [11]. The 2-Finger-Electric-Gripper PG 70 [12] is controlled over Profibus which, for the intact functioning, presupposes master and slave components. Therefore the electric gripper is projected for the use via Control panel MP277 (Siemens) and integrated visualization system, which has an integrated Profibus master function [13]. Technical details of the system realization will not be described in total, with exception of the basic elements used. The system enables I/O communication directly or via protocols. So, the Profibus master device must communicate via the robot control unit R-30iA with the electric gripper PG70, because the electric gripper commands are a parts of the robot program which needs to be written on the robot control unit. The commands for the robot movements are, because of the safety reasons and the observance of the modes of robot system operation T1, T2 and AUTOMATIC, exclusively to be programmed via the robot control unit. In order to develop a functioning program for the control of the robot and the electric and pneumatic gripper over the HMI-Control panel and robot control unit, software components as e.g. Step7, WinCC flexible 2008 SP1 und WinAC MP 2008 [14] are used. Those are products of the Siemens company and are chosen because they are the most used systems in the German industry. During the lay down procedure of the

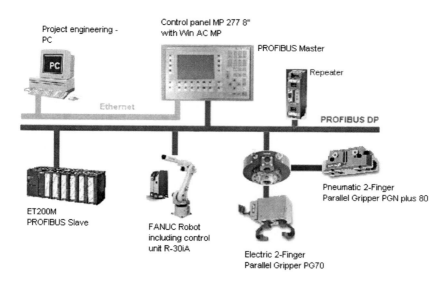

Fig. 2. Structural system overview

electric gripper PG70 by using of the Gripper-Change-System SWS21 (electric gripper is laid down on the shelf), the terminating resistor (terminator), necessary in the Profibus DP interface is missing because the connection between the segments SWS21 and PG70 does not exist in that moment.

As a problem solution a so called "repeater" was used. A repeater has the function to couple two segments with each other. Besides, it makes for both segments terminator available. To prevent an error message with absence of the gripper PG70 (and with it the terminator) in the Profibus DP net, the gripper is disconnected in the network before is laid down on the shelf. This is realized with the software library component SFC12 used in the Step7. Following figure presents the used Gripper-Change-System.

Fig. 3. PG70 in action (left) and shelf for the SWS21 (right)

In order to realize all functions used in standard automation, an automation-process has been designed, which satisfies the didactic and qualitative requirements needed for the realization of the certified university courses. The generation of an automation-process is carried out by the programming, which is divided into two parts. The first part is carried out by using the project engineering PC. On this occasion, an inter-program and a sequential program are developed with PLC software on the basis of function modules. The inter-program is used for the manual steering of the components over the robot-operating device (robot hand panel used for programming the robot). Then, the program is loaded on the operating device MP277 and can be started there. The second part of the automation-project is compiled on the FANUC robot control unit. A sequential program with the adequate robot control commands is written by using the robot control panel. By the execution of the automated process both sequential programs are redundant processed.

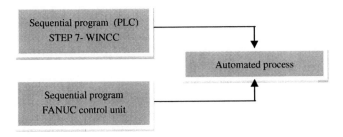

Fig. 4. Block diagram of the automation-process

The practical task which students needs to realize is to be done within 4 hours and is carried out in the single robot cell per student. The place of examination in Stuttgart is presented in the following figure.

Fig. 5. Training hall - FANUC Robotics in Stuttgart

Time frame has been defined by testing the realization of the task by experienced applicants adding the additional time supplement for inexperienced applicants. It means that students have enough time for the realization of the task. During the realization, only in security related matter they get the assistance, otherwise the task is carried out without any assistance. At the Rheinische Fachhochschule Köln GmbH the same robot system exists and is used for the preparation of the students for the practical part as well as for the understanding of the theoretical transferred knowledge. Because in the same time many students have to be prepared for the assessment robot simulation software from FANUC so called RoboGuide is parallel used for preparation purposes. It is an inexpensive and effective solution. The practical task which has to be realized consists of 4 parts. These are:

1. System setting and initial startup of the robot cell
2. Configuration of basic position program (HOME)
3. Creation of the interpolation program (JLC)
4. Production (PROD)

System setting and initial startup of the robot cell includes setting of the tools coordinates (Toolframe), users defined coordinates (Userframe) and axis limits. Also PLC Profibus master and all other side devices needed for control of the electrical gripper system need to be started up and adjusted to the task. In the following figure robot used for the task is presented by using of RoboGuide software.

Fig. 6. Setting of the axis limits with RoboGuide

Configuration and generation of basic position program comprises the creation of the HOME program which is used to define the beginning and the final position of the production (PROD). After it, interpolation program (JLC) with the available interpolation modes joint, linear and circular mode needs to be created. Arrows with numbers displayed at the picture belows shows the track which robots needs to follow by using of different interpolaiton modes.

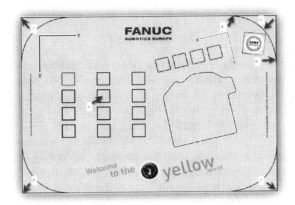

Fig. 7. Creation of the interpolation program (JLC)

After creation of the JLC program, the production program (PROD) needs to be created. It includes the establishment of the I/O signals in the program, which on the one side needs to be simulated with the robot control unit and on the other after the simulation side in real created and integrated into production program by using of PLC device, which has to be parallel programmed for the task. PLC device has also to be integrated in the programming of the electrical gripper, which is the part of the robot program. So, direct interaction between PLC and robot control unit by using of the I/O ports and Profibus connection is required. In the following figure the position of the parts which has to be handled is presented.

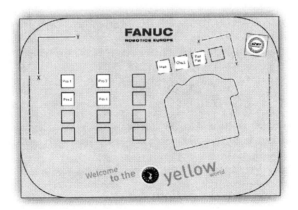

Fig. 8. Creation of the production program (PROD)

For the case that the task is successfully accomplished, the examinee gets in the same day the certificate as so called Fanuc Certified Technician (FCT) or Engineer (FCE) in dependence of which kind of the education examinee he/she had to pass trough and which kind of assessment he/she had to make. The whole university-industry concept includes further types of examination, which is related to the registered job-seeker and is realized under co-assistance of the German Federal Employment Office.

5 Conclusion

Against the general image that in highly-developed industrial countries like in Germany the collaboration between industrial enterprise and universities flourishes, the example in this paper shows that there are no as much mature and fully developed didactic-technical concepts for joint university-industry certified lectures. In this paper a successful university-industry cooperation in the field of the robots and advanced automation, is presented including the analysis of conceptual backgrounds of realization of the collaboration, with the emphasis on the didactical and technical part. These results can serve as a didactic-technical suggestion for the other companies and universities which intend such collaboration. In further paper the key success factor of such cooperation will be analysed and presented.

References

1. Harlan, R.: Adding robotics to the curriculum. Industrial Robot: An International Journal 11(1), 22–23 (1984)
2. Buchstab, A.: KUKA AG, Annual Report 2008: Business and Business enviroment (2008),
   http://www.kuka.com/res/media/geschaeftsberichte/
   gb_2008/en/business-and-business-environment.html
3. Yoshiharu, I.: Neues von Fujiyama (News from Fujiyama). Automation, 24–27 (January 2009)
4. Kösel, E.: Die Modellierung von Lernwelten. Die Theorie der Subjektiven Didaktik (The modeling of learning worlds. Volume I: the theory of the subjective didactics), 4th edn., Bahlingen (2004)
5. Rheinische Fachhochschule Köln gGmbH, University of Applied Sciences Studienordung (Regulations for the students), Intranet (January 2011), http://www.rfh-koeln.de
6. Pädagogische Hochschule Ludwigsburg: What is ECTS (January 2010),
   http://www.ph-ludwigsburg.de/html/
   9e-aaax-s-01/-seiten/english/e_ects1.htm0
7. Reich, K.: Konstruktivistische Didaktik: ein Lehr- und Studienbuch mit Methodenpool auf CD (Constructivistic didactics: a textbook and study book with method pool on CD), 3rd edn., Beltz, Weinheim (2006)
8. FANUC Robotics Deutschland GmbH: System R-30iA Controller - Basic Description (January 2011),
   http://www.kmtgroup.com/opencms/en_ZZ/ba_robotic_solutions/
   -resources/processes/downloads/R-30iA_Controller.pdf

9. Schunk AG: PGN-plus80 Pneumatic 2-Finger Parallel Gripper Universal Gripper (January 2011),
   `http://www.schunk.com/schunk_files/attachments/`
   `PGN-plus_80_En.pdf`
10. Schunk AG: Assembly and Operating Manual for Gripper-Change-System Type SWS, Precision Workholding Systems,
    `http://www.schunk.com/schunk_files/attachments/`
    `OM_AU_SWS_DE_EN.pdf` (January 2011)
11. Monkman, G.J., Hesse, S., Steinmann, R., Schunk, H.: Robot Grippers. Wiley, Berlin (2007)
12. Schunk AG: Electrical 2-Finger Parallel Gripper Universal Gripper PG70 (January 2010),
    `http://www.schunk.com/schunk_files/attachments/PG_70_En.pdf`
13. Weigmann, J., Kilian, G.: Dezentralisieren mit PROFIBUS-DP/DPV1. Aufbau, Projektierung und Einsatz des PROFIBUS-DP mit SIMATIC S7 (Decentralize with PROFIBUS-DP/DPV1/. Construction, project engineering and application of the PROFIBUS-DP with SIMATIC S7), 3rd edn., Siemens Verlag (November 2008)
14. Siemens AG: Bedienen und Beobachten mit WinCC V6 - Modul_F05 Teil 1 (Serve and observing with WinCC V6–module F05 part 1), pp. 2–193 (September 2006),
    `http://www.automation.siemens.com/fea/ftp/module/de/`
    `f05/f0-5_wincc_1.pdf`

Author Index

Abduramanov, Pavel   158
Alvarez Caro, Irene   10
Alves, João Bosco da Mota   236
Alves, Silas F.R.   17
Assaf, Dorit   29
Ax, Markus   277

Bajic, Jovan   202
Bedkowski, Janusz   40
Beitelschmidt, Michael   288
Bendersky, Diego   68
Bittel, Oliver   55, 102, 130
Blaich, Michael   55, 102, 130
Borovac, Branislav   263
Brkic, Miodrag   202

Caccavelli, Javier   68
Caldeira, Marco A.C.   17
Castellanos, Jose A.   221
Čermák, Petr   78
Chistyakov, Mikhail   187

de Cristóforis, Pablo   68
Dessimoz, Jean-Daniel   88
Durst, Valentin   102

Faigl, Jan   172
Ferasoli Filho, Humberto   17
Fišer, Daniel   172

Gauthey, Pierre-François   88
Gottscheber, Achim   114
Grabmair, Gernot   123
Greuter, Matthias   130

Hagel, Daniel   102
Hanzel, Jaroslav   144
Hochlehnert, Andreas   114
Horáková, Jana   1

Jahoda, Václav   210
Jurišica, Ladislav   144

Kandoba, Victor   158
Katz, Andrea   68

Kelemen, Jozef   78
Kľúčik, Marian   144
Kobayashi, Nobuaki   300
Kononchuk, Dmitry   158
Krajník, Tomáš   172, 210
Kuhnert, Klaus-Dieter   277
Kuhnert, Lars   277
Kuturov, Andrey   187

Lukač, Duško   335
Lukic, Milan   202

Mairon, Lukas   114
Masłowski, Andrzej   40
Montano, Luis   221
Mosteo, Alejandro R.   221
Mudrová, Lenka   210
Murillo, Ana C.   221

Neves Jr., Othon da Rocha   236
Nikolić, Milutin   263

Okulovsky, Yuri   158

Pashinskiy, Igor   187
Pastorek, Lukas   310
Pedre, Sol   68
Pegoraro, Renê   17
Pfeifer, Rolf   29
Pierlot, Vincent   248
Porges, Oliver   210

Raković, Mirko   263
Ramos, Josué J.G.   236
Rezankova, Hana   310
Rosário, João M.   17
Rosenfelder, Michael   130

Schlemper, Jens   277
Schollenberger, Werner   335
Semyonov, Mikhail   321
Stier, Johannes   288
Suzuki, Ryoichi   300

Urbin-Choffray, Maxime   248

Vander, Jan   102
Van Droogenbroeck, Marc   248
Vintr, Tomas   310
Vitko, Anton   144
Vonásek, Vojtěch   172

Yonezawa, Wilson M.   17
Yudin, Anton   187, 321

Zechel, Gero   288
Zhigalov, Sergey   158